Who Goes?
Who Stays?
What Matters?

Accessing and Persisting

in Post-Secondary

Education in

Canada

Who Goes?
Who Stays?
What Matters?

Accessing and Persisting

in Post-Secondary

Education in

Canada

Edited by

Ross Finnie, Richard E. Mueller,

Arthur Sweetman, and Alex Usher

School of Policy Studies, Queen's University
McGill-Queen's University Press
Montreal & Kingston · London · Ithaca

SCHOOL OF
Policy Studies

Publications Unit
Policy Studies Building
138 Union Street
Kingston, ON, Canada
K7L 3N6
www.queensu.ca/sps/

Library and Archives Canada Cataloguing in Publication

Who goes? Who stays? What matters? : accessing and persisting in postsecondary education in Canada / edited by Ross Finnie ... [et al.].

Includes abstracts in French.
Includes bibliographical references.
ISBN 978-1-55339-222-4 (bound).—ISBN 978-1-55339-221-7 (pbk.)

1. College attendance—Canada. 2. College students—Canada—Economic conditions. 3. College students—Canada—Social conditions. 4. Postsecondary education—Canada. I. Finnie, Ross II. Queen's University (Kingston, Ont.). School of Policy Studies

LA417.5.W48 2008   378.1'619   C2008-904695-1

Contents

Preface

Ensuring that young people have the chance to pursue their studies beyond high school is not only a matter of social equity; it is also crucial to Canada's economic future. Above all, if Canada is to build the skilled workforce that will keep it competitive in an increasingly global and knowledge-based economy, it must recruit college and university students from among those young people now under-represented in higher education – a group that has too often been left behind in this country, as in others.

Improving access – or getting individuals started in their post-secondary studies – is the first step. The rest of the challenge is to ensure that students who begin post-secondary education are able to make their way successfully through the system.

For governments, institutions, and other stakeholders, accurate and up-to-date information on these issues is central to developing efficient "evidence-based" policies and programs. Such information must offer a clear portrait of those who pursue post-secondary studies and those who do not. It must also identify which students face challenges in successfully completing their studies, and shed light on the underlying factors that make it difficult for them to do so. The articles in this book offer in-depth empirical analysis of these issues by skilled, policy-oriented researchers.

When the Canada Millennium Scholarship Foundation launched its access bursaries in 2005, it committed itself to evaluating their impact on student outcomes. It called on the research community for proposals regarding the collection and analysis of data on the students receiving the bursaries. The Educational Policy Institute and Queen's School of Policy Studies put together their MESA (Measuring the Effectiveness of Student Assistance) team, which came up with a winning proposal to not only gather new data but also exploit existing datasets to carry out an original program of research on access and persistence.

The timing was ideal, as Statistics Canada's Youth in Transition Survey (YITS) was coming to maturity, meaning that, with the arrival of the 2006 data, researchers could follow 15-year-old and 18-to-20-year-old survey respondents over a period of up to six years. This is a period in which youth make crucial decisions: Will they finish high school? Attend post-secondary education? Stay in once they have started? The YITS data are unequalled even at the international level in their richness for addressing such questions.

These unique data have allowed the MESA researchers to investigate the factors that explain why some young people enter post-secondary education and others do not. They have also allowed us to better understand which youth persist in their studies and which of them drop out – and why. The findings presented in this book will therefore enrich discussions among researchers, policy-makers, and practitioners as they confront the related issues of post-secondary access and persistence.

> *Norman Riddell*
> Executive Director and CEO,
> Canada Millennium Scholarship Foundation

Acknowledgements

The volume *Who Goes? Who Stays? What Matters? Accessing and Persisting in Post-Secondary Education in Canada* grew out of the Canada Millennium Scholarship Foundation's desire to better understand post-secondary access and persistence in order to aid Canadians. The Education Policy Institute (EPI) and the School of Policy Studies at Queen's University partnered to create the Measuring the Effectiveness of Student Aid (MESA) project (Le Projet Mesurer l'efficacité de l'aide financière aux étudiants – MEAFE) to study the issues and this volume is one of the results.

We would like to thank staff at the School of Policy Studies Publication Unit, Mark Howes and Valerie Jarus for their many efforts, copyeditor Maureen Garvie, and research associate Christina Lazarova for her proofreading. Thanks also go to the research assistants for the MESA project, Stephen Childs, Viorela Diaconu, Theresa Hanqing Qiu and Yan Zhang, for their excellent work with the YITS data. Academic guidance and peer review of the chapters in this book were undertaken by the members of the MESA Research Advisory Committee, and we would like to thank Keith Banting, Charles Beach, Lorne Carmichael, Jane Friesen, Clément Lemelin, Garnet Picot and Hans Vossensteyn. Special thanks go to Anne Motte of the Foundation, who has been invaluable to the MESA project and in the preparation of this book.

Ross Finnie
Associate Professor
School of Public and International Affairs
University of Ottawa

Richard E. Mueller
Associate Professor
Department of Economics
University of Lethbridge

Arthur Sweetman
Director
School of Policy Studies
Queen's University at Kingston

Alex Usher
Vice-President and Director
(Canada)
Educational Policy Institute (EPI)

Part I

Introduction and Background

1

Introduction: A Framework for Thinking about Participation in Post-Secondary Education

ROSS FINNIE, ARTHUR SWEETMAN, AND ALEX USHER

On reconnaît de plus en plus que l'accès aux études postsecondaires (EPS) est tributaire d'un ensemble complexe de facteurs reliés entre eux et qui vont bien au-delà d'éléments de nature financière comme les frais de scolarité ou l'aide financière offerte aux étudiants. Sont également en jeu la préparation des jeunes et leur attitude face aux EPS, leurs aspirations et d'autres facteurs fortement associés au milieu familial et qui s'enracinent tôt dans la vie des individus. Ce texte d'introduction propose un cadre qui tient compte de toutes ces influences et aborde les questions de l'analyse et de l'interprétation des résultats d'études empiriques, des politiques publiques et des recherches qui seront nécessaires. Chacun des articles présentés dans cet ouvrage est réinterprété dans cette optique.

Access to post-secondary education (PSE) is the result of a complex set of relationships involving not only financial factors such as the costs of schooling and student aid but also students' attitudes to PSE, their preparation, their aspirations, and other factors rooted in family background that start early in an individual's life. This chapter develops a framework that incorporates such influences and discusses the implications for estimating the underlying relationships, interpreting the findings of empirical analyses, policy, and future research needs. The research papers that follow in the volume are reviewed in this context.

Who Goes? Who Stays? What Matters? Accessing and Persisting in Post-Secondary Education in Canada, eds. R. Finnie, R.E. Mueller, A. Sweetman, and A. Usher. Montreal and Kingston: McGill-Queen's University Press, Queen's Policy Studies Series. © 2008 The School of Policy Studies, Queen's University at Kingston. All rights reserved.

Policy-Related Research on Access and Persistence

Driven by the gains in standards of living, productivity, and global competitiveness associated with post-secondary education (PSE), governments around the world, including those in Canada, are working to increase participation in higher education (OECD 2008). Alongside this push to increase overall numbers, concerns regarding the equity of access to PSE have become more pressing. Such interests are long-standing in Canada but gained strength and a sense of immediacy in the 1990s as tuition fees rose, student debt levels increased, and various empirical studies identified important differences in PSE participation rates by certain family characteristics, including socio-economic status and the family income component of it in particular. Few would insist that everyone should attend PSE. Some individuals will simply prefer careers – and lives – that do not involve going to college or university, and others lack the ability. But it is widely accepted, at least in Canada, that access to PSE and its associated benefits should be open to all those who have the desire to participate and the talent to succeed. Access both addresses equity goals and helps drive the engine of the knowledge economy.

The policy question thus becomes one not simply of increasing overall PSE participation rates but also of providing the opportunity to obtain a post-secondary education to all interested and qualified individuals, including those from lower socio-economic backgrounds who have traditionally had lower participation rates, especially at the university level. Effectively addressing these issues from an evidence-based policy perspective requires an understanding of who gains *access* to PSE (typically defined as starting a program), as well as who *persists* (i.e., advances from one year to the next, on through graduation), and the underlying factors determining these dynamics.

The Youth in Transition Survey (YITS) enables the essays in *Who Goes, Who Stays, What Matters* to offer fresh, empirically related insights on these dynamics. Two characteristics of the YITS data contribute, in particular, to their value in this regard. First, the data longitudinally track young people from their mid-teens through late twenties as they move through the adolescent years preceding PSE, make decisions about and progress through PSE, and then enter the labour market. Second, the information contained in the files is very rich.[1]

Based predominantly on analyses undertaken with the YITS, a source of policy-relevant data on education with few equals anywhere in the world, the papers in this volume provide an important contribution to the empirical basis of the public policy debate on access and persistence in Canada. The book thus conforms to the fundamental purpose of the Measuring the Effectiveness of Student Aid (MESA) Project from which it stems. That is, the project brings scholars together to engage in research that provides new empirical evidence and otherwise enhances our understanding of access to PSE and persistence through to completion in a way that informs and advances the relevant policy discussions, and makes these advances accessible to a wide audience.[2]

The purpose of this introductory chapter is to put the volume's papers in context, summarize their contributions and draw the most important inferences. In doing so, however, it first peels back the relevant issues to their fundamentals and presents a more general model of access and persistence and the various factors that determine them. Using this framework, it then identifies some of the limitations of past approaches to analyzing access and persistence, draws a roadmap for future research, and discusses related policy issues. Especially when paired with the literature review chapter provided by Richard Mueller, the chapter thus offers a useful general starting point for thinking about access and persistence in the Canadian context.

An Extended View of Barriers to Participation in Post-Secondary Education

Many discussions of access to PSE focus on the identification of barriers that may block individuals' access to higher education or prevent them from continuing in their studies after starting. But the term "barriers" is often poorly defined and not placed in the broader context necessary for addressing the full set of relevant issues from a conceptual, empirical, or policy perspective.

We might, for example, agree that not being able to afford the required tuition fees or associated living costs represents a potential (financial) barrier to PSE, and be concerned that for this reason individuals from lower income families, in particular, might not have the same opportunities to access PSE as others. This definition of a barrier is in fact the predominant one used in public discourse regarding access to PSE. But there are also "softer" barriers, such as an individual not being sufficiently prepared for PSE, not being well informed regarding the monetary benefits and costs of higher education, or simply not being able to see the broader worth of going to university or college, all of which seem to be related to family background.

These latter barriers are a bit trickier than, for example, the question of affordability. Because they are typically related to family background, there is no obvious and simple (though perhaps expensive) government-action-only intervention such as a cash transfer that will causally improve outcomes. To some degree these barriers follow from the interaction between an individual's environment and the *choices* he or she makes over long periods of time. But if the end result is unequal access to PSE and, in particular, if these inequalities are related to family or other background factors such as socio-economic status, surely they should be regarded as *inequities* or otherwise considered as barriers, representing different sets of PSE – and life course – opportunities. From this perspective, all-too-common discussions of barriers to PSE that focus exclusively on financial aid can be seen as narrow and limiting.

If we accept this broader perspective of "barriers," it follows that we need to better understand *all* the myriad factors that affect access and persistence. In short, any factor that determines PSE participation should be of concern, especially if it is related to family background or other factors beyond an individual's control. Finnie, Lascelles, and Sweetman (2005) find that many early-in-life outcomes that are correlated with family background are predictors of post-secondary access. So, it is not just financial barriers in which we are interested but also "preparation barriers," "interest barriers," and so on. The papers presented here generally embrace this broader notion of barriers and provide new evidence informing a range of topics regarding access to PSE while also opening up new ones.

Access issues from this broader perspective are conceptually and empirically complex. In contrast to focusing on affordability, access and persistence might also relate to differences in information and perceptions (e.g., those related to the costs or benefits of attending PSE), differences in preferences (e.g., the enjoyment of school), or differences in the preparation for PSE (academic and otherwise), all of which may be correlated with socio-economic status.

Constructing access in this way is not just a matter of academic interest. It also has fundamental policy implications. If access in general, and differences in access among different socio-economic groups, are primarily a matter of money, then policy solutions would presumably lie in the realm of student financial aid or tuition fees. But if access and its relationship to family income have more to do with information, preferences, preparation, and other such factors, then our interventions need to line up along these dimensions as well. In short, if our notion of barriers is wide, then so too should be the range of policy tools under consideration.

In our opinion, research and debate about access to PSE are moving in the direction of the broader model: that is, towards recognition of the importance of non-financial factors, even as these are often found to be correlated with family income and parental education. Yet much policy – and many public policy debates – are focused on money and on affordability in particular. The most recent measures, at least at the federal level as announced in the federal 2008 budget, are a case in point: increased grants, rather than loans, for low income students. While the specific measures to be put into place are not bad, they do nothing to address the need to go beyond such conventional initiatives.

How Barriers Interact and Related Implications for Empirical Analysis

Adopting this broader perspective of barriers can help us to better understand and investigate the range of factors that may affect participation in PSE as well as differences in participation rates among different groups in the population. However, this perspective also points to certain challenges regarding the empirical estimation of the relevant relationships. For example, various papers in this volume identify family income as an important determinant of access to PSE. But when parental education is added to the analysis, the income effect falls dramatically, and education seems to exert a much stronger independent influence than parental income.

Furthermore, when aspirations for PSE (expressed by students, their parents, and their peers) and preparations for PSE (as represented by high school grades and other measures) are included in the estimation, aspirations are also found to be significantly related to access and to play important roles in explaining differences in access rates between various groups. When the additional variables are added, it is mostly the effect of parental education that is reduced, while the remaining income effects change only slightly. Variables such as post-secondary aspirations have a much stronger relationship with parental education than with income.

From this we conclude that family income, parental education, aspirations for PSE, and the preparation for higher education are all important determinants of who goes to PSE; and parental education as well as family income operate both through their effects on the "intermediate" outcomes we use as regressors such as aspirations and preparations, and also "directly" on PSE access. However, the direct effect of parental education appears to be larger than that for family income. These findings have useful policy implications. If non-monetary factors that start relatively early in life seem to matter much more than monetary ones (at least at the margin – see below on this), we probably need to shift access policies from the present focus on "affordability" to emphasizing these early life-course influences of educational pathways.

But we cannot stop there. The effects of the various "early influence" factors are complex. Those who aspire to go on to PSE may, for instance, tend to have this orientation because they will face fewer financial barriers (perhaps because their parents have more money or are otherwise more willing to support them), because they are already on the path to being better prepared for PSE (they might go to better schools, have advantageous extracurricular experiences or be getting higher grades), or because they have simply already decided to go to PSE. Meanwhile, overcoming any financial or other point-of entry barriers might in turn depend on the choices individuals have already made regarding PSE, their related preparations in anticipation of that choice, and the family support they may receive in a variety of other forms, financial and otherwise.

Furthermore, any of these variables might also be related to other omitted factors not included in the analysis. Perhaps, for example, "stick-with-it-ness" is a personal attribute of significant importance in determining not only access to PSE but also grades, aspirations, and other variables included in the analysis. The observed relationships will reflect such omitted factors, further complicating any analysis.

In short, the new factors identified in these analyses – important and significant as they are – might in turn be related to each other, to the access outcome itself, or to other omitted influences, potentially biasing the estimates of their effects.[3] When, therefore, a model is estimated in which access is taken to be determined not just by, say, family income and other background factors but also by high school grades and PSE aspirations, we are identifying some empirical relationships of potentially substantial importance. But we need to be cautious in the interpretation of those relationships, particularly with respect to ascribing causality (e.g., "the effect of grades on access"), and seek even better estimates that take these concerns into effect.

The research presented here thus contributes to our understanding of some important new relationships regarding access to PSE and persistence, including aspirations, attitudes, and preparation. It also sheds light on how these variables relate to certain key background factors such as parental education and family income. The policy implications of these findings are of immediate and great importance. At the same time, the work brings us up against a new set of questions and empirical challenges – an outcome in many cases recognized and pointed out by the authors.

A Broader Model of Access, Empirical Estimation, and the YITS

Though estimating more complex models extends our understanding of access and persistence, in Canada data limitations have previously impeded such investigations. The unprecedented richness of the YITS data has, however, opened up new opportunities. The conceptual framework discussed above will help illustrate the broader approach, point to the data needed to estimate it, and place the YITS – and the papers included in this volume – in this context.

The two ways of thinking about participation in PSE and how it may be related to different sets of influences are presented in Figures 1 and 2. The first figure represents what we will term the "student aid policy model" (or just "policy model") and shows a very simple approach that symbolizes a narrow view of access issues.

FIGURE 1
A Simple Model of PSE, Access, and Attainment

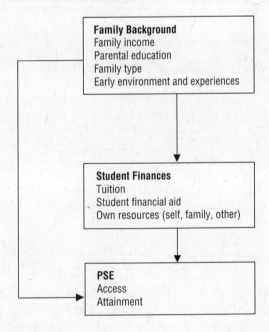

Source: Authors' compilation.

FIGURE 2
Full Model of PSE Causal Pathways

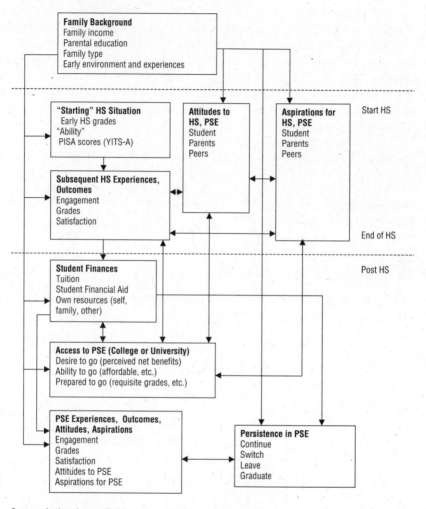

Source: Authors' compilation.

In the simple model, participation in PSE – perhaps measured as "access to PSE" or as final PSE attainment – is deemed to be related to family background, as measured by family income, parental education, or some other such relatively limited set of variables (e.g., family type), and another limited set of variables representing early environment and experiences (e.g., province or rural-urban residence). PSE participation is also postulated to be related to student finances (i.e., tuition, student financial aid, and the student's and family's own resources), which are in turn linked to family background, including the extent of parental support and the availability of student financial aid (which depends on income). Any associated empirical analysis may identify the relationship between PSE outcomes and these variables. The interpretation of any empirical findings based on this model, as well as any policy inferences drawn from it, will likely be commensurately simple and limited. It may also be quite misleading. Such ways of thinking have, for example, caused Canadian governments and those in other countries to focus on financial factors as the most important barriers to PSE, and thus on tuition policy and student financial aid as the proposed remedies. Such a policy focus is not only inadequate but wrong-headed if the more important determinants of participation in PSE include much more than "financial factors," especially if they begin to operate long before the nominal point of decision-making with respect to participation in PSE at the end of high school.

Figure 2 represents a much more general and extended model of participation in PSE, corresponding to what we have called the (emerging) "research model" above. Family background again comes first chronologically among the myriad effects shown (see its placement at the top of the figure), since it can be assumed to be at least largely "predetermined" and thus "exogenous" to the rest of the access process,[4] but, beyond this, the relationships are complex, with many potential interconnections.

So, for example, PSE attitudes, aspirations, and preparations (the last represented here by the young person's performance in high school) might affect PSE outcomes. But these influences might themselves be at least partly determined by not only family background (which thus has an indirect effect on PSE outcomes as well as a direct effect) but also by PSE decisions. See the "Access to PSE" box in the bottom part of the figure, which should perhaps be depicted to extend chronologically upward into the high school region of the figure, because such access and related decisions are often made well before the end of high school and thus influence the "earlier" variables (i.e., attitudes, aspirations, preparation). These different relationships are represented in the figure by the relevant arrows going to and from the various boxes.

Other potential influences on access to PSE shown here include the student's "engagement" and "satisfaction" while in high school. Note also the potential interactions between student finances and other factors, now including not just family background but also additional variables. And throughout, there will also be the sorts of unobserved factors (not shown here), discussed in the preceding section, which will present other complications and further challenges to estimation, whether at the student or family level, or even beyond; these may include differences across provinces in high schools, PSE systems, and anything else that can affect access.

The general upshot of this more general model is that there exists a complex set of relationships that is relevant to our theoretical view of PSE outcomes, to our strategies for the empirical estimation of these effects, to our interpretation of those findings, and to the policy implications we draw from them. Furthermore, access and persistence are shown to be two distinct processes that together represent the two main components of "participation" in PSE and, ultimately, PSE attainment.

The extended model implies vastly widened opportunities, as well as greater challenges, when used as a guide for empirical work on access or persistence. This kind of large-scale empirical work has previously been impossible in Canada due to the lack of suitable data, though the education research literature has addressed parts of it. In contrast, the YITS datasets with their wide range of information, including great depth on the various blocks of variables in Figure 2, open new opportunities for exploring the full set of factors determining participation in PSE.

We might debate the particular details of the model in Figure 2, including the specific labelling of the different blocks of variables shown, the precise elements included in each block, and the specified causal pathways. However, the major point would remain: access to and persistence through PSE are the result of a complex set of processes typically starting early in a person's life. Understanding these processes requires a model, an empirical approach, and data that capture these. The work presented here represents a first installment of such a broad research agenda

The Papers

The papers in this volume, which in all cases but one use the YITS dataset, set the context for the questions they ask, present the principal findings, and discuss the implications for policy. Discussions of methodology are minimized, and the more technical elements are explained in intuitive terms, with the related material confined to footnotes, appendices, and especially the underlying research papers, which interested readers may consult.[5]

The first two papers provide context and lead-in material for those that follow. Richard Mueller's literature review gives a general overview of previous work on access and persistence, and underlying ways of thinking about these issues, with an emphasis on Canada. Significantly, many of the key limitations and gaps he identifies stem from a lack of better data, a problem largely resolved by the YITS. The papers in this volume thus begin to fill some of the more important of these gaps.

Bussiere et al. discuss the YITS in detail, providing a valuable cross-reference for the other papers, which refer back to this chapter instead of repeating general discussions of the YITS. These authors also discuss the unprecedented opportunities for policy-related research afforded by the two YITS cohorts, YITS-A and YITS-B. Apart from its usefulness for this volume, this discussion of the YITS should offer a valuable reference for other researchers and policy-makers thinking about where to take future explorations.

Access

According to the YITS-A cohort, 31 percent of young people from the bottom income quintile (i.e., the lowest 20 percent) had attended university by the age of 19, compared to 50 percent of those from the top quartile (see Frenette, below). While significant, this gap does not appear to have changed appreciably in the last decade or so; for example, Statistics Canada (2001) found similar patterns using data from the Survey of Labour and Income Dynamics (SLID) in the late 1990s. Identifying the size of this gap and putting it in historical context is interesting in itself, but the real strength of the YITS dataset is that it allows researchers to look well beyond such simple participation statistics to study the reasons behind this gap in ways that the SLID and other data have not previously permitted.

One of the central focuses of the papers included here is to identify how much of the access gap is related to financial factors and how much is explained by other influences (preparations, choices, etc.) with which family incomes are correlated. In short, are income differences the root cause of the associated access gaps, or are they just a marker for other factors?

Finnie and Mueller use regression techniques and the YITS-A to address these issues, focusing on university attendance, where the greatest differences are observed.[6] Although parental income appears to be an important driver of university attendance when looked at using a simpler model (i.e., including fewer explanatory variables), when parental education is added to the analysis, it is found to be much *more* important than family income and causes the estimated income effect to be driven sharply downward, although (significantly) family income does not disappear entirely as a factor. In extending their models further, Finnie and Mueller also find a significant relationship between success in secondary school and access to PSE; however, in contrast to Adelman's (1999) and others' results, which show the primacy of mathematics grades to access in the PSE, they find that the overall secondary school mark has the greatest impact on access.

The international PISA (Programme for International Student Assessment) reading score is also an important predictor of university attendance, while the inclusion of high school "engagement" as well as personal characteristics and attitudes indicates that the effort students make in high school counts more than their social integration, that "self efficacy" also matters, and that parental behaviour (as measured by parents' "monitoring consistency") has a small but in some cases statistically significant effect. Importantly, the parental education effect falls as these other factors are added to the models, thus pointing to at least some of the pathways by which parental education likely has its effects – stronger high school performance, better study habits and attitudes, and so on – and suggesting where we might look for other ways in which parental education matters.

The Finnie-Mueller results thus strongly suggest that the cause of the participation gap between rich and poor is less financial than "cultural." Using a different approach aimed explicitly at explaining the rich-poor participation gap, Marc Frenette picks up on this theme in the first of his two articles. Applying standard decomposition techniques to data from the YITS-A to understand the relative importance of various observable characteristics, Frenette shows that it is largely differences in academic preparation that explain the gap, with perceived financial barriers accounting for only 12 percent of the variance between high and low income students. This does not imply that money is never an issue, but it does suggest that the approximately $6 billion currently spent on student aid is in most cases sufficient to help students pay their schooling costs (tuition, and other fees and expenses) while attending college or university. The specific implication of Frenette's paper is that moves to redress inequalities in access likely need to focus on the secondary level education system, not on financial factors.

But inequalities in access also have an important gender component, and one that may surprise readers who have not been following the relevant literature. Across the western world, the past thirty years have seen a major shift in the patterns of post-secondary enrolment, with female enrolment catching up to and then significantly surpassing male enrolment. In Canada, the YITS-A data show that at age 19 (as captured in 2004), 60 percent of all university students were female. Frenette and Klarka Zeman use these data to again apply decomposition techniques to identify the relative importance of various observable characteristics on the gender access gap. Factors related to academic preparation (again), including grades, the international-standardized PISA test scores, and better study habits, seem to predominate, explaining well over half the gender gap in participation, while parental expectations are also important.

Parental income and education have a very small effect on the gap in access by socio-economic status; this is largely by construction, because males and females come from the same kinds of families. Indeed, for this reason we must look beyond differences in family-specific characteristics to explain the gender gap, although the possibility of different "returns" to family characteristics remains a potential subject for future research – even though the Frenette-Zeman analysis finds no important differences in this regard.

The paper also casts some doubt on the importance of differential economic rates of return from a university education as being important in explaining the gender gap in participation – unless the differences in rates of return start to influence behaviour well in advance of high school graduation (i.e., the idea that females are more likely to go to university because they receive a greater economic benefit is not supported unless that motivation starts to act very early), but it also points out that this factor is inherently difficult to quantify. In the end, in identifying the importance of good academic habits in driving the gender access gap, the findings beg the follow-up questions about where the roots of academic performance lie, how and why these differ for males and females, and what can – or should – be done about it. These are important empirical and policy issues, and will only become more so in the future.

Hoy et al. address a related question, finding that aspirations for PSE attendance significantly influence the decision to attend university, that this influence comes in addition to qualifications as reflected by grades as well as other explanatory variables such as parental education levels, and that male-female differences in aspirations seem to play an appreciable role in explaining the differences in PSE access rates between males and females.

These authors also take full advantage of the longitudinal structure of the YITS to focus on how aspirations for PSE evolve during the run-up to PSE, and find that there is a gender gap from the beginning but that it increases over time: girls start (at age 15) with higher overall aspirations for PSE, university in particular, but are also more likely to revise their aspirations upwards by age 17. Of course a new set of questions again arises from these findings: why do females have these different aspirations, why do they evolve in this way, what are other related factors, and – again – what can or should be done about them? The research agenda has once more been pushed forward in an interesting and important way by this analysis in what it tells us and in where it points us for further work.

One ongoing question related to access issues is the effect of high school students' paid work outside of school. Does such work lessen students' ability to concentrate on their studies and thus hurt academic achievement, causing those who work longer hours to be less likely to make it into PSE and succeed when they get there? The issue is not cut and dried, since there are arguments and some existing empirical evidence suggesting that moderate amounts of work may be good for students, perhaps teaching them to handle workloads, budget their time, and so on. Jorgen Hansen addresses the issue by looking at the relationship between work during high school and students' high school grades (which are themselves strongly related to access and future PSE outcomes). Exploiting the richness of background variables and the information available on high school grades available in the YITS-A, Hansen finds that simpler models do in fact indicate an upside-down "U-shaped" relationship, where smallish amounts of work appear to have beneficial effects on high school grades but longer hours are damaging.

But when the additional controls for individual attributes available in the YITS are included in the analysis, this result is reversed. The effect of work is everywhere found to be negative: *any* amount of paid work appears to have an adverse effect on high school grades. This contrasts, interestingly, with the effects of extracurricular activities, which are uniformly positive. However, Hansen's alternative approach of attempting to come up with exogenous variation in students' work through instrumental variables methods yields less conclusive results, quite possibly because the statistical challenges characterizing this approach are inherently formidable in this context (i.e., the difficulty of finding a variable that affects work but has no direct effect on grades).

Hansen's findings naturally raise many new questions. Do the effects hold up using other methods and with other data? If the effects are correct, can the PSE opportunities of youth in lower income families be increased by providing the means by which they do not have to work during high school – or by otherwise encouraging them to *choose* not to work? What are the effects of work *during* PSE on PSE outcomes?

Persistence

Access is, however, just one part of the PSE story. Since many of the benefits of PSE come only with obtaining a completed credential, persistence through to completion is equally important in terms of determining which individuals gain the benefits of PSE. We therefore need to better grasp the persistence dynamic and to better understand 1) the rates of persistence and depth of the persistence "problem," 2) the factors to which persistence is related, and 3) the policies that might be adopted to help get students on the right PSE track from the beginning and to provide the assistance some students need in getting through the programs they choose.

In Canada, unfortunately, there has been an almost total lack of data on measured completion rates that include students who change from one institution to another, as well as those who leave PSE entirely and then return to their studies at their original institution (and in their original program) or another, or on other patterns related to PSE pathways and the diverse routes students take to obtain PSE credentials. PSE pathways – persistence, mobility, and, ultimately, graduation – are dynamic processes that require similarly dynamic (or longitudinal) data to be studied, and such longitudinal data on students have not previously been available. This is why the creation of the YITS and the analysis undertaken by Finnie and Qiu is so important.

Using the YITS-B, Finnie and Qiu show that while about 50 percent of all students fail to finish their *initial* programs of study within five years, only about 10-15 percent are what might be called true dropouts – that is, they have neither completed a credential nor remain in school. The difference between the two sets of numbers represents those who finished a different program from the one in which they started, sometimes at a different institution or even at a different level of study, as well as those who are still continuing in their studies, again in many cases in a different program or at a different institution from the one in which they started, sometimes after a break from their studies.

Included in these dynamics are the findings that among those who leave PSE at some point, 40 percent of college students and 54 percent of university students return to PSE within three years, and that there are relatively low rates of movement between college and university sectors, either among (direct) "switchers" or "leaver-returners." Finnie and Qiu's results thus suggest that the dropout problem in Canada is not nearly as large as was previously thought (based primarily on estimates derived from data restricted to single institutions) and that the PSE experience takes many different pathways. They also find that it is only rarely financial factors that cause students to leave their studies, and that family background tends to have smallish effects as well, which contrasts with the strong effect of family background on access (more for college than university students). Schooling experiences such as the perceived quality of teaching and the relevance of the schooling to future job opportunities also appear to play a relatively minor role in these dynamics, although these effects are generally more important for college students than university students.[7]

Felice Martinello adds to the Finnie-Qiu findings and focuses on the issue of students who switch programs, examining the characteristics of switchers and their prospects of success after switching. He finds, like Finnie and Qiu, that most switchers appear to change to other programs at the same level of study (i.e., they stay within either the college or university system rather than changing across) but, intriguingly, those who switch levels appear to be more likely to complete their second program than those who do not. He also finds that although parental education does not have as strong an effect on switchers as it does on access, those with high parental education seem likelier to switch than to drop out, but then have no advantage when it comes to completing a second program. Individuals' finances are also related to completion: although Martinello is not able to distinguish between need-based and merit-based aid, students with either of these appear to be more likely to complete their first program than those without financial aid, but less likely to start a second program if they did not finish their first.

What about the longer-run pathways of students and how they relate to time to completion in PSE? Lesley Andres and Maria Adamuti-Trache are the only authors to use non-YITS data, instead exploiting a 15-year panel of students in British Columbia to examine the relationship between student loans and educational and other life course outcomes (e.g., marriage). The sample, length of the follow-up, and information available in the file is unique, and some of the relationships uncovered point to avenues for future research, especially with respect to the relationship between time to graduation, student loans, and early life course events. Their findings, in this paper and related ones they cite, point to the value of looking beyond how student aid affects in-school activities. Student loans can constrain life choices beyond graduation, sometimes for many years, in very fundamental ways.

Financial Factors

David Johnson looks at student finances, in this case the effects of tuition fees on access and persistence. In the tradition of Coelli (2004), Neill (2005), and Johnson and Rahman (2005),[8] Johnson makes use of inter-provincial differences in tuition and tax credits and changes in these over time, using a "differences-in-differences" approach (thus controlling for provincial fixed effects that may be correlated with tuition levels and PSE participation patterns) to measure the effects on enrolment of changes in tuition and "net" tuition (i.e., tuition after tax credits). Using the YITS, he finds little evidence of any effect of tuition on access or persistence, even in the case of the sharp changes in tuition of 30 percent or more that occurred in British Columbia early in this decade. (Like the other researchers discussed here, Johnson finds that "social" variables such as parental education matter a great deal for access decisions but very little for persistence decisions.)

It could be argued that access and persistence effects might operate with a lag as plans that are already in place are executed, as opposed to students changing their choices immediately when they find themselves with suddenly higher prices. This might be especially true in the case of persistence, where students have already begun to invest in their schooling.

Johnson also presents some evidence, although it is weaker, that increases in tuition might have effects on access for young persons from families whose parents have limited PSE experiences themselves. At this point these possibilities remain not much more than conjectures, with Johnson's main findings clearly pointing to the absence of price effects – at least at the general level and in the short run, where those who argue for tuition decreases would presumably have expected to find at least some effect.

The problem of all this for policy-makers is that it does not provide much in the way of guidance for how best to provide financial aid to students. While the $6 billion currently provided in student aid each year is probably responsible in large part for the finding that financial factors do not loom large among the barriers to access and completion at the margin, it is possible that this money could be more effective still if it were reconfigured. Martinello provides few clues on this point because need-based and merit-based aid are aggregated in his analysis. Johnson looks at the effects of tax credits but not of loans or grants; the Frenette papers, being more concerned with pre-access characteristics, do not deal with student aid at all except as it affects the financial barriers variables they employ; and Finnie and Qiu are wary of interpreting the financial aid variables they include in some of their models due to concerns regarding omitted variable effects.

Kathleen Day tackles this issue directly by looking into the separate effects of student loans and merit-based aid. In some respects, her paper is one of the most significant recent pieces on student financial aid in Canada, not so much for the empirical evidence it provides (which is hardly definitive) as for the way it poses certain questions. Although she begins by finding some weak positive effects of student aid on persistence (the outcome on which she focuses), she then questions whether or not student financial aid can be considered an exogenous variable, which has important implications for the estimation of its effects.

What does the presence of aid really capture? Having a loan or grant is likely to be related to parental income, family size, schooling costs, the individual's willingness to take on paid work, province of residence, and other factors that determine whether a student receives aid, and how much, and these factors are likely to exert their own effects on persistence. Hence, the estimated "effects" of student financial aid are likely to be biased. Even when attempts are made to control for these other factors (as in the case of family income), the controls might not be perfect, thus leaving aid to be related to various factors not fully captured by the model. When Day re-analyses the data, adjusting for endogeneity using standard methods, she finds that the loan effect disappears or in some specifications even becomes negative.

Further compounding the problem is the issue of what effect a loan (or other form of aid) is capturing. In some cases, the presence of loans – or differences in levels of loans – might represent additional aid being given to offset higher costs. In other cases, more loans might be made available (and be taken up by the student) for a *given* level of need. We would expect "the loan effect" to be different in each of these cases, meaning that researchers who attempt to estimate a single loan effect are in reality likely to be estimating the weighted average of a number of different effects. It is not even clear what direction "the loan effect" should take in such circumstances, since in some cases the effects of loans on persistence (or access) should presumably be positive (e.g., when more generous aid is provided for a given set of costs), while in others it might be negative (e.g., when loans are replacing grants). Researchers and policy-makers alike thus need to think carefully about what "loan effect" they are interested in, what is being identified in any given research undertaking, and how the relevant estimates should be interpreted.

Although its effects are difficult to estimate, even with data as good as the YITS, financial aid is clearly important, and it is not only the *amount* but also the *type* that is relevant. These are the issues addressed by Carmichael and Finnie: what is the role of loans, and when is there a role for grants rather than loans in student financial aid packages? The theoretical model they develop posits a role for family income based on the (unconditional) financial support parents provide for their children *whether or not* they go to PSE, and thus represents an effect that will operate in addition to any that operates through the amount of (conditional) support provided should the child in fact decide to pursue PSE.

Importantly, the effect Carmichael and Finnie describe does not operate by relieving financial constraints on participating in PSE faced by the student or otherwise making the schooling more *affordable* – in which case the problem could be addressed with loans. Instead, it affects even those students who have the means of paying for their schooling but decide not to go because of the relative hardship they would experience while in school because of the lower transfers they receive from their families.

The empirical work carried out by Carmichael and Finnie with the YITS-A supports this hypothesis, as they find that family income does in fact affect whether a student goes to PSE even for those who say the reason they did not participate in PSE had nothing to do with being able to afford it. The upshot of the research is that grants, and not just loans, are needed to level the PSE playing field between young people from richer and poorer families.

Policy Implications

Identifying Barriers: Who Goes, Who Stays, What Matters?

The policy implications of the findings in these papers – and the broader view of access to PSE represented in the "research model" we are proposing (as opposed to the narrower "policy model" that still seems to be driving government actions on the issue) – are profound. Many (policy) discussions are predicated on the common empirical finding that access to PSE is related to family income and other such basic relationships. Policy then turned to solutions involving student funding largely on the assumption that the income-access relationship, in particular, must imply an affordability issue: the reason low income students weren't going was because they didn't have enough money to do so. Grants, loans, and other forms of targeted student aid have therefore been duly administered and adjusted, and related tuition policies such as freezes or limited increases have been implemented, but inequalities in access have remained stubbornly fixed – in Canada as indeed in most other developed countries, even where student aid is extremely generous and tuition is in some cases free.

Meanwhile, the effects of more general forms of student financial aid not specifically targeted at lower income and other under-represented students, including education-related tax credits and family savings incentives programs, are hard to identify because it is difficult to know what the access and persistence patterns and other behaviour (e.g., how PSE is financed) would have been in their absence. That said, most experts believe that the effects of these programs have probably been largely to subsidize the PSE of middle and upper income students who would have gone anyway, thus having little effect on access or persistence rates generally, or on differences in these rates by socioeconomic background, and that the money could be better spent on individuals at the margin of participating in PSE and / or not remaining to graduation.[9]

The research presented in this book offers an explanation for the relatively slow progress, especially with respect to under-represented groups such as those from low income families or those whose parents do not have PSE. For the greatest part, it appears that "culture dominates money," where "culture" is a shorthand reference for the various non-monetary and significantly family-based influences that cause one kind of student to steer towards and prepare for PSE, often from a relatively early age, while another has no such orientation, undertakes no such preparations, and ultimately winds up making different PSE choices. If money in general and affordability in particular are not the determining barriers to PSE, it is hardly surprising that money-based policies aimed at making PSE more affordable have left wide inequities in access.

It is important to emphasize that we are talking about the effect of money *at the margin,* and that current access patterns might look quite different were the existing student financial aid system not in place. There are too many testimonies to the effect that students would not have been able to go to PSE had they not received the financial aid they did, and the limited direct empirical evidence available on the issue points to a similar effect.[10] The issue, however, is not about the effects of the existing student aid system in its entirety. Instead it is to identify the access levers that operate *at the margin*: what policies can bring currently non-participating but deserving and potentially able students into PSE? Put another way, where should the next dollars be spent, or how should current spending on student financial aid be shifted in order to effect the improvements in access patterns we seek? If it is not affordability that determines access, then what *are* the relevant factors? How, and when, do they operate to affect access outcomes? What is their relationship to family background? And what can be done in terms of policy to change access patterns in the face of these relationships?

Unfortunately, here we are stymied anew, because although we can now be relatively certain that student funding is not central to increasing access for those from low socio-economic backgrounds (at the margin), few solid answers exist regarding the next most beneficial avenue to increase access for disadvantaged groups. We are still unsure about precisely what influences parental education is capturing, how such influences operate, and what policy can do in the face of such apparently strong family-based factors to affect access patterns and reduce differences in access across different kinds of families.[11]

We can therefore move the policy agenda to the necessary next step first of all by changing its focus (i.e., going beyond money). Although we do not yet have the answers to all the next sets of questions that have been identified, we can at least point to the research agenda that will help get us there, and consider policy approaches that could be adopted in the nearer term.

Where Research Needs to Go Now

Using the YITS: Where should research go next? We suggest a number of routes. To start, we cannot overstate how we have only just begun to take advantage of the YITS. The work carried out with it thus far has – among other things – revealed a much richer set of determinants of access to PSE and has permitted the first complete analyses of persistence in PSE ever to have been carried out in this country. These steps can be built upon in a number of ways.

One direction would be to go beyond the identification of the associations made thus far to tease out the ever more detailed nature of the relationships in question. Parental education has, for example, been identified as being key to access, but what exactly does parental education provide that leads to college or university attendance? The influences seem to be partly related to test scores, grades, high school engagement, schooling aspirations, and other such outcomes, but how exactly do these linkages work? Further research could drill into these and other related relationships, bringing into the analysis other variables in the YITS that have not yet been investigated. What matters, when do the relevant factors begin to take effect, how do they operate? The more we know, the better.

However, causal relationships, not simple correlations, are of greatest interest. We have already discussed some of the problems related to omitted variable and endogeneity bias – and there are other estimation and interpretation problems associated with the complexity of the access and persistence dynamics. The YITS data do not represent a general panacea to such problems; no single dataset could. But the richness of the YITS data certainly allows for more extensive sets of controls to be included in any analysis and can thus help reduce various omitted bias problems. It may also help address some of the endogeneity problems if identifying "instruments" suitable for addressing those issues can be found, thus allowing researchers to better tease out some of the relevant causal effects.

As an alternative estimation strategy focused on obtaining true causal effects, "natural experiments" – typically represented by changes in policy across different jurisdictions and/or groups over time – offer interesting opportunities for studying the effects of student financial aid and tuition policies on access and persistence. If, for example, student loans were made more generous in a given province at a specific time, that "natural experiment" could provide the means of identifying the relevant effects on access and persistence. Johnson uses such methods to look at the effects of tuition fees on access and persistence, and we are confident that as researchers deepen their thinking about the related estimation problems and understand better how the YITS might be helpful for addressing them in this way, more such work will unfold.

In summary, the use of the YITS for policy related research on access and persistence should continue to be expanded. We believe this will happen as a matter of course as the YITS datasets and all their strengths continue to become better known and the number of experienced researchers working with the data grows. But this agenda could also benefit from making the YITS data – which are very complex and thus relatively difficult to work with – more accessible for researchers.

Using other datasets: Although the strengths of the YITS data are unique, other datasets are probably still worth using for research on access and persistence. The Labour Force Survey (LFS), and the related Survey of Consumer Finances (SCF), for example, while lacking in sample size and variables of interest, are long-running cross-sectional datasets with at least some information related to PSE attainment and current enrolment that can be appropriate for addressing certain research/policy questions, even if in a limited way.

The Survey of Labour and Income Dynamics (SLID) has the benefit of being longitudinal, allowing researchers to track young people in the years leading up to, and through, PSE (like the YITS). But unlike the YITS, it is a general survey rather than youth/PSE-focused, and so again the relevant sample sizes are small and the schooling information is limited. But the SLID has already been used to some effect for addressing certain specific issues related to access (e.g., Drolet 2005), and could prove useful in other specific applications.

The Post-Secondary Education Participation Survey (PEPS), while now getting old (the information dates from 2002), is also focused on young people and their PSE experiences, and still has the best data on student financial aid, and therefore continues to be useful for looking at issues related to participation in PSE.

The National Longitudinal Survey of Children and Youth (NLSCY) has significant research potential related to PSE, since it has the richest background information available (longitudinally gathered) on a co-hort of youth now beginning to arrive at the normal age for entering PSE. Sample sizes, missing information, and attrition are issues, but at the very least the NLSCY should be of some complementary use to the YITS due to the uniqueness of the information available.

The recently developed Post-Secondary Student Information System (PSIS) is an administrative file that has been constructed by Statistics Canada from data provided by participating PSE institutions. The PSIS theoretically represents a census (as opposed to sample) of students from the covered institutions, and contains a wealth of institutional and student based data that could prove complementary to the YITS, especially for issues pertaining to persistence (as individuals can be tracked from their point of entry into PSE). That said, PSIS coverage is mixed so far, ranging from essentially 100 percent for Atlantic Canada to lower rates in other provinces.

Finally, the Longitudinal Administrative Database (LAD), which is constructed from tax data, contains information related to PSE participation derivable from the related tax credits. Although the PSE information is somewhat lacking in detail and precision, careful use of the dataset would allow it to be employed for the analysis of access and persistence patterns, especially as they relate to family background – past income (longitudinal) profiles in particular. Also, the continuous time series of data available makes the LAD well suited to the "natural experiment" approach described above. In this regard, analyzing the effects of specific changes in student financial aid, tuition levels, and related finance-based policies on access and persistence seems particularly promising.

Other data, including the wealth of more specific, administratively based files that exist across the country, could also be used in interesting, creative ways. Thus, while the YITS will probably dominate research into access and persistence in this country in the coming years, other sources may be profitably exploited as well.

Random assignment experiments: Another potentially important line of research on access and persistence is random assignment experiments. These could be done in two main areas. The first would be their use to more definitively identify the effects on access and persistence of student aid – the types of aid (loans, grants, etc.), the amounts that are required to effect changes in outcomes, and how it should be targeted.

Past research on the effects of student assistance using existing datasets – including the YITS – has been plagued by the classic estimation problems noted above, since aid is inherently related to a range of personal/family characteristics that determine eligibility for student assistance and other elements of the broader policy environment. For example, student aid is frequently linked to tuition strategies and supply-side policies, which vary by province and are difficult to isolate. Identifying the effects of aid has therefore been difficult. Random assignment experiments, however, can resolve such issues through the construction of control and treatment groups that equalize other factors across the groups. Through such methods, it is possible to identify which kinds of aid work best, and, assuming the sample size is large enough, how the effects vary according to the way in which the aid is targeted.

Why, then, are random assignment experiments not used more often? One reason is that ethical barriers can arise, since such experiments can be seen as "using students as guinea pigs" or otherwise treating individuals unequally and therefore "unfairly." Designing experiments so that no student is made worse off, obtaining informed consent on the part of all participants, emphasizing the social benefits of the research, and following other established experiment implementation strategies can minimize these barriers but do not always overcome them. Also, such experiments are, like any policy intervention, very specific regarding the implementation details, and an experiment with one program design provides limited information about other options. So, a failure for a specific design need not imply that a different design will not succeed.

Another problem with experiments is that they can be relatively expensive. If, for example, the policy to be tested is to give students, say, $2,000 in grants, something like a thousand individuals might have to be given the grant in order to estimate its effects with sufficient precision to make those estimates meaningful, thus costing close to $2 million in grants alone, before other expenses have even been considered (e.g., implementation/administration costs, analysis of the findings, etc.). Each particular version of the policy being tested would drive up the numbers needed, and costs, commensurately. These costs might seem small in comparison to the hundreds of millions of dollars or even more spent on such programs in any given year, and they can be well worthwhile if such an experiment makes it possible to better identify the effects of the programs in question or to learn how to target them more effectively. Million-dollar-plus research projects, however, are rare.

One random assignment experiment worth noting is the Future to Discover project currently being implemented in New Brunswick and Manitoba in partnership with the Canada Millennium Scholarship Foundation. In this experiment a group of high school students have, starting in grade nine, been enrolled in programs that essentially orient them towards PSE by providing information on PSE options, helping them explore different careers, and so on. In some permutations of the experiment, money has also been placed in accounts in students' names, and they will be able to draw upon these funds to help pay for their PSE later on. The experiment should provide interesting and important evidence on the initiatives being tested. A number of initiatives to help disadvantaged students improve their likelihood of high school graduation and of transitioning to PSE have been attempted over the years, and serious evaluations are required to identify what works. More efforts in this area are clearly desirable, and the research in this volume suggests that much of it should be focused on the early high school, and even elementary school, years.

Conclusion

The major findings of the papers included in this book can be summarized as follows. First and foremost, access is clearly the outcome of a detailed, complex, interrelated set of factors that begins to operate early in a young person's life and depends heavily on family background and early schooling experiences.

Second, although family income has typically been seen as a key determinant, access is in fact dominated by parental education, high school grades, test scores, schooling aspirations and other such factors, which also explain most of the differences in access across families of different income levels. We might sum up these findings by saying that "culture matters more than money" in determining who gains access to PSE.

Third, although the influence of family income is much reduced when parental education is taken into account, a modest statistically significant effect remains. For some students, financial issues have a direct effect on access.

Fourth, the substantially higher female access rates that we now observe, especially at the university level, appear to be related to male-female differences in PSE aspirations, preparations, and related factors, which increase through the high school years.

Fifth, once a fuller set of personal characteristics are controlled for, the number of hours that students work at paid jobs while in high school is found to have a uniformly negative effect on grades, which are in turn strongly related to access.

Sixth, PSE pathways are much more diverse and dropout rates much lower than previously thought. For university students, for example, five year dropout rates decline from about 50 percent when viewed at the program level to approximately 30 percent when those who finish other programs are counted (including those at other institutions and at college), and to about 10 percent when those still in PSE are included. The adjustment is almost as great for college students. The effects of family background on persistence are also found to be generally much smaller than they are for getting into PSE, although in some cases they remain statistically significant, especially for college students. Switchers show some evidence of benefit from changing programs, but the patterns are complex and require further analysis.

Seventh, there is little evidence that tuition fees affect students' access or persistence, at least in the short run.

Eighth, the effects of receiving student financial aid – loans, grants, scholarships, etc. – on persistence must be disentangled from individual and family characteristics and other factors to which receiving aid is related, which have their own effects on access and persistence. But doing so represents a significant methodological challenge, and has led to little in the way of precisely identified effects. Further complicating the issue is that student aid in general and loans in particular are provided in various different contexts: sometimes to help students cover increased costs, sometimes to give students more money to meet a given set of needs, sometimes (in the case of loans) as substitutes for grants. Since the effects of the aid are likely to vary in these different circumstances, we need to think carefully about what having a loan (or other form of aid) is meant to capture, and how to estimate that effect – or more properly, the associated *range* of effects associated with the different circumstances in which loans are given.

Ninth and finally, following students for a longer period of time suggests that there might be important relationships among student loans and time to graduation and early life course events, but pursuing such issues presents significant methodological challenges and requires data of a type that is difficult to come by.

Apart from reviewing the papers in the volume, this introduction emphasizes the need to look at the determinants of access and persistence using a framework that goes beyond the finance-oriented factors such as costs and student financial aid that often dominate discussions. We present such a framework, and then discuss the methods and findings of past studies, suggested directions for future research, and associated policy implications from this perspective. We conclude that government policy is highly relevant for alleviating barriers to PSE, but that it must include early interventions for disadvantaged youth, providing information and academic support and other opportunities related to the "culture" of PSE.

Notes

1. See Motte et al. (2008) for detailed discussion of the YITS data, which comprise two different datasets: the YITS-A, which tracks a sample of youth aged 15 in 2000 with subsequent interviews every two years, and the YITS-B, which follows a sample of 18 to 20 year olds in similar fashion.

2. The MESA project includes a research review committee composed of scholars in the area of post-secondary education, whose job it is to select, provide feedback on, and ultimately approve or reject specific projects, including those upon which the papers included in this volume are based. This structure has been instrumental in ensuring the focused nature (including the policy relevance) and quality of the research that has resulted. The research papers from which those in this volume are drawn and other information regarding MESA may be found at www.mesa-project.org.

3. In statistical terms, we are looking at "endogeneity" and "omitted variable bias," meaning that some of the important factors that appear to affect participation in PSE should themselves be considered in any full treatment as outcomes themselves (rather than be assumed to be "exogenously" given) or to otherwise be capturing effects not otherwise controlled for in the analysis.

4. Even this assumption could be challenged on the grounds that family income is chosen, perhaps with an eye to the family's children's future PSE

opportunities, but we make this assumption for now to keep the arguments that follow a little simpler. Relaxing this assumption would be but another step in the direction we advocate.

5.   These can be found at www.mesa-project.org.

6.   College attendance rates tend to be more similar across income groups, but this pattern can be misleading. It is *not* that income does not affect college attendance; it does – children from higher income families are in fact more likely to go to college than not to go to PSE at all. It is just that among those who decide to do some PSE, higher family income is also related to going to university rather than college, and the two effects essentially cancel out, leading to increased university participation rates, relatively equal college rates, and lower rates of no PSE among those from higher income families. See the underlying Finnie-Mueller research paper for the full set of results, which includes the effects on college attendance.

7.   These insights thus contrast to some degree with those of U.S. researchers including Paulsen and St. John (2002), St. John and Starkey (1995), and the United States Government Accounting Office (1995), which generally find that finances do affect persistence, especially in the first year, while results from both Dynarski (2005) and Stinebrickner and Stinebrickner (2003) show that cultural variables such as parental education play a more important role in determining PSE completion.

8.   See also Corak, Lipps, and Zhao (2003) or Christophides et al. (2001).

9.   See, for example, Finnie, Usher, and Vossensteyn (2005) and the references therein.

10.   Finnie and Laporte (forthcoming) report, for example, that based on data taken from the Post-Secondary Education Participation Survey (PEPS), approximately 70 percent of all PSE students who held student loans said they would not have been able to go to PSE without them, these numbers applying approximately equally for college and university students.

11.   The various writings of James Heckman and co-authors (e.g., Heckman 2006a, and Heckman, Knudsen, Cameron and Shonko, 2006) in the last few years have helped to focus attention on these sorts of factors at the international level. The research reported here can be seen as lying in this new tradition.

References

Adelman, C. 1999. *Answers in the Tool Box: Academic Intensity, Attendance Patterns, and Bachelor's Degree Attainment*. Washington: U.S. Department of Education.

Christofides, L.N., J. Cirello, and M. Hoy 2001. "Family Income and Postsecondary Education in Canada." *Canadian Journal of Higher Education* 31 (1): 177-208.

Coelli, M.B. 2004. "Tuition Increases and Inequality in Post-Secondary Education Attendance." University of British Columbia Working Paper.

Corak, M., G. Lipps, and J. Zhao. 2003. *Family Income and Participation in Post-Secondary Education.* Analytical Studies Branch Research Paper Series. Statistics Canada No. 11F0019MIE2003210, Ottawa.

Drolet, M. 2005. *Participation in Post-Secondary Education in Canada: Has the Role of Parental Income and Education Changed over the 1990s?* Analytical Studies Branch Research Paper Series. Statistics Canada No. 11F0019MIE2005243, Ottawa.

Dynarski, S.M. 2005. "Building the Stock of College-Educated Labour." NBER Working Paper 11604.

Finnie, R. 2005. "Access and Capacity in the Canadian Post-Secondary Education System: A Policy Discussion Framework." In *Preparing for Post Secondary Education: New Roles for Governments and Families,* edited by P. Anisef and R. Sweet, 17-54. Montreal and Kingston: McGill-Queen's University Press.

Finnie, R., and C. Laporte. Forthcoming. "Lending Opportunity: Student Loans and Access to Post-Secondary Education." Statistics Canada Analytical Studies Branch Research Paper, Ottawa.

Finnie, R., E. Lascelles, and A. Sweetman. 2005. "Who Goes? The Direct and Indirect Effects of Family Background on Access to Postsecondary Education." In *Higher Education in Canada,* edited by C.M. Beach, R.W. Boadway, and R.M. McInnis, 295-338. Montreal and Kingston: McGill-Queen's University Press.

Finnie, R., A. Usher, and H. Vossensteyn. 2005. "Meeting the Need: A New Architecture for Canada's Student Financial Aid System." In *Higher Education in Canada,* edited by C.M. Beach, R.W. Boadway, and R.M. McInnis, 495-536. Montreal and Kingston: McGill-Queen's University Press. Also published in August 2004 under the same title in *Policy Matters* 5 (7) by the Institute for Research on Public Policy.

Heckman, J. 2006. "Skill Formation and the Economics of Investing in Disadvantaged Children." *Science* 312 (5782): 1900-2.

Heckman, J., E. Knudsen, J. Cameron and J. Shonko. 2006. "Economic, Neurobiological, and Behavioral Perspectives on Building America's Future Workforce." *Proceedings of the National Academy of Sciences* 103 (27): 10155-62.

Johnson, D., and F. Rahman. 2005. "The Role of Economic Factors, Including the Level of Tuition, in Individual University Participation Decisions in Canada." Wilfrid Laurier University Working Paper.

Motte, A., H.T. Qiu, Y. Zhang, and P. Bussière. 2008. "The Youth in Transition Survey: Following Canadian Youth through Time." In *Who Goes? Who Stays? What Matters? Accessing and Persisting in Post-Secondary Education in Canada*, edited by R. Finnie, R.E. Mueller, A. Sweetman, and A. Usher. Montreal and Kingston: McGill-Queen's University Press and School of Policy Studies, Queen's University.

Neill, C. 2005. "The Impact of Tuition Fees on University Enrollments and Students' Work in Canada." Working Paper: Preliminary Draft.

OECD. 2008. *Tertiary Education for the Knowledge Society.* OECD thematic review of tertiary education: synthesis report. Paris: OECD.

Paulsen, M.B., and E.P. St. John. 2002. "Social Class and College Costs." *Journal of Higher Education* 73 (2): 189-236.

St. John, E.P., and J.B. Starkey. 1995. "An Alternative to Net Price: Assessing the Influence of Prices and Subsidies on Within-Year Persistence." *Journal of Higher Education* 66 (22): 156-86.

Statistics Canada. 2001. "Participation in Postsecondary Education and Family Income." *The Daily.* Ottawa, 7 December.

Stinebrickner, R., and T.R. Stinebrickner. 2003. "Understanding Education Outcomes of Students from Low Income Families: Evidence from a Liberal Arts College with a Full Tuition Subsidy Program." *Journal of Human Resources* 38 (3): 591-617.

United States Government Accounting Office. 1995. *Higher Education: Restructuring Student Aid Could Reduce Low-Income Student Dropout Rate.* Washington.

2

Access and Persistence of Students in Canadian Post-Secondary Education: What We Know, What We Don't Know, and Why It Matters

RICHARD E. MUELLER

Faire ou non des études post-secondaires (EPS) ? Dans quel type d'institutions ? Comment répondre aux exigences que cela comporte et obtenir ainsi un diplôme ? Voilà autant de questions complexes auxquelles font face les jeunes Canadiens. Différents facteurs – des considérations financières, le contexte familial, des habiletés personnelles – interagissent pour amener les jeunes à entreprendre ou non des EPS, et, le cas échéant, à les poursuivre ou non jusqu'à l'obtention d'un diplôme. Dans cet article, je trace un bilan des connaissances actuelles sur l'accès aux EPS et sur la persévérance des jeunes qui les entreprennent. Je mets l'accent sur la situation des jeunes de familles défavorisées, car ils constituent un groupe qui, historiquement, n'a pas bénéficié autant des EPS que les jeunes de familles à revenus moyens ou élevés. Ensuite, j'indique les failles qui existent actuellement dans les connaissances que nous possédons dans ce domaine.

Whether to attend post-secondary education (PSE), which institution to attend, and how to complete its degree or diploma requirements are extraordinarily complex decisions faced by young Canadians. Factors such as financial considerations, family background, and inherent ability all interact to determine whether or not they will attend – and ultimately graduate from – any PSE institution. This paper reviews the state of knowledge regarding access to and persistence in PSE. The emphasis is on the experiences of students from low-income families, a group that has historically not benefited from PSE as much as those from middle- and high-income families. Some gaps in the current research are identified.

Introduction

The Canadian system of higher education has historically been viewed as functioning reasonably well, as assessed by its ability to attract eligible students from diverse backgrounds. This perception was undoubtedly due to the fact that post-secondary education was conducted at public institutions where tuition and other fees were considered to be affordable. For students from modest family backgrounds, there were government-subsidized student loans available to bridge the short-term financing gap. There may have been problems with access to post-secondary education, but there was a general perception that the system was reasonably fair and those students who desired a post-secondary education could attain it.

The general perception began to change in the 1990s. When provincial governments cut spending, public institutions were forced to do their part. The pressure of competition from abroad and a few private institutions within Canada started to be felt. Provincial governments across Canada started scrutinizing what occurred in their ivory towers, and the governments' business agendas dictated that these institutions provide performance indicators to justify their funding. Universities responded by discussing public accountability and quality (although often unable to define either) and by increasing tuition fees (usually within government-established guidelines) to partially offset declines in provincial grants. Student loan programs often failed to keep pace with the increasing costs of attending post-secondary institutions, and grant programs were reduced.

Given the increasing costs of attendance, policy-makers and academics have become concerned with the accessibility of post-secondary education (PSE) in Canada, especially amongst students from low-income backgrounds. Have these cost increases had a more profound negative effect on students from families with more modest or lower incomes? Furthermore, accountability as well as revenue considerations have led these same institutions to concern themselves with retention and graduation rates: it is one thing to admit students (i.e., access), but it is another to ensure that they make reasonable progress towards graduation (i.e., persistence).

The popular perception in Canada is that post-secondary education has become less accessible and that student indebtedness continues to rise, in both cases as a result of tuition increases outpacing the rate of inflation. If true, these changes have the potential to put PSE out of reach of many Canadians, especially those from low-income families.

Indeed, data show that over the past 40 years, students have become increasingly reliant on part-time work during the school years and on student assistance (both grants and loans, but especially the latter) to finance their education. At the same time, parental contributions have declined sharply (Cervenan and Usher, 2004), and student borrowing has increased, as has the debt-to-earnings ratio, resulting in some students struggling to pay back their loans (Finnie, 2002). Still, demand for PSE has increased over this period of time, due at least in part to the increased rates of return of a PSE qualification versus a high school diploma (Boothby and Drewes, 2006).

This paper summarizes the current state of knowledge regarding access and persistence of students in PSE, especially amongst those from low-income families. In particular, it looks at what factors have been shown to influence students' ability to attend PSE and also to remain in PSE over the longer term (presumably to graduation). The volume of literature is large; to keep the review more manageable and focused, it is necessary to work within certain parameters. First, the studies reviewed are limited to those addressing the factors behind post-secondary education access and persistence in Canada.[1] Although the U.S. literature is more advanced in both depth and breadth, the potential to derive Canadian policy implications from this body of work is limited by the substantial institutional differences between PSE systems in the two countries. Second, what follows focuses predominantly on studies using more sophisticated empirical techniques; the attendance and persistence decisions of young people are complex, and studies that use only simple correlations do not add much light to this complex issue, although these types of studies are sometimes useful for providing stylized facts that can be used in empirical modelling. Readers interested in broader reviews of less technical papers are directed to Junor and Usher (2004), Looker and Lowe (2001), and Looker (2001), all of which provide excellent reviews of the Canadian literature. De Broucker (2005) also provides a good review of the factors that limit access and persistence of low-income students.[2] Finally, this paper does not discuss the current Canadian data available. Readers interested in this topic should see Junor and Usher (2004) and Statistics Canada and CMEC (2003) for discussion of the Canadian microdata available, or Motte et al. (2008) for specific information on the Youth in Transition Survey – likely the best Canadian data available to date.

The following section addresses the current state of knowledge about access to PSE in Canada. The next two sections address what we currently know about persistence in PSE and discuss some policy implications I am able to draw from this body of work. The final section concludes and offers advice for how researchers might proceed in studying PSE in Canada.

Access to Post-Secondary Education

In its simplest form, human capital theory says that individuals will pursue education up to the point where the increase in its expected present value (in terms of lifetime salary) is positive net of the direct and indirect costs of the education. In the presence of perfect information and efficient credit markets, the implication is that students from low-income families would find pursuing higher education equally worthwhile as those from higher-income families, all else equal. Further, this theory would suggest that the form of financing for PSE does not matter, so that, say, a grant for an entering student would have the same effect as an equivalent decrease in tuition or an equal credit on income taxes. In other words, basic human capital theory suggests that no barriers exist to entering PSE.

Although the theory suggests that financially constrained students are able to borrow to overcome this constraint, it is well known that high school students from lower-income families are less likely to attend post-secondary education than those from more affluent backgrounds. There may be a number of reasons for this: the cost of higher education may be perceived as too high, and this may be exacerbated if the information given to low-income students – whether by their parents, school counsellors, or others – is incorrect. These students may not understand the value of PSE in terms of future earnings; they may apply a discount rate that is too high (thus underestimating the present value of future earnings); or they may be risk averse and so not want to borrow to finance an education. Furthermore, students are human, and assumed to maximize utility, and will therefore take factors other than the rate of return into account when deciding whether to pursue post-secondary education. Moreover, although consensus seems to be emerging on the variables important in the decision to access PSE, there is less agreement on the pathways taken, and this provides researchers with methodological and empirical challenges. For example, students may access PSE right out of high school, or they may delay entering for a year or more. They may choose between various types of PSE – university, college, or trade-vocational schools – or they may elect not to attend at all. The existing evidence on each of these factors is considered in turn below.[3]

Financial Factors

Tuition Effects: Researchers have spent considerable time and effort addressing the impact of finances on access to PSE. Most recent research in Canada has focused on the impact of tuition increases that occurred in the 1990s as some provincial governments cut funding to colleges and universities and, as transfers to post-secondary institutions declined, tuition increased to fill the funding gap (Finnie and Usher, 2005). Current research debates the full impact of tuition increases and whether these have resulted in decreased student enrolments, particularly those students from low-income families, since this group may be more sensitive to tuition hikes compared to those from families with higher incomes.

Junor and Usher (2004) in their extensive review look at simple trends in tuition and PSE participation and find little evidence that tuition has been a barrier to PSE access overall. By contrast, Johnson and Rahman (2005) find that including province-specific trend variables in the model indicates that higher tuition fees reduce participation. They also find that the opportunity costs of attendance, as well as the expected payoff of university education, are also important in determining the probability of participation. Neill (2005) too finds a negative relationship between tuition and participation, even though there is little overall correlation between fees and enrolments, and the instrument she uses to determine this relationship is questionable. Strictly in terms of the participation of students from lower-income families, Coelli (2005) finds the tuition increases in the late 1990s had a negative impact on the university attendance rates of individuals from low-income families and a smaller effect on those from middle- and high-income backgrounds. The effect of tuition increases on attendance at non-university PSE institutions was essentially zero, with no discernable differences amongst parental income levels.

Despite the apparent negative relationship between tuition and access, paradoxically there is no support for a widening attendance gap between students from low-income and high-income families. De Broucker (2005) reviews the Canadian literature and finds that the university attendance gap between children from low-income and high-income families is consistent in the literature; there is no evidence that the gap has widened over time, despite fears that participation amongst low-income families would decline as tuition increased dramatically in the 1990s. He argues that financial considerations are only one of many determinants of PSE attendance. Similarly, Drolet (2005) finds that the relationship between participation in PSE and parental income remained rather stable through the 1990s, despite this being a period in Canada of rapid tuition increases. Although the cost of education may not have much effect on overall participation rates, evidence does suggest that cost considerations may be influencing the choice between college and university. Statistics Canada and CMEC (2003) show that about 25 percent of college students in Canada are enrolled in university transfer programs, and this number increased slightly in the 1990s. Whether this increase is in response to higher university tuition, limited availability of university spots, or other factors is unclear. Similarly, it is not clear from these results if students from lower-income families are more likely to begin their university studies at the college level.

Christofides et al. (2001) use data between 1975 and 1993 and find that the PSE participation rates of 18 to 24 year olds increased, but this increase was larger for children from families in the lowest income quantile. Higher incomes explain some of this increase in participation rates, but there is still a strong secular increase in participation from all income groups – especially lower income groups – so that participation rate convergence occurred. Tuition, however, is generally found to be an insignificant predictor of participation. This may have to do with the time period studied, when there was little variation across provinces in real tuition fees and annual increases were small as compared to the large rises in the years after this study as reported by Coelli (2005). Corak et al. (2003) use more recent data but also find that tuition had little impact on the participation of PSE students, largely because increases in student loan availability kept pace with tuition increases in the 1990s.

In sum, the literature on tuition effects in Canada is incomplete and often contradictory, the result of the employment of different data and different methodologies. While drawing a definitive conclusion is difficult, the evidence does show that any tuition effect is small at best, but that tuition increases are likely to have a larger effect on participation amongst students from low-income families. Still, other factors exist that may be more important determinants of PSE participation.

Parental income: Economic theory shows that the demand for normal goods tends to increase as personal income increases. Education is likely to be a normal good, with family income playing a decisive role in the participation of young people. Thus, when parental income increases, so does children's demand for PSE. Corak et al. (2003) find that parental income is important for university attendance but not for PSE in general, since participation in college is not as sensitive to income as university participation. Frenette (2005) investigates this point further, using a model with three choices: university, college, and no PSE. He finds no significant differences in the probability of college attendance between income quartiles. He argues that these results are misleading, however, since he also finds that the probability of college attendance is lower amongst lower-income students when the sample is limited to those who did not attend university. Drolet (2005) looks at the attendance gap somewhat differently but still finds a similar result. Conditioning her sample on those young people who did not go to university, she finds that the college attendance rate between young people from high-income and low-income families is similar to that for university attendance. These studies imply that the PSE attendance gap is narrowed when we include colleges as well as universities, but young people from low-income families are less likely to attend either type of institution and are more likely to attend college rather than university when they do go.

Rivard and Raymond (2004) argue that there are methodological problems with many studies that could misrepresent the true effects of financial variables. For example, students who are already in the system (and thus nearer to graduation) are less likely to be affected by tuition increases. The authors attempt to correct for these methodological problems and still find that the transition into PSE from high school is not particularly sensitive to family income or tuition. More important factors are academic preparation and parental education. They also argue that government student loans were able to meet the growing tuition burden in the 1990s and/or the increased returns to education over this period made PSE completion worthwhile, even as tuition increased.

Insofar as families use accumulated wealth to pay for PSE-related expenses, the use of family income as a determinant of PSE participation could give misleading results (although the two are positively correlated). There are no Canadian studies on family wealth and access to PSE, but the scant evidence that does exist suggests that programs designed to enhance wealth for the purpose of financing PSE are more likely to benefit families with higher incomes. For example, Milligan (2005) shows that the use of Registered Education Savings Plans (RESPs) and the related Canada Education Savings Grants (CESGs) is concentrated amongst both high-income families and families where the parents are highly educated. This is in direct conflict with the program's intent of increasing post-secondary education accessibility amongst children from lower-income families. This result is supported by Shipley et al. (2003), who show the positive correlation between income quintile and savings for post-secondary education. The CMSF (2005) analyzes two commissioned surveys and shows that family income is positively correlated with the probability of saving for PSE as well as RESP participation. Furthermore, the amount of time that parents have been saving for their children's post-secondary education is also positively correlated with family income. These results mean that children from higher income families will have a larger pool of assets to draw on to finance their college or university attendance. The implication of these studies is that RESPs and similar programs represent a wealth transfer from low- to higher-income groups, as the latter group would be saving for PSE even without the government incentives.

Student loans: As previously mentioned, a well-functioning student loan system is important for the participation of students who are otherwise financially constrained. Finnie (2000) studies four graduating classes between 1982 and 1995 and finds that the use of student loans has been increasing, and repayment problems have been increasing as well. Allen, Harris, and Butlin (2003) have similar findings. Both studies show that the state of the economy (i.e., lower incomes, higher unemployment, etc.) affects the ability of graduates to pay back loans. Furthermore, college graduates are more likely to have these problems than university graduates. The limitation of both these studies is that they suffer from sample selection bias since only PSE graduates were surveyed in the data. As a result, the authors have no way of knowing how many students either did not pursue PSE or left before completing their education owing to concerns about high debt burdens. In short, these results do not tell us if credit markets are functioning to assist students in accessing PSE, but they do show that repayment problems are most common amongst college graduates who enter a poor labour market.

More recently, Finnie and Laporte (2007) use a sample of 17 to 24 year olds and show that about two-thirds of the sample had accessed PSE at the time of the interview. About one-third of these had taken out a student loan, and about 70 percent of this group said that they would not have been able to pursue PSE without the loans. Other loan holders pointed to the wider range of options available to them as a result of the loans. In any case, the rate of borrowing was higher among students from lower socio-economic backgrounds (as measured by parental education or family income). The authors further argue that the loan system does appear to be working in aiding young Canadians to access PSE and that non-monetary factors (such as family background) should be looked at if the policy goal is to increase PSE participation rates. In a previous paper Finnie and Laporte (2006) suggested that students with loans from private sources and students who worked while attending PSE might be evidence of unmet need in the government loan system.

Although the availability of student loans may assist some students to participate in PSE, there are still distributional implications. Kapsalis (2006) notes that use of the Canada Student Loans Program (CSLP) increases as parental income decreases. This report also notes that the average loan amongst students from low-income families is only slightly more than that of students from high-income families – a factor that could be due at least in part to their higher attendance in colleges (which cost less). Given that those with college diplomas will be paid less on average than those with university degrees, the loan burden as a percentage of income could be greater for low-income students; this possibility is worthy of further investigation.

Scholarships: Student loans have to be paid back, while scholarships do not. Two types of scholarships or aid programs generally exist: needs-based aid, which is for students who might not otherwise have the means to attend PSE, and non-needs based aid (including merit-based aid), which is competitive and based on criteria such as athletic ability, ethnicity, gender, and high school grades. While needs-based aid is targeted at students from low-income families, thus enhancing their ability to attend PSE, recently the amount of this type of aid has been decreasing in real terms at the same time that non-needs-based aid has increased (Finnie and Usher, 2005). Gucciardi (2004) discusses the increase in the number of merit-based scholarships in Canada over the past 15 years. Although merit scholarships have become increasingly diverse (for example, awarded for both merit and need), the majority of these scholarships are still awarded on the basis of academic achievement; most are given to first-year students on a non-renewable basis and represent a relatively small portion of the total costs of education. Since high school grades and parental income tend to be positively correlated, the corollary is that many low-income students could be shut out of this type of aid. Gucciardi also notes that it is not clear that these merit scholarships improve students' probability of success at post-secondary education, and clearly there is need for more Canadian research in this area. If merit scholarships are not enhancing the probability of program completion, then government and private money might be better spent elsewhere. In a similar vein, Ouelette (2006) finds that while 29 percent of PSE students in 2001-02 received some form of grant or scholarship, the dollar amounts were only large enough to cover the full education costs for 5 percent of all students.

Even the term "needs-based assistance" in Canada is largely a mis-
nomer, and it could be an inefficient means of helping low-income students. Much of this aid is actually targeted at higher-income students,
based on the ease with which students in Canada are able to claim independent status, generally deemed to have no parental support; they
are thus eligible for higher amounts of aid, even if their families continue to provide support. Furthermore, individuals' "need" is increased
if they attend institutions or enrol in programs that are more expensive
(e.g., university instead of college, or medical school instead of general
arts). The conclusion is that high need and low income are not necessarily positively correlated. Usher (2004, 21) notes: "The real way to get
grants is to study expensively, refrain from working, and move away
from home. Is this the message Canadian governments want to send to
students?" He recommends that the Canadian system move toward that
of most other countries where income-based grants are more prevalent.

Other financial factors: While tuition costs and the availability of loans
and grant aid have attracted the attention of researchers, these are not
the most common forms of PSE financing in Canada either in terms of
usage or amount of funds coming from these sources. Usalcas and
Bowlby (2006), for example, have found that money from personal
savings was the most common source of funds for financing PSE and
that employment income was the largest dollar amount of funds used.
Of course, low-income students may not have savings and thus would
not be included in this figure.

Another popular alternative is working while studying, and both the
probability of working as well as the number of hours worked per week
during the academic year by Canadian post-secondary students appear
to be on the rise (Usalcas and Bowlby, 2006). Junor and Usher (2004)
note that students work to pay for their education-related expenses, to
sustain a certain lifestyle, or to gain work experience that will enhance
their future prospects. They cite sources indicating that amongst students who work, the first reason is the most important, but that amongst
all students only about one-third cite the need to work to pay for education. This gives rise to the importance of the other two reasons for
working. Unfortunately, it is not possible to disentangle "wants" from
"needs," nor can students from different income strata be identified in
their data.

The details of the tax system also seem to have important ramifica-
tions for PSE access. For example, Junor and Usher (2004) note that the
largest financial program in Canada for post-secondary education is
tax-based assistance, whereby students are given tax benefits not

available to their non-student peers. In fact, the financial benefit of this program is larger than that of all student loans and grant programs combined, as students can earn almost twice as much as non-students before their incomes become taxable. Despite its significance, no research has been done on the effects of this tax-based assistance on accessibility to PSE. Collins and Davies (2005) also address the importance of the tax system in Canada, but argue that income taxes following graduation can impact the decisions of young people. They reason that it is not expected income but *net* expected income that drives attendance in PSE. Furthermore, they state that it is usually the direct costs of higher education that are considered by the Canadian public (i.e., tuition, transfers to institutions, etc.), but that tax reforms have lowered taxes on returns to higher education, and this has represented a substantial benefit and is hence an encouragement for students to pursue higher education.

Non-Financial Family Background Factors

The research discussed above indicates that financial constraints have been important determinants in limiting access to PSE for many students, especially students from low-income families. These constraints, however, tend to be highly correlated with other factors such as family background that also impact the probability of PSE participation. Knighton and Mirza (2002), for example, find that parental education is a stronger predictor of PSE participation than parental income, and that this is particularly true of participation in university. Similarly, Rahman et al. (2005) show that youth whose parents had post-secondary education were much more likely to attend PSE, especially university, while those from low-income families were less likely to participate in either college or university. Drolet (2005) too shows the positive relationship between parental and child attendance of PSE and adds that this factor is a more important determinant of attending university than parental income. Over this same period Finnie, Laporte, and Lascelles (2004) argue that the importance of parental education on PSE participation increased throughout the 1990s for children with highly educated parents but increased less or even declined for individuals from families with lower parental education. De Broucker and Underwood (1998) also find that this correlation between parental education and PSE participation holds across the 11 countries they studied. These results, coupled with the general increase in admissions criteria to Canadian institutions, suggest that parental education, not parental income, is the more important factor in young people accessing PSE.

Finnie, Lascelles, and Sweetman (2005) go a step further and find that family background has both indirect and direct effects. Regression analysis usually captures only the total effect, whereas these authors use a block-recursive technique that permits the separation of each factor. They find that parental background is important in determining PSE (especially university) participation directly, but also indirectly through its influence on pre-PSE schooling. In other words, parental influence is an important determinant of PSE participation long before the period immediately preceding PSE attendance. In an earlier study de Broucker and Lavallée (1998) show the importance of parental education on youths' educational attainment, but they also argue that low parental education can be mitigated with high socio-economic status (as defined by parental occupation).

The current family situation, not just the family background, of potential PSE attendees is also a factor in determining participation. While Butlin (1999) finds that lone parent versus two parent families has no significant effect on attending any of three levels of PSE (loosely university, college, and trades), he does find that having dependent children reduces participation significantly.

After being relatively stable over the 1990s, university (but not college) participation rates have begun to increase in the new millennium. But while demand has increased, capacity or supply may not have kept up as provinces cut back on provincial funding to universities. Finnie and Usher (2005) use the average entering grades of students compiled in the *Maclean's* magazine annual ranking of Canadian universities, and – consistent with the situation of rising excess demand – find the average entering high school mark has been increasing over the past decade, although how much of this is due to grade inflation is unclear. As students from low-income backgrounds do tend to be less prepared than those from higher-income backgrounds, this phenomenon could also harm access.

Similarly, Fortin (2005) uses a simple demand and supply explanation to compare the market for university education in Canada and the United States. She argues that reduced government contributions to universities limit the supply of spaces available, and this becomes a binding constraint limiting access to these institutions. Her econometric estimates confirm this hypothesis. She argues that whereas state grants in the U.S. increased in the 1990s, provincial grants to Canadian universities fell in the 1990s, which explains the flat enrolment growth rates in Canada.

Butlin (1999) finds that the only socio-demographic factor influencing PSE attendance is parental level of education (although the study did not simultaneously control for parental income). He also finds that school-related variables such as average high school grades (especially in math and English or French) and student participation in class and extracurricular activities affect attendance in PSE. He concludes by counselling against lumping all PSE together since the determinants of participation in each differ. The studies by Frenette (2005) and Drolet (2005) support this conclusion. Junor and Usher (2004, 113) perhaps sum it up best: "Youth with higher secondary school marks are more likely to come from higher income strata while those with lower marks are more likely to come from lower income strata. The former tend to desire a university education, and the latter tend to desire a college education. These two groups do not compete against each other for access to post-secondary spaces. They are, in effect, two separate 'markets.'"

Other Factors

Although financial factors and (to a lesser extent) family background capture most attention in the literature on access to PSE, a number of other factors may also influence the decision of young people as to whether to attend PSE and, if so, at what level. This section outlines some of these influences, even though it is often difficult to disentangle the effects of a number of factors owing to high correlation between two or more variables. Nevertheless, an exposition of the importance of these influences is necessary, if only to start debate on how to appropriately identify their effects on access to PSE.

Foley (2001) studies Canada and focuses on those who had completed high school and were thus eligible to attend PSE but did not, or else attended and then dropped out. Although the decision not to attend PSE is complex, the main reason dropouts gave was that they did not have enough money to continue. While this was the most popular response, the remaining 77 percent of respondents cited non-financial reasons for not attending. This does not mean that financial factors were not important in non-attendance, only that respondents did not consider them the most important factor. Finnie and Laporte (2007) also find that financial barriers were no more important a deterrent to PSE attendance than a decade earlier, despite the fact that tuition increased while needs-based aid fell in real terms over this period.

Bowlby and McMullen (2002) discover that amongst those 18-20 year olds surveyed who did not attend PSE, less than half cited any barriers. Of these, the most common barrier was financial, with about two-thirds citing this obstacle. Other barriers were inability to get into programs and lack of motivation. Tomkowicz and Bushnik (2003) also find that not receiving a grant or scholarship predicted delayed enrolment in PSE compared to those who entered right after high school. But other factors such as province of residence and high school grades tend to be better predictors of delayed entry. The same study shows that having parents with lower levels of education is a good predictor of not going on to PSE from high school. The study, however, covers a relatively short period (approximately three years) after high school graduation. Tomkowicz, Shipley, and Ouelette (2003) show that those with higher debt loads, all else being equal, are more likely to perceive financial barriers to PSE. However, these authors also note that there was no definitive relationship between the perception of financial barriers and the receipt of scholarships, grants, and bursaries, although this may be due to the relatively small amounts of money in this category.

Mueller and Rockerbie (2005b) find that when demand for entrance spaces at Ontario universities increases, it is not tuition that increases to clear the market but rather the entering GPA of high school students rises to ration these limited spaces. Coupled with other evidence (presented above) that relates socio-economic status and high school grades, this suggests that low-income students are put at a disadvantage compared to those from higher-income families. In a related paper, Mueller and Rockerbie (2005a) find distinct demographic differences in demand: males tend to be more price sensitive than females, and students applying from Ontario high schools exhibit less sensitivity to tuition and median incomes in their applications behaviour compared to "other" students who include college transfers and those not applying while in high school. In other words, as discussed above, applicants are not a homogenous group: some students are destined for university and are not sensitive to tuition or income changes, while others have less attachment to the idea of attending university and are sensitive to these variables.

Looker and Lowe (2001) provide a good look at various factors determining post-secondary educational access and note a lack of data to analyze many issues regarding the participation of lower-income students. To be useful, they argue, data must allow researchers to interact socio-economic status with other characteristics such as gender, ethnicity, and Aboriginal status normally associated with lower educational attainment. They also point to Canada's lack of time-series data on the total direct costs of post-secondary education, which include housing, food, books, transportation, relocation costs, and other education-related expenses. More recently, Usher and Steele (2006) provide information on many of these variables by province and state in their comparison of PSE affordability in Canada and the United States.

These other costs of attending PSE are of particular importance for low-income families. Distance between home and the post-secondary educational institution, for example, has been shown to be more of a deterrent for Canadian students from low-income families, especially for those wishing to attend university (Frenette, 2002, 2004). This effect, however, is mitigated for low-income students living close to a college.[4] Whether these students graduate and ultimately attend university, however, is not known. Since those in rural areas are more likely to live further from a university, there may be other factors correlated with distance. McMullen (2004) synthesizes this line of research and discusses the importance of losing social capital in the decision to move away to attend university, which is almost always necessary for rural students. In addition, the fact that individuals in rural areas tend to have a lower probability of having a university education means that young people in those areas may not be fully aware of the benefits of attending university. Students who attend rural high schools are less likely to attend university than those schooled in an urban area. Rural status, however, does not decrease the odds of attending other types of PSE (Butlin, 1999). Rahman et al. (2005) also find no difference in the PSE participation probabilities of rural versus urban youth and find no difference in choosing university over college. They do find, however, that both college and university attendance is higher amongst youth from high-income families, which suggests that low income rather than residency in a rural area is driving this result, although the two are positively correlated.

Working may also have an impact on the decision to attend PSE. Indeed, working more than twenty hours per week in the final year of high school significantly reduces participation in university compared to not working at all, but working does not appear to affect those high school students intending to pursue a college or trades education (Butlin, 1999). This result may be owing to the fact that working during school is endogenous to the decision to attend PSE and may have different effects on university attendance versus college and trade school attendance.

The amount of competition amongst an entering class also seems to play an important role in access. Coelli (2005) found that large cohorts had a negative effect on university attendance, even after controlling for other variables, especially for youth from low-income cohorts (although this may be correlated with lower measured achievement during high school, thus reducing their probability of acceptance at university).

Using a unique longitudinal survey of young people and their parents from three Canadian cities, Looker (1997) discusses the importance of student attitudes towards schooling and knowledge of post-secondary programs as well as other variables that are important in determining both access and educational attainment. She finds the main differences arise between those who went to university and those who attended other post-secondary educational institutions (often considered inferior to universities), not between those who pursued PSE and those who did not. She argues that knowledge is important, especially information about the non-university options available. A survey of Alberta high school graduates (Ipsos-Reid, 2001) found that the earlier the decision to pursue PSE, the more likely a student was to attend a post-secondary institution. In reviewing some of the recent American literature, Ehrenberg (2005) observes that the most successful programs in preparing students from low-income families for PSE start early and continue to provide services throughout middle and high school. Although this factor is especially important in the United States, since low-income students tend to live in districts where schools are underfunded, the lesson likely applies to Canada as well.

Persistence in Post-Secondary Education

The issue of persistence in higher education is much less studied in the economics literature than the issue of access. This is undoubtedly due, at least in part, to the lack of longitudinal data regarding student outcomes. While access to PSE is obviously a necessary condition for graduation, it is not a sufficient condition, yet program completion is likely more important than mere attendance. Indeed, program completion (or the "sheepskin effect") has been shown to be important in recent Canadian studies (Ferrer and Riddell, 2001, 2002), although completion of education credentials may be correlated with other unobservable characteristics such as perseverance and work effort, both of which are also rewarded in the labour market.

Grayson and Grayson (2003) in their review of the literature observe that different institutional settings and other factors explain attrition, so that it is misleading to make general statements about the conditions that lead to withdrawal. There appears to be only a weak relationship between leaving PSE and finances. Still, students often cite both academic and financial reasons for withdrawing. Some 50 percent of Canadian students cited lack of interest in their programs or PSE in general as the main reason for dropping out; whether or not they returned is not known from these data. Financial considerations rated a distant second at 29 percent (Barr-Telford et al., 2003). Lambert et al. (2004) come to a similar conclusion but note that 40 percent of leavers from PSE returned within two years. This underlines the importance of understanding the full diversity of students in terms of their personal, academic, and economic realities.

Cervenan and Usher (2004) also find that very few of the students surveyed claimed that they were forced to withdraw from PSE for financial reasons, and this number (3 percent) was the same in 2002 as it was in 1965 when the real costs of education were significantly less. On the surface it would seem that financial reasons have little impact on persistence. Still, the Canadian Undergraduate Survey Consortium survey used by these authors only captures those students who returned to school and not those who left for financial reasons and did not return. Foley (2001) cites the most popular reason for not attending (which includes leaving) PSE as not having enough money to continue (23 percent). Amongst those who dropped out, however, only 9 percent cited this reason. All things considered, she finds that non-financial reasons are more important determinants of persistence than financial reasons.

Students are most likely to leave PSE during their first year, and the probability of leaving thereafter decreases, although large numbers of students return to PSE later in life. Bowlby and McMullen (2002) find that those students who continued their post-secondary studies were more likely to receive money from parents as well as scholarships and grants compared to those who dropped out of their studies, although these differences do not appear to be large. Those who left also seemed to have more trouble adjusting to their studies compared to those who continued.

Although financial factors may have a limited effect on persistence, the type and amount of financial aid are likely important in determining a student's decision to remain in PSE. McElroy (2005) defines aid as government student loans, grants, or both, and annualizes the amount of aid received based on the amount that would have been received to complete one year of the program on a full-time basis. She finds that persistence (defined as completion of the degree requirements or progress toward completion) is highest for those who received both grants and loans, especially when the annualized amount is less than $3,000. By contrast, persistence is lowest for those who receive only loans, especially those with annualized loan amounts over $3,000; persistence decreases (by both measures) as this amount increases. Family income and academic preparedness are not significant factors. McElroy argues that debt aversion may be responsible for the negative relationship between loans and persistence, perhaps since students with both grants and aid had accumulated less debt for the same total amount of money received (loans plus grants).

There is also evidence that sources of financial assistance are related to age. The CMSF (2001) finds that parental financing of PSE decreases with age, while debt increases. Furthermore, debt from private sources is increasing as education costs increase at the same time that earnings from summer employment remain modest. Finnie and Laporte (2007) show that older students are more likely to have student loans. They argue that this is because older students are no longer constrained by the income of their parents, and thus this type of financing may not be as targeted as it could be. Prairie Research Associates (2005) find a similar pattern amongst college students. Another interpretation might be that older students are more likely to be in the final years of their programs and the resources they used for earlier years of education might be diminished or at least diminishing. This could affect the persistence of older students.

Junor and Usher (2004) note that working students spend less time in class, and they provide mixed evidence about the relationship between number of hours working and number of hours studying (although any negative correlation could be related to the fact that students may be taking fewer classes per semester). In fact, the authors note that students working more than 30 hours per week tend to maintain their grades, but this is the result of cutting back on the number of courses taken in order to devote the same amount of time to studying per course. The cost is that the time-to-completion is increased, and it is likely – but not certain – that persistence is negatively affected.

Summary, Conclusions, and Policy Implications

Attending and completing post-secondary education in a timely manner involves a series of extraordinarily complex decisions. The state of research in this area in Canada, while not in its infancy, is in the toddler years. The factors that influence the decision to attend and complete PSE and the variety of pathways taken (and perhaps abandoned) by individuals are the subject of active research. This paper has reviewed this literature on access and persistence of students, especially those from low-income families. A few conclusions and policy implications can be drawn, although many questions remain to be answered.

In terms of financing higher education, governments can pursue two broad options: first, increasing the availability of aid such as loans, grants, and scholarships, or second, decreasing tuition costs. Aside from certain advocacy groups, almost no one suggests that increasing subsidies to post-secondary education is an efficient way to increase access and persistence, since this would simply represent a windfall to middle-

and upper-income families who are able to pay (or at least borrow) for higher education. Rather, the call has been for such subsidies (be it grants or interest subsidies of student loans) to be directed to individual students (Laidler, 2002). Scholarships or merit-based aid tend to benefit those most qualified academically, but academic preparedness is positively correlated with family income and so again provides a subsidy to higher-income families. This leaves grants and loans as options. Finnie (2005) discusses these two options, arguing that there are two ways in which financing PSE can increase enrolment. The first is that it decreases the direct cost of education. The second way is that the rate of return to higher education is increased. In the case of student loans and perfect capital markets, only loans with a below-market rate of interest (such as the CSLP) will have any positive effect on enrolment by increasing the rate of return to education. Targeted grants, by contrast, affect both the rate of return and affordability. That said, grants have a stronger effect than loans, but loans can be spread over a larger number of students. A number of studies (e.g., Vossensteyn 2004) have noted that loans are more cost effective than outright grants or scholarships, as the former have to be repaid by those benefiting whereas the latter do not. Furthermore, subsidized loans are less expensive than grants or scholarships of the same amount, so that limited government resources can be spread over a larger number of beneficiaries.

One lesson we can take from existing research is that not all aid is created equal. The empirical evidence suggests that loans are less effective than grants at attracting lower-income students to PSE. This, coupled with the fact that governments have been granting more merit-based awards at the expense of needs-based aid, does not bode well for the access and persistence of students from low-income families. Indeed, this realization appears to be making its way into educational policy, at least in Ontario. The report by former Ontario Premier Bob Rae recommends, among other measures, increasing grants to students from low-income families as a way of improving accessibility.[5]

The evidence suggests, moreover, that the expanded use of the Canadian college system may be an option worth pursuing since entrance requirements, both monetary and academic, tend to be less onerous than those at universities. This may be more easily said than done. Andres and Krahn (1999) study the post-secondary education systems in Alberta and British Columbia; both systems are "articulated" and intended to provide access to a wide group of students by offering the relatively easy transfer of credits between institutions. Still, they are at a loss to explain why so few non-academic high school students take advantage of the less onerous entry requirements at non-university

institutions, especially amongst students in Alberta. Junor and Usher
(2004) too observe that colleges in Alberta and British Columbia have
become increasingly integrated into the university system, and they
are also becoming more selective in their admission choices, compared
to the other eight provinces, which effectively have open access policies. Thus, while integration of community college and university cur-
ricula may be beneficial to students from low-income families, the
benefits are lost as colleges start to behave more like universities in
their admission procedures.

Although the financial aspects of higher education are important,
especially for students from low-income families, an increasing body
of literature suggests that other factors are at least as important.

De Broucker (2005) recommends programs such as early intervention in school to level the playing field between children from different
family backgrounds, and information and counselling to help students
make the right PSE decisions. On the financial front, he recommends
universities reduce tuition risk by fixing tuition levels for the length
of a student's program, as well as government aid that focuses more
on low-income students. This last measure includes rethinking the
use of tax credits (which are regressive), reassessing the criteria used
in needs assessment, and ensuring that low-income students do not
graduate with huge debt loads (in order to prevent inequality after
graduation).

We know little about what influences the access and persistence of
non-traditional students, even though these are becoming an increasing share of students at both universities and colleges in Canada. Similarly, students who follow the traditional route of completion (i.e., four
years in university) are no longer necessarily the norm. This suggests
that researchers must expand their time horizons to capture students
who may interrupt but ultimately complete their programs, as well as
the factors responsible for this behaviour.

We have focused here on financing PSE through loans, scholarships,
or grants, or some combination of these three. Students may also finance their higher education through working more hours, both during the school year and during the summer and holidays. We still know
little about the effects of working on access and persistence in PSE, aside
from the fact that students who work most tend to either do less well in
school or increase their time to graduation. But does working during
PSE help or hinder the employment prospects of graduates? The only
detailed empirical evidence that exists for Canada is at the high school
level and shows that working is an important determinant of dropout
behaviour, although it is correlated with a number of other factors

(Bushnik, 2003). Involvement in cooperative education programs may enhance the employment prospects of graduates, but what about those who take McJobs in order to pay PSE-related expenses? Does this increase the time to graduation or decrease the probability of graduating? What about low-income students who tend to be risk averse and may choose to work over taking out student loans?

Related to this, student loan burdens have been increasing at the same time that the CSLP has become more generous. How much of this increase is used for education and how much is used for current (perhaps unnecessary) consumption? Finnie and Laporte (2007) show that almost 60 percent of students who held loans in 2002 would have liked to borrow more, but they could not determine if it was due to need (i.e., expenditures related to PSE), to maintain a certain lifestyle, or for savings (i.e., interest-free money).

Little Canadian evidence exists about the choice of institution once the decision to attend PSE has been made. Are students directed towards different institutions and/or fields of study as the result of financial considerations, and could this result in a mismatch between students' skills and interests and their program of study? If so, it could be an inefficient outcome for both the student and society as a whole.

We have assumed throughout this paper that more education is a good thing for both the individuals who receive private benefits from it and for all Canadians because of the positive externalities that are created. Much literature in the United States discusses the movement of the university model from, in essence, cultural finishing schools for the elite to the mass-access model where product branding is important to differentiate competitors. While most studies implicitly assume that increased access and persistence are good for society, this may not be the case. PSE may not be worthwhile for every student, and there may in fact be a number of students for whom PSE credentials do not improve earnings. Thus, enticing marginal students to remain in PSE may not be a socially optimal policy. As de Broucker (2005, 36) argues, "We need more vocational options that would offer a real alternative to post-secondary education and provide a smooth and rewarding school-to-work transition for high school students who do not want to pursue post-secondary studies."

We have also implicitly assumed throughout that the supply of PSE spots would passively increase as the result of increased participation of students from low-income families. This assumption should be put to rigorous investigation. Even if the benefits to educating more students are positive, the net benefit to society may be low or negative if the costs of providing additional education are increasing.

We know practically nothing about the influences of various factors on post-graduate education. The ability for Canada to be competitive in the knowledge or post-industrial economy has been on the radar screen of policy-makers for some time (to wit, the Canada Research Chairs program), yet most research is focused on access to colleges and universities rather than on persistence. As graduate education increases in importance, it is vital to understand if the models used for college and undergraduate university education also apply to graduate students.

The Canadian literature is also rather thin on the longer-term family background effects on PSE attendance and persistence. The U.S. literature by Heckman and his colleagues (e.g., Cameron and Heckman, 2001; Carneiro and Heckman, 2002) is particularly useful since it adds new evidence supporting the paramount importance of long-term factors (such as family background) over short-term factors (such as credit constraints) in determining PSE participation. Since many of these short-term factors are correlated with family income in the short-term period when PSE decisions are made, it is often erroneously stated that this short-term credit constraint is what prohibits low-income individuals from attending PSE. The implication is that policy should be directed towards students earlier in life if the long-term goal is to increase PSE participation.

Similarly, we do not know much about the PSE experiences of immigrants to Canada. We do know something about the higher rates of return for a post-secondary education obtained in Canada versus elsewhere (Hum and Simpson, 1999; McBride and Sweetman, 2003), differences between rates of return by immigrants' region of origin (Ferrer and Riddell, 2008), the level of post-secondary educational attainment amongst first- and second-generation immigrants (Aydemir and Sweetman, 2008) and amongst those who entered Canada at different ages (Schaafsma and Sweetman, 2001), but we still have no evidence on any differentials on access and persistence compared to the Canadian-born. Given that the average immigrant has more PSE than the average person born in Canada, coupled with the evidence of the high degree of intergenerational transfer of education within Canadian ethnic groups and the slow convergence of education levels to those of the Canadian-born (Sweetman and Dicks, 1999), it is probable that second-generation immigrants are also likely to access PSE at higher rates than the Canadian-born. Furthermore, this education is likely to be obtained in Canada rather than abroad, and will be rewarded more highly in the Canadian labour market. This hypothesis is certainly worth investigating more rigorously, given the current and future reliance of the Canadian labour market on immigrants.

A reason for this lack of Canadian research in these areas is the paucity of appropriate data to study these questions. The lack of longitudinal microdata, in particular, has hampered our understanding of persistence patterns among students. Often surveys are cross-sectional, and include only those who are already in PSE, limiting the usefulness of the data for studying the experiences of students who do not participate in PSE. Furthermore, researchers must often utilize complex statistical techniques to control for biases inherent in cross-sectional data. Other datasets contain only graduates, again limiting their usefulness, while still others use a limited number of variables, and even though they allow us to follow students over time, the small sample sizes often prevent meaningful inference. Perhaps the most promising widely available study is the Youth in Transition Survey (YITS), which includes only young Canadians and follows them as they transition between high school, work, and PSE. These data will allow researchers to follow and estimate the impact of many of the factors listed above on the education or PSE access, persistence, and ultimately the completion probabilities of Canadian youth.

Notes

This is an abbreviated version of a report prepared for the Canada Millennium Scholarship Foundation through the MESA project managed by the Educational Policy Institute and Queen's University. Bryce van Sluys provided outstanding research assistance on this project, and Marc Frenette, Anne Motte, and Theresa Qiu gave numerous useful comments. Special thanks to Ross Finnie and Arthur Sweetman for their careful reading of an earlier version of this paper. The longer report is entitled "Access and Persistence of Students from Low-Income Backgrounds in Canadian Post-Secondary Education: A Review of the Literature" and is available on the CMSF website.

1. Mueller (2007) is a longer and broader version of this paper that explicitly addresses the U.S. literature.
2. Ehrenberg (2004) provides a brief but comprehensive review of (mainly) recent econometric studies of higher education with emphasis on the U.S. Long (2005) also has an excellent review of the U.S. literature.
3. Some factors are beyond the scope of this chapter. One is the influence of information constraints; the evidence to date suggests that lack of information may be influential in the decisions of many young people in

deciding to pursue PSE. Also beyond the chapter's scope is the effect of many of the factors outlined here on graduate education. See Mueller (2007) for an exposition of these arguments.

4.   Frenette (2002) demonstrates that distance to a university or college should not be confused with the urban or rural residency of an individual.

5.   See Beach et al. (2005) and the papers therein for an assessment of the Rae Report.

References

Allen, M., S. Harris, and G. Butlin. 2003. "Finding Their Way: A Profile of Young Canadian Graduates." Statistics Canada, Education, Skills and Learning Research Papers (February).

Andres, L., and H. Krahn. 1999. "Youth Pathways in Articulated Postsecondary Systems: Enrolment and Completion Patterns of Urban Young Women and Men." *Canadian Journal of Higher Education* 29 (1): 47-82.

Aydermir, A., and A. Sweetman. 2008. "First and Second Generation Immigration Educational Attainment and Labor Market Outcomes: A Comparison of the United States and Canada." *Research in Labor Economics* 27: 215-70.

Barr-Telford, L., F. Cartwright, S. Prasil, and K. Shimmons. 2003. "Access, Persistence and Financing: First Results from the Postsecondary Education Participation Survey (PEPS)." Statistics Canada, Education Skills and Learning Research Paper No. 81-595-MIE – No. 7.

Beach, C.M., R.W. Boadway, and R.M. McInnis, eds. 2005. *Higher Education in Canada*. Montreal and Kingston: McGill-Queen's University Press.

Boothby, D., and T. Drewes. 2006. "Returns to Postsecondary Education in Canada." *Canadian Public Policy* 32 (1): 1-21.

Bowlby, J.W., and K. McMullen. 2002. *At a Crossroads: First Results for the 18- to 20-Year-old Cohort of the Youth in Transition Survey*. Ottawa: Human Resources Development Canada and Statistics Canada.

Butlin, G. 1999. "Determinants of Postsecondary Participation." *Education Quarterly Review* 5 (3): 9-35.

Bushnik, T. 2003. "Learning, Earning and Leaving: The Relationship between Working While in High School and Dropping Out." Statistics Canada, Education, Skills and Learning Research Paper No. 4, No. 81-595-MIE.

Cameron, S.V., and J.J. Heckman. 2001. "The Dynamics of Educational Attainment for Black, Hispanic, and White Males. *Journal of Political Economy* 109 (3): 455-99.

Canada Millennium Scholarship Foundation. 2005. "Closing the Access Gap: Does Information Matter?" Millennium Research Note No. 3.

Carneiro, P., and J.J. Heckman. 2002. "The Evidence on Credit Constraints in Post-Secondary Schooling." *Economic Journal* 112: 705-34.

Cervenan, A., and A. Usher. 2004. "The More Things Change: Undergraduate Student Living Standards after 40 Years of the Canada Student Loan Program." Educational Policy Institute (March).

Christofides, L.N., J. Cirello, and M. Hoy. 2001. "Family Income and Post-Secondary Education in Canada." *Canadian Journal of Higher Education* 31 (1): 177-208.

Coelli, M. 2005. "Tuition, Rationing and Inequality in Post-Secondary Education Attendance." University of British Columbia Working Paper.

Collins, K.A., and J.B. Davies. 2005. "Carrots and Sticks: The Effect of Recent Spending and Tax Changes on the Incentive to Attend University." C.D. Howe Institute Comment No. 220 (October).

Corak, M., G. Lipps, and J. Zhao. 2003. "Family Income and Participation in Post-Secondary Education." Statistics Canada, Analytical Studies, Research Paper No. 210.

De Broucker, P. 2005. "Getting There and Staying There: Low Income Students and Post-Secondary Education: A Synthesis of Research Findings." Canadian Policy Research Networks, Research Report W-27.

De Broucker, P., and L. Lavallée. 1998. "Intergenerational Aspects of Education and Literacy Skills Acquisition." In *Labour Markets, Social Institutions, and the Future of Canada's Children*, edited by Miles Corak. Statistics Canada No. 89-553-XPB.

De Broucker, P., and K. Underwood. 1998. "Intergenerational Education Mobility: An International Comparison with a Focus on Post-Secondary Education." *Education Quarterly Review* 5 (2): 30-51.

Drolet, M. 2005. "Participation in Post-Secondary Education in Canada: Has the Role of Parental Income and Education Changed over the 1990s?" Statistics Canada, Analytical Studies Branch Research Paper Series No. 243.

Ehrenberg, R.G. 2004 "Econometric Studies of Higher Education." *Journal of Econometrics* 121 (1-2): 19-37.

– 2005. "Reducing Inequality in Higher Education: Where Do We Go from Here?" Paper presented at the conference on Economic Inequality and Higher Education: Access Persistence and Success, Syracuse University, 23-24 September 2005.

Ferrer, A., and W.C. Riddell. 2001. "Sheepskin Effects and the Return to Education." In *Towards Evidence-Based Policy for Canadian Education*, edited by P. de Broucker and A. Sweetman, 423-45. Kingston, Ont.: Queen's University, John Deutsch Institute for the Study of Economic Policy; and Ottawa: Statistics Canada/McGill-Queen's University Press.

Ferrer, A., and W.C. Riddell. 2002. "The Role of Credentials in the Canadian Labour Market." *Canadian Journal of Economics* 35 (4): 879-905.

– 2008. "Education, Credentials, and Immigrant Earnings." *Canadian Journal of Economics* 41 (1): 188-216.

Finnie, R. 2000. "Student Loans: The Empirical Record." Queen's University, School of Policy Studies Working Paper 6 (September).

– 2002. "Student Loans, Student Financial Aid and Post-Secondary Education in Canada." *Journal of Higher Education Policy and Management* 24 (2): 155-70.

– 2005. "A Simple Model of Access and Capacity for Post-Secondary Schooling in Canada." Queen's University, School of Policy Studies, Working Paper 40 (February).

Finnie, R., and C. Laporte. 2006. "The Demand for Student Loans and Access to Post Secondary Education." Mimeo.

– 2007. "Lending Opportunity: Student Loans and Access to Post-Secondary Education." Mimeo.

Finnie, R., C. Laporte, and E. Lascelles. 2004. "Family Background and Access to Post-Secondary Education: What Happened in the 1990s?" Statistics Canada, Analytical Studies Research Paper Series No. 226.

Finnie, R., E. Lascelles, and A. Sweetman. 2005. "Who Goes? The Direct and Indirect Effects of Family Background on Access to Postsecondary Education. In *Higher Education in Canada*, edited by C.M. Beach, R.W. Boadway, and R.M. McInnis, 295-338. Montreal and Kingston: McGill-Queen's University Press.

Finnie, R., and A. Usher. 2005. "The Canadian Experiment in Cost-Sharing and Its Effects on Access to Higher Education, 1990-2002." Queen's University, School of Policy Studies, Working Paper 39 (January).

Foley, K. 2001. "Why Stop after High School? A Descriptive Analysis of the Most Important Reasons that High School Graduates Do Not Continue to PSE." Canada Millennium Scholarship Foundation.

Fortin, N.M. 2005. "Rising Tuition and Supply Constraints: Explaining Canada–U.S. Differences in University Enrolment Rates." In *Higher Education in Canada*, edited by C.M. Beach, R.W. Boadway, and R.M. McInnis, 369-413. Montreal and Kingston: McGill-Queen's University Press.

Frenette, Marc. 2002. "Too Far to Go On? Distance to School and University Participation." Statistics Canada, Analytical Studies Research Paper Series No. 191.

– 2004. "Access to College and University: Does Distance to School Matter?" *Canadian Public Policy* 30 (4): 427-43.

– 2005. "Is Post-Secondary Access More Equitable in Canada or the United States?" Statistics Canada, Analytical Studies Research Paper Series No. 244.

Grayson, J.P., with K. Grayson. 2003. *Research on Retention and Attrition.* Canada Millennium Scholarship Foundation.

Gucciardi, F. 2004. "Recognizing Excellence: Canada's Merit Scholarships." Canada Millennium Scholarship Foundation (March).

Hum, D., and W. Simpson. 1999. "Wage Opportunities for Visible Minorities in Canada." *Canadian Public Policy* 25 (3): 379-94.

Ipsos-Reid. 2001. *Post-Secondary Accessibility Study*. Study prepared for Alberta Learning (April).

Johnson, D.R., and F. Rahmad. 2005. "The Role of Economic Factors, Including the Level of Tuition, in Individual University Participation Decisions in Canada," *Canadian Journal of Higher Education* 35 (3): 101-27.

Junor, S., and A. Usher. 2004. *The Price of Knowledge 2004: Access and Student Finance in Canada*. Montreal: Canada Millennium Scholarship Foundation.

Kapsalis, C. 2006. "Who Gets Student Loans." *Perspectives on Labour and Income* 7 (3). Statistics Canada No. 75-001-XIE (March), 12-18.

Knighton, T., and S. Mirza. 2002. "Postsecondary Participation: The Effects of Parents' Education and Household Income." *Education Quarterly Review* 8 (3): 25-32.

Laidler, D. 2002. "Renovating the Ivory Tower: An Introductory Essay." In *Renovating the Ivory Tower: Canadian Universities and the Knowledge Economy*, edited by David Laidler. Toronto: C.D. Howe Institute.

Lambert, M., K. Zyman, M. Allen, and P. Bussière. 2004. "Who Pursues Postsecondary Education, Who Leaves and Why: Results from the Youth in Transition Survey." Statistics Canada No. 81-595-MIE – No. 26.

Long, B.T. 2005. "Contributions from the Field of Economics to the Study of College Access and Success." Harvard Graduate School of Education Working Paper.

Looker, E.D. 1997. "In Search of Credentials: Factors Affecting Young Adults' Participation in Postsecondary Education." *Canadian Journal of Higher Education* 27 (2 and 3): 1-36.

– 2001. "Why Don't They Go On? Factors Affecting the Decisions of Canadian Youth Not to Pursue Post-Secondary Education." Canada Millennium Scholarship Foundation, Research Series.

Looker, E.D., and Graham S. Lowe. 2001. "Post-Secondary Access and Student Financial Aid in Canada: Current Knowledge and Research Gaps." Canadian Policy Research Network.

McBride, S., and Arthur Sweetman. 2003. "Immigrant and Non-Immigrant Earnings by Postsecondary Field of Study." In *Canadian Immigration Policy for the 21st Century*, edited by C.M. Beach, A.G. Green, and J.G. Reitz, 413-62. Montreal and Kingston: McGill-Queen's University Press.

McElroy, L. 2005. "Student Aid and University Persistence: Does Debt Matter?" Canada Millennium Scholarship Foundation, Research Series No. 23.

McMullen, K. 2004. "Distance as a Post-Secondary Access Issue." *Education Matters* 1. Ottawa: Statistics Canada.

Milligan, K. 2005. "Who Uses RESPs and Why." In *Higher Education in Canada*, edited by C.M. Beach, R.W. Boadway, and R.M. McInnis, 467-94. Montreal and Kingston: McGill-Queen's University Press.

Motte, A., H.T. Qiu, Y. Zhang, and P. Bussière. 2008. "The Youth in Transition Survey: Following Canadian Youth through Time." In *Who Goes? Who Stays? What Matters? Accessing and Persisting in Post-Secondary Education in Canada,* edited by R. Finnie, R.E. Mueller, A. Sweetman, and A. Usher. Montreal and Kingston: McGill-Queen's University Press and School of Policy Studies, Queen's University.

Mueller, R.E. 2007. "Access and Persistence of Students from Low-Income Backgrounds in Canadian Post-Secondary Education: A Review of the Literature." Mimeo.

Mueller, R.E., and D. Rockerbie. 2005a. "Determining Demand for University Education in Ontario by Type of Student." *Economics of Education Review* 24 (4): 469-83.

– 2005b. "Do the *MacLean's* Rankings Affect University Choice? Evidence for Ontario." In *Higher Education in Canada,* edited by C.M. Beach, R.W. Boadway, and R.M. McInnis, 339-67. Montreal and Kingston: McGill-Queen's University Press.

Neill, C. 2005. "Tuition Fees and the Demand for University Places." Wilfrid Laurier University Working Paper.

Ouellette, S. 2006. "How Students Fund Their Post-Secondary Education: Findings from the Postsecondary Education Survey." Culture, Tourism and the Centre for Education Statistics Research Paper No. 42, Statistics Canada No. 81-595-MIE (April).

Prairie Research Associates. 2005. "Canadian College Student Finances." 3rd ed. Canada Millennium Scholarship Foundation, Research Series, No. 19.

Rahman, A., J. Situ, and V. Jimmo. 2005. "Participation in Post-Secondary Education: Evidence for the Survey of Labour and Income Dynamics." Culture, Tourism and the Centre for Education Statistics Research Paper No. 36, Statistics Canada No. 81-595-MIE.

Rivard, M., and M. Raymond. 2004. "The Effect of Tuition Fees on Post-Secondary Education in Canada in the Late-1990s." Department of Finance Working Paper No. 2004-09.

Schaafsma, J., and A. Sweetman. 2001. "Immigrant Earnings: Age at Immigration Matters." *Canadian Journal of Economics* 34 (4): 1066-99.

Shipley, L., S. Ouellette, and F. Cartwright. 2003. "Planning and Preparation: First Results of Approaches to Educational Planning (SAEP) 2002." Education, Skills and Learning Research Paper No. 10, Statistics Canada No. 81-595-MIE.

Statistics Canada and Council of Ministers of Education, Canada (CMEC). 2003. *Education Indicators in Canada: Report of the Pan-Canadian Education Indicators Program 2003.* Toronto: Canadian Education Statistics Council.

Sweetman, A., and G. Dicks. 1999. "Education and Ethnicity in Canada: An Intergenerational Perspective." *Journal of Human Resources* 34 (4): 668-96.

Tomkowicz, J., and T. Bushnik. 2003. "Who Goes to Post-Secondary Education and When: Pathways Chosen by 20-Year-Olds." Statistics Canada, Education, Skills and Learning Research Papers (July).

Tomkowicz, J., L. Shipley, and S. Ouelette. 2003. "Perception of Barriers to Education in a Group of 18- to 20-Year-Olds: For Whom Does Money Matter?" Paper presented at the Education, Schooling and Labour Market Conference, Ottawa, Ontario, May 29-30.

Usalcas, J., and G. Bowlby. 2006. "Students in the Labour Market." *Education Matters: Insights on Education, Learning and Training in Canada* 3 (1). Statistics Canada No. 81-004-XIE.

Usher, A. 2004. *Are the Poor Needy? Are the Needy Poor? The Distribution of Student Loans and Grants by Family Income Quartile in Canada.* Toronto: Educational Policy Institute.

Usher, A., and K. Steele. 2006. *Beyond the 49th Parallel II: The Affordability of University Education.* Toronto: Educational Policy Institute.

Vossensteyn, H. 2004. "Fiscal Stress: Worldwide Trends in Higher Education Finance." *Journal of Student Financial Aid* 34 (1): 39-55.

3

The Youth in Transition Survey: Following Canadian Youth through Time

Anne Motte, Hanqing Qiu, Yan Zhang, and
Patrick Bussière

Cet article porte sur le fonctionnement et les résultats de l'Enquête auprès des jeunes en transition (EJET). Cette étude, qui suit, au cours des ans, deux cohortes de jeunes Canadiens, offre des possibilités sans précédent aux chercheurs qui s'intéressent aux questions de l'accès aux études postsecondaires et de la persévérance des jeunes qui décident d'entreprendre de telles études. La richesse des données accumulées par l'EJET permet d'élargir considérablement notre compréhension des divers facteurs qui jouent un rôle dans ce domaine. Par conséquent, les décideurs politiques sont maintenant mieux outillés pour choisir les mesures et les programmes qui aideront les jeunes à acquérir une meilleure formation et à mieux réussir sur le marché du travail.

The Youth in Transition Survey (YITS), which follows two cohorts of Canadian youth, offers unprecedented opportunities to look at issues of access and persistence in PSE. Indeed, the richness of the information contained in the YITS allows researchers to further their understanding of what is at play. In turn, policy-makers are better equipped to make informed decisions on programs that should be implemented to help improve youth educational and labour market outcomes. This article provides key information on the sample, the structure, and the content of this unique survey.

Who Goes? Who Stays? What Matters? Accessing and Persisting in Post-Secondary Education in Canada, eds. R. Finnie, R.E. Mueller, A. Sweetman, and A. Usher. Montreal and Kingston: McGill-Queen's University Press, Queen's Policy Studies Series. © 2008 The School of Policy Studies, Queen's University at Kingston. All rights reserved.

Introduction

Attempts at answering questions such as "Who goes to post-secondary education (PSE)?" "Who stays in PSE?" or "What matters around these issues?" naturally call for data. While data collected at one point in time (cross-sectional data) provide important and necessary indicators for governments and society in general, getting a sound understanding of the process or the mechanisms by which people adopt certain behaviours or make choices – for example, to pursue further studies after high school – requires tracking individuals through time. The need for longitudinal data is particularly acute when the questions above are tied to important policy questions such as how to determine when governments should intervene to encourage PSE participation and success.

Fortunately, the Youth in Transition Survey (YITS) enables researchers and policy-makers to study the intricate pathways of two cohorts of Canadian youth. The creation of the YITS stemmed from the mid-1990s when it became clear that, to ensure Canada's prosperity, efforts would be needed to improve the educational outcomes of Canadian youth. However, before tweaking or elaborating new policies to make sure that youth would be equipped to integrate into the "knowledge economy," there was a need to shed light on some key issues. As described in the YITS project overview (Statistics Canada, 2000), a better understanding was necessary of the costs and benefits of educational investments, the reasons why some youth decide to pursue or not to pursue education, and the ways in which youth transition into the labour market. The case was made to "start collecting information about students before they have begun their transition process, and to follow their progress through the education system (i.e., their educational pathways) and into the labour market for several years" (Statistics Canada, 2000, 9).

About eight years after its inception, with four cycles of data, the YITS is bearing fruit in a number of articles.[1] While we are only beginning to tap into the great potential of the YITS, our vision or understanding of issues is already evolving. The YITS is confirming that pathways of youth are far from being linear: not all youth go in an orderly fashion from high school to post-secondary education to finally enter the labour market and live happily thereafter. Moreover, in trying to understand post-secondary participation, the richness of the information contained in the survey is allowing us to investigate how family background, peer influences, work experiences, and other characteristics interact.

To take stock of this richness, the next sections provide more detailed information on the YITS. An important point to make from the outset is that while we talk of "the YITS" as if it were a single survey, there are in fact two distinct surveys, making it a relatively complex instrument. Indeed, the YITS has two target populations: a cohort of individuals who were 15 years old on 31 December 1999 (cohort A) and a cohort who were 18 to 20 years old on 31 December 1999 (cohort B). While the overarching policy and research questions are the same for both cohorts (getting a better understanding of youths' transitions), the sampling and specific content of the surveys for each cohort differ substantially.

The section that follows provides information on the 15-year-old cohort (cohort A). We then provide details on the cohort of youth aged 18 to 20. A final section addresses some of the challenges with collecting longitudinal data.

The YITS Cohort A: Youth Aged 15 Years Old on 31 December 1999

Sampling

The sampling methodology for the cohort A of YITS (YITS-A) is described by two different stages. In the first stage, a stratified sample of 1,242 schools, all located within the 10 Canadian provinces, was selected. In the second stage, students aged 15 on 31 December 1999 were selected from these schools. This sampling strategy enables researchers to model high school effects when using the YITS-A for analysis. Once in the sample, respondents are surveyed every other year. More specifically, four cycles of data are now available: information was collected in 2000 (cycle 1), 2002 (cycle 2), 2004 (cycle 3), and 2006 (cycle 4).

Content

As respondents get older, the questions in a longitudinal survey change. Some questions may be dropped as they become irrelevant for an older group of respondents (for example, questions about high school experiences), while other questions are added to reflect new realities (for example, entry into the labour market). Such changes or adjustments to questions are seen in the YITS. While it is beyond our scope here to make an exhaustive list of such changes, it is important to point out the unique composition of the first cycle of YITS-A.

The first cycle is best described as being composed of four different entities. Indeed, it gathers information from four different sources. First, high school students in the sample responded to a survey (also referred to as the student questionnaire). Secondly, they participated in the Program for International Student Assessment (PISA) testing conducted by the Organization for Economic Co-Operation and Development (OECD).[2] Thirdly, the parents or guardians of the YITS-A students participated in a YITS parent survey. Finally, the principals or head administrators of the school where the YITS-A students were selected also participated in a PISA/YITS school survey.

In subsequent cycles, neither school administrators nor parents of participating youth were followed up. Only those students who completed a YITS student questionnaire in cycle 1 were interviewed in later cycles. The themes for survey questions for subsequent cycles are similar to those in the student survey of the first cycle.

In the remainder of this section, we provide more details on the content of the four entities: the student survey, PISA, the parent survey, and the school survey.

The Student Survey

The student survey gathers information on different themes described below.

Demographic and family characteristics: A number of demographic characteristics such as the student's age, gender, visible minority status, and immigrant and citizenship status are collected. These characteristics are the traditional candidates for analyzing differences in PSE access or persistence issues.[3]

In addition, researchers can find information about a student's perceptions of his or her parents' expectations concerning his or her postsecondary attainment as well as the student's own expectations. This latter question is asked in each cycle, which allows researchers to investigate how educational expectations evolve through time (Christofides, Hoy, Li, and Stengos, 2008). An interesting feature of the survey is that the same question is asked in the parental questionnaire, making it possible to compare differences in expectations between parents and students (see section on parent questionnaires).

The student questionnaire also captures some complex notions such as self-perception. This concept is measured by three subscales: 1) self-esteem, which measures respondents' self-worth or self-acceptance; 2) self-efficacy, which measures confidence in achieving a positive outcome; and 3) self-mastery, which measures sense of mastery – the extent to which respondents regard their chances as being under their control. Specifically, self-mastery and self-esteem can be used as measures for non-cognitive abilities in the analysis of PSE access (Frenette, 2008).

High school experience: Because the first cycle of YITS-A surveyed high school students, it should not be surprising that high school experiences represent a key component of the survey. Researchers have access to a wealth of information on students' high school experience, such as average overall grade, high school courses taken and students' performance in these courses, extracurricular activities they attended while in high school, and their feelings about different aspects of high school life.

In the analysis of PSE access and persistence, researchers can exploit high school information to measure students' abilities. They can also use this information to capture and analyze students' pre-postsecondary activities, which are proven to have significant influence on subsequent PSE access and persistence. A range of questions such as "How many of your friends were planning to pursue their education after high school?" can be used to capture peer influences on students' educational outcomes (Frenette and Zeman, 2008).

The YITS-A also contains two scale variables measuring high school experience. The first measures high school social engagement. Respondents were asked a series of questions related to their social life in high school. A scale variable was constructed from their responses. The second measure relates to high school academic engagement. A scale variable was constructed from students' responses. The scale variables were standardized to have a mean of zero.[4]

Traditional family background variables such as family income and parental education may work directly on PSE access and persistence or/and work indirectly through certain channels such as high school engagement or social support. Researchers can use these scale variables to enrich their model (Finnie and Mueller, 2008).

Post-secondary education and labour market activities: Given the age of respondents, the first cycle of YITS-A collects limited information on students' employment and no information on post-secondary education. However, later cycles collect a considerable amount of information on both these themes. (See the following section on the YITS cohort B.) In the specific case of the YITS-A, the data collected allow researchers to follow young people from high school to higher education (PSE access) or into the labour market.

PSE financial factors: In later cycles of YITS-A,[5] the survey gathers information on the sources of money that respondents use to fund their PSE, including government sponsored student loans, bank loans, loans from family, scholarships, awards, prizes, grants, or bursaries. The YITS also asks a series of questions on students' applications for government loans.

Students' PISA Scores

The PISA is an international standardized test to assess the skills and knowledge acquired by 15 year olds in reading, mathematics, and science. Tests are administered in the language of instruction of the school – in Canada, either English or French. In cycle 1, all YITS-A respondents participated in a two-hour written test for the assessment of reading, mathematics, and science. Since reading was the major domain in 2000, all respondents were assessed in reading. Also, some students (five-ninths of them) were assessed in mathematics or science, while others (two-ninths) were assessed in both disciplines.

The reading component consists of students' performance in retrieving information from, reflecting on, and interpreting texts. The texts included standard prose passages and various types of documents such as lists, forms, graphs, and diagrams. Test results were then standardized to scores with a mean of 500 and a standard deviation of 100 (which means that two-thirds of respondents had a score between 400 and 600). Researchers use PISA scores as a standardized measurement of cognitive ability. After controlling for cognitive ability, the effects of non-cognitive ability can be separated out (Frenette, 2008; Finnie and Mueller, 2008).

One popular measurement is the PISA overall reading, science, and mathematics score. Another prevailing measurement is the students' overall high school grade average. These two measurements can be used together. Conditioning on an individual's performance on the PISA standardized test, the student's high school overall average may reflect that individual's non-cognitive ability to capitalize on these abilities in a more structured setting (Frenette, 2008).

The Parent Questionnaire

The YITS-A parent questionnaire provides us with a chance to explore family and cultural effects on youth transitions as never before. Information on the family circumstances as well as the student's early education and other demographic characteristics is reported by the parent, which implies greater accuracy than if it were reported by the student. For example, family income is rarely collected when only students are surveyed. This is generally a shortcoming of data, as income in terms of its influence on PSE access remains a hot research topic.

In the analysis of the effect of parental expectations on their child's educational outcome, scrupulous researchers may doubt the accuracy of information provided by children themselves. Using the YITS-A data obviates this concern, since the survey asked parents and children the same question about "the highest level of education that parents hope child to get." The parent-reported variable satisfies researchers' need of preciseness. Moreover, the difference between the student's and the parent's answer could be used to measure the accuracy of information provided by students themselves.

The parental questionnaire also includes a series of questions on parental behaviour. The scale is composed of three items measuring the parents' monitoring behaviour, nurturance behaviour, and inconsistent discipline or rejection-oriented behaviour.

The School Questionnaire

The YITS school questionnaire was completed during cycle 1 by school administrators. It covers issues such as demographics of the school, school staffing, school environment, human and material educational resources, selection and transfer policies, and educational and decision-making practices.

The availability of this information allows researchers to investigate the influence of school quality on PSE access. For example, researchers used school quality factors such as the education level of teachers to enrich their analysis of peer effect on aspirations (Christofides, Hoy, Li, and Stengos, 2008).

Finally, geographical information on the high school is available at a level smaller than the province. For example, it is possible to know the census metropolitan area or census agglomeration area (CMA/CA) of the school that students attended, in turn making possible an exploration of the neighborhood effect. An application is the link of regional university premium relative to high school from the census to YITS-A (Frenette and Zeman, 2008).

The YITS Cohort B: Youth Aged 18 to 20 Years Old on 31 December 1999

As it would take a few years before researchers would be able to observe youth from cohort A making transitions into the labour market, it was decided that the YITS would also follow an older cohort of youth. Youth aged 18 to 20 years old on 31 December 1999 represent the second population target of the YITS. This cohort is referred to as YITS cohort B (YITS-B).

Cohort B is differentiated from cohort A not only by the age when respondents were first interviewed but also by the sampling strategy and survey content, described below.

Sampling

The YITS-B was sampled from eligible in-scope Labour Force Survey (LFS) households, in which at least one household member was between 18 and 20 years old on 31 December 1999. As the individuals in this sample are older and also because they do not share a common trait aside from their age, respondents in YITS-B had a different status with respect to educational activities and the labour market.

Content

The YITS-B respondents participated only in a comprehensive survey conducted by Statistics Canada. That is, unlike in the YITS-A, their parents or school administrators (for those in school) were not interviewed. This means that some variables available in YITS-A are not available in YITS-B. The family income variable constitutes one such example.

Demographic characteristics and family background: Respondents to the YITS-B are asked a number of questions on their demographic characteristics and their family background. These questions are asked about their current situation (at the time of the interview). In the first cycle, some of the questions are also asked about a past period. For example, YITS-A respondents are asked with whom they lived in their last year of high school.

In terms of family background, the YITS-B respondents provide the education attainment and occupation of their parents. Parental income is not collected for this cohort.

High school experience: The YITS-B contains a number of questions on high school experiences – more specifically, a series of questions on the respondents' experiences during their last year in high school. However, as these respondents are older and thus less likely to be in high school, the questions are often retrospective. While such questions can be subject to recall error (because people forget), it remains that they provide valuable information in understanding youth pathways.

Post-secondary education and labour market activities: The YITS-B gathers a considerable amount of information on all post-secondary education programs that students have taken during the period covered by the survey (1999 to 2005) as well as retrospectively for those who entered PSE before 1999. Data are gathered on the province of study, type of institution (trade school, college, university), level of the program (undergraduate level, bachelor's, etc.), start and end date of each program, final status in each program (graduate, leave, continue), and major field of study, etc. The wealth of program information enables researchers to capture detailed transitions between programs, such as a switch from a college diploma to a university degree, or a change in major field of study (Martinello, 2008). Moreover, by using the variable "province of study," PSE choices can be linked to provincial policy – for example, tuition – in a certain jurisdiction (province), and specific regional effects on PSE access or persistence can be analyzed and identified (Johnson, 2008).

The YITS-B also collects information on early PSE experiences, including average grades during the first year in PSE, quality of teaching, workload challenges, perceived relevance of the program to the job skills being sought, and the presence of a social support network. According to Tinto's (1975) "student integration model," this institution-related information could modify students' initial goals and commitments to PSE study and therefore have influence on PSE persistence.

Finally, the YITS-B collects information on jobs that respondents worked at during each cycle's reference period, as well as information on "first job after leaving full-time schooling," including start and end date, tenure, province, and occupation and industry of work. Hence, the YITS-B enables researchers to capture and analyze various transitions through post-secondary education and the labour market.

PSE financial factors: The YITS-B gathers information on the sources of money that respondents use to fund their PSE, including government-sponsored student loans, bank loans, loans from family, scholarships, awards, prizes, grants, or bursaries. The survey also asks a series of questions on students' applications for government loans. Researchers can get a sense of who would have liked to get a loan and did not by analyzing questions like "Have you ever applied for a government sponsored student loan to fund your education?" and "Have you ever been turned down for a government sponsored student loan?"

While the YITS-B provides information on the dollar amounts of different types of financial aid, it does not provide the information on an annual basis. In cycle 1, respondents are asked to report the total amount of each type of aid received up to December 1999. From cycle 2 onwards, they are asked to report the total amount of each type of aid received for a two-year period. Because it is impossible to allocate the amount of money to a specific year or semester, it is difficult to use the YITS-B data to examine how financial aid influences persistence (Day, 2008). Furthermore, for students who enrol in multiple programs over the course of the two years that correspond to a given reference period, it is impossible to link the receipt of a source of funds with a particular program, thus getting a deeper understanding of the effect of financial aid on changing PSE programs.

The YITS over Four Cycles: The Challenges of Longitudinal Data

As mentioned earlier, the key feature of the YITS is that it is a longitudinal survey that follows the same respondents over time. Following individuals through time represents important challenges for surveyors as respondents may not be found or may refuse to take part in the survey. Like any other longitudinal survey, the YITS is thus the subject of sample attrition that occurs between cycles (interviews). As attrition can lead to important analytical issues that researchers cannot ignore, this section provides more information on the phenomenon.

Table 1 presents the number of respondents in the YITS survey between cycle 1 and cycle 4 for each cohort. In 2006, 55 percent of the original cohort A sample was still participating in the survey. This was the case for 42 percent of cohort B.

TABLE 1
Number of Observations in Cycles 1–4

Cycle (Year)	Cohort A		Cohort B	
	Observations	Longitudinal response rates	Observations	Longitudinal response rates
Sample	34,275	100.0	29,164	100.0
Cycle 1 (2000)	29,687	86.6	22,378	76.7
Cycle 2 (2002)	26,854	78.4	18,743	64.3
Cycle 3 (2004)	22,626	66.0	14,753	50.6
Cycle 4 (2006)	18,762	54.7	12,360	42.4

Source: Authors' compilation.

Attrition issues cause two main problems. First, it is quite likely that the sample will become unrepresentative of the original cohort, as attrition is unlikely to be random. In other words, some individuals with specific characteristics are more likely to "disappear" from one cycle to the next. To ensure that the sample in a given cycle remains representative of the original cohort, Statistics Canada creates weights for each observation. These weights are adjusted separately depending on a set of observable individual characteristics, such as province of residence, income, gender, language of interview, and family structure. A sample bias may still be introduced as weights do not control for all changes in the sample composition from one cycle to the next. For example, if those who are least successful academically are less likely to be retained in the sample, it is possible that when analyzing PSE persistence patterns, leaving (or dropout) rates may be underestimated.

Second, attrition reduces sample size substantially, and in turn, implies a lower number of observations in particular sub-groups (for example, immigrants). To deal with this problem, some researchers adopt a survival analysis set-up (Finnie and Qiu, 2008). As is standard in survival analyses, individuals are excluded from the analysis (censoring) at the point they can no longer be tracked for attrition reasons, but enter the analysis up to the point of censoring, meaning that all the information available in the data is used in the most efficient manner.

Conclusion

Launched in 2000, the Youth in Transition Survey allows new light to be shed on issues of access and persistence in post-secondary education. Given its longitudinal nature, the YITS paints a picture of the evolution of youths' pathways over time. Most importantly for policy-makers, the richness of the information contained in the YITS provides the means as never before to understand what is at play. While a single dataset can rarely answer all policy questions, the YITS is an essential component of the education policy-making toolbox.

Differences in population target, sampling methodology, and survey structure distinguish the two cohorts of the YITS, meaning that researchers need to determine which of the two cohorts is appropriate for their purpose. The data of cohort A contain extremely rich information about family background, parents' attitudes, high school characteristics, and standardized cognitive ability measurements when the student was 15 years old. As the parents themselves report parental information, it is thus more accurate. This makes the YITS-A data a good resource to examine the transition from high school to PSE.

On the other hand, youth in the YITS-A are just 21 years old at the latest cycle available (cycle 4), which limits the possibility of studying their PSE persistence and labour market outcomes. Youth from cohort B were 24 to 26 years old when they were last interviewed, which corresponds to an age when most respondents who would have undertaken a PSE program would have finished it. The YITS-B data allow for drawing a detailed picture of transitions between PSE and labour market activities. However, the background information in the YITS-B data is not as rich as that of the YITS-A.

The investment and the commitment made by governments in the Youth in Transition Survey have enabled a new wave of research on PSE issues. Indeed, the papers resulting from the analysis of the YITS are strengthening an effort towards evidence based policy-making in post-secondary education by increasing our understanding of the issues (de Broucker and Sweetman, 2002).

Notes

1. See the articles in *Who Goes? Who Stays? What Matters? Accessing and Persisting in Post-Secondary Education in Canada*, edited by R. Finnie, R.E. Mueller, A. Sweetman, and A. Usher (Montreal and Kingston: McGill-Queen's University Press and Queen's University School of Policy Studies), the collection in which this paper appears. Most of these articles use only the first three cycles of the data, as the fourth cycle of the YITS was not available until early 2008.
2. The PISA is an internationally recognized test to evaluate the knowledge and skills of 15 year olds in reading, mathematics, and science.
3. Note that more demographic and family characteristics are collected in the parent survey.
4. A scale variable summarizes the response from students to a series of related questions that share an empirical or logical structure.
5. These questions are not included in the first cycle, as respondents were then in high school.

References

Christofides, L.N., M. Hoy, Z. Li, and T. Stengos. 2008. "Evolution of Aspirations for University Attendance: A Gender Comparison." In *Who Goes? Who Stays? What Matters? Accessing and Persisting in Post-Secondary Education in Canada*, edited by R. Finnie, R.E. Mueller, A. Sweetman, and A. Usher. Montreal and Kingston: McGill-Queen's University Press and Queen's University School of Policy Studies.

Day, K. 2008. "The Effect of Financial Aid on the Persistence of University and College Students in Canada." In *Who Goes? Who Stays? What Matters?*, ed. Finnie et al.

de Broucker, P., and A. Sweetman, eds. 2002. *Towards Evidence-Based Policy for Canadian Education/Vers des politiques canadiennes d'éducation fondées sur la recherche.* John Deutsch Institute Series. Montreal and Kingston: McGill-Queen's University Press.

Finnie, R., and H. Qiu. 2008. "Is the Glass (or Classroom) Half-Empty or Nearly Full? New Evidence on Persistence in Post-Secondary Education in Canada." In *Who Goes? Who Stays? What Matters?*, ed. Finnie et al.

Finnie, R., and R.E. Mueller. 2008. "The Effects of Family Income, Parental Education and Other Background Factors on Access to Post-Secondary Education in Canada: Evidence from the YITS." In *Who Goes? Who Stays? What Matters?*, ed. Finnie et al.

Frenette, M. 2008. "Why Are Youth from Lower-income Families Less Likely to Attend University? Evidence from Academic Abilities, Parental Influences, and Financial Constraints." In *Who Goes? Who Stays? What Matters?*, ed. Finnie et al.

Frenette, M., and K. Zeman. 2008. "Why Are Most University Students Women? Evidence Based on Academic Performance, Study Habits, and Parental Influences." In *Who Goes? Who Stays? What Matters?*, ed. Finnie et al.

Johnson, D.R. 2008. "Inter-Provincial Variation in University Tuition and the Decision to Continue to Attend University: Evidence from the Youth in Transition Survey in Canada." In *Who Goes? Who Stays? What Matters?*, ed. Finnie et al.

Martinello, F. 2008. "Student Transitions and Adjustments in Canadian Post-Secondary Education." In *Who Goes? Who Stays? What Matters?*, ed. Finnie et al.

Statistics Canada. 2000. *T-00-5E (September 2000) Youth in Transition Survey – Project Overview.* Catalogue no. MP32-30/00–5E, Statistics Canada.

Tinto, V. 1975. "Dropout from Higher Education: A Theoretical Synthesis of Recent Research." *Review of Education Research* 45 (1): 89-125.

Part II
Access

4

The Backgrounds of Canadian Youth and Access to Post-Secondary Education: New Evidence from the Youth in Transition Survey

ROSS FINNIE AND RICHARD E. MUELLER

Dans cet article, nous examinons l'influence du milieu familial et de divers autres contextes sur l'accès des jeunes Canadiens aux études post-secondaires. Nos résultats montrent que le revenu parental semble fortement relié au fait que les jeunes décident de fréquenter l'université, mais que cette influence est de beaucoup moindre quand on prend en compte le niveau de scolarité des parents, dont l'effet est de loin plus important. Cela nous permet donc de mieux situer, dans l'ensemble de la problématique, le rôle du milieu familial, qui devient ainsi plus une question de « culture » qu'une question d'« argent ». Toutefois, les résultats montrent également que l'influence relative du niveau de scolarité des parents diminue quand on tient compte des résultats scolaires des jeunes, de leur participation à la vie étudiante et de leurs résultats aux tests d'aptitude en lecture normalisés ; on obtient ainsi une meilleure indication de la façon dont le niveau de scolarité des parents a un effet sur l'accès des jeunes aux études post- secondaires. L'étude montre donc qu'il est nécessaire de mettre en place des politiques et des mesures qui ciblent ces influences de type culturel, et ce, dès le bas âge.

This paper investigates the nature of various family and other background influences on access to post-secondary education. We find that parental income appears to be strongly related to university attendance but that this effect is greatly diminished once parental education, which is the far greater influence, is taken into account. This re- frames the family background issue as being one that is more about "culture" than "money." The parental education effect is, however, itself reduced once high school grades, academic engagement, and standardized reading test scores are included, thus pointing to the more specific influences through which parental education operates. These findings indicate the need to target policy on these cultural influences and to start early when doing so.

Who Goes? Who Stays? What Matters? Accessing and Persisting in Post-Secondary Education in Canada, eds. R. Finnie, R.E. Mueller, A. Sweetman, and A. Usher. Montreal and Kingston: McGill-Queen's University Press, Queen's Policy Studies Series. © 2008 The School of Policy Studies, Queen's University at Kingston. All rights reserved.

Introduction

Plenty of attention has recently been focused on attracting students to post-secondary education (PSE), not only in Canada but also around the Western world. Much of this attention is driven by the view that Canada will need increasing numbers of educated workers to maintain its position – let alone gain ground – against competitors in the increasingly integrated global economy. University and college administrators too are well aware that the demographic trends that have favoured the latest tide of enrolments cannot be sustained in the future. As the size of the potential applicant pool decreases, they are looking for ways to maintain admissions by increasing the rate at which young people choose to attend PSE.

To date, many of the studies conducted on PSE access have tended to concentrate on the financial constraints that may keep qualified students from attending higher education. From an economist's point of view – and economists have done the lion's share of work in this area – this makes a great deal of sense, given that the inverse relationship between price and demand has the lofty status of a "law" within the discipline. Thus economists expect that if the price (or tuition) increases, fewer students will desire to attend PSE. Indeed, a number of Canadian studies on the impact of tuition hikes at post-secondary institutions have recently been conducted (e.g., Coelli, 2005; Neill, 2005; Johnson and Rahmad, 2005). Up until the fiscal problems of many provincial governments in the mid-1990s, tuition at Canadian PSE institutions was low as a percentage of the total cost of education, ensuring that most students who were able and willing to attend could do so. If low-income families were financially constrained in their ability to send their children, then the student loan system would fill this financial void. As provincial governments reduced their funding to institutions in the 1990s, universities and colleges were forced to make up for shortfalls by increasing revenue from other sources, mainly tuition (Finnie and Usher, 2005). This tuition increase led to concerns that individuals, especially those from low-income backgrounds, may be excluded from participating in PSE.

These changes to the PSE funding regime have not gone unnoticed by the mainstream media, often encouraged by student interest groups whose mandate is to lobby federal and provincial governments for more favourable financial conditions for those attending PSE. Tuition increases are constant fodder for the media, and student protests are frequently front-page news. Indeed, the relationship between low-cost tuition and PSE access has become conventional wisdom – and therefore not to be questioned – for what seems like all but those few who seriously study the issue. To wit, a recent *Globe and Mail* opinion piece entitled "The Sacred Cow of Low Tuition" ran on the same day as PSE students across the country rallied against high tuition.

As Mark Twain once mused, "Sacred cows make the best hamburger." In what follows, we address the importance of some of the non-financial barriers and assess their impact on the PSE participation decision. In particular, we focus on the background of young adults at age 15 and evaluate the importance of these factors on entering either college or university. The availability of the Youth in Transition Survey (YITS) allows an unprecedented look at the importance of many variables that could potentially determine the success or failure of students in accessing PSE in Canada.

What differentiates this research from previous Canadian research on this topic is that we are able to explicitly control for a variety of family background characteristics, most importantly parental income and education, in determining access to PSE. While the YITS has been used in previous research, it has not included the same variety of controls, nor has it been used to model the choice between college and university.[1] What follows is a user-friendly exposition of two much longer and more technical papers. Readers desiring the full details are directed to Finnie and Mueller (2007a, b).

The paper is organized as follows. The following section contains a review of the pertinent literature. The next two sections discuss the data along with a brief outline of the methodology employed, followed by the major results of the descriptive and multivariate analysis. The final section concludes the paper and offers a few policy recommendations based on the major results of the empirical work.

Literature Review

A comprehensive review of the literature that addresses the factors related to PSE participation has been done elsewhere in this volume (Mueller, 2008), as well as by other authors: De Broucker (2005); Junor and Usher (2004); Looker (2001); and Looker and Lowe (2001) for the Canadian literature, and Ehrenberg (2004) and Long (2005) for the U.S. literature. In what follows we briefly describe the evolution of our knowledge about access to PSE in Canada and then outline how the subsequent work in this paper fits into this evolving literature.

A good share of the Canadian and international literature has addressed the impacts of financial variables on access to PSE amongst young people. The accumulated evidence, however, suggests that the demand for PSE is price inelastic (Junor and Usher, 2004). The negligible impact of tuition is important for our purposes, since we are unable to control for this influence in our data. Both Christofides et al. (2001) and Corak et al. (2003) include parental income in their models of PSE participation and find that tuition generally has little effect, but that parental income is important for university attendance but not for PSE in general. Frenette (2005) and Drolet (2005) also find that the PSE attendance gap between high- and low-income families is narrowed when colleges and universities are both considered, but that students from low-income families are less likely to attend either, especially university. Frenette (2008) finds that 12 percent of the gap in university participation between students at the top and those at the bottom income quartiles can be explained by financial constraints. Rivard and Raymond (2004) also find that entrance into PSE is not particularly sensitive to either tuition or family income. More important factors are parental education and academic preparation, although the authors argue that increased returns to PSE as well as increased student loan amounts are also likely important in reducing the significance of income and tuition variables. The data these authors utilize make these conclusions possible: namely that the financial variables that were hitherto considered important become much less so when the appropriate variables are included.

The U.S. evidence also points to the lack of importance of financial factors when the appropriate background variables and data are utilized. Cameron and Heckman (2001) show that parental income in students' pre-PSE years is positively correlated with schooling attainment, but this is due to the long-term correlation with family and environmental factors. Keane and Wolpin (2001) perform simulations that suggest that financial transfers from parents to students have only a modest effect on PSE attendance for individuals from low-income families. Carneiro and Heckman (2002) argue that since many long-term factors are correlated with short-term financial factors in the period when PSE decisions are made, the latter are often cited as being important when in fact it is the former influences that carry the most weight. These studies together suggest that it is not financial constraints that prohibit young people from attaining PSE but rather other factors correlated with parental income.

Finnie, Laporte, and Lascelles (2004) use the 1991 School Leavers Survey (SLS) and the 2000 YITS-B – both of which contain a variety of family background variables – to analyze the influences of these factors on PSE access. They find that participation rates in the 1990s increased most amongst students whose parents were highly educated, which may partially reflect the fact that education is highly correlated with income. This correlation may be particularly important in the 1990s since tuition increased rapidly in most jurisdictions throughout Canada. Finnie, Lascelles, and Sweetman (2005) address the indirect channels through which parental influences work in a paper that also uses the 1991 SLS as well as its follow-up in 1995. The authors find that family background is related to PSE participation both directly and indirectly through variables such as high school marks and attitudes towards education. Furthermore, the direct effects are generally attenuated when the indirect effects are included, and are strongest for university attendance compared to other types of PSE participation.

What we have learned from these recent studies is that the decision to attend (and ultimately to complete) PSE is complex and depends on a variety of financial and non-financial variables related to students' family background, preparedness for post-secondary studies in terms of courses, and activities undertaken during secondary studies. The existing work has also taught us that the inclusion of many relevant variables seems desirable, since many control variables in earlier studies were highly correlated with excluded variables, thus biasing coefficient estimates and (potentially) resulting in misguided policy recommendations. For example, recent Canadian studies generally show that the effect of tuition on the decision to attend PSE is practically nil once family income is taken into consideration, and family income itself is shown to be less important statistically and economically once parental education is included. Ironically, policy discussions still tend to focus on financial-related barriers to entry.

This is the point of departure for the current paper. We utilize the extensive background information contained in YITS-A to address access to PSE in Canada. Specifically, we add to the existing literature by including a comprehensive set of background variables that are determined before entry into PSE to assess both the direct and indirect impact of these variables on access to college and university.

Data and Methodology

The Youth in Transition Survey Sample A (YITS-A) initially interviewed 15 year olds, their parents, and their high school administrators in 2000. Two follow-up surveys of the young people only were conducted in 2002 and again in 2004. In this final wave of the survey, the young people were 19 years of age, a time when most people have already entered either PSE or the labour force.

We limit the sample to include only those in nine of the ten provinces, Quebec being the exclusion. Because Quebec has a special system of PSE, Collège d'Enseignement Général et Professionnel, or CEGEP, students in Quebec only attend secondary education up to the equivalent of grade 11 and then attend CEGEP to either prepare for a university degree (an additional two years) or to complete a technical program (usually an additional three years). Because of the structure of this system, those attending university in Quebec normally can complete their PSE studies in three years compared to four years outside of the province. We drop Quebec from our analysis since there is no way in these data to disaggregate the two streams, and this could potentially confound our analysis (i.e., university-bound students could be incorrectly classified as college students or vice versa). The differentiation of college- and university-bound students is key to the analysis that follows. Observations from the territories are also eliminated, owing to small sample sizes.

PSE participation refers to the first program that a student entered, rather than the highest level attended. This is owing to the fact that more information is available on the first program than on subsequent programs for each individual, as well as the fact that we are concerned in this research with the transition from high school to PSE. Since individuals who have studied outside of Canada might have quite different backgrounds and experiences, we eliminate them from the sample. For the same reason, non-Canadian citizens and those with unknown immigration status are dropped. Finally, we drop those individuals for whom there are missing data as well as those who are continuing in high school, since for this latter group we obviously do not observe any transition into PSE. A full accounting of the observations dropped from the sample is contained in Finnie and Mueller (2007a). The final unweighted sample size consists of 16,163 observations from 7,852 males and 8,311 females, although missing observations sometimes change these numbers slightly in selected estimations.

All estimates that follow are derived from a multinomial logit model whereby young people chose among university, college (including trade school), and not attending PSE. All models control for urban (versus rural) location, province in which the young person attended high school, French minority status, family type (two parents, mother or father only, other), and indicators for minorities and immigrants, and their interaction.[2] This methodology was used in earlier work on access by Finnie, Sweetman, and Lascelles (2004), albeit on a much less detailed dataset.

Results

Table 1 shows participation rates of males and females in any PSE, then separated into participation at colleges and universities. A few patterns are present from these data and worthy of note. PSE participation is much higher for females than for males – 69.2 percent versus 55.9 percent. This total differential can entirely be accounted for by the higher university participation rates of young women – 44.7 percent versus 30.9 percent for males. College participation rates for the sexes are almost identical. The higher university participation rate for young women is well known, at least amongst researchers. Any other differences between the young males and females in our sample are not obvious from the data in this table.

The table shows that young people from urban areas are much more likely to attend university. The Maritime provinces and Ontario have the highest rates of PSE participation in the country, while Alberta has the lowest, followed by Saskatchewan. Much of Ontario's high overall participation rate is owing to the proportion of young people attending college rather than university, whereas for the Maritimes high university participation rates – the highest in the country – explain the high overall rates. Family background also appears to be an important determinant of PSE attendance. Young people from two-parent families are much more likely to attend PSE than those from other types of families, entirely due to their higher university participation rates. Interestingly, minorities in Canada (whether visible minorities, immigrants, or linguistic minorities) all have higher overall PSE participation rates in general, usually the result of higher university participation rates.

Figures 1 through 4 use the data from Table 1 to show participation rates by parental income and parental education for both males and females. First, Figures 1 and 2 show participation rates at college and university by parental income for males and females, respectively. Here college participation rates are at or above 20 percent for both males and females regardless of family income; the lone exception is for females from the lowest family income group. Also of note is that college participation rates are relatively flat for males and only a little less so amongst females. With the exception of both males and females with the lowest parental incomes, university participation rates are increasing with income, especially for females, approximately double for those in the highest income category compared to those in the second lowest category. A similar pattern is observed for males, although overall participation rates are lower than those for females.[3]

TABLE 1
PSE, College and University Participation Rates by Individual Characteristics,
Males and Females

	Any PSE		College		University	
	Males	*Females*	*Males*	*Females*	*Males*	*Females*
Overall	55.9	69.2	25.0	24.5	30.9	44.7
HS region						
Rural	47.8	67.1	26.3	30.8	21.4	36.3
Urban	58.4	69.9	24.5	22.4	33.9	47.4
HS province						
Newfoundland and Labrador	53.7	68.4	23.9	21.7	29.8	46.7
Prince Edward Island	62.0	73.1	18.7	15.1	43.3	58.0
Nova Scotia	66.3	75.2	19.3	15.8	47.1	59.4
New Brunswick	55.2	72.4	19.3	18.6	35.9	53.7
Ontario	61.8	75.8	31.3	28.8	30.5	47.1
Manitoba	45.0	64.1	11.6	16.7	33.4	47.4
Saskatchewan	46.1	59.3	16.4	18.2	29.8	41.1
Alberta	43.5	56.3	18.2	21.3	25.3	35.0
British Columbia	54.0	62.3	22.6	22.8	31.4	39.5
French minority outside QC						
No	55.7	68.9	24.7	24.2	31.1	44.7
Yes	60.6	76.1	33.0	30.2	27.6	45.9
Family type						
Two parents	57.5	70.9	25.3	24.3	32.2	46.7
Mother only	46.7	63.6	22.7	26.4	24.0	37.1
Father only	49.8	57.7	26.3	23.2	23.6	34.6
Other	40.7	40.0	20.6	17.7	20.1	22.3
Visible minority						
Visible minority	69.4	79.0	24.0	22.6	45.5	56.5
Non-visible minority	53.7	67.5	25.1	24.8	28.6	42.7
Immigrant status						
Canadian by birth	54.8	68.1	25.1	24.9	29.7	43.2
Canadian by immigration	67.6	79.8	23.8	19.7	43.8	60.1
Visible minority and Canadian **by immigration**						
No	55.4	68.6	25.0	24.7	30.4	44.0
Yes	66.7	80.2	24.1	20.5	42.6	59.6

... continued

TABLE 1
(Continued)

	Any PSE		College		University	
	Males	*Females*	*Males*	*Females*	*Males*	*Females*
Parent/guardian education						
Less than HS	28.7	43.8	18.9	24.6	9.8	19.2
HS completed	44.2	59.8	27.3	28.8	16.9	31.1
Some PSE	48.9	68.2	26.7	32.8	22.1	35.5
Trade/college	53.0	65.5	28.8	27.4	24.2	38.0
University – below BA degree	62.2	83.3	27.7	19.4	34.5	63.9
University – BA	71.5	84.9	21.3	18.9	50.2	66.0
University – grad	82.0	88.1	16.3	11.3	65.6	76.8
Other/unknown	-	-	-	-	-	-
Parental income level						
Extremely low ($0-$5,000)	49.8	55.7	25.7	14.1	24.2	41.6
$5,000 to $25,000	44.9	54.9	23.6	23.1	21.3	31.8
$25,000 to $50,000	48.8	59.9	25.3	25.1	23.5	34.8
$50,000 to $75,000	51.1	70.0	24.3	26.3	26.8	43.6
$75,000 to $100,000	62.3	74.2	25.8	25.0	36.5	49.2
$100,000 and up	68.6	83.5	24.6	20.5	44.0	63.0

FIGURE 1
PSE Participation Rate by Parental Income, Males

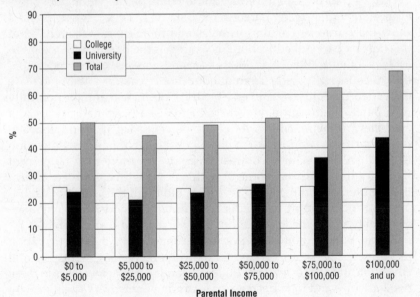

Source: Finnie and Mueller, 2007a.

FIGURE 2
PSE Participation Rate by Parental Income, Females

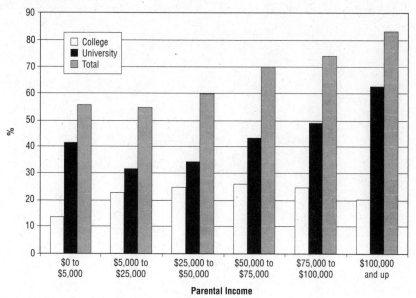

Source: Finnie and Mueller, 2007a.

The raw data on parental education and PSE participation rates show even more variance compared to the data on income. Figures 3 and 4 show these results – again for males and females, respectively – but this time by parental education (measured as the parent with the highest level of education). For both males and females, college participation rates increase with parental education, peak, and then decrease thereafter. By contrast, university education increases monotonically with parental education, and these increases are dramatic, especially for males. Young men have about a 10 percent participation rate when they come from a family where the highest level of parental education is less than high school; contrast this with the more than 60 percent figure for those who have one or both parents with a graduate education. For females, the pattern is similar, although the jump not as dramatic: an increase from just under 20 percent to the mid-70 percent range as we move from the least educated to the most educated parents.

To summarize, the results from our sample show that participation in PSE, especially university, tends to be increasing with parental education and family income. College attendance first increases in these two variables and then decreases for young people from families with the highest levels of education and income. Of course, one lesson we

FIGURE 3
PSE Participation Rate by Parental Education, Males

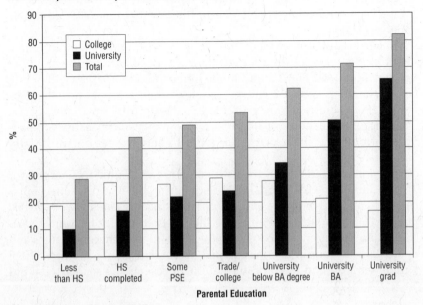

Source: Finnie and Mueller, 2007a.

FIGURE 4
PSE Participation Rate by Parental Education, Females

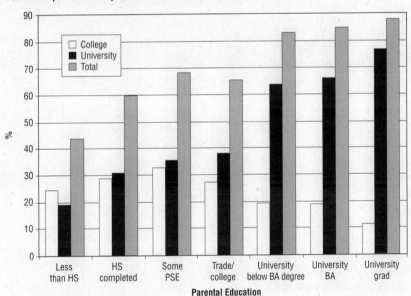

Source: Finnie and Mueller, 2007a.

have learnt quite clearly from the literature is that these education and income effects tend to be positively correlated, and the only way to tease them (and other effects) out of the data is to use a multivariate analysis.

In what follows we present the results from estimating a multinomial logit model whereby individuals attend college, attend university, or do not attend either. Changes in the independent variables will jointly affect the university and college decisions of individuals, and the marginal effects are what are presented in the figures. Since most of the significant results are for university attendance and because of space limitations, we limit our comments to the effects on university attendance.[4]

The initial results from the estimation are presented in Figure 5 for males and Figure 6 for females. In both figures the marginal effects presented are relative to the omitted parental income category of $50,000 to $75,000. Four sets of results are shown: first with only control variables and the parental income variable; second with these variables and parental education added; next as in the second case but with high school grade variables added; and in the fourth case as the second case but

FIGURE 5
Marginal Effects of Parental Income on Access to University, Males

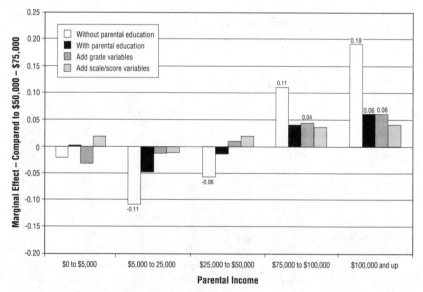

Note: Bars with data labels denote statistical significance at at least the 5 percent level.
Source: Finnie and Mueller, 2007a, b.

with various scale variables added intended to measure engagement in high school, self-perception, etc.[5] In all cases, bars with data labels are those where coefficients estimates are significant at least at the 5 percent level.

As expected, these results differ in a number of important ways relative to the simple summary measures outlined in Figures 1 to 4. University attendance is increasing with parental income for both males and females regardless of the specification. However, once controls for parental education are added to the model, the importance of income is diminished greatly, and becomes insignificantly different from zero in many cases, especially amongst males. For example, in the cases without parental education in Figure 5, each level of parental income (except for the lowest) has a significant effect on university attendance. Once parental education is added, however, only the top income group continues to have an effect on attendance, albeit at a much reduced level. The results for females in Figure 6 follow the same general trend but are less pronounced. When high school grade variables and scale/score variables are added (in separate estimates), the effects of parental income do not change by much if at all.

FIGURE 6
Marginal Effects of Parental Income on Access to University, Females

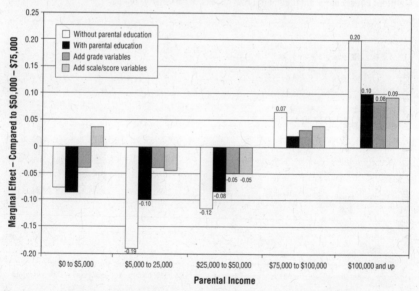

Note: Bars with data labels denote statistical significance at at least the 5 percent level.
Source: Finnie and Mueller, 2007a, b.

Figures 7 and 8 look at the results of the model somewhat differently: the marginal effects of parental education relative to the omitted case (i.e., high school completed). Here we see a similar pattern to that in the previous two figures: namely, that participation in university is increasing in relation to parental education. This is hardly surprising given the positive correlation between education and income. What is more surprising is that parental income tends to become less influential on university attendance as more explanatory variables are added to the model; the same does not hold for parental education, which continues to exert a strong influence on participation even as new regressors are added to the model.

Another interesting feature of these results is that parental education exerts a much more potent influence on participation than income. Even though it is somewhat difficult to compare these two since they are measured differently, we see that once parental education is added to the model in Figures 5 and 6, the increase in participation for those from the richest families – relative to the control group at the $50,000-$75,000 range – is never above 10 percentage points for females or 6 percentage points for males. By contrast, having one parent with at least a bachelor's degree would increase the likelihood of participation by at

FIGURE 7
Marginal Effects of Parental Education on Access to University, Males

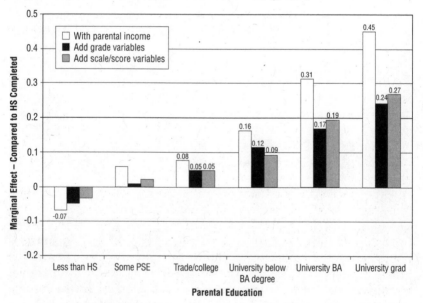

Source: Finnie and Mueller, 2007b.

FIGURE 8
Marginal Effects of Parental Education on Access to University, Females

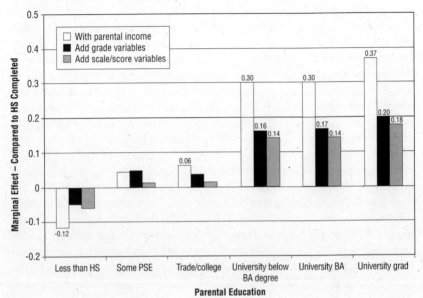

Source: Finnie and Mueller, 2007b.

least 17 percentage points for males and 14 percentage points for females relative to those from the control group (at least one parent with a high school diploma). This general result – that parental education is a stronger predictor of university participation than parental income – has also been found in the Canadian studies by Knighton and Mirza (2002), Drolet (2005), and Rahman et al. (2005).

A further interesting result from this set of estimates requires a little more explanation. Here we compare the results in Figures 5 and 7 (males) and Figures 6 and 8 (females). The effect of parental income remains relatively unchanged in Figures 5 and 6 when we add the grade variables to the model, whereas the effect of parental education on university attendance is attenuated greatly in both cases (Figures 7 and 8). This suggests that the influence of parental education works at least in part through high school grades. This result is worthy of further investigation since the mechanism through which this influence operates is not clear. Finally, when we substitute the scale/score variables for the grade variables, the result is very similar: little impact on the marginal effect of parental income but a greater effect (over 50 percent in some cases) on the marginal effect of parental education.

Next we turn our attention to a detailed analysis of the grades that students received in high school at the time of the first wave of the survey in 2001 when these young people were 15 years old, and the influence that these have on access to PSE. The results of these estimations are in Figures 9 and 10 where the model estimated includes both parental income and education as well as all other controls mentioned above. We outline the marginal effects of high school grades from models in which grades are added in both individually and jointly.[6] Adding the overall numerical high school grade to the model results in higher university participation. The estimates suggest that a 10-percentage point higher grade average in high school will result in about a 21 percentage point increase in university participation for males and a 22 percentage point increase for females. Numerical high school grades in each of math, language, and science also yield positive coefficients in each case, although of a smaller magnitude, suggesting that, rather than any individual grade, overall grades are important in determining participation in university. Indeed, when the model is jointly estimated with all grades included, it is still the overall grade that is of paramount importance in determining university attendance.

FIGURE 9
Marginal Effects of HS Grades on Access to University, Males

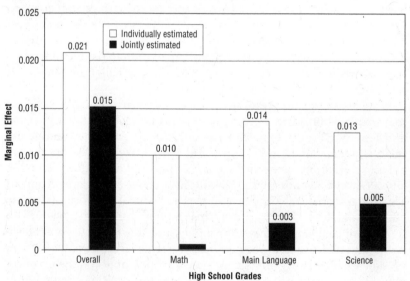

Source: Finnie and Mueller, 2007b.

FIGURE 10
Marginal Effects of HS Grades on Access to University, Females

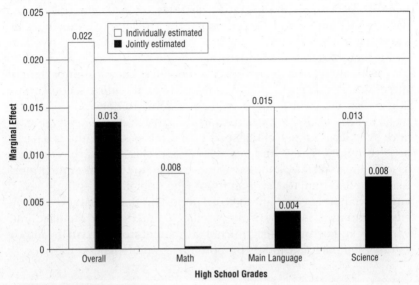

Source: Finnie and Mueller, 2007b.

An interesting result is that the math grade is numerically the least important in determining university attendance, whether this enters the model individually or jointly. The lack of numeracy skills (at least as reflected by the math grade) does not appear to be as important as the language grade in any of the specifications for either sex. The same can be said for the science grade. This is somewhat surprising, since the importance of high school science and math grades has become conventional wisdom. While this wisdom may be correct for gaining entrance directly into certain university programs – engineering, for example – most students enter a general studies program before declaring a major, so it is not unexpected that the overall grades rather than individual subject grades are what is important.

The YITS survey includes a number of "scale" variables, which are indices derived from the data collected for the survey. These variables are designed to measure various aspects of a student's engagement in high school, the student's self-esteem, parental behaviours, and the PISA (Programme for International Student Assessment) reading score. Each of these variables is normalized at mean zero (mean five for the PISA score) and a standard deviation of one. This is important when interpreting the results below. Details of these variables can be found in Appendix Table A-1.

The influence of scale variables on college and university attendance is addressed in Figures 11 and 12 for males and Figures 13 and 14 for females. As before with the grades variables, these are entered into the basic model individually and then jointly. The latter case includes all the variables in both figures for both males and females. The two academic variables (academic identification and academic participation) are positively related to university attendance. The most important of these is academic participation (a measure of attending school, doing homework, etc.). For females, being one standard deviation above the mean on this academic participation scale increases university attendance by at least 8.8 percentage points. For males, this figure is 6.8 percentage points. Thus, students who attend class regularly, complete assignments on time, and spend more time studying are much more likely to attend university than those who do not. Interestingly, social engagement, often thought to be an important determinant of university attendance, is numerically smaller than either of the academic variables and becomes insignificantly different from zero in the jointly estimated model. This holds for both males and females.

FIGURE 11

Marginal Effects of Scale Variables of HS Engagement and Self-Perception on Access to University, Males

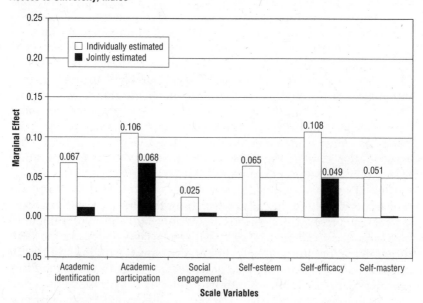

Source: Finnie and Mueller, 2007b.

FIGURE 12
Marginal Effects of Scale Variables of Social Support, Parental Behaviours, and
PISA Reading Score on Access to University, Males

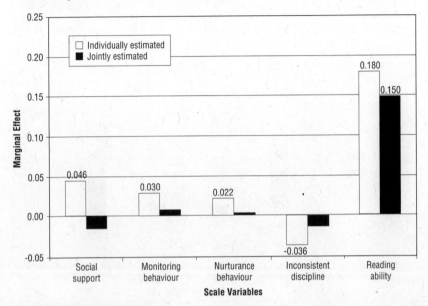

Source: Finnie and Mueller, 2007b.

Self-perception would also seem to be an important determinant of PSE participation. This category is divided into three subcategories: self-esteem is a measure of self-worth and self-acceptance; self-efficacy is the student's own perception of his or her competence and confidence in performing class work; and self-mastery is a measure of being in control of one's own destiny. Students who score high on these measures might be more prepared to enter PSE. The results do show that all three are positively and significantly correlated with university attendance, at least when entered individually. Self-efficacy, however, has the largest coefficient for both males and females – about double the value of the others in this category, at least when estimated separately. Furthermore, it remains at about 5 percentage points and significant for both males and females in the jointly estimated model. Social support is important for males but not for females in the first case, but unimportant statistically for males in the second. Indeed, for females the marginal effect is negative and significant.

Parental behaviour is divided into three subcategories: "monitoring behaviour" addresses how well parents feel informed about the activities

FIGURE 13
Marginal Effects of Scale Variables of HS Engagement and Self-Perception on Access to University, Females

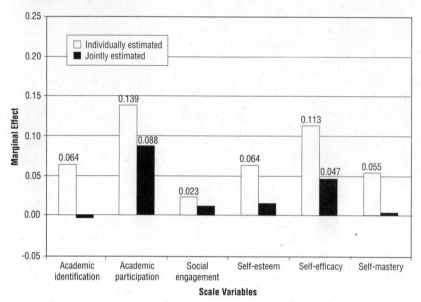

Source: Finnie and Mueller, 2007b.

of their children, while "nurturance behaviour" and "inconsistent discipline" are both fairly self-explanatory. Of these, monitoring behaviour is positively related to university attendance for both males and females, although nurturing is important only for males. Finally, inconsistent discipline is negatively related to participation in university. Still, these values are numerically smaller than many of the other influences. Indeed, in the jointly estimated model, none remains important for males, while monitoring behaviour and inconsistent discipline remain significant but decrease in size for females.

Reading ability is also an important correlate of university attendance. This variable has a mean of five and a standard deviation of one and was created from the PISA reading test results. The point estimates show that females who are one standard deviation above the mean will on average have about a 19-23 percentage point increase in attending university. For males, the figure is 15-18 percentage points. Considering the mean probability of attending university for the sample is 30.9 percent for males and 44.7 percent for females, these reading scores account of about one-half of these figures. The PISA reading score is a

FIGURE 14
Marginal Effects of Scale Variables of Social Support, Parental Behaviours, and
PISA Reading Score on Access to University, Females

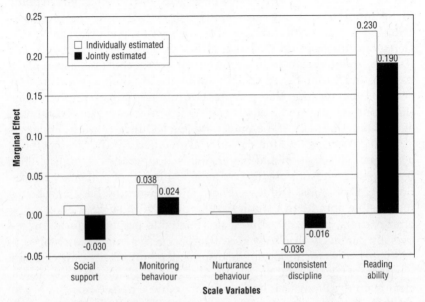

Source: Finnie and Mueller, 2007b.

standardized test, and these results are similar to those obtained by Carneiro and Heckman (2002) who also use standardized test scores to explain differences in college attendance in the United States. It is important to note that the PISA results are from administrative data collected from high schools, whereas the high school grades are self-reported. Finnie and Meng (2005) have shown that these types of test score measures of skill perform better than self-assessments of skill. In particular, they use literacy as an example using both types of measures, and find that the self-assessed measure tends to lead to a significant underestimation of the effect of literacy on employment compared to the test measure. In the present work, this bias may also be present, as indicated by the lower coefficients on the high school language variable (which are self-reported) versus the PISA reading score.

When all these scale variables are considered together, only three stand out for both sexes: academic participation, self-efficacy, and reading ability. When the model is jointly estimated, it is only these three coefficients that are both economically and statistically significant for both males and females. This latter result is particularly interesting.

Since reading ability is a skill derived over a period of time, this result is also consistent with the earlier work on this subject by Cameron and Heckman (2001) and Carneiro and Heckman (2002), both of which point to the importance of long-term family factors in determining success in PSE. The general results presented above are consistent with the sparse Canadian literature on this subject. Finnie, Lascelles, and Sweetman (2005) also find that including a variety of high school grades and other background variables reduces the influence of parental education on access. They also find that parental education is still an important influence after these grades and background variables are taken into consideration, especially at the university level. Our results are similar.

What can we make of these results taken together? The fact that more academic participation and better high school grades or higher PISA reading ability results are important determinants of university education seems obvious. The lesson here is that working hard and being responsible about one's studies are important. In short, a good work ethic matters. This work ethic is also related to parental education (especially parents with a BA or above) as the coefficients on parental education become less important determinants of university participation when these background variables are added to the model. What is not clear from this analysis is how this work ethic is passed from parent to child: do highly educated parents push their children harder, or is this work ethic transmitted by some other mechanism? The generally small and often insignificant coefficients on the parental behaviour variables seem to provide some supporting evidence for the latter explanation. In any case, they do underline the importance of family background and natural skill endowments as emphasized by Cameron and Heckman (2001), Keane and Wolpin (2001), and Carneiro and Heckman (2002), to name but three such studies.

Conclusions and Policy Implications

This research has addressed how the backgrounds of high school graduates are related to access to PSE in Canada. Several interesting results can be derived from this work.

First, in accordance with earlier studies, the impact of parental income is reduced once the level of parental education is taken into account. In particular, higher levels of parental education tend to increase the probability that an individual will attend university and reduce the probability that he or she will attend college.

Second, parental education exerts a much stronger influence on university attendance than does parental income. Although obviously young people have no choice in the matter, they would do better to have at least one university-educated parent rather than one with a high income.

Third, overall high school grades, as well as the three subject grades under consideration, tend to be positively correlated with university attendance. Further, it is the overall high school grade rather than any individual subject grade that has the largest influence on university attendance. This is an interesting result since it is often assumed that language arts and mathematics grades are what are the most important. Still, this result makes sense if in fact most students take a general-studies program upon entering university, so it is not surprising that the universities themselves might prefer individuals who are better overall academically compared to students who excel at one or two subjects.

Fourth, engagement at high school, especially academic participation, is an important determinant of university participation. In fact, it is the most important of all the scale variables included, although self-efficacy (or a feeling of competence and confidence at school) is also demonstrably important. The largest determinant of university participation, however, is the score on the reading portion of the PISA.

Fifth, when any of high school grades, academic participation, or PISA reading score is added to the basic model, the direct effect of parental education is diminished but not eliminated. Although not shown above, the largest drop in parental education comes from the inclusion of the PISA reading ability score, arguably a much more reliable indicator of ability compared to the other background variables (which are self-reported). In other words, parental education works through both of these sets of variables to influence PSE choice. We cannot tell from these estimates the path that this influence takes, although it seems certain that hard-working students do better at finding a spot in university. This could be the result of highly educated parents expecting more of their children – and having this expectation realized, on average – or it could be the result of some other characteristic passed on from parent to child which is correlated with parental education but not observed nor controlled for in the estimates. Further disentangling this result would not only be a fruitful avenue for future research but an understanding of this dynamic is also essential for prescribing appropriate policy.

The policy implications of this research are not straightforward. We know that parental education and parental income are important determinants in whether students access PSE and also at what level. But parental education is correlated with other background variables that are themselves important determinants of PSE participation. It is unrealistic to expect policy to change the exigent level of parental education, although policy could influence its level for today's young people when they themselves are parents. Therefore, the short-term policy focus must be on the correlates of parental education, in particular those that can be changed by policy. In our model, these are factors such as academic participation and reading ability, as well as high school grades, all of which are positively correlated to the probability of PSE attendance. How these factors are determined is currently unclear, but as they are likely developed early in life, targeting these characteristics seems like an important consideration for policy-makers.

Notes

This research was financed by the Canada Millennium Scholarship Foundation through the MESA project, an undertaking based at the School of Policy Studies at Queen's University in Kingston and the Educational Policy Institute. We thank Yan Zhang for her exceptional research assistance throughout this project. René Morissette provided useful comments on an earlier draft of this paper. We are also grateful to the MESA research committee, especially Charles Beach, for the thoughtful comments given on the penultimate version of this paper.

1. For example, Finnie, Laporte, and Lascelles (2004) do not use the family income variable, since they try to match the YITS with the SLS (which does not contain this variable). Frenette (2007) does include a wide array of controls, including family income, but addresses only university attendance.

2. Details of the models estimated can be found in Finnie and Mueller (2007a, 2007b).

3. Although not reported in these figures, total PSE participation is 62.6 percent for all youth in our sample but is much higher for females than for males – 69.2 percent versus 55.9 percent. This total differential can entirely be accounted for by the higher university participation rates of young women – 44.7 percent versus 30.9 percent for males. See Finnie and Mueller (2007a) for more details.

4. This is not to imply that studying access to college is any less important than studying access to university, but only that most of the statistically important results pertain to university access. Readers interested in these results are referred to Finnie and Mueller (2007a, b).

5. In these and all figures that follow, the model specification also includes controls for the province where the respondent's high school was located (urban or rural area, as well as province), a dummy variable for French

minority status outside of Quebec, a categorical variable for family type (two parents, mother or father only, and other), and dummy variables for both visible minorities and immigrants and their interaction. Parental education is the maximum of either the mother's or father's education. Similarly, family income is the higher of the mother or the father in the two-parent family case, or the parent who is present in the one-parent case. Grade variables are at the time of the survey in which the respondent was 15 years of age and include the overall grade as well as grades for math, main language (i.e., English or French), and science. Scale variables include measures of academic, social, and overall engagement at high school; and measures of self-perception, social support, and parental behaviours. The score variable is the grade attained on the PISA (Programme for International Student Assessment) reading ability test. See Finnie and Mueller (2007b) and/or Appendix Table A-1 for details.

6. In other words, each grade is entered into the model by itself before including all the grade variables together. This results in four individual regressions, each with a unique grade variable included, and a fifth regression with all grade variables included together.

References

Cameron, S.V., and J.J. Heckman. 2001. "The Dynamics of Educational Attainment for Black, Hispanic, and White Males." *Journal of Political Economy* 109 (3): 455-99.

Carneiro, P., and J.J. Heckman. 2002. "The Evidence on Credit Constraints in Post-Secondary Schooling." *Economic Journal* 112: 705-34.

Christofides, L.N., J. Cirello, and M. Hoy. 2001. "Family Income and Post-Secondary Education in Canada." *Canadian Journal of Higher Education* 31 (1): 177-208.

Coelli, M. 2005. "Tuition, Rationing and Inequality in Post-Secondary Education Attendance." University of British Columbia Working Paper.

Corak, M., G. Lipps, and J. Zhao. 2003. "Family Income and Participation in Post-Secondary Education." Statistics Canada, Analytical Studies, Research Paper Series No. 210.

De Broucker, P. 2005. "Getting There and Staying There: Low Income Students and Post-Secondary Education: A Synthesis of Research Findings." Canadian Policy Research Networks, Research Report W-27.

Drolet, M. 2005. "Participation in Post-Secondary Education in Canada: Has the Role of Parental Income and Education Changed over the 1990s?" Statistics Canada, Analytical Studies Research Paper Series No. 243.

Ehrenberg, R.G. 2004 "Econometric Studies of Higher Education." *Journal of Econometrics* 121 (1-2): 19-37.

Finnie, R., C. Laporte, and E. Lascelles. 2004. "Family Background and Access to Post-Secondary Education: What Happened over the 1990s?" Statistics Canada, Analytical Studies Research Paper Series No. 226.

Finnie, R., E. Lascelles, and A. Sweetman. 2005. "Who Goes? The Direct and Indirect Effects of Family Background on Access to Postsecondary Education." In *Higher Education in Canada*, edited by Charles M. Beach, Robin W. Boadway, and R. Marvin McInnis, 295-338. Montreal and Kingston: McGill-Queen's University Press.

Finnie, R., and R. Meng. 2005. "Literacy and Labour Market Outcomes: Self-Assessment versus Test Score Measures," *Applied Economics* 37 (17): 1935-51.

Finnie, R., and R.E. Mueller. 2007a. "High School Student Characteristics and Access to Post-Secondary Education in Canada: Evidence from the YITS." Mimeo, October 2007.

– 2007b. "The Effects of Family Income, Parental Education and Other Background Factors on Access to Post-Secondary Education in Canada: Evidence from the YITS." Mimeo, December 2007.

Finnie, R., and A. Usher. 2005. "The Canadian Experiment in Cost-Sharing and Its Effects on Access to Higher Education, 1990-2002." Queen's University, School of Policy Studies, Working Paper 39 (January).

Frenette, M. 2005. "The Impact of Tuition Fees on University Access: Evidence from a Large-Scale Price Deregulation in Professional Programs." Statistics Canada, Analytical Studies Research Paper Series No. 263.

– 2008. "Why Are Lower-Income Students Less Likely to Attend University? Evidence from Academic Abilities, Parental Influences, and Financial Constraints." In *Who Goes? Who Stays? What Matters? Accessing and Persisting in Post-Secondary Education in Canada*, edited by R. Finnie, R.E. Mueller, A. Sweetman, and A. Usher. Montreal and Kingston: McGill-Queen's University Press and School of Policy Studies, Queen's University.

Johnson, D.R., and F. Rahmad. 2005. "The Role of Economic Factors, Including the Level of Tuition, in Individual University Participation Decisions in Canada." *Canadian Journal of Higher Education* 35 (3): 83-99.

Junor, S., and A. Usher. 2004. *The Price of Knowledge 2004: Access and Student Finance in Canada*. Montreal: Canada Millennium Scholarship Foundation.

Keane, M.P., and K.I. Wolpin. 2001. "The Effect of Parental Transfers and Borrowing Constraints on Education Attainment." *International Economic Review* 42 (4): 1051-1103.

Knighton, T., and S. Mirza. 2002. "Postsecondary Participation: The Effects of Parents' Education and Household Income." *Education Quarterly Review* 8 (3): 25-32.

Long, B.T. 2005. "Contributions from the Field of Economics to the Study of College Access and Success." Harvard Graduate School of Education Working Paper.

Looker, E.D. 2001. "Why Don't They Go On? Factors Affecting the Decisions of Canadian Youth Not to Pursue Post-Secondary Education." Canada Millennium Scholarship Foundation, Research Series.

Looker, E.D., and G.S. Lowe. 2001. "Post-Secondary Access and Student Financial Aid in Canada: Current Knowledge and Research Gaps." Canadian Policy Research Network.

Mueller, R.E. 2008. "Access and Persistence of Students in Canadian Post-Secondary Education: What We Know, What We Don't Know, and Why It Matters." In *Who Goes? Who Stays? What Matters? Accessing and Persisting in Post-Secondary Education in Canada*, edited by R. Finnie, R.E. Mueller, A. Sweetman, and A. Usher. Montreal and Kingston: McGill-Queen's University Press and School of Policy Studies, Queen's University.

Neill, C. 2005. "Tuition Fees and the Demand for University Places." Wilfrid Laurier University Working Paper.

Pearlin, L., and C. Schooler. 1978. "The Structure of Coping." *Journal of Health and Social Behaviour* 19: 2-21.

Rahman, A., J. Situ, and V. Jimmo. 2005. "Participation in Post-Secondary Education: Evidence for the Survey of Labour and Income Dynamics." Culture, Tourism and the Centre for Education Statistics Research Paper No. 36, Statistics Canada Catalogue No. 81-595-MIE.

Rivard, M., and M. Raymond. 2004. "The Effect of Tuition Fees on Post-Secondary Education in Canada in the Late 1990s." Department of Finance Working Paper No. 2004-09.

Rosenberg, M. 1965. *Society and the Adolescent Self-Image*. Princeton, NJ: Princeton University Press.

APPENDIX

TABLE A-1
Explanation of Scale Variables

Variable	Definition
Academic identification	Measures a respondent's academic identification with high school; the focus of attention is on two components of identification, valuing and belonging. A student who fails to identify with school is expected to have a lack of valuing for the school and a lack of feelings of belonging to the school.
Academic participation	Focusing on the first three levels of taxonomy to academic participation: the acquiescence to the need to attend school, to be prepared and to respond to directions and questions; students demonstrating initiative-taking behaviours; and participation in the social, extracurricular, and athletic aspects of school life in addition to or as a substitute for extensive participation in academic work.
Social engagement	Defined as the identification with and behavioural involvement in the social aspects of school (the school social life). It involves both a feeling of belonging to the school's social environment and a sense of fit between the individual and the school. This connection reflects the extent to which students feel personally accepted, respected, included, and supported by others in the school's social environment.
Self-esteem	The self-esteem scale that was chosen for YITS is Morris Rosenberg's 22 self-esteem scale (RSE) (Rosenberg, 1965: 17). Rosenberg defines self-esteem as favourable or unfavourable attitudes towards self and proposes a series of ten questions to measure it. Within the context of YITS, RSE attempts to measure adolescents' global feelings of self-worth or self-acceptance.
Self-efficacy	Defines academic self-efficacy as the student's competence and confidence in performance of class work as perceived by the student. This concept should be distinguished from global self-efficacy or mastery, which is the belief that one has control over one's own destiny.
Self-mastery	The powerlessness scale chosen by YITS is based upon the work of Pearlin and Schooler (1978). This scale, referred to as the mastery scale 25, assesses a feeling of powerlessness without reference to concrete life situations. Mastery can be defined as a measure that assesses "the extent to which one regards one's life chances as being under one's own control in contrast to being fatalistically ruled" (Pearlin and Schooler, 1978). Hence, if one scores high on the mastery scale, one does not feel powerless.

... continued

TABLE A-1
(Continued)

Variable	Definition
Social support	Measures the availability of social supports, via friends, family, and other sources for the youth. Three aspects are included: reliable alliance (the assurance that others can be counted upon for practical help), attachment (emotional closeness), and guidance (advice or information). These aspects are most directly related to problem-solving within the context of stress. Two items were proposed to measure each of these aspects for a total of six items.
Monitoring behaviour	Measures parents' monitoring behaviour. A monitoring parent is defined as one who believes that he or she is knowledgeable about his or her child's activities, whereabouts, and friends.
Nurturance behaviour	Measures parents' nurturing behaviours. Nurturance represents child-centred, effective parenting practices such as nurturance, involvement, and positive reinforcement.
Inconsistent discipline	Measures parents' inconsistent discipline or rejection-oriented behaviours.
Reading ability	Weighted likelihood estimate in reading ability, which is provided for all students who answered at least one reading question. It was transformed to a scale with a mean of 5 and a standard deviation of 1 by using the data for the participating OECD countries only (except the Netherlands).

Source: Finnie and Mueller, 2007b.

5

The Evolution of Aspirations for University Attendance

LOUIS N. CHRISTOFIDES, MICHAEL HOY,
ZHI (JANE) LI, AND THANASIS STENGOS

Dans cet article, nous examinons l'importance du rôle que jouent, dans la décision d'entreprendre ou non des études postsecondaires (EPS), les aspirations qu'ont les élèves du secondaire face à de telles études. Les résultats montrent que de hautes aspirations face aux EPS, associées à des compétences suffisantes (évaluées à partir des résultats scolaires) et à d'autres variables explicatives – comme le niveau de scolarité des parents –, influencent de façon significative le choix de fréquenter l'université. Par ailleurs, en général, les filles commencent dès l'âge de 15 ans à avoir de plus hautes aspirations que les garçons face aux EPS ; de plus, elles ont tendance à réfléchir de nouveau favorablement aux EPS à l'âge de 17 ans, ce qui contribue à expliquer l'écart entre les sexes que l'on observe à l'université. Nous concluons qu'il serait nécessaire d'analyser de plus près le rôle des aspirations des jeunes dans leur décision d'entreprendre ou non des EPS, et qu'il serait important d'agir, dès le bas âge, pour développer leur motivation en ce sens.

This paper explores the importance of aspirations among high school students about participation in post-secondary education (PSE). We find that high aspirations regarding PSE, in addition to qualifications as reflected by grades and other explanatory variables such as parental education levels, significantly influence the decision to attend university. Girls begin at age 15 with higher overall aspirations about PSE and are more likely to revise their aspirations upwards by age 17, which helps to explain the gender gap in university attendance. Our results point to the need to further investigate the role of aspirations in leading to attainment of post-secondary education and the importance of efforts to influence aspirations at a young age.

Who Goes? Who Stays? What Matters? Accessing and Persisting in Post-Secondary Education in Canada, eds. R. Finnie, R.E. Mueller, A. Sweetman, and A. Usher. Montreal and Kingston: McGill-Queen's University Press, Queen's Policy Studies Series. © 2008 The School of Policy Studies, Queen's University at Kingston. All rights reserved.

Introduction

A striking pattern known as the gender gap has emerged in university attendance in Canada. Since the mid-1980s, women have been increasingly more likely than men to attend universities and now outnumber men by approximately three to two.[1] Given the public concern in trying to increase the overall rate of post-secondary education (PSE) attainment in Canada, understanding the role of aspirations regarding PSE generally and any gender differences in this process has important policy implications.

Several recent studies have attempted to explain the growing gender gap. It has been documented that females and males differ in their preparedness for PSE (i.e., school achievement) as well as in their non-cognitive abilities; see, for example, Jacob (2002) and Goldin et al. (2006). However, a significant percentage of youth of both genders who reach a sufficiently high achievement level in high school to qualify for university admission do not take up the opportunity – at least not by age 19. It is therefore important to also consider why it is that some youth develop aspirations to obtain PSE while others do not.

A number of studies, primarily in the sociology literature, have addressed the importance and timing of aspirations to attend PSE. Hosssler, Schmit, and Vesper (1999) found that most students develop aspirations about PSE attendance by the end of the ninth grade.[2] Carter (2001), for example, found that a long-held desire to go to university was important in leading to the actual decision to attend.[3] More specifically on this point, Alexander and Cook (1979) found students who planned to go to university by the tenth grade were 47 percent more likely to attend than those who didn't make such a plan until twelfth grade. A link between aspirations and PSE participation was also found by Carpenter and Fleishman (1987, 79), who note that "favourable attitudes toward higher education, parental encouragement, and friends' college plans all lead to the formation of intentions to enter college. Intentions, in turn, predict actual college attendance." These results point to the importance of studying how such aspirations are developed earlier in life rather than focusing attention only at the time the decision to attend PSE is made.

We consider both the importance of youths' aspirations (desire) for attending university while in high school as well as their preparedness in terms of high school grades as factors leading to PSE attendance. We use the panel dataset called Youth in Transition Survey Cohort A (YITS-A) to explore factors underlying the formation of aspirations regarding future PSE experience at age 15 and how these aspirations are updated by age 17. We then analyze how these aspirations, along with grades and other individual, peer group, and family characteristics, influence choices regarding PSE attendance.[4] The determination of separate influences from grades and aspirations on PSE decisions is complicated by the fact that some of the same explanatory variables, including innate ability and family background factors, are likely to influence both grades and aspirations. Moreover, grade achievement is likely to affect aspirations, and vice versa. Finally, the decision to attend university is likely to be influenced by factors such as family background characteristics – both directly and indirectly – through grades and aspirations.

We find that girls at the outset (i.e., age 15) are more likely to hold high aspirations regarding future PSE attendance and that girls are more likely to revise their aspirations upwards (at age 17). We also see that the PSE aspirations held at age 17 are an important predictor for students' later participation in PSE. Not only are girls more likely to achieve grades required to enter university but, conditional on these grades, they are more likely to have high aspirations of going to university and are more likely to follow through on them.

In our examination of the determinants of PSE aspirations, we find that measures of school quality regarding the expertise of teachers do not appear to matter, although peer effects, which may be influenced by the school environment, do matter and especially for boys. Parental expectations regarding PSE attendance and their children's view of these expectations turn out to be significant variables in explaining the evolution of aspirations to attend PSE. Also, parental education exerts an independent influence – over and above grade attainment in high school – in determining PSE choices. We tentatively suggest that more attention should be paid to developing these students' aspirations for PSE (e.g., through high school counselling) in order to provide them with a more equitable opportunity for PSE attendance, and that this is particularly important for boys.

In the following section we lay the groundwork for our analysis. We focus on the decision to attend university rather than other forms of PSE because this allows for a sharper econometric analysis and also because it is primarily at the university level that boys' and girls' attendance rates have become dramatically different over the past three decades. We draw some comparisons with other relevant studies but do not attempt to provide a comprehensive review of the field. In the next two sections we explain the data used for our empirical analysis and describe our econometric methodology. Results and policy implications are followed by our conclusions.

A Brief Literature Review

Before explaining how our research fits into the literature on PSE attendance in general and the gender imbalance issue in particular, we briefly describe some types of empirical research in this literature. A much more complete survey can be found in Mueller (2007).

The most common type of empirical study regarding the determinants of university attendance uses datasets that allow the linking of PSE decisions of youths to the characteristics of their family, especially parental education and income. Not surprisingly, most of these studies find each of these two latter variables contributes significantly to the explanation. Recent examples using Canadian data include Christofides, Cirello, and Hoy (2001), Corak, Lipps, and Zhao (2003), Johnson and Rahman (2005), and Christofides, Hoy, and Yang (2006a, b). Knighton and Mirza (2002) in particular find that family income is a statistically significant determinant but that parental education is the more powerful predictor of university participation.

Many of these studies cover a long period of time through use of a series of cross-section datasets. This provides useful evidence on long-term trends, and the gender imbalance is one very interesting and striking trend observed in Canada over the past few decades. Documenting the gross pattern between family income and university attendance can be useful for determining the extent of some aspects of inequity associated with differential attendance rates by family income. In particular, since government subsidizes university education, understanding this relationship allows the measurement of one facet of the degree of regressivity of such a policy.

Naturally, the ability of parents to help finance a child's university education is a plausible reason for low family income to reflect a barrier to access to PSE. However, family income is not likely to be a direct reason for this relationship in its entirety, as income levels can also represent many other indirect influences. For example, higher income families may spend more on nurturing children in ways that allow them to prepare better cognitive and non-cognitive skills related to successful entry into PSE. General social environment differs, on average, across income classes. Also, family income may be a signal of innate ability that is inherited by children.[5] There are other datasets, such as the YITS-A dataset which we use, or the School Leavers Survey, that allow for more detailed investigation into the role of income and other characteristics influencing the decision to attend post-secondary education. Using the YITS-A dataset, Frenette (2007, 4), for example, discovers that "96% of the gap in university attendance between youth from the top and bottom income quartiles can be accounted for by differences in observable characteristics," with only 12 percent of this gap being related to financial constraints. Finnie, Laporte, and Lascelles (2004) also use the YITS-A dataset, as well as the School Leavers Survey, to investigate the importance of family background on PSE attendance in the 1990s. They find that parental education is indeed a very important variable, but that its effect varies across income classes and gender. Finnie, Lascelles, and Sweetman (2005) use the 1991 School Leavers Survey and the 1995 School Leavers Follow-up Survey and find that there are important indirect effects of family background variables that affect high school outcomes and related attitudes and behaviours.

Although all the above studies offer insights into the determinants of university education, the reason for the rather recent rise in the female-male ratio in university attendance is still not completely settled. One argument put forward to explain this trend is the claim that the education system has been *feminized* over recent decades. This process, it is argued, includes a trend towards more female teachers in elementary and high school as well as pedagogical changes, such as more frequent testing, that favour girls. If one accepts this claim, then studies such as ours and that of Frenette and Zeman (2007) and Jacob (2002) offer important insights into how this feminization process has led to an advantage for girls in creating a successful path to university. If non-cognitive (behavioural) attributes of girls are better suited to a changing education system, then analysis based on a single cohort may indeed explain the increasing gender imbalance at Canadian universities.

There is, however, substantial debate about the merits of the feminization hypothesis. In many countries the ratio of women teachers at the elementary and especially high school level has been increasing, and some researchers have argued that girls do better when taught by women teachers. As Dee (2005, 2) notes, however, "empirical evidence on whether these interactions actually matter is limited and contradictory." More generally, studies that follow several cohorts of boys and girls and can address changes in non-cognitive abilities and the relative impact they have in a changing school system are, not surprisingly, difficult to carry out. Moreover, it is not clear that girls have not always been "better students" at the high school level. Goldin, Katz, and Kuziemko (2006), for example, point out that over the past century girls in the United States have consistently outperformed boys in postsecondary education. They argue that this advantage for females has only relatively recently led to a higher PSE attendance rate for females because of the increased premium for educated labour for women compared to men in conjunction with increasing female attachment to the labour force.[6]

Besides the increased fraction of female teachers, some argue that the style of education and curriculum has recently changed to favour females. Burman (2005, 353) points out, for example, that the new AS-level systems in the U.K. have been predicted to benefit girls since girls do best on continuous assessment. Or more generally, it is often suggested that society might be becoming "more difficult" for boys (family dissolutions, for example, are argued to be more problematic for boys). Such changes are hard to document, let alone measure objectively. The problem in resolving this question is that datasets that include PSE decisions taken by populations over long periods of time do not have the sort of detailed information about non-cognitive abilities and academic preparedness as do panel datasets such as the YITS-A. Therefore, we suggest that both types of studies can make important complementary contributions to our understanding of the growing gender gap.

Our particular objective is to understand better why it is that females have recently been more likely to attend university by exploiting the interesting features concerning PSE aspirations available in the YITS-A dataset. As noted above, it has been recognized in the literature that formation of aspirations by children concerning possible future post-secondary educational attainment is an important consideration in understanding enrolment rates and patterns. Hossler and Stage (1992) present an excellent summary of both the methodologies used to understand the factors that influence youths' predisposition (aspirations) towards post-secondary education and a review of findings up to 1992. Lakshmanan (2004) provides a recent update on findings. We take as our premise that individuals will attend university only if they (1) wish to attend and so apply, and this is where aspiration formation is an important consideration; (2) are qualified, and hence are admitted; and (3) can obtain the financial resources to do so. We focus on the first two of these conditions.

As for existing evidence on the gender difference in the formation of aspirations, some studies that have included this factor have simply looked at whether there is an "intercept term difference," while others have looked for differences in the relationship of the aspiration formation process. Results have been mixed. Coleman (1962), for example, found little difference in the effect on boys and on girls of the high school attended, although he found a significant high school effect on aspirations for both boys and girls when using data from (larger) metropolitan schools. Stage and Hossler (1989, 301) found "subtle differences in family influence on male and female students' college-going plans." In their review of the existing literature (304), they note that "gender was unrelated to post-secondary plans; however, research suggested that family and environmental factors differentially affected the aspirations of males and females (Carpenter and Fleishman, 1987; Marini and Greenberger, 1978)." Stage and Hossler (1989) find, unlike previous studies, that level of father's education had a stronger effect than mother's education on student (ninth-grader) plans, although they also found (312) that "parents may be less committed to post-secondary education for their daughters than their sons."

Data and Background Information

We now turn to the basic data describing the evolution of aspirations by youths in high school. One of the main advantages of the YITS-A data is its panel style, with a group of students having been surveyed at ages 15, 17, and 19; this allows us to follow each student before and during PSE education attendance (at least the beginning of PSE for many of the youths). We focus on analyzing the different PSE aspiration formation of boys and girls from ages 15 to 17 in order to help understand the role of aspirations in leading to a decision about PSE attendance and in particular at the university level. The specific question about aspirations is "What is the highest level of education you would like to get?" The possible responses include "one university degree" and "more than one university degree." We code both responses as "university" and the other responses as "below university," except for those who choose the response "don't know" or those who do not choose a response to this question. These latter two categories represent a little more than 13 percent of respondents, and we ignore this group. We also exclude respondents from Quebec where students attend CEGEP before university, and so only a very few Quebec youths in our dataset have attended university by age 19.

Another advantage of the YITS-A dataset is the availability of information on the aspirations on PSE participation from both students and their parents, including parents' expectations of their children, students' perceptions of the importance their parents place on PSE attendance for their children, and students' aspirations about themselves. This allows us to understand the rather complex relationship between parental expectations, youths' expectations, the youths' beliefs about their parents' expectations, and how these combine to influence the decisions of youths to attend university.

We turn our attention to summarizing the data on aspirations and university attendance, as well as relating this information with grade achievement. From Figures 1 and 2 we see that at age 15, girls are more likely to have aspirations of attending university (78 percent for girls compared to 67 percent for boys). This higher level of aspiration for girls is magnified by age 17, as a larger fraction of girls who did not have aspirations of attending university at age 15 revise these aspirations upward (41 percent for girls compared to 26 percent for boys). Also, girls with high aspirations at age 15 are more likely to stick with these high aspirations than are boys (86 percent for girls and 81 percent for boys). Thus, the initial gap at age 15 of 11 percentage points between girls' and boys' aspirations for university has by age 17 grown to 13 percentage points (76 percent for girls compared to 63 percent for boys).

We also see how these aspirations carry over into actual PSE decisions by age 19. Again, girls increase their "advantage" over boys in that they are more likely to meet their high aspirations, with 60 percent

FIGURE 1
Tree Format of Evolution of Aspirations for Boys

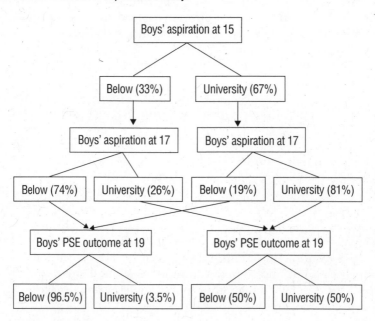

Source: Authors' compilation.

FIGURE 2
Tree Format of Evolution of Aspirations for Girls

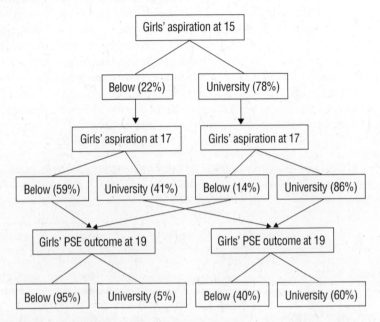

Source: Authors' compilation.

of girls with university aspirations enrolling in university by the age of 19 compared to only 50 percent of boys with university aspirations. Very few of either gender attend university by age 19 if their aspirations were "below university" at age 17. One must, however, interpret these figures with caution as many may attend university at a later age, and delayed attendance may not be a symmetric phenomenon for boys and girls.[7]

It is, of course, one thing to have high aspirations about PSE but another to actually obtain the grades required to meet one's aspirations. Moreover, obtaining low grades could affect one's aspirations directly.[8] Table 1 describes the relationship between students' aspirations in cycle 2 (age 17) based on their most recent high school performance. Among students with high overall high school grades (80 percent or higher), most (88 percent) have high aspirations regarding their future PSE decision, and this is the same for boys and girls. There is, however, a pronounced gender difference for those with low (below 70 percent) or medium (between 70 percent and 80 percent) overall grades. Boys with low or medium overall grades in high school are less likely to have aspirations about attending university than are girls with equivalent grades. Although one could interpret this as saying "boys hold more reasonable aspirations, given their previous grades," the direction of causality in these two-way tables cannot be inferred. We simply note here that girls with low or medium grades are more likely to still consider university as a goal in life, and a lower percentage of girls in fact obtain low grades.[9] This suggests that there is more to the story of gender imbalance than "girls simply do better than boys in high school and so are more likely to be admitted to university."

TABLE 1
Boys' and Girls' Aspirations in Cycle 2 (Age 17) Dependent on Most Recent Overall Grades

Most recent grades	Aspirations in cycle 2 BOYS		Aspirations in cycle 2 GIRLS	
	Below	University	Below	University
Low	61	39	53	47
Medium	38	62	29	71
High	12	88	12	88

Source: Authors' compilation.

Finally, we describe the relationship between students' overall high school grades at age 18 and their participation outcomes at age 19 in Figures 3 and 4. We find (not surprisingly) that most students with low grades do not attend university (4 percent for boys and 6 percent for girls). However, gender differences arise again when we look at university attendance for boys and girls with medium overall grades, with only 23 percent of boys in this category attending university compared to 31 percent of girls.

We conclude that it is a mix of both differential grade-level achievement in high school and different aspirations that lead to the current gender imbalance in university attendance. In the next section of this paper we develop an econometric model to explore the reasons for the difference in aspirations of boys and girls and how these impact on the decision to attend university.

Econometric Methodology

The dependent variables in our estimations have been discussed in detail in the preceding sections. Explanatory variables are for the most part

FIGURE 3
PSE Attendance by Grades for Boys

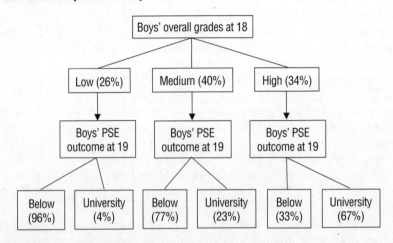

Source: Authors' compilation.

FIGURE 4
PSE Attendance by Grades for Girls

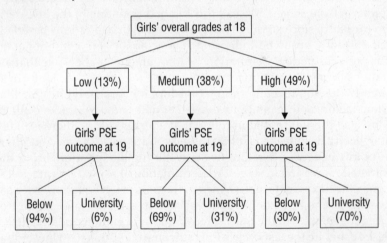

Source: Authors' compilation.

as defined and coded in the original dataset (YITS-A) provided. However, we also construct a variable reflecting family equivalent income and mother's income share. Equivalent income is taken to be family income divided by the square root of family size (number of family members), while mother's income share is the income earned by the mother divided by total family income.

In order to find out the determinants of PSE attendance in general, we adopt an information updating approach to study a student's decision path. In this updating process, we make full use of the panel style of the dataset and also of the aspiration information collected from both parents and students. By updating we mean the updating of PSE aspirations from the first to the second cycle and then further to the third cycle to study the PSE participation decisions. We compare students' aspirations for PSE in the first and second cycles and then find out how the final outcomes of their PSE participation in the last cycle are determined. One can think of this updating process as a survival analysis of PSE aspiration or a belief updating process, conditional on previous environmental changes.

In our empirical analysis, we make use of information about students' aspirations on PSE participation at the ages of 15 and 17 as well as of a general analysis of the determinants of final PSE outcome at the age of 19. We construct a triangular system of equations describing a three-stage model for this information updating process. The first stage is to find out how students' characteristics at the age of 14 can affect their PSE aspirations at the age of 15. The second stage is to perform a similar estimation for cycle 2 aspirations conditional on their predicted PSE aspiration from stage 1. We call this the first updating of the PSE decision (or path), since students have updated their aspirations based on their currently observed individual characteristics but conditional on their previous period's aspirations. Although one might argue that aspirations formed at a younger age (15) are exogenous to those formed at age 17 due to the temporal relationship, it is probably the case that certain factors and mental processes that determine aspirations at age 17 are also present in that individual at age 15. That is, there is likely endogeneity despite the fact that these aspirations are formed at different points in time. Therefore, we use the fitted aspirations from the estimated regression in stage 1 (determination of aspirations at age 15) as one of the explanatory variables in the regression equation, with aspirations at age 17 as dependent variable in order to take account of any endogeneity.[10] In the third stage of this information updating process, we estimate the last cycle's PSE outcome conditional on individual information surveyed in cycle 3 and predicted aspiration estimated in stage 2. Although we use the probit model for estimation purposes (including when predicted values are generated and used as regressors), below we provide only the constituent parts of the probit index in order to avoid excessive mathematical notation.

Stage 1: $Exp_{15} = \beta_0 + \beta_1 X_{15} + \beta_2 Y_{15}$

where the subscript of 15 denotes the age of students. X_{15} is a vector for individual characteristics. Y_{15} is a vector for family background and other variables.

Stage 2: $Exp_{17} = \alpha_0 + \alpha_1 X_{17} + \alpha_2 \hat{Exp}_{15} + \alpha_3 Y_{17}$

where $\hat{Exp}_{15}$ denotes the expected level of aspiration as estimated from stage 1.

Stage 3: $PSE_{19} = \gamma_0 + \gamma_1 X_{19} + \gamma_2 \hat{Exp}_{17} + \gamma_3 Y_{19}$

$$+\gamma_4(\hat{Exp}_{17} - \hat{Exp}_{15} \mid_{\hat{Exp}_{17} > \hat{Exp}_{15}}) + \gamma_5(\hat{Exp}_{15} - \hat{Exp}_{17} \mid_{\hat{Exp}_{15} > \hat{Exp}_{17}})$$

where PSE_{19} is the PSE participation outcome observed in cycle 3. In this final stage, we use both the predicted previous cycle's aspiration and the differences between the previous two cycles' (fitted) aspirations as regressors in order to investigate the path dependence among all three cycles. X_{19} used in cycle 3 includes the grade levels immediately before the PSE participation decision. The final two terms of the stage 3 equation represent, in absolute value terms, the increase or decrease in fitted aspirations between ages 15 and 17. These terms are included to see if a change in either direction in aspirations at age 17 from age 15 has any impact on the decision to attend university.

Note that there is a generated regressor problem in our estimation, since the aspiration level variables that we use on the right-hand side of stage 2 and 3 are generated from the previous stages. The inclusion of a generated regressor introduces an adjustment to the variance-covariance matrix in order to obtain reliable inferences (see Pagan, 1984, for a discussion of econometric issues that are used in the context of generated regressors).

Using this three-stage updating process has a number of advantages. The first advantage of running three separate probit regressions is that we can test for differences among the same explanatory variables in different stages rather than pooling them together, in which case we could only see the impact on the final participation outcome. This distinction could also be valuable for policy considerations; we may need to concentrate on different factors in different secondary education stages in order to have the most effective impact on the final PSE participation outcome. Secondly, by conditioning on the predicted aspiration of cycle 2, we are in essence estimating a pooled model, since the estimated aspiration is fitted through the individual information observed in cycle 2 along with the fitted aspiration of cycle 1, where the fitted aspiration of cycle 1 is estimated by using the individual information observed in cycle 1. Thus we use the whole information set but take the endogeneity issue into consideration. This information-updating process makes the best use of the available information set and has some useful by-products from the method of information updating. We summarize our econometric results in the following section.

Results and Policy Implications

In what follows, we explain the empirical results from the methodology introduced above and discuss the effect of those variables that are statistically significant (at the 10 percent level of better) in our regressions at each relevant stage. These effects are reported in Tables 2 and 3 below. More detail on the description of the variables used in the analysis, as well as tables with full numerical regression results, are available in the full research paper, which is available at http://www.mesa-project.org/pub/pdf/MESA_Christofides.pdf.

In Table 2 we capture all the variables that have a statistically significant effect either on aspiration levels at age 15 (cycle 1) or on the updated aspiration levels at age 17 (cycle 2). Positive and negative effects are noted simply by POS or NEG, respectively, followed by the cycle (age) for which the variable was found to be significant. So, for example, if a variable had a positive and significant effect at least at the 10 percent level of significance but only in the second cycle (aspirations at age 17), this is indicated by the entry POS_c2, while if it had such an effect in both cycles (aspirations at ages 15 and 17), this is indicated by the entry POS_c1_c2. Table 3 performs the same summarizing function but for the stage 3 regression; that is, it indicates which variables are statistically significant in the explanation of the decision to attend university.

First and foremost, fitted values of aspirations from cycle 1 have a positive and significant effect in the cycle 2 regression explaining aspirations. Moreover, even though we include a comprehensive battery of

TABLE 2
Summary of Cycle 1 and 2 Effects

	Girls	Boys
Initial (fitted) aspirations		
Aspirations_c1	POS_c2	POS_c2
School characteristics		
% girls enrolled in the school	NEG_c1	POS_c2
Highly educated teachers – English	POS_c1	
Highly educated teachers – Science		NEG_c1
Private school (independent of government)		POS_c1_c2
Peer effects		
Most of friends cause trouble	POS_c2	
Most of friends dropped out of high school	NEG_c2	
Most of friends smoke cigarettes	NEG_c1_c2	NEG_c1
Most of friends think it is okay to work hard at school		POS_c1_c2
Most of friends have plans for PSE_c1_c2		POS_c1_c2
Family characteristics (minority/immigrant/income/etc.)		
Mother is an immigrant	POS_c1	
Father is an immigrant		POS_c2
Child is of minority status	POS_c2	POS_c1
Family income (equivalized)	POS_c1	
Mother's share of income		POS_c1
Parents have a plan to save for child's PSE	POS_c2	
Family characteristics (parental education)		
Father has a college education	POS_c1	
Father has a university education	POS_c1_c2	POS_c1_c2
Mother has a college education	POS_c2	POS_c1
Mother has a university education	POS_c1_c2	POS_c1
Child has a sibling who dropped out of high school	NEG_c2	
Parental expectations (etc.)		
PSE viewed important		POS_c2
Expect child to obtain some PSE	POS_c1_c2	POS_c1_c2
Confident in child's pursuit of PSE	POS_c1_c2	POS_c1_c2
Parents often help with homework	POS_c2	
Child's view of parents' expectations		
Child thinks mother views PSE attainment important_c1	POS_c1	POS_c1
Child thinks parents view PSE attainment important _c2	POS_c2	POS_c2
Region		
Atlantic	POS_c1	POS_c1_c2
Manitoba or Saskatchewan	POS_c1	POS_c1
Alberta		POS_c1_c2
BC	POS_c2	POS_c2

Notes:
1. First row is effect of fitted aspirations from cycle 1 on actual aspirations in cycle 2.
2. In all cases _c1 means "information or result from cycle 1" and similarly for _c2.
3. Variables with no "cycle designation" represent information at initial interview.
Source: Authors' compilation.

TABLE 3
Summary of Actual Decision Effects

	Girls	Boys
Initial (fitted) aspirations and change		
Aspirations_c2	POS	POS
Aspirations (fitted) fell in c2	POS	
Grades at age 18		
Overall grades high (80% plus)	POS	POS
Overall grades mid (70% to 80%)		POS
English grades high (80% plus)		POS
English grades mid (70% to 80%)	POS	
Math grades high (80% plus)		POS
"Natural ability"		
PISA reading score at age 15	POS	POS
School characteristics		
Private school (independent of government)		POS
Peer effects		
Most of friends smoke cigarettes	NEG	NEG
Family characteristics (minority/immigrant/income/etc.)		
Child is of minority status		POS
Mother's share of income		POS
Parents had a plan to save for child's PSE		POS
Child has at least one non-birth parent	NEG	NEG
Child has a sibling who dropped out of high school	NEG	
Family characteristics (parental education)		
Father has a university education		POS
Mother has a university education	POS	POS
Parental expectations (etc.)		
Confident in child's pursuit of PSE	POS	
Child's financial preparation		
Child has a plan to save for PSE	POS	POS
Region		
Atlantic	POS	POS
Manitoba or Saskatchewan		POS
Alberta	NEG	
BC		NEG

Note: Grades are self-reported and refer to grade 12. Low grades would be 60 to 70 percent.
Source: Authors' compilation.

grade outcomes from cycle 3 for the year before the decision to go to university is made (i.e., final year high school grades), fitted values of aspirations from cycle 2 have a positive and significant effect on the decision to go to university. This suggests that over and above the ability to learn and do well at high school, early formation of aspirations is indeed an important factor in leading to university attendance. Moreover, the PISA test score[11] (taken at age 15 and so reflecting an ability "at age 15" measure) also exerts a statistically significant positive effect on the attendance decision even in the presence of final-year high school grades.

These two results suggest that early attention to learning and aspirations may make an important contribution in leading to a youth's eventual decision to attend PSE. Many variables are important in explaining the formation and updating of aspirations, and since aspirations have a role to play in determining university attendance decisions, these variables are worth considering as factors leading to a positive decision to attend university. Since cycle 1 aspirations are important in determining cycle 2 aspirations, which in turn are important in determining the decision to go to university, we have established a chain of effects that is useful in thinking about how to enhance the likelihood of youths eventually deciding to obtain a university education.

The variables below are statistically significant in explaining the formation of initial aspirations (at age 15) and/or the updating of aspirations (at age 17):

School characteristics: The percentage of girls enrolled in the school oddly has a negative effect on girls' aspirations at age 15 and a positive effect on boys' aspirations at age 17. The percentage of highly educated teachers in English has a positive effect on girls' aspirations (age 15), but the same "quality variable" for science has a negative effect on boys' aspirations (age 17). Thus these aspects, or at least measures, of school quality do not paint a very clear or compelling picture regarding the importance of school quality on the formation of aspirations. However, going to a (government-independent) private school[12] does have a consistently positive effect (for both cycles and decision time) for boys, so this is a clear and consistent effect for boys and not for girls. This is noteworthy since this effect is over and above parental expectations, peer group effects, quality of teachers, grades, PISA score (natural ability), gender mix at the school, etc. This result suggests that the option of being able to send boys to a private school may indeed promote PSE attendance for boys but not for girls. However, given the broad range of private schools covered by these variables (i.e., religious, academically or financially elite, etc.), it is not very clear just what is the cause of this effect, and so this finding represents a question for further research.

Peer effects: Here we see a mostly consistent story from our variables. Except for the characteristic "many of my friends have a reputation for causing trouble," which has a positive effect on girls' cycle 1 aspirations, all other peer effects are as one might expect. Having most of one's friends smoke has a negative effect in all cases of aspiration formation except for cycle 2 aspirations for males (including a negative effect even at decision time). Interestingly, boys with friends who think it is okay to work hard at school and/or who expect to go on to university are consistently affected in cycle 1 and 2 aspiration formation – although no additional effect exists at decision time. This points to the importance of peer effects throughout high school on the formation of aspirations to attend university, and hence is worthy of consideration as a target for parents and schools in order to enhance PSE opportunity take-up for students, especially boys.

Family characteristics: Our results do not point to a disadvantage for children of immigrants or minority groups per se in terms of developing a positive attitude towards PSE attendance. Of course, if these groups disproportionately have characteristics that reduce the likelihood of PSE attendance for their children, then some particular attention may be warranted, but not simply because children are from minority or immigrant backgrounds.[13] In fact, there is evidence of a positive effect on aspirations from being the child of a minority group (cycle 2 aspirations for girls and cycle 1 aspirations for boys) or from having immigrant parents (cycle 1 for girls and cycle 2 for boys). Family income is mostly not a statistically significant variable, except in the case of aspiration formation for girls at age 15. Mother's share of income has a positive effect on boys' aspirations in cycle 1. The effect of parents saving for PSE for their children is mostly not statistically significant in the process of aspiration formation (except for cycle 2 for girls) but is important for the ultimate decision to go to university for boys.[14] For girls, having a sibling who has dropped out of high school has a negative impact on aspirations in cycle 2.

Parental education: As one would expect, parental education has a consistent and entirely expected impact on aspiration formation, especially whether the father and/or mother has a university degree. This variable continues to have an additional independent effect at the decision stage. Thus, it may be particularly useful for school counsellors to focus on drawing the attention of children from families with lower levels of education to the merits of a university education.

Parental expectations: We see that parental expectations regarding their children's PSE attainment, importance placed on PSE by parents, and confidence in their child to attain PSE have an expected and quite consistent effect on students' aspiration formation. This effect diminishes at the decision stage, but this just means that beyond the impact of high parental expectations regarding PSE on students' aspiration formation, there appears to be no additional effect on their PSE attendance decision.[15] Overall, then, these results point to an important effect of parental expectations. It is worth considering how schools could reinforce together both students' and parents' aspirations about PSE attendance.

Students' view of parental expectations: Interestingly, both girls' and boys' initial aspirations are affected by their understanding of their parents' views about the importance of obtaining a university education. This reinforces our discussion in the above paragraph in that not only is it helpful for parents to have high expectations about their children's future education choices but also it appears important to clearly communicate this to children.

Additional Remarks Concerning the "Decision Stage"

Typically, students with low grades would not qualify for university programs, or at least not many of them, and so it is natural to include grades in the decision stage regression. We included available results of grades from students' final year of high school in the categories of overall grades, grade in English, and grade in mathematics. Not surprisingly, having good grades (mid to high) shows up often in positive and significant variables. Natural (or early developed) ability as measured by the PISA reading test score at age 15 is also an important predictor of deciding to attend university over and above grades in coursework. The fitted aspirations of students from age 17 is also statistically significant, indicating the continued importance of aspiration formation in addition to ability and grade achievement in leading to a positive decision to attend university.

Parents' confidence in their children's PSE participation turns out to be positively significant at the decision stage for girls but not boys, and there is also a significant negative effect for girls on having a sibling who has dropped out of school, but not for boys. The variable "non-birth parent," which indicates the presence of at least one parent who is not the student's birth parent, has a statistically significant negative effect for both boys and girls on the decision to attend university. This may be the result of a stressful family environment earlier in the student's life, although it is interesting to note that this variable does not show up as significant in any of the aspiration formation regression equations.

Students engaging in some savings for PSE turns out to be a statistically significant factor for university attendance for both boys and girls. Parents having a savings plan for their child to attend PSE is statistically significant for boys. Note, however, that the direction of causality with respect to these variables is difficult to assign; that is, is saving for PSE done in anticipation of a positive decision or existing plan by children to attend university, or is the decision affected by parents' and students' financial commitment to keep university attendance as a viable option?

We also explored the impact of revisions to aspirations between cycles 1 and 2 to see if there is an "extra effect" from persistence of aspiration. This exercise produced no consistent or clear result and no support for the importance of "unchanging" aspirations – and earlier aspirations – leading more strongly to university participation, as has been found in some of the literature. However, from our updating methodology we do see that aspirations at age 15 have a positive effect on aspirations at age 17, and so in this sense there is a special importance in forming aspirations about PSE relatively early in life.

Differences between Boys and Girls in Aspiration Formation

In our regression analysis we also checked for statistically significant differences in coefficients of regressors for boys and girls in order to help shed further light on this question, as well as in terms of the eventual decision-making stage. Although we do not report the formal statistical analysis here, from our results we see some statistically significant differences in the channels for the formation of boys' and girls' aspiration levels. The results reinforce the observation that confidence of parents in their children's pursuit of PSE is more important for girls (for both cycle 1 aspirations and the decision stage), while the effect of what friends are thinking regarding further education is more important for boys (cycle 1 aspirations). Evidence on the difference in the importance of minority status is mixed (more important for boys in cycle 1 but more important for girls in cycle 2, a positive influence in both cases). The fact that the percentage of girls in school is positive and significant for boys (cycle 2 aspirations) but insignificant for girls is reinforced by the fact that there is a statistically significant difference between boys and girls for this variable.

Conclusions

We have taken a three-stage evolutionary, or information-updating, approach to examine how youths form aspirations about PSE and also to determine whether these aspirations ultimately exert an effect on the decision to attend university over and above their performance levels at high school and their natural or developed abilities. Early stage aspirations – as of age 15 – turn out to significantly affect aspiration formation or updating at age 17, and these aspirations exert a statistically significant and positive effect on the decision to attend university. We find that girls at age 15 are more likely to hold positive aspirations about attending university than are boys, by an 11 percentage point gap. This gender gap is reinforced at age 17 when the gap grows to 13 percentage points. Among youths previously holding high aspirations about future university attendance, girls are more likely to continue to hold such aspirations than are boys at age 17. Moreover, among youths not holding high aspirations, girls are more likely to revise these upwards than are boys. Since aspirations at age 17 are found to exert a statistically significant influence on the decision to attend university by age 19, even in a regression that includes several indicators of grade achievement, a natural ability measure (PISA score at age 15), and the usual parental and other control variables (e.g., parental education level), the gender gap in aspirations appears to be one of the sources of the gender gap in university participation. It is, of course, not the only source, but the higher aspirations of girls reinforce the gender imbalance that arises from the fact that girls as a group out-perform boys in high school grade achievement. Thus, more girls achieve the high school grades required to qualify for admittance to university, and conditional on grades being the same (especially those in the "medium" category), girls are more likely to hold high aspirations about attending university. These forces combine to lead to a substantially greater fraction of girls currently attending university. We emphasize, however, that although our analysis sheds some light on the current gender imbalance, it does not explain the growing trend of this imbalance.

Our results point to some possible areas in which policies may be developed to redress the gender imbalance and/or enhance PSE attendance levels for both genders. We have examined a number of forces that influence aspiration formation for girls and boys. In the literature on the effect of schools on youths' aspirations and grade attainment, two of the channels that have been suggested are a direct pedagogical effect and a peer group effect; see, for example, Boyle (1966) and Turner (1964). Our measures of school quality, including those regarding the expertise of teachers, suggest little effect of school characteristics on the formation of aspirations or the decision to attend university. The fact that several of our variables reflect peer-group characteristics through variables reflecting friends' views (e.g., whether most of friends think it is okay to work hard at school) and behaviour (e.g., whether most of friends smoke) indicates that school quality from a pedagogical perspective may be less important than the implicit effect of the types of peers at the school in determining students' aspirations for PSE in the Canadian context.

There is, however, one exception regarding school characteristics, and that is the result that for boys, but not for girls, going to a (government-independent) private school does have a consistently positive effect on aspiration formation and the decision to attend university. Understanding the source of this effect and its gender difference may point to some changes in the way education is delivered in the public system in order to help redress the growing gender imbalance at university.

Parental education has the expected influence in our regressions. Since having a university education significantly enhances the likelihood of a child developing aspirations to attend university as well as taking the decision to attend university, it is worth keeping this in mind when developing counselling programs in high schools; in particular we should consider a focus on students from families without this advantage. Perhaps even more interesting is that we find parental expectations, including parents' confidence in their children's pursuit of PSE, are also very important predictors of students' aspirations. Moreover, students' beliefs about the importance that their parents place on a university education are also significant in explaining their formation of aspirations. High schools might consider better integrating their counselling activities for students by including their parents.

Finally, although our regression analysis indicates the importance of the evolution of aspirations in affecting eventual participation in university education, very few explanatory variables in the aspiration formation equations proved to have statistically significant differences by gender. Therefore, determining the reasons for the gender difference in aspiration levels – especially at age 15, when girls' aspirations regarding future university education exceed those of boys – is an important topic for future research.

Notes

We thank MESA for financial and logistical (data) support and participants at the Canadian Economics Association meetings in Halifax in 2007 for many helpful comments, and especially thanks to Marc Frenette and Charlie Beach for perceptive comments and suggestions. While the research and analysis are based on data from Statistics Canada, the opinions expressed do not represent the views of Statistics Canada.

1. The same pattern has established itself in other countries (see Goldin, Katz, and Kuziemko, 2006 for a discussion of this pattern in the United States). Also of interest are changes in the proportion of women across various fields (see Andres and Adamuti-Trache, 2006).

2. Others have concluded that these aspirations evolve beyond tenth grade and later (see Parish, 1979).

3. Lakshmanan (2004) provides a review of the literature on the development of aspirations to PSE and the importance this has on actual attendance.

4. Being able to follow the evolution of aspirations allows us to explore whether the stability of aspirations is relevant in making PSE decisions, as the previous literature has suggested. As Lakshmanan (2004, 23) notes, "most studies so far mainly focused on studying factors that influence the educational and occupational aspirations of students at one point in time." This is one way in which our work adds to the existing general literature on the role of aspirations.

5. Empirical work by Plug and Vijverberg (2003) and Rothstein (2004) suggests that parental intelligence has substantial impact on the ability of children to succeed in university. Income and intelligence (of this sort) are likely to be positively correlated, although we have no ability to check this with our dataset.

6. Goldin, Katz, and Kuziemko (2006) also attribute some of the gender imbalance to changing marital and fertility patterns for young women.

7. By comparing the YITS-A and -B datasets, Lambert, Zeman, Allen, and Bussière (2004) were able to show that in the age category 18 to 20, 17 percent of males and 24 percent of females had attended university, while in the age category 20 to 22, these numbers had risen to 28 percent of males and 38 percent of females. These figures do not suggest a strong gender difference, with the male rate increasing by 65 percent and the female rate increasing by 58 percent by extending the age category.

8. As noted earlier, some of the same characteristics that affect both grades and aspirations (e.g., family background variables, innate ability, etc.) could lead to a correlation between the two even across time periods that is not causal in either direction.

9. In cycle 2 (age 17) we find 18 percent of females but 32 percent of males have "low overall grades," while 44 percent of females and only 27 percent of males have "high overall grades."

10. Suppose, for example, that some unobserved characteristic influences aspirations generally. This is likely to mean both higher than expected aspirations at 17 as well as high values of actual aspirations at 15. That is, the error in the equation explaining aspirations at 17 will be correlated with the RHS variable "aspirations at 15," leading to bias. By using the predicted value of aspirations at 15, which is uncorrelated with the missing unobserved characteristic, the problem of a biased coefficient estimate is avoided.

11. PISA refers to the OECD Program for International Student Assessment that surveys 15 year olds in the principal industrialized countries.

12. This type of school is managed by a non-government organization (e.g., church or business organization) and receives less than 50 percent of its funding from government.

13. It is also not clear from our data and results if there may be differential effects according to which minority status pertains.

14. Of course, the direction of causality between financial preparation for PSE and the decision to attend PSE is not easy to ascertain, and we were not able to find effective instruments for the variable "parental savings for child's PSE."

15. Note, however, that parental confidence in their daughters does have an "additional" positive impact at the decision stage. There is also a significant impact of a sibling dropping out of school in reducing girls' cycle 2 aspirations.

References

Alexander, K.L., and M.K.A. Cook. 1979. "The Motivational Relevance of Educational Plans: Questioning the Conventional Wisdom." *Social Psychology Quarterly* 42 (3): 202-13.

Andres, L., and M. Adamuti-Trache. 2007. "You've Come a Long Way, Baby? Persistent Gender Inequality in University Enrolment and Completion in Canada." *Canadian Public Policy* 33 (1): 93-116.

Boyle, R.P. 1966. "The Effect of the High School on Students' Aspirations." *American Journal of Sociology* 71 (6): 628-39.

Burman, E. 2005. "Childhood, Neo-liberalism and the Feminization of Education." *Gender and Education* 17 (4): 351-67.

Carpenter, P.G., and J.A. Fleishman. 1987. "Linking Intentions and Behavior: Australian Students' College Plans and College Attendance." *American Educational Research Journal* 24 (1): 79-105.

Carter, D.F. 2001. *A Dream Deferred? Examining the Degree Aspirations of African-American and White College Students*. New York: Routledge Farmer.

Christofides, L.N., J. Cirello, and M. Hoy. 2001. "Family Income and Post-Secondary Education in Canada." *Canadian Journal of Higher Education* 31 (1): 177-208.

Christofides, L.N., M. Hoy, and L. Yang. 2006a. "The Determinants of University Participation." Department of Economics, University of Guelph discussion paper no. 2006-8.

– 2006b. "The Gender Imbalance in Participation in Canadian Universities, 1977-2003." Department of Economics, University of Guelph discussion paper no. 2006-10.

Coleman, J. S. 1962. *The Adolescent Society*. New York: Free Press.

Corak, M., G. Lipps, and J. Zhao. 2003. "Family Income and Participation in Post-Secondary Education." Statistics Canada, Analytical Studies Branch Research Paper Series No. 210.

Dee, T.S. 2005. "Teachers and the Gender Gaps in Student Achievement." NBER Working Paper No. 11660.

Finnie, R., C. Laporte, and E. Lascelles. 2004. "Family Background and Access to Post-Secondary Education: What Happened in the 1990s?" Statistics Canada, Analytical Studies Research Paper Series, No. 226.

Finnie, R., E. Lascelles, and A. Sweetman. 2005. "Who Goes? The Direct and Indirect Effects of Family Background on Access to Postsecondary Education." Statistics Canada, Analytical Studies Research Paper Series, No. 237.

Frenette, M. 2007. "Why Are Youth from Lower-Income Families Less Likely to Attend University? Evidence from Academic Abilities, Parental Influences, and Financial Constraints." Statistics Canada, Analytical Studies Branch Research Paper Series No. 295.

Frenette, M., and K. Zeman. 2007. "Why Are Most University Students Women? Evidence Based on Academic Performance, Study Habits and Parental Influences." Statistics Canada, Analytical Studies Branch Research Paper Series No. 303.

Goldin, C, L.F. Katz, and I. Kuziemko. 2006. "The Homecoming of American College Women: The Reversal of the College Gender Gap." *Journal of Economic Perspectives* 20 (4): 133-56.

Hossler, D., and F.K. Stage. 1992. "Family and High School Experience Influences on the Postsecondary Education Plans of Ninth-Grade Students." *American Educational Research Journal* 29 (2): 425-51.

Hossler, D., J. Schmit, and N. Vesper. 1999. *Going to College: How Social, Economic, and Educational Factors Influence the Decisions Students Make*. Baltimore, MD: Johns Hopkins University Press.

Jacob, B.A. 2002. "Where the Boys Aren't: Non-Cognitive Skills, Returns to School and the Gender Gap in Higher Education." *Economics of Education Review* 21 (6): 589-98.

Johnson, D.R., and F. Rahman. 2005. "The Role of Economic Factors, Including the Level of Tuition, in Individual University Participation Decisions in Canada." *Canadian Journal of Higher Education* 35 (3): 83-99.

Knighton, T., and S. Mirza. 2002. "Postsecondary Participation: The Effects of Parents' Education and Household Income." *Education Quarterly Review* 8 (3): 25-32.

Lakshmanan, A. 2004. "A Longitudinal Study of Adolescent Educational Aspirations and Their Relationship to College Choice Using Hierarchical Linear Modeling and Group-Based Mixture Modeling." Ph.D. dissertation, Louisiana State University.

Lambert, M., K. Zeman, M. Allen, and P. Bussière. 2004. "Who Pursues Postsecondary Education, Who Leaves and Why: Results from the Youth in Transition Survey." Ottawa: Statistics Canada, 81-595-MIE-No. 026.

Marini, M.M., and E. Greenberger. 1978. "Sex Differences in Educational Aspirations and Expectations." *American Educational Research Journal* 15 (1): 211-30.

Mueller, R.E. 2007. "Access and Persistence of Students from Low-Income Backgrounds in Canadian Post-Secondary Education: A Review of the Literature." Working Paper, version 1.1.

Pagan, A. 1984. "Econometric Issues in the Analysis of Regressions with Generated Regressors." *International Economic Review* 25: 221-47.

Parish, R. 1979. *Survey of Educational Goals: Ocean County High School Juniors and Seniors.* Tom River, NJ: Ocean County College.

Plug, E., and W. Vijverberg. 2003. "Schooling, Family Background and Adoption: Is It Nature or Is It Nurture?" *Journal of Political Economy* 111 (3): 611-41.

Rothstein, J. 2004. "College Performance Predictions and the SAT." *Journal of Econometrics* 121 (1-2): 297-317.

Stage, F.K., and D. Hossler. 1989. "Differences in Family Influences on College Attendance Plans for Male and Female Ninth Graders." *Research in Higher Education* 30 (3): 301-14.

Turner, R.H. 1964. *The Social Context of Ambition.* New York: Free Press.

6

Understanding the Gender Gap in University Attendance: Evidence Based on Academic Performance, Study Habits, and Parental Influences

Marc Frenette and Klarka Zeman

Dans cette étude, nous analysons les différences, entre les hommes et les femmes, dans les constantes que l'on observe depuis plusieurs décennies en matière d'études universitaires. En 2003, par exemple, parmi les jeunes de 19 ans, 38,8 % des filles fréquentaient l'université, contre 25,7 % chez les garçons (EJET-A). Nous montrons que, dans une proportion de 76,8 %, cet écart s'explique par certaines caractéristiques qui avantagent les filles. Par ordre d'importance, ces caractéristiques sont : de meilleures notes à l'école, de meilleurs résultats aux tests normalisés en lecture, de meilleures habitudes d'étude, de plus grandes attentes de la part des parents et l'attrait de la rémunération supérieure que procurent des études universitaires relativement aux études secondaires.

This study addresses the gender differences in patterns of university attendance that have emerged over the past several decades. Among 19-year-old youth in 2003, 38.8 percent of females had attended university, compared with only 25.7 percent of males (YITS-A). We find that three quarters (76.8 percent) of the gender gap in university participation can be accounted for by more favourable characteristics held by females. In order of importance, these include higher school marks, higher standardized test scores in reading, better study habits, greater parental expectations, and a higher university earnings premium relative to high school.

Who Goes? Who Stays? What Matters? Accessing and Persisting in Post-Secondary Education in Canada, eds. R. Finnie, R.E. Mueller, A. Sweetman, and A. Usher. Montreal and Kingston: McGill-Queen's University Press, Queen's Policy Studies Series. © 2008 The School of Policy Studies, Queen's University at Kingston. All rights reserved.

Introduction

In recent history, universities have been the domain of male students. Over the last 30 years or so, however, a dramatic reversal has taken place on Canadian university campuses. According to the 1971 Census, 68 percent of 25- to 29-year-old university graduates were male. Ten years later, women had more or less caught up to men, as only 54 percent of graduates were male. By 1991, women had become the slight majority, comprising 51 percent of graduates. In the 2001 Census, universities had clearly become the domain of women, as they made up 58 percent of all graduates.[1]

Recent Canadian data on university attendance suggest that the female advantage is persisting. In 2003, 38.8 percent of 19-year-old women had attended university, compared with only 25.7 percent of 19-year-old men (Figure 1). However, in that same year young men and women were about equally likely to attend "college" (i.e., all forms of non-university post-secondary schooling).

The large gender divide in university participation may have several important demographic and economic implications. First, completing university and starting a career may require women to delay their first child. Second, more and more professionals are female, which may have

FIGURE 1
University and College Participation Rates by Sex

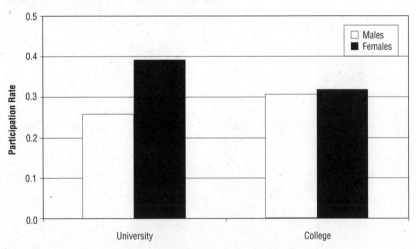

Source: Statistics Canada, Youth in Transition Survey, Cohort A.

implications for skilled labour shortages. For example, the proportion of medical doctors who are women has increased in recent years. Given that female doctors tend to work far fewer hours than male doctors,[2] this may exacerbate the existing pressures to increase the number of doctors in light of the aging population and the associated increase in the demand for health care services. Third, the rising educational attainment of women may help reduce the raw (or unconditional) gender wage gap.[3] Fourth, given marital homogamy (i.e., the tendency of like to marry like), rising educational attainment of young women could lead to the emergence of "power couples" (i.e., couples comprised of two high-earners), which may contribute to increased inequality of family earnings. This may already be happening in Canada: Hou and Myles note an increase in the proportion of couples with the same level of education between 1971 (42 percent) and 2001 (54 percent), while Heisz documents a rise in family earnings inequality in the 1980s and 1990s. Furthermore, Kentworthy and Pontusson (2005) find evidence that increased marital homogamy is a large part of the reason why family earnings inequality has increased in several countries.

Despite its importance, very little is known about the gender divide in university participation. In the United States, Jacob (2002) examines the issue by using a survey containing detailed socio-economic information of youth. He is able to account for 90 percent of the gender gap in the university participation rate by differences in non-cognitive abilities (including school marks) and the university earnings premium relative to high school. However, the data that Jacob uses date back to the early 1990s, a period when the gap in the university participation rate was only about 5 percentage points – quite small by today's standards. Explaining such a small gap may be less informative than understanding the larger gap that exists today.

In a related branch of the literature, some U.S. authors have attempted to explain the rising female advantage in higher educational participation (Goldin et al., 2006; Cho, 2007). Analogously, they also find that academic performance and relative labour market opportunities account for a large portion of the trend in the gender gap in educational attainment. In Canada, Christofides et al. (2006) associate the changing gap mainly with the rising university earnings premium. Unfortunately, their data did not contain measures of academic performance.

The objective of the current study is to shed light on the large gender gap in university participation that exists at a point in time by using a new data source, namely the Youth in Transition Survey, Cohort A. This survey contains very detailed information on youth including school marks, performance on standardized reading tests, study habits, and parental expectations, among many other characteristics. Although the study largely follows Jacob (2002), it also adds to the literature in two important ways. First, it provides Canadian evidence on the topic. Second, it focuses on a more recent period (2003), when the gender gap in university participation was very large (13.1 percentage points).

In the next section, we describe the methodology employed in the study. To provide some context for the remainder of the study, the following section pieces together a profile of girls and boys from birth to age 15. This brings us to the core of the study, where we examine the extent to which the advantages held by girls at age 15 account for the large gender gap in university participation at age 19. The result of this exercise suggests that more than three-quarters (76.8 percent) of the gender gap in the university participation rate can be accounted for by differences in observable characteristics. In order of importance, the main factors are differences in school marks, standardized test scores in reading, study habits, parental expectations, and the university earnings premium relative to high school.

Methodology

The data for the study are drawn from the Youth in Transition Survey (YITS), Cohort A, which is described in detail by Motte, Qiu, Zhang, and Bussière (2008) in this book.[4] We select all youth in the survey. In Frenette (2008), only students who had completed high school by age 19 were considered; this is because the focus of that study was on illustrating to what extent financial constraints (i.e., the ability to pay for university) may or may not explain the income access gap in university participation. Since high school graduation is normally required to attend university,[5] it would be difficult to ascribe a lower university attendance rate for high school dropouts to financial constraints.

The main outcome is university participation by 31 December 2003. The main advantage of the data lies in the large number of explanatory variables. Four measures of academic performance are used in the study. The first is the PISA (Programme for International Student Assessment) overall reading score. Since Frenette (2007) demonstrates that performance in reading is more strongly associated with university participation than performance in mathematics or science, we focus exclusively on the reading component of PISA in this study. The second measure of academic performance is the student's overall mark in school at age 15, which is self-reported by the student. Since school marks largely reflect performance on curricula-based tests, they are indicative of "non-cognitive" abilities, according to Jacob (2002). In the same vein, study habits may also be considered a form of "non-cognitive" abilities. Study habits may in fact serve as a proxy for motivation to pursue further studies. To this end, YITS contains information on the number of hours the student spends per week doing homework, which we consider as a third measure of academic performance. The final measure of academic performance is the ability to progress through the schooling system at the usual pace (i.e., whether or not the student repeated a grade). Jacob (2002) suggests that being held back may signal a lack of maturity.

To capture "peer effects," we include variables that capture how many of the respondents' friends were planning to pursue their education after high school. Answers were grouped into three categories: *some or none, most,* and *all.*

Finally, students may also consider the economic benefits of completing a university degree. To this end we turned to the 2001 Census and calculated the ratio of mean earnings of university graduates to the mean earnings of high school graduates who were paid employees and had no self-employment income during the year 2000.[6] For university graduates we looked at 24- to 29-year-olds, while for high school graduates we looked at 18- to 23-year-olds. This approach has been used to control for the expected differences in the number of years of experience between high school and university graduates (e.g., Burbidge, Magee, and Robb, 2002). We did this calculation for males and females in every city – i.e., census metropolitan area or census agglomeration area – and matched it to the sex and city of students in YITS. For students living outside of cities, we looked at the earnings ratio of each gender in all areas in the rest of the province – i.e., outside of all cities in the province. Although this measure does not draw its variation across the time dimension, which may yield more variability, it nevertheless has 135 potentially different values for each sex (125 cities plus 10 provincial rural areas). The drawback of using the local university premium is that some students may consider the national premium in making their choices (especially if they do not plan on working in the city where they attended high school).

Parental characteristics were also added as controls. The first characteristic is parental presence in the home (one parent present; two parents present but neither are birth parents; two parents present but only one is a birth parent; or two birth parents present). The sex of the parent most knowledgeable of the student is also used, as is the highest level of education of either parent (no post-secondary certificate, a non-university post-secondary certificate, an undergraduate degree, or a graduate or professional degree). Although parental income is not expected to vary much by gender, it too is included. We use the quartile of total income in 1999 – including earnings, investment income, and government transfer income.[7] Finally, we include parental expectations of the highest level of educational outcome of the child (a university degree or not).

The goal of the study is to decompose the gap in university attendance into an explained component and an unexplained component (i.e., portions of the gap that are accounted for and not accounted for by differences in observable characteristics, respectively). The explained portion of the gap provides an estimate of the reduction in the total gap that we would expect to see if the males and females had the same observable characteristics. Specifically, the explained portion is simply the difference in the characteristics of males and females, multiplied by the "impact" that the characteristic has on the probability of university attendance.

An example may help illustrate. Suppose the rate of university attendance for group A is 10 percentage points higher than for group B. This is the total gap in university attendance. Suppose also that group A scores 50 points higher on a test of academic abilities. For every additional point scored on this test, assume that the probability of going to university rises by 0.01 percentage point. In that case, the portion of the gap in university attendance explained by differences in test scores would be 50*0.01=0.5, which represents 5 percent of the total gap (0.5/ 10=5 percent). A similar exercise would be performed for all other characteristics. Any portion of the total gap that could not be explained by differences in these characteristics would be called the unexplained component.[8]

A Profile of Girls and Boys from Birth to Age 15

In this section, we document gender differences in several characteristics in the early years. Establishing a link between these characteristics and future educational outcomes is obviously very difficult and beyond the scope of this chapter. In fact, most of the statistics to follow come from data sources that do not contain information on university attendance. As such, these statistics will simply serve as contextual information. The one exception is the description of the characteristics of boys and girls at age 15. This information will subsequently be used in the university attendance patterns.

Gender Differences in the Early Years

From birth, it would seem that boys and girls are very different on several fronts. This is true in the physical, developmental, and behavioural aspects of life. Physically, boys tend to have poorer health outcomes than girls. Out of every 1,000 live births, 5.8 boys die in the first year of life, compared with 4.7 girls (Statistics Canada, 2005). From the ages of one to four, boys are considerably more likely to be hospitalized than girls. Specifically, 7,793 out of 100,000 boys are hospitalized during this period, compared with only 5,726 out of 100,000 girls (Canadian Institute of Child Health, 2000). According to the National Longitudinal Survey of Children and Youth (NLSCY), Cycle 4 (2000/ 2001), boys are also far more likely to be categorized as having activity limitations (15 percent) than girls (11 percent). Boys also lag behind girls on the developmental side of things in the early years. For example, from birth to three years only 12 percent of boys are categorized as having advanced motor and social development, compared with 21 percent of girls (Canadian Institute of Child Health, 2000). On average, five-year-old boys score 97.2 on a test of copying and symbol use compared with 104.3 for girls (Thomas, 2006). Some 78 percent of five-year-old boys often display independence in dressing compared with 87 percent of girls (Thomas, 2006). Finally, boys have more behavioural problems than girls in the early years. For example, five-year-old boys display less attention (a score of 8.5) than girls (a score of 9.3), according to Thomas (2006). Some 16 percent of four- to 11-year-old boys display aggressive behaviour compared with only 9 percent of girls (Canadian Institute of Child Health, 2000). Similarly, 14 percent of four- to 11-year-old boys display hyperactivity compared with only 6 percent of girls (Canadian Institute of Child Health, 2000).

Gender Differences in the Elementary School Years

Additional gender differences appear during the elementary school years. For instance, 83 percent of elementary school teachers are women (2001 Census). This means that girls are far more likely to be taught by a same-sex teacher than boys during the first several years of school. A recent U.S. study using the National Education Longitudinal Survey found that both boys and girls benefited from a same-sex teacher (Dee, 2007). The size of the effect was quite large. For example, it is estimated that just one year with a male English teacher would eliminate nearly one-third of the gender gap in reading performance among 13-year-olds and would do so by improving the performance of boys and simultaneously harming that of girls. Similarly, a year with a female teacher would help girls partially catch up to boys in science and mathematics. Specifically, it would close the gender gap in science achievement among 13-year-olds by one-half and entirely eliminate the smaller achievement gap in mathematics.

Independent of the teacher's gender, several other important gender differences are worth noting. According to Julien and Ertl (2000), 10- to 11-year-old boys are less likely to work neatly and carefully (61 percent) than girls (82 percent), more likely to get into many fights (35 percent) than girls (13 percent), more likely to be restless, display hyperactivity, or be unable to sit still (49 percent) than girls (23 percent), and less likely to show sympathy when someone else has made a mistake (32 percent) than girls (49 percent).

Gender Differences in Parental Influences

Throughout the early and elementary school years, boys are also less likely to have a same-sex parent present in the home. Following family dissolution, the mother is more likely than the father to take care of the children. According to the 2001 Census, 14.3 percent of boys lived with a lone mother, while only 2.9 percent of boys lived with a lone father. Even among two-parent families, the mother is usually the parent most knowledgeable of the child: 78.7 percent of cases among girls compared to only 24.3 percent of the time among boys (YITS, Cohort A).

Gender Differences at Age 15

So far we have described gender differences in the early years in order to provide contextual information. No direct link can be made between those early differences and the gender gap in university participation. However, it is clear that by age 15, boys and girls continue to have very different characteristics (Table 1). These differences will, in fact, serve to explain observed differences in university participation rates in the core of the paper.

On the academic stage, boys trail behind girls on several fronts. For example, boys have weaker performances on standardized reading tests. Only 20.4 percent of boys score in the top 25 percent of the reading distribution. By contrast, 30.1 percent of girls score in the top 25 percent. Analogously, 30.3 percent of boys score in the bottom 25 percent, while only 19.5 percent of girls do so. There is an equally large gender divide in terms of overall school marks. While only 31.9 percent of boys

TABLE 1
Means of Variables by Sex

	Men	Women
University participation	0.257	0.388
Reading score<P5	0.075	0.028
P5 Reading score<P10	0.064	0.036
P10 Reading score<P25	0.164	0.131
P25 Reading score<P50	0.256	0.237
P50 Reading score<P75	0.237	0.267
P75 Reading score<P90	0.124	0.180
P90 Reading score<P95	0.042	0.056
Reading score P95	0.038	0.065
Overall mark<60%	0.104	0.057
60% Overall mark 69%	0.220	0.160
70% Overall mark 79%	0.356	0.320
80% Overall mark 89%	0.261	0.368
Overall mark 90%	0.057	0.096
Does no homework	0.085	0.025
Does less than 1 hour of homework per week	0.219	0.154
Does 1 to 3 hours of homework per week	0.394	0.409
Does 4 to 7 hours of homework per week	0.230	0.281
Does 8 to 14 hours of homework per week	0.055	0.103
Does 15 or more hours of homework per week	0.017	0.028
Repeated a grade	0.099	0.065
One parent	0.144	0.175
Two parents, neither from birth	0.100	0.027
Two parents, one from birth	0.031	0.094
Two birth parents	0.725	0.703
Person most knowledgeable of youth is same sex	0.235	0.798
Parents have no PS certificate	0.339	0.358
Parents have a non-university PS certificate	0.381	0.363
Parents have an undergraduate degree	0.190	0.178
Parents have a graduate or professional degree	0.090	0.101
1st parental income quartile	0.237	0.265
2nd parental income quartile	0.254	0.246
3rd parental income quartile	0.250	0.251
4th parental income quantile	0.259	0.238
Parents expect university degree	0.604	0.696
Few or no friends plan to further education after high school	0.244	0.158
Most friends plan to further education after high school	0.496	0.481
All friends plan to further education after high school	0.260	0.361
University premium	2.554	2.809
Sample size	6,223	7,403

Note: Percentiles are denoted by "P."
Source: Statistics Canada, Youth in Transition Survey, Cohort A.

report marks of at least 80 percent, almost half of girls fall in the same category (46.3 percent). At the opposite end of the spectrum, 8.4 percent of boys report overall marks below 60 percent compared with only 2.5 percent of girls. Boys and girls are also quite different in terms of the amount of time they spend on homework. While 8.5 percent of boys spend no time on homework, only 2.5 percent of girls make the same claim. By contrast, only 30.3 percent of boys spend at least four hours per week on homework, compared with 41.2 percent of girls. Almost one in 10 boys (9.9 percent) repeat a grade in school, compared with 6.5 percent of girls.

Boys and girls are also different in terms of their parental influences. Beginning with parental presence, boys are less likely than girls to be in lone-parent families or in two-parent families where only one parent is biological. However, boys are more likely to be in two-parent families where neither parent is biological. In terms of direct parental influence, the parent most knowledgeable of girls is far more often a parent of the same sex (79.8 percent) than is the case of boys (23.5 percent). In terms of socio-economic background, there is no clear advantage based on parental education or parental income. However, parents of 15-year-old girls are more likely to expect their 15-year-olds to complete a university degree (69.6 percent) than parents of 15-year-old boys (60.4 percent).

Peers may also influence future plans. On that front, boys are once again at a disadvantage. Boys (26.0 percent) are less likely than girls (36.1 percent) to report that all of their friends plan on pursuing further education following high school. At the other end of the spectrum, boys (24.4 percent) are more likely to report than girls (15.8 percent) that few or none of their friends plan on pursuing further education following high school. Finally, the direct economic benefits of completing a university degree are weaker for boys than for girls. Specifically, the ratio of mean annual earnings of university graduates to the mean annual earnings of high school graduates is smaller for males (2.55) than for females (2.81).

Results

The gender differences in socio-economic characteristics noted in the previous section may go some distance towards explaining the gap in university participation, but only to the extent that the characteristics themselves are associated with university participation. The detailed regression results are available in Frenette and Zeman (2007). To summarize these results, performance on standardized reading tests, overall marks, and time spent doing homework are all positively associated with university participation. Students who repeat a grade are less likely to attend university four years later, although the difference is not statistically significant once factors such as overall marks and performance on the standardized reading test are taken into account. The number and type (birth or other) of parents present in the home play a minimal role in the decision to attend university. Parental education, on the other hand, is very strongly associated with university participation. Youth with at least one university-educated parent enjoy a large advantage in university participation over youth with no post-secondary-educated parent. The same is true for parental expectations: students whose parents expect them to complete a university degree are far more likely to do so. Parental income, on the other hand, is very weakly associated with university participation once other socio-economic characteristics are taken into account. Students who report that all of their friends plan to pursue further education after high school are moderately more likely to pursue university than students who report that few or none of their friends plan to further their education after high school. Finally, a higher earnings premium for university relative to high school[9] is positively associated with a greater probability of attending university.[10]

We now proceed to decompose the overall gender gap in university participation (Figure 2). Recall from Figure 1 that the overall gender gap in university participation at age 19 is 13.1 percentage points. The decomposition results suggest that more than three-quarters (76.8 percent) of this gap can be accounted for by differences in observable socio-economic characteristics. We note that the main factor is differences in overall marks, accounting for nearly one-third (31.8 percent) of the overall gap in university participation. Differences in performance on standardized reading tests account for a more modest 14.6 percent of the gap in university participation.

These results are interesting in light of the findings in Frenette (2008). In that study, differences in performance on standardized reading tests accounted for a larger proportion of the gap than differences in overall marks between students from the top and the bottom income quartiles. In other words, the gender gap in university participation is more strongly linked to differences in performance at school, whereas the income gap in university participation is more strongly linked to differences in performance on tests of abilities that are not necessarily taught in school.

FIGURE 2
Proportion of Gender Gap in University Participation Explained by
Differences in Characteristics

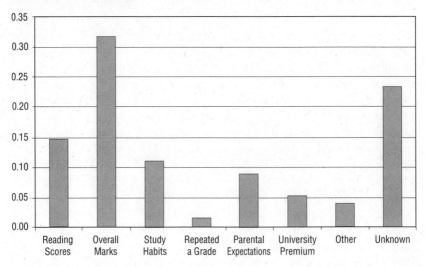

Source: Statistics Canada, Youth in Transition Survey, Cohort A.

Another important factor behind the gender gap in university participation is the difference in study habits (i.e., time spent doing homework). This accounts for 11.1 percent of the gap in university participation. Note that in Frenette (2008), where the sample is divided into parental income categories, this factor had no explanatory power and was dropped early on in the study. The higher propensity of boys to repeat a school grade accounts for only a negligible portion of the gap in university participation (1.5 percent).

Of course, it is very difficult to separate the effects of certain academic measures (such as marks) from others (such as time spent studying). A more meaningful conclusion that can be drawn from the analysis is that the four academic measures used in the study – overall marks, performance on standardized reading tests, study habits, and repeating a grade – collectively account for 58.9 percent of the gender gap in university participation.

Another notable factor is differences in parental expectations. Overall, this accounts for 8.5 percent of the gender gap in university participation.

The other factors considered in the study each account for less than 6 percent of the gap. Included in this list is the difference in the university premium relative to high school, which accounts for only 5.3 percent of the gap. This is in contrast to an American study by Jacob (2002) that finds that the university premium explains about one-half of the gender gap. Aside from the fact that the Jacob study looked at U.S. data, the difference between his estimate and ours may largely relate to the time period examined. The Jacob study focused on the early 1990s, a period when the gender gap in university participation was much smaller (about 5 percentage points in the United States). By contrast, the gender gap in university participation in our study is more than 13 percentage points. It is also worth noting that the evidence in our study suggests that although the university premium is higher for women, they do not seem to respond to this signal. We noted earlier that the university premium was positively associated with university participation among males, but among females there was no statistical association. Furthermore, girls report about the same level of importance of education in shaping their future career success as boys (Youth in Transition Survey, Cohort A). A final point relates to the importance one attaches to *relative* premiums. In absolute terms, males actually gain more from a university degree compared with a high school diploma. The absolute gap for males is $22,766, while for females it is only $18,490. If youth are responding to absolute rather than relative benefits, this would explain why the relative earnings premium does not account for a large portion of the gender gap in university participation. To test this hypothesis, we ran a pooled regression of males and females, and included both the relative and absolute premium variables. Although both coefficients were positive, only the coefficient for the absolute premium variable was statistically significant. This suggests that the differential absolute premium between males and females may actually work towards reducing the gender gap in university attendance. In fact, this is what a decomposition exercise suggests: the differential absolute premium accounts for -14 percent of the total gap in participation. The other results were invariant to replacing the relative premium with the absolute premium.

The upshot of this discussion is that some doubt is cast on the notion that women are more likely to attend university because of the greater economic benefits of doing so, although further research in the area is needed to be more conclusive on the issue. One possibility is to examine changes in the earnings premium over time. Christofides et al. (2006) did just that, and largely correlated the faster increase in the premium observed among women with the rising female composition in universities between 1977 and 2003. Unfortunately, their data do not contain detailed information on men and women such as academic performance, among others. Furthermore, they show with the same data that the university earnings premium fluctuated substantially from year to year. Had they picked 2002 as their end date instead of 2003, men and women would have seen the same increase in their premium since 1977. In fact, the male premium rose slightly faster over the period. Of course, women also made dramatic gains in terms of university enrolment between 1977 and 2002, despite the fact that the university earnings premium they faced rose no faster than it did for men.

Conclusion

In 2003, some 38.8 percent of 19-year-old women had attended university, compared with only 25.7 percent of 19-year-old men. However, young men and women were about equally likely to attend college. Despite the importance of the gender divide, very little is known about its significance in university participation. In this study we have used Canadian data containing detailed information on standardized test scores, school marks, parental and peer influences, and other socio-economic background characteristics to try to account for the large gender gap in university attendance.

We find that gender differences in observable characteristics account for more than three-quarters (76.8 percent) of the gender gap in university participation. In order of importance, the main factors are: differences in school marks (31.8 percent), standardized test scores in reading (14.6 percent), study habits (11.1 percent), parental expectations (8.5 percent), and the university earnings premium relative to high school (5.3 percent). Altogether, the four measures of academic performance used in the study – overall marks, performance on standardized reading tests, study habits, and being held back a grade – collectively account for 58.9 percent of the gender gap in university participation. Overall marks account for a larger share of the gender gap in university participation than do reading scores.

Performance on standardized tests has been treated as an indicator of cognitive abilities (e.g., Carneiro and Heckman, 2002). Overall marks, study habits, and repeating a grade, on the other hand, have been treated as non-cognitive abilities by others, *once cognitive abilities are taken into account* (e.g., Jacob, 2002). That is, overall marks may reflect one's ability to capitalize on cognitive abilities in a more formal setting, i.e., school. It may also reflect one's level of motivation or maturity, as can time spent on homework or repeating a grade. According to Heckman, Stixrud, and Urzua (2006), cognitive abilities are only malleable in the early years, while non-cognitive abilities are malleable well into the teenage years. If this is the case, then this factor has important implications for the findings in this study, as well as in Frenette (2007). In that paper, performance on standardized reading tests accounts for a larger share of the income access gap in university participation than school marks. The implication, from a research point of view, is that the key to understanding the income access gap in university participation may lie in the early years – the pre-school years. By contrast, the findings in the current study suggest that a very large proportion of the gender gap in university participation relates to non-cognitive abilities displayed at school. As a result, understanding the female advantage in attending university may critically depend on understanding why girls outperform boys in elementary and high school. This may, in part, depend on the physical, developmental, and behavioural gender differences observed early in life.

Notes

This article was adapted from Frenette and Zeman (2007). The authors gratefully acknowledge helpful comments by Evelyne Bougie, Dafna Kohen, Michael Hoy, René Morissette, and Garnett Picot. Evelyne Bougie and Dafna Kohen were particularly helpful in providing references and insight on child development. The authors are responsible for all remaining errors.

1. The improvements registered by women were larger at the graduate degree level. In 1971, 22 percent of 25- to 29-year-old graduate degree holders were women. This figure rose to 58 percent by 2001. By contrast, 35 percent of bachelor degree holders in 1971 were women, compared with 58 percent in 2001.

2. Information on physician work hours by sex is available from the Canadian Medical Association at www.cma.ca/multimedia/CMA/Content_Images/Inside_cma/Statistics/pwr-average1.pdf

3. Frenette and Coulombe (2007) investigate this issue for the period 1980 to 2000 in Canada. They find that rising educational attainment of women was linked to a falling gender earnings gap in the 1980s and (to a lesser extent) in the 1990s. Cutbacks in public administration (a common career choice area of highly educated women), as well as rapid expansion in the high-tech sector (an employer of many highly educated men), may have prevented the gender gap from declining further in the 1990s.

4. Note also that to account for the complex survey design of YITS, all variance measures were bootstrapped with 1,000 replicate weights.

5. Older high school dropouts may qualify to enter university as mature students. However, they are not included in the data.

6. We also used the ratio of median earnings, and there was no discernable change to the results.
7. To account for differences in family size and their associated economies of scale, we calculated "equivalent" income by dividing parental income by the square root of the family size. Based on equivalent income, students were categorized by quartile. The threshold levels of equivalent income for each quartile are $20,409 (25th percentile), $30,531 (50th percentile), and $41,000 (75th percentile). For a family of four, these are equivalent to twice these levels in unadjusted terms: $40,819 (25th percentile), $61,062 (50th percentile) and $82,000 (75th percentile). See Skuterud, Frenette, and Poon (2004) for a more detailed discussion of equivalent income.
8. For more technical readers, please see Frenette and Zeman (2007) for a more detailed description of the approach used. Note that we only show results from method 3 described in Frenette and Zeman (2007) in the current study since the findings are largely invariant to the choice of the method.
9. See the methodology section for the construction of this variable.
10. Interestingly, this is true for males but not for females when we estimate the models separately.

References

Burbidge, J.B., L. Magee, and A.L. Robb. 2002. "The Education Premium in Canada and the United States." *Canadian Public Policy* 28 (2): 203-17.

Canadian Institute of Child Health. 2000. *The Health of Canada's Children: A CICH Profile*. 3rd ed. Ottawa: Canadian Institute of Child Health.

Carneiro, P., and J.J. Heckman. 2002. "The Evidence on Credit Constraints in Post-Secondary Schooling." *Economic Journal* 112 (482): 705-34.

Cho, D. 2007. "The Role of High School Performance in Explaining Women's Rising College Enrollment." *Economics of Education Review* 26 (4): 450-62.

Christofides, L., M. Hoy, and L. Yang. 2006. *The Gender Imbalance in Participation in Canadian Universities (1977-2003)*. University of Guelph, Department of Economics, Working Paper No. 2006-10.

Dee, T.S. 2007. "Teachers and the Gender Gaps in Student Achievement." *Journal of Human Resources* 42 (3): 528-54.

Frenette, M. 2007. *Why Are Lower-income Students Less Likely to Attend University? Evidence from Academic Abilities, Parental Influences, and Financial Constraints*. Analytical Studies Research Paper Series. No. 11F0019MIE2007295. Ottawa: Statistics Canada.

– 2008. "Why Are Lower-Income Students Less Likely to Attend University? Evidence from Academic Abilities, Parental Influences, and Financial Constraints." In *Who Goes? Who Stays? What Matters? Accessing and Persisting in Post-Secondary Education in Canada*, edited by R. Finnie, R.E. Mueller,

A. Sweetman, and A. Usher. Montreal and Kingston: McGill-Queen's University Press and School of Policy Studies, Queen's University.

Frenette, M., and S. Coulombe. 2007. *Has Higher Education among Young Women Substantially Reduced the Gender Gap in Employment and Earnings?* Analytical Studies Research Paper Series No. 11F0019MIE2007301. Ottawa: Statistics Canada.

Frenette, M., and K. Zeman. 2007. *Why Are Most University Students Women? Evidence Based on Academic Performance, Study Habits and Parental Influences.* Analytical Studies Research Paper Series No. 11F0019MIE2007303. Ottawa: Statistics Canada.

Goldin, C., L.F. Katz, and I. Kuziemko. 2006. "The Homecoming of American College Women: The Reversal of the College Gender Gap." *Journal of Economic Perspectives* 20 (4): 133-56.

Heckman, J.J., J. Stixrud, and S. Urzua. 2006. "The Effects of Cognitive and Non-Cognitive Abilities on Labor Market Outcomes and Social Behaviour." *Journal of Labor Economics* 24 (3): 411-82.

Heisz, A. 2007. *Income Inequality and Redistribution in Canada: 1976 to 2004.* Analytical Studies Research Paper Series No. 11F0019MIE2007298. Ottawa: Statistics Canada.

Hou, F., and J. Myles. 2007. *The Changing Role of Education in the Marriage Market: Assortative Marriage in Canada and the United States since the 1970s.* Analytical Studies Research Paper Series No. 11F0019MIE2007299. Ottawa: Statistics Canada.

Jacob, B.A. 2002. "Where the Boys Aren't: Non-Cognitive Skills, Returns to School and the Gender Gap in Higher Education." *Economics of Education Review* 21 (6): 589-98.

Julien, A.-M., and H. Ertl. 2000. "Children's School Experiences in the NLSCY, 1994/1995." *Education Quarterly Review* 6 (2): 20-34. Statistics Canada, Catalogue no. 81-003-XIE. Ottawa: Statistics Canada.

Kentworthy, L., and J. Pontusson. 2005. *Rising Inequality and the Politics of Redistribution in Affluent Countries.* Luxembourg Income Study Working Paper No. 4000. Luxembourg: Luxembourg Income Study.

Motte, A., H.T. Qiu, Y. Zhang, and P. Bussière. 2008. "The Youth in Transition Survey: Following Canadian Youth through Time." In *Who Goes? Who Stays? What Matters? Accessing and Persisting in Post-Secondary Education in Canada,* edited by R. Finnie, R.E. Mueller, A. Sweetman, and A. Usher. Montreal and Kingston: McGill-Queen's University Press and School of Policy Studies, Queen's University.

Skuterud, M., M. Frenette, and P. Poon. 2004. *Describing the Distribution of Income: Guidelines for Effective Analysis.* Income Research Paper Series No. 75F0002MIE2004010. Ottawa: Statistics Canada.

Statistics Canada. 2005. *Health Indicators.* No. 82-221-XIE. Ottawa: Statistics Canada.

Thomas, E.M. 2006. *Readiness to Learn at School among Five-Year-Old Children in Canada.* Children and Youth Research Paper Series No. 89-599-MIE2006004. Ottawa: Statistics Canada.

7

The Effect of School and Non-School Activities on High School Performance in Canada

Jorgen Hansen

Dans cet article, j'analyse les effets, sur la moyenne pondérée cumulative des élèves du secondaire, de la participation à la vie étudiante et à certaines activités extrascolaires. Les données montrent d'abord que les élèves qui participent à des activités parascolaires ou qui ont des activités extrascolaires sont nombreux : c'est le cas d'environ deux tiers des élèves en 10ᵉ année. Pour ce qui est des effets de la participation à ces activités, on observe que, chez les élèves de 10ᵉ année qui un ont emploi pendant l'année scolaire, cette activité entraîne une baisse significative de la moyenne pondérée cumulative, et ce, à la fois en 10ᵉ année et en 11ᵉ année. À l'inverse, la participation à des activités parascolaires a des effets bénéfiques et améliore de façon significative la performance scolaire des élèves.

This paper analyzes the effects on students' grade point average of participating in school and non-school related activities during high school. Data show that participation is common: around two-thirds of grade 10 students participate in school and/or non-school related activities during the school year. The results indicate that working in the 10th grade significantly reduces students' grade point averages, both in grade 10 and in grade 11. Contrary to the effects of working, participation in school organized activities has beneficial effects and significantly improves academic performance.

Who Goes? Who Stays? What Matters? Accessing and Persisting in Post-Secondary Education in Canada, eds. R. Finnie, R.E. Mueller, A. Sweetman, and A. Usher. Montreal and Kingston: McGill-Queen's University Press, Queen's Policy Studies Series. © 2008 The School of Policy Studies, Queen's University at Kingston. All rights reserved.

Introduction

Over the past two decades a number of researchers have examined whether or not high school employment is beneficial; see, for example, Ruhm (1997), Light (1998, 1999, 2001), Eckstein and Wolpin (1999), Oettinger (1999), Dagenais et al. (2001), Tyler (2003), and Parent (2006). Given that youth employment is common, the interest in the topic is easily justified, and the findings may have important implications. For instance, if research shows that working while in high school has a harmful effect on academic performance, a reasonable policy would be to restrict youths' employment behaviour. On the other hand, if it is found that working during high school improves academic outcomes, then the laws that regulate employment among youth should be relaxed.

Unfortunately, it has proven difficult to determine whether high school employment is harmful or not. Although extensive research on the topic exists, that work has been unable to reach a consensus. For instance, Ruhm (1997), who provides an extensive survey of research on the subject, concludes that "there is currently no consensus whether student employment improves or worsens school performance" (738). Working while in high school may crowd out time that students instead could have spent on school work and other activities that foster further educational investments; in this case, working leads to lower grades and lower educational attainment. Conversely, working during high school may not be detrimental, as by working, students may gain skills such as work ethics, responsibility, and discipline that complement their school performance. Further, by working, students may gain valuable work experience, which may ease the transition from school to work.

Since economic theory does not provide us with any unambiguous predictions regarding the effects of high school employment, we need to rely on empirical assessments. However, it is difficult to assess the causal or true effect of working on academic achievement because it is unlikely that the decision to work (and also how many hours to work) is exogenous. For example, students who fare well academically in school may be more motivated in general and therefore also more likely to work. If this is the case, and motivation is unobserved, then the variation in scholastic ability that is attributed to differences in working is spurious and should be attributed to motivation. Thus, the estimated effects obtained using simple regression techniques may be overstated.

It is generally very difficult to deal with this "endogeneity" problem. Most previous work has focused on using instrumental variables (IV) estimators. However, it can be a challenging task to find instruments that are unrelated to academic performance (and thus can legitimately be excluded from the primary equation) but explain a significant portion of the variation in the incidence of work. Examples of instruments that have been used include geographic characteristics (Ruhm, 1997 and Light, 2001), and state child labour laws (Tyler, 2003).[1]

A perhaps more natural way to estimate the causal effect of both incidence and intensity of working (and other activities) on different outcome variables is to use a proxy method (e.g., Ruhm, 1997 and Light, 2001). In this case the unobserved variables that are presumed to be correlated with employment behaviour – such as motivation and ability – are approximated using combinations of variables such as measures of family background and test scores. However, in most data sources, such information is not available.

A third alternative to obtain a causal effect of working while in school is to use a fixed-effects (FE) estimator. This, however, requires access to data where students are observed over time, along with an assumption that the unobserved variables causing the "endogeneity" problem are time invariant.

In this paper I utilize data from the Youth in Transition Survey (YITS) to examine both the extent of participation in different activities during the school year and the effect of such participation on academic performance. Contrary to most of the previous literature, which has focused mainly on working while in school, this paper also considers non-work activities that may be organized by schools or by other organizations. Further, this paper utilizes longitudinal information that allows us to consider the sequential nature of students' decisions and outcomes. For instance, it is possible that current academic performance is partially determined by work status and participation in other activities during the *previous* year. Moreover, students' decisions regarding employment and enrolment in post-secondary education are likely to depend on prior academic achievement. Understanding these relationships is extremely important because they relate to how higher education should be financed and to the skill level of new entrants in the labour force.

The data show that participation in various activities outside regular school hours but during the school year is common. Around two-thirds of grade 10 students in Canada participated in activities organized by schools (e.g., school clubs, teams, or other school organizations). A slightly higher proportion participated in non-working activities that were not organized by schools (e.g., non-school clubs, teams, volunteering, or other organizations), while around 60 percent worked. At grade 11 the participation rate in all activities had increased, especially that for working.[2]

Since it is likely that all activities considered in this paper are endogenously chosen, alternative methods have been used to examine the impact of participation on academic outcomes. Regarding working while in school (and during the school year), the results firmly show that this negatively affects academic performance in grade 10. Moreover, the negative effect of working in grade 10 appears to be persistent over time and significantly affects academic performance in grade 11. However, working while attending 11th grade has no significant effect on grade point averages in grade 11. Finally, there are no indications that working a modest amount of hours during the school year is beneficial in either grade. While working less than five hours per week does not significantly worsen grades, neither does it improve them. Working more than five hours per week significantly reduces students' grade point average, and the negative effect increases with hours worked. While working is found to have no positive effects on students' achievements, participation in school activities has significant and positive effects.

The remainder of the paper is organized as follows. The next section provides a brief review of the literature. The data are then described, the methodology is discussed, and the results are presented. The paper concludes with some policy implications of the main findings.

Literature Review

Over the past two decades much work has been done on establishing whether working while in school is beneficial or harmful. This section briefly reviews a selection of these studies.

Lillydahl (1990) uses the 1987 National Assessment of Economic Education Survey to further research the effects on academic achievement of employment while in school. Her data shows that nearly one-third of all 10th graders and approximately 70 percent of high school seniors hold part-time jobs during the school year. Her results indicate that modest levels of employment (less than 15 hours per week) for high school students may not interfere with their academic achievement. However, students who work more than 15 hours per week are more absent from school, spend less time on homework, and have lower grade point averages (GPAs).

Ruhm (1997) provides a detailed summary of research on this topic and concludes that there is no agreement in the literature about the effect of employment during high school. Reasons for the divergence in findings include the use of different samples and different method-ologies. Earlier work generally treated youth employment as exogenous, and those researchers who addressed the endogeneity problem were faced with the difficulty of finding credible instrumental variables. Apart from providing a thorough summary of previous work, Ruhm (1997) also estimates the effect of youth employment on future wage outcomes. The endogeneity problem is dealt with using geographic characteris-tics as instruments, and the results suggest that there are no harmful effects of working during high school. Instead, Ruhm finds that jobs held in the senior year of high school yield substantial and lasting benefits.

Oettinger (1999) uses data from the 1979 National Longitudinal Sur-vey of Youth (NLSY) and presents results using ordinary least squares (OLS) and fixed-effects estimators. While the OLS estimates generally indicate that working has a negative impact on school performance (measured as grade point average), the fixed-effects estimates are small and not significant. When Oettinger splits the sample according to ethnic status, he finds that extensive school-year employment seems to re-duce academic performance for minority students.

Tyler (2003) uses the variation in labour supply of 12th grade stu-dents created by interstate variations in child labour laws to estimate the effects of school-year work on their 12th grade math achievement. He develops a model that both illustrates the potential problems with OLS estimation of the effects of work on achievement and provides a framework for IV estimation. The IV estimates show a much larger nega-tive effect of working on 12th grade math scores than the OLS estimates.

As is apparent from the above review, most of the previous work on employment and academic performance has been conducted on U.S. data. One exception is the paper by Dagenais et al. (2001). Using Cana-dian data extracted from the 1991 School Leavers Survey, this study estimates a system of equations with three outcomes: high school grade point average, hours of work during the last year of high school studies, and student persistence at high school. The effect of working on aca-demic performance is identified using information on minimum wage levels and on unemployment rates. The findings suggest that working reduces high school grade point averages, especially when weekly hours of work exceed 15. Further, they show that working also increases the likelihood of dropping out of high school, and this likelihood increases as weekly work hours increase.

Finally, Parent (2006) uses the same Canadian survey to estimate the effects of working while in high school on high school completion and on future wages. Similar to the findings of Dagenais et al. (2001), Parent finds that working reduces the likelihood of graduating from high school. Further, the results suggest that high school employment has no beneficial effect on future wages, a result that contrasts the findings of Ruhm (1997), among others.

Overall, findings in the previous literature indicate that working while in high school appears to hamper students' performance in high school. This is especially true if students spend more than 15 hours per week working. However, it is not clear whether working during high school has beneficial or harmful effects on future wages. Most of the findings have been obtained using U.S. data, and few Canadian studies are available. Finally, past work has focused almost exclusively on working and has ignored the effects of other activities that, like working, are time consuming and reduce time for school work. This paper hopes to provide some new evidence on this issue.

Data

The data used in this paper are obtained from the first three cycles of the youngest cohort of the Canadian Youth in Transition Survey (YITS).[3] The empirical analysis requires longitudinal information on both academic performance and school year participation in different activities. To be included in the sample, an individual respondent must have completed both the math and the reading PISA (Programme for International Student Assessment) tests. This requirement, which reduced the sample to 8,125 individuals, is imposed since the test scores will play a central role in obtaining estimates of the true impact of working on high school performance. Moreover, all individuals with incomplete information on their participation in school and non-school activities (including work) were removed. This reduced the sample to 7,711. Finally, respondents with no information on their grade point average or any of the included family background variables were dropped. This reduced the sample to 5,754 respondents.

The analysis in this paper uses information extracted from all three cycles. In particular, information on whether respondents lived with both biological parents most of the time during high school, parents' education, and parents' income (only available for the youngest cohort) was obtained from the first cycle. For the youngest cohort, information on high school grade averages and participation in various activities was obtained from cycles 1 and 2. Students' grade point averages are measured on a six-point scale, where 6 corresponds to overall grades ranging from 90 percent to 100 percent and 1 corresponds to less than 50 percent. Finally, sample weights provided by Statistics Canada have been used throughout this paper, both when calculating descriptive statistics and when estimating regression equations. The results are therefore representative of the corresponding population of Canadian youths.

Table 1 shows a description of participation in different activities for respondents from cohort A.[4] In this paper we consider three different activities: (1) school related activities (including participation in school clubs and teams as well as in other school organizations); (2) non-school related activities (including participation in non-school clubs and teams or in other organizations); and (3) paid or unpaid work (including working in the family's farm or business with or without pay). As can be seen in the table, participation in these types of activities is common. During the 1999-2000 school year, 67.4 percent of the respondents participated in some activities organized by the school. A slightly higher

TABLE 1
Participation in Different Activities during the 1999-2000 and 2000-01 School Years, YITS Cohort A

| | Type of activity | | |
	School related	Non-school related	Paid or unpaid work
Proportion participating			
School year 1999	0.674	0.702	0.601
School year 2001	0.740	0.740	0.761
Proportion spending (given participation)			
Between 1 and 3 hours per week			
School year 1999	0.634	0.494	0.039
School year 2001	0.476	0.460	0.063
Between 4 and 7 hours per week			
School year 1999	0.277	0.318	0.157
School year 2001	0.276	0.308	0.146
More than 7 hours per week			
School year 1999	0.089	0.188	0.804
School year 2001	0.189	0.227	0.791
Sample size		5,754	

Source: Calculations are based on survey data extracted from cohort A of the Youth in Transition Survey (YITS), cycles 1 and 2. The proportions are weighted by sample weights. School activities include participation in school clubs, teams, or other school organizations. Non-school activities include participation in non-school clubs, teams, volunteer work, or other organizations. Paid or unpaid work includes working in the family's farm or business with or without pay. For details on sample selections, see text. In 1999-2000 most students were in grade 10, while in 2000-01 most students were in grade 11.

fraction, 70.2 percent, participated in non-working activities that were not organized by the school. Finally, just over 60 percent worked some time during this school year. In the 2000-01 school year, participation in all activities had increased, especially working (just over 76 percent). The lower panels of Table 1 provide some information on how much time students spend on each of these activities conditional on participation. Clearly, among students who work, a majority (around 80 percent for both years) spend on average more than seven hours per week at work. Non-work activities appear to consume less time, and most students who participate spend less than four hours per week on such activities.

To examine who participates in different types of activities, participation in each of the three activities was regressed on a number of observable characteristics. The results are in Tables 2a (for the 1999-2000 school year) and 2b (for the 2000-01 school year). For example, during

TABLE 2a
Determinants of Participation in Different Activities in the 1999-2000 School Year

	Type of activity		
	School related	Non-school related	Paid or unpaid work
Female	0.025**	-0.003	0.150**
	(1.99)	(0.24)	(11.80)
Number of siblings	-0.002	0.004	0.039**
	(0.41)	(0.67)	(6.75)
Nuclear family	-0.009	0.028	0.023
	(0.48)	(1.57)	(1.20)
Family income ($1,000)	0.236**	0.355**	0.192
	(2.08)	(3.21)	(1.64)
Mother's education			
High school	0.051**	0.071**	0.036
	(2.17)	(3.15)	(1.49)
Some post-secondary education	0.089**	0.132**	0.040*
	(3.92)	(5.93)	(1.69)
Father's education			
High school	0.077**	0.048**	0.020
	(3.54)	(2.25)	(0.90)
Some post-secondary education	0.100**	0.065**	-0.023
	(4.93)	(3.27)	(1.11)
Sample size	5,754	5,754	5,754

Source: The regressions were conducted on the sample presented in Table 1 (cycle 1, cohort A). Robust t-statistics are presented in parentheses. ** and * signify statistical significance at the 5 percent and 10 percent level, respectively. In 1999-2000 most students were in grade 10.

TABLE 2b
Determinants of Participation in Different Activities in the 2000-01 School Year

	Type of activity		
	School related	Non-school related	Paid or unpaid work
Female	0.031**	0.018	0.056**
	(2.73)	(1.60)	(5.01)
Number of siblings	0.009*	0.005	0.011**
	(1.71)	(1.04)	(2.26)
Nuclear family	0.059**	0.037**	-0.008
	(3.40)	(2.12)	(0.44)
Family income ($1000)	0.033	0.198*	0.216**
	(0.31)	(1.86)	(2.08)
Mother's education			
High school	0.066**	0.018	0.042
	(2.99)	(0.82)	(1.98)
Some post-secondary education	0.060**	0.074**	0.024
	(2.79)	(3.47)	(1.15)
Father's education			
High school	0.005	0.017	-0.026
	(0.26)	(0.81)	(1.32)
Some post-secondary education	0.049**	0.066**	-0.069**
	(2.54)	(3.49)	(3.72)
Sample size	5,754	5,754	5,754

Source: The regressions were conducted on the sample presented in Table 1 (cycle 1, cohort A). Robust t-statistics are presented in parentheses. ** and * signify statistical significance at the 5 percent and 10 percent level, respectively. In 2000-01 most students were in grade 11.

the first school year, participation in both school and non-school related activities are significantly and positively correlated with parents' education and family income. This may indicate that students from less affluent backgrounds are unable to participate in these activities because of monetary constraints. Participation in work does not show this pattern. Much of the pattern remains for the following school year. While it is possible that the reasons for working may differ depending on the age of the student, the entries in Tables 2a and 2b do not indicate that there are substantial changes between the two school years in the composition of those who work.

Methodology

The basic empirical model used to estimate the effect of non-academic activities on academic performance is a linear regression model where the dependent variable is a measure of academic achievement (high school GPA). The independent variables include information on parents' level of education, family income, family composition, province, gender, and measures of different activities (school organized activities, non-school organized activities, and work).

As mentioned in the introduction, the OLS estimates of the effects of activities on academic performance will be biased if these variables are correlated with the error term. For example, this will happen if those who participate in activities also are more motivated in their school work. If we ignore this possible correlation and use OLS, the estimated effect of activities will be overstated and include the effect of motivation as well. One possibility for overcoming this problem is to include proxy variables for the unobserved characteristics that we believe are correlated with activities. For instance, the PISA math and reading scores may be used for this purpose.

As an alternative to the use of proxy variables – and given that we have access to panel data – we can take the difference of the regression equation over time. This difference will remove any unobserved characteristics of the respondents that are time invariant and that we expect are correlated with participation in activities. In this paper, I look at differences in grade point averages between cycle 1 and cycle 2 and regress that difference on differences in participation. Least squares estimates of this regression specification will be consistent so long as the between-grade change in the unobserved transitory component of GPA is uncorrelated with the between-grade change in participation in activities. Given the likely importance of unobserved, time-invariant individual heterogeneity, this orthogonality assumption seems reasonable. However, it is possible that the transitory component of the error term is correlated with participation in activities. In this case, the fixed effects estimates do not necessarily measure the causal effect of participation. In such a case, a natural candidate is the instrumental variables (IV) estimator. This requires that we define a primary outcome equation as well as an "auxiliary" regression equation in which the dependent variable equals the presumed endogenous variable in the primary equation. To be able to identify the parameters in this context, we need to include observed characteristics in the auxiliary regression equation that we can exclude from the primary equation (exclusion restrictions). Generally, it is very difficult to find valid exclusion restrictions (instruments), and the results may be sensitive towards the choice of such restrictions. Given these concerns, I do not report any IV estimates in this paper.

While the above has focused on participation in activities, the intensity of such activities may also be important. To investigate this, we consider regression equations where the indicator variables are replaced by intensity measures. It should be noted that the endogeneity problems remain, and they are addressed using similar methodologies.

Results

The first column of Table 3 presents weighted least squares estimates using information on activities from the 1999-2000 school year. These estimates suggest that participation in both school and non-school activities significantly improves a student's GPA, especially participation in school related activities. Employment appears to have a small and (statistically) insignificant effect on academic performance. In column 2, the same regression was estimated but was instead based on activities and outcomes in the 2000-01 school year. The pattern remains, and the estimates are close to those reported in column 1. Finally, in column 3, outcomes in 2000-01 were regressed on activities in both years. One reason for including lags of activities is that participation in such activities may have effects on both current and future outcomes. The entries in column 3 suggest that the beneficial effects of participation in school related activities last (or persist), while this is not the case for non-school activities. Further, the effects of current activities on current outcomes are similar to those found in the first two columns.

From these results we may conclude that working while in high school is neither beneficial nor harmful. Participation in other activities such as clubs or teams do have positive effects on GPA, especially if these activities are organized by the school. However, as discussed earlier in the paper, it is likely that these estimates simply reflect systematic unobserved differences among students choosing whether or not to participate in different activities. For example, the most talented and motivated students might be much more likely to participate in school organized activities, and the estimates above are unable to control for this possibility. Consequently, the estimates provided in Table 3 may be biased.

One way to reduce the potential bias in the OLS estimates is to include proxy variables for the unobserved individual characteristics that exist. Table 4 contains results when PISA scores were added to the set

TABLE 3
The Effect of Participation in Activities on High School Grade Point Average (GPA)

	Dependent variable GPA school year		
	1999-2000	*2000-01*	*2000-01*
Activities in school year 1999			
School related activities	0.322**		0.154**
	(11.05)		(5.73)
Non-school related activities	0.128**		0.028
	(4.24)		(1.03)
Paid or unpaid work	0.029		0.046*
	(1.05)		(1.81)
Activities in school year 2001			
School related activities		0.368**	0.310**
		(13.54)	(10.80)
Non-school related activities		0.159**	0.132**
		(5.78)	(4.65)
Paid or unpaid work		0.033	0.008
		(1.19)	(0.29)
Sample size	5,754	5,754	5,754

Source: The regressions were conducted on the sample presented in Table 1 (cycles 1 and 2, cohort A). Robust t-statistics are presented in parentheses. ** and * signify statistical significance at the 5 percent and 10 percent level, respectively. The regressions also include controls for number of siblings, nuclear family, family income, mother's education, father's education, and provincial dummies. In 1999-2000 most students were in grade 10, while in 2000-01 most students were in grade 11.

of regressors. From column 1 we see that participation in non-work activities is still beneficial and has a positive effect on students' GPA. This is again especially true for school organized activities. As expected, the estimates are somewhat smaller than the comparable ones in Table 3. This indicates that there is a positive correlation between participation in school activities and scholastic ability and that when such ability measures are omitted, the participation variables pick up their effect as well.

While the effects of participating in non-work activities were reduced slightly, the effect of working on GPA changes quite dramatically. The estimate is now negative (-0.110) and significant, suggesting that working in grade 10 significantly reduces students' GPA. The corresponding estimate when PISA scores were omitted was positive and

TABLE 4
The Effect of Participation in Activities on High School Grade Point Average (GPA),
with Controls for PISA Test Scores

| | Dependent variable GPA school year | | |
	1999-2000	2000-01	2000-01
Activities in school year 1999			
School related activities	0.251**		0.119**
	(10.04)		(5.00)
Non-school related activities	0.093**		0.018
	(3.59)		(0.72)
Paid or unpaid work	-0.110**		-0.053**
	(4.57)		(2.31)
Activities in school year 2001			
School related activities		0.288**	0.248**
		(11.97)	(9.77)
Non-school related activities		0.112**	0.099**
		(4.65)	(3.96)
Paid or unpaid work		-0.041*	-0.027
		(1.68)	(1.04)
PISA math score	0.003**	0.002**	0.002**
	(15.30)	(14.08)	(14.13)
PISA reading score	0.004**	0.003**	0.003**
	(24.33)	(21.23)	(21.21)
Sample size	5,754	5,754	5,754

Source: The regressions were conducted on the sample presented in Table 1 (cycles 1 and 2, cohort A). Robust t-statistics are presented in parentheses. ** and * signify statistical significance at the 5 percent and 10 percent level, respectively. The regressions also include controls for number of siblings, nuclear family, family income, mother's education, father's education, and provincial dummies. In 1999-2000 most students were in grade 10, while in 2000-01 most students were in grade 11.

close to zero (0.029). Clearly, the inclusion of test scores has an important impact on the estimates, especially the one associated with working. The estimates for the PISA scores have expected signs (positive correlation between scores and GPA). In column 2, the outcome is GPA in 2000-01.[5] The effects of non-work activities change very little compared to the effects found in column 1. However, the negative effect of working is reduced (the estimate is reduced by more than half), and the estimate is now only significant at the 10 percent level (two-sided alternative). Finally, in column 3, outcomes are measured in 2000-01, while activities are measured in both years. Similar to the specification without ability measures, there is persistence in the effect of participation in school activities, and such activities significantly improve GPA. Working in grade 10 reduces students' GPA in grade 11, while working in grade 11 has no significant negative effect. Thus, the results again provide strong indications that school organized activities are beneficial. This finding is robust, and the effect is larger in grade 11 than in grade 10. Moreover, working in grade 10 appears to harm academic performance. The effect also persists and negatively affects performance one year later.

While the entries in Table 4 show that participation has a statistically significant effect on academic achievement, it is somewhat difficult to assess the magnitude of this effect from the OLS regression results. This is so because the dependent variable is categorical rather than continuous. Hence, OLS may not be the best suited estimation method. To evaluate whether the results are sensitive towards the choice of methodology, the regression specifications described in Table 4 were re-estimated using ordered logit models instead. This methodology is designed to deal with ordered outcomes. Using estimates from such a model, it is possible to calculate the effect of a change in an independent variable on the predicted probability that a certain grade point average is obtained.

The effects for the 1999-2000 school year are reported in Table 5a.[6] In the first column, the effects of participation in school organized activities are shown. They suggest that such participation reduces the probability of having a grade point average below (or increases the probability of having a grade point average above) 80. The magnitudes of these effects are quite large. For instance, the predicted probability of having a grade point average above 90 increases from 0.047 to 0.069, an increase of almost 50 percent. The effects for non-school organized activities show a similar pattern, although the magnitudes are smaller.

The effect of working is presented in column 3. The pattern is the opposite of that shown for school organized activities: working increases the probability of having a grade point average below 80. Although the sizes of the effects are smaller than those for school activities, they are still large. As an illustration, the effect of working reduces by 30 percent the probability of having a grade point average above 90, and it reduces by 16 percent the probability of having a grade point average between 80 and 89. These changes are not negligible, and they are also statistically significant.

The marginal effects from participation on grade point averages in the 2000-01 school year are shown in Table 5b. The effects of participa-

TABLE 5a
The Effect of Participation in Activities on High School Grade Point Averages (GPA) in 1999-2000, with Controls for PISA Test Scores; Marginal Effects from an Ordered Logit Model

	Type of activity		
	School related	Non-school related	Paid or unpaid work
Effect on the probability of having a GPA less than 50 (predicted proportion in this range is 0.003)	-0.002**	-0.001**	0.001**
Effect on the probability of having a GPA 50-59 (predicted proportion in this range is 0.026)	-0.015**	-0.006**	0.007**
Effect on the probability of having a GPA 60-69 (predicted proportion in this range is 0.138)	-0.060**	-0.024**	0.031**
Effect on the probability of having a GPA 70-79 (predicted proportion in this range is 0.440)	-0.044**	-0.019**	0.030**
Effect on the probability of having a GPA 80-89 (predicted proportion in this range is 0.346)	0.099**	0.041**	-0.056**
Effect on the probability of having a GPA 90- (predicted proportion in this range is 0.047)	0.022**	0.009**	-0.013**

Source: The regressions were conducted on the sample presented in Table 1 (cycles 1 and 2, cohort A). Robust t-statistics are presented in parentheses. ** and * signify statistical significance at the 5 percent and 10 percent level, respectively. The regressions also include controls for number of siblings, nuclear family, family income, mother's education, father's education, and provincial dummies. In 1999-2000 most students were in grade 10.

tion in non-work activities are similar to those in Table 5a, although the magnitudes of the effects of school organized activities are somewhat smaller. The effects of working are substantially smaller than those presented in Table 5a, and they are not statistically significant. Hence, similar to the findings in Table 4, they suggest that working is harmful for grade 10 students, but this negative effect does not appear for grade 11 students.

An alternative way to deal with the potential endogeneity of participation in activities is to assume that the unobserved effects – which are possibly correlated with activities – do not change over time. If this assumption holds, we may be able to obtain valid estimates by taking

TABLE 5b
The Effect of Participation in Activities on High School Grade Point Average (GPA) in 2000-01, with Controls for PISA Test Scores; Marginal Effects from an Ordered Logit Model

	Type of activity		
	School related	Non-school related	Paid or unpaid work
Effect on the probability of having a GPA less than 50 (predicted proportion in this range is 0.002)	-0.0015**	-0.0004*	0.0001
Effect on the probability of having a GPA 50-59 (predicted proportion in this range is 0.011)	-0.009**	-0.003**	0.001
Effect on the probability of having a GPA 60-69 (predicted proportion in this range is 0.120)	-0.084**	-0.026**	0.009
Effect on the probability of having a GPA 70-79 (predicted proportion in this range is 0.493)	-0.065**	-0.027**	0.011
Effect on the probability of having a GPA 80-89 (predicted proportion in this range is 0.331)	0.133**	0.047**	-0.017
Effect on the probability of having a GPA 90- (predicted proportion in this range is 0.043)	0.026**	0.010**	-0.004

Source: The regressions were conducted on the sample presented in Table 1 (cycles 1 and 2, cohort A). Robust t-statistics are presented in parentheses. ** and * signify statistical significance at the 5 percent and 10 percent level, respectively. The regressions also include controls for number of siblings, nuclear family, family income, mother's education, father's education, and provincial dummies. In 2000-01 most students were in grade 11.

first differences in order to remove these time-invariant and unobserved individual characteristics. The results are shown in Table 6. The dependent variable is defined as the difference in GPA between the two school years 2000-01 and 1999-2000. This difference is regressed on changes in participation in different activities. Hence, the effects here are identified by those who change their participation status between the two years. From Table 1, it appears as if more students change (increase) their work status than their school activities status. This fact may have an impact on the results, and it is possible that we do not have enough changers for school and non-school activities to consistently estimate the impact of these activities on GPA. The estimates show that participation in school organized activities improves GPA but the effect is not statistically significant (this may be a result of

TABLE 6
Fixed Effects Estimates from a Regression of High School Grade Point Averages (GPA) on Participation in Activities

	Dependent variable *Difference in grade averages*
School related activities	0.016
	(0.79)
Non-school related activities	0.020
	(1.01)
Paid or unpaid work	-0.035*
	(1.78)
Intercept	-0.060
	(5.47)
Sample size	5,754

Source: The regressions were conducted on the sample presented in Table 1 (cycles 1 and 2, cohort A). Robust t-statistics are presented in parentheses. ** and * signify statistical significance at the 5 percent and 10 percent level, respectively.

the relatively few "changers"). However, the effect of working is estimated with precision (it is significant at the 5 percent level for a one-sided alternative) and again indicates that working worsens students' academic performance.

Much of previous research on the effects of working on academic achievement have found that working a few hours per week may be beneficial to academic performance, while working many hours (generally more than 15 hours per week) negatively affects academic outcomes. In Table 7 this issue is examined using a regression specification that includes PISA scores. In the first column the dependent variable of the regression is GPA in 1999-2000, while in the second column the dependent variable is GPA in 2000-01. In 1999-2000 there is a strong and positive relationship between participation in school activities and GPA. Interestingly, the positive effect increases the more hours that are spent on these activities although the increase is small. A similar pattern is found for non-work activities that are not organized by schools, but the magnitudes of the estimates are smaller. Finally, the effects of working show that – contrary to much earlier research – working is never beneficial, not even at very low hours (less than five hours per week). A significant and negative effect appears already for 6-10 hours per week, and the negative effect increases with hours worked. One implication of these findings is that the negative effect associated with working

TABLE 7
Intensity of Activities and High School GPA, with Controls for PISA Test Scores

| | Dependent variable: GPA | | | |
| | School year 1999-2000 | | School year 2000-01 | |
	Estimate	T-stat.	Estimate	T-stat.
School related activities				
Between 1 and 3 hours per week	0.250**	9.35	0.212**	8.16
Between 4 and 7 hours per week	0.278**	8.07	0.354**	11.77
More than 7 hours per week	0.297**	5.59	0.298**	8.78
Non-school related activities				
Between 1 and 3 hours per week	0.109**	3.80	0.105**	3.87
Between 4 and 7 hours per week	0.095**	2.89	0.125**	4.15
More than 7 hours per week	0.115**	2.94	0.084**	2.57
Working				
Between 1 and 5 hours per week	0.007	0.14	-0.031	0.83
Between 6 and 10 hours per week	-0.091**	2.50	-0.030	0.89
Between 11 and 15 hours per week	-0.096**	2.67	0.054	1.60
Between 16 and 20 hours per week	-0.169**	4.31	-0.092**	2.69
More than 20 hours per week	-0.163**	4.78	-0.102**	3.29
Sample size	5,754		5,754	

Source: The regressions were conducted on the sample presented in Table 1 (cycles 1 and 2, cohort A). Robust t-statistics are presented in parentheses. ** and * signify statistical significance at the 5 percent and 10 percent level, respectively. The regressions also include controls for PISA test scores, number of siblings, nuclear family, family income, mother's education, father's education, and provincial dummies. In 1999-2000 most students were in grade 10, while in 2000-01 most students were in grade 11.

arises not only because students who work spend more hours on this activity than students who participate in school activities (a fact that was observed in Table 1); instead, the negative effect appears to be due to the type of activity the students engage in. It seems as if the jobs that students hold do not provide any skills they can use to their benefit in school.

In the 2000-01 school year, the positive effects of non-work activities remain while the negative effects of working are only significant for hours exceeding 15 hours per week. Working less than 15 hours does not significantly affect academic performance. It is, however, important to note that many of the students who work in 2000-01 work many hours per week (79 percent worked more than seven hours per week).

In order to further illustrate the impact of hours of work on high school performance, Table 8 shows the marginal effects from an ordered logit model. For example, working more than 20 hours per week reduces by 36 percent the probability of having a grade point average above 90, and it reduces by 24 percent the probability of having a grade point average between 80 and 89. Again, these changes are not negligible, and they are also statistically significant.

TABLE 8
Intensity of Working and High School GPA, with Controls for PISA Test Scores in 1999-2000; Marginal Effects from an Ordered Logit Model

| | Average hours of work per week | | | | |
	1-5	6-10	11-15	16-20	21-
Effect on the probability of having a GPA less than 50 (proportion in this range is 0.003)	-0.0001	0.001*	0.001**	0.002**	0.002**
Effect on the probability of having a GPA 50-59 (proportion in this range is 0.026)	-0.0005	0.007**	0.008**	0.012**	0.013**
Effect on the probability of having a GPA 60-69 (proportion in this range is 0.138)	-0.002	0.028**	0.034**	0.049**	0.052**
Effect on the probability of having a GPA 70-79 (proportion in this range is 0.440)	-0.002	0.020**	0.024**	0.030**	0.033**
Effect on the probability of having a GPA 80-89 (proportion in this range is 0.346)	0.004	-0.046**	-0.056**	-0.077**	-0.082**
Effect on the probability of having a GPA 90- (proportion in this range is 0.047)	0.001	-0.010**	-0.012**	-0.016**	-0.017**

Source: The regressions were conducted on the sample presented in Table 1 (cycles 1 and 2, cohort A). Robust t-statistics are presented in parentheses. ** and * signify statistical significance at the 5 percent and 10 percent level, respectively. The regressions also include controls for number of siblings, nuclear family, family income, mother's education, father's education, and provincial dummies. In 1999-2000 most students were in grade 10.

Summary

This paper examines the effect on different academic outcomes of participating in different activities during high school. Unlike previous research in this area, which has generally focused on the effects of working while in school, this paper considers both school and non-school related activities and their effects on students' grade point average. It is likely that these activities are endogenously chosen, and the paper considers alternative approaches to deal with this issue. Descriptive statistics show that participation is common: about 75 percent of high school students participate in school and / or non-school related activities. The proportion of high school students who work during the year (not including the summer months June-August) in Canada appears to be similar to those reported in the earlier literature for the United States.

The estimation results suggest that participation in activities, especially working, is endogenously chosen. In the paper, two alternative approaches to deal with the endogeneity problem were suggested and implemented. While each of these alternatives has advantages and disadvantages, they both indicate that participation in school organized activities is beneficial.

Moreover, the two estimation methods both suggest that working while in high school may harm student performance as measured by the grade point average. The negative effect is larger at younger ages. Furthermore, the negative impact increases as hours of work increase. However, contrary to the general impression in the literature, working is never beneficial, not even at very low hours (less than five hours per week). In grade 10 a significant and negative effect appears already for 6-10 hours per week, and the negative effect increases with hours worked. The negative effect associated with working not only arises because students who work spend more hours on this activity than students who participate in school activities; the negative effect may also be due to the type of activity the students engage in. The jobs that students hold are unlikely to provide them with skills they can use to their benefit in their school work.

A number of policy implications can be drawn from the findings in this paper. First, the robust finding that working in grade 10 reduces academic performance suggests that labour laws should be designed so that students are not encouraged to start working at this early age (at least not during the school year). Further, parents and school administrators may want to caution students about the likely negative impact that working may have on their school performance, both in the short run (a lower grade point average) and the long run (lower likelihood of acquiring higher education). Secondly, this paper is one of the first to show the effect on high school grades of participating in non-work activities during the school year. The results suggest that participating in such activities is beneficial and improves academic performance. Thus, a second policy implication is that non-work activities should be encouraged. This could be accomplished by policy measures such as increased government subsidies or tax rebates.

Notes

Financial support from Human Resources and Social Development Canada (HRSDC) is gratefully acknowledged. The views expressed in this paper are those of the author and do not necessarily reflect the opinions of Human Resources and Social Development Canada or the federal government. I am grateful to the editors of this volume for many useful comments on an earlier version of this paper.

1. Stinebrickner and Stinebrickner (2003) use an exogenous job assignment process as an instrument in their study of the effect on academic performance of working while in college.
2. The participation rates were measured during the following two school years: 1999-2000 and 2000-01. Since respondents were 15 years of age in 1999, most students attended grade 10 during the first school year. Similarly, most students attended grade 11 during the second school year.
3. Details on the general properties of the YITS-A database used here are described in chapter 3 of this volume (Motte et al., 2008).
4. Average values of other variables are shown in Table A1 in the appendix.
5. The question refers to average or overall grade during the last year of high school. Thus, if a respondent did not attend high school in 2001, the variable measures the average GPA the year before leaving high school.
6. A full set of parameter estimates and marginal effects is available upon request.

References

Dagenais, M., C. Montmarquette, and N. Viennot-Briot. 2001. "Dropout, School Performance and Working While in School: An Econometric Model with Heterogeneous Groups." CIRANO working paper 2001s-63.

Eckstein, Z., and K.I. Wolpin. 1999. "Why Youths Drop out of High School: The Impact of Preferences, Opportunities, and Abilities." *Econometrica* 67 (6): 1295-339.

Light, A. 1998. "Estimating Returns to Schooling: When Does the Career Begin?" *Economics of Education Review* 17 (1): 31-45.

– 1999. "High School Employment, High School Curriculum, and Post-School Wages." *Economics of Education Review* 18 (1): 291-309.

– 2001. "In-School Work Experience and the Returns to Schooling." *Journal of Labor Economics* 19 (1): 65-93.

Lillydahl, J.H. 1990. "Academic Achievement and Part-Time Employment of High School Students." *Journal of Economic Education* 21 (3): 307-16.

Motte, A., H.T. Qiu, Y. Zhang, and P. Bussière. 2008. "The Youth in Transition Survey: Following Canadian Youth through Time." In *Who Goes? Who Stays? What Matters? Accessing and Persisting in Post-Secondary Education in Canada*, edited by R. Finnie, R.E. Mueller, A. Sweetman, and A. Usher. Montreal and Kingston: McGill-Queen's University Press and School of Policy Studies, Queen's University.

Oettinger, G.S. 1999. "Does High School Employment Affect High School Academic Performance?" *Industrial and Labour Relations Review* 53 (1): 136-51.

Parent, D. 2006. "Work While in High School in Canada: Its Labour Market and Educational Attainment Effects." *Canadian Journal of Economics* 39 (4): 1125-50.

Ruhm, C. 1997. "Is High School Employment Consumption or Investment?" *Journal of Labor Economics* 15 (4): 735-76.

Stinebrickner, R., and T.R. Stinebrickner. 2003. "Working during School and Academic Performance." *Journal of Labor Economics* 21 (2): 473-91.

Tyler, J.H. 2003. "Using State Child Labor Laws to Identify the Effect of School-Year Work on High School Achievement." *Journal of Labor Economics* 21 (2): 381-408.

APPENDIX

TABLE A1
Descriptive Statistics

Variable	Mean
School year 1999-2000	
Grade point average (GPA) 1999-2000	4.201
Proportion with GPA in the 90-100 range	0.092
Proportion with GPA in the 80-89 range	0.329
Proportion with GPA in the 70-79 range	0.339
Proportion with GPA in the 60-69 range	0.176
Proportion with GPA in the 50-59 range	0.055
Proportion with GPA less than 50	0.008
School year 2000-01	
Grade point average (GPA) 2000-01	4.257
Proportion with GPA in the 90-100 range	0.082
Proportion with GPA in the 80-89 range	0.324
Proportion with GPA in the 70-79 range	0.395
Proportion with GPA in the 60-69 range	0.170
Proportion with GPA in the 50-59 range	0.024
Proportion with GPA less than 50	0.004
Number of siblings	1.783
Nuclear family	0.867
Female	0.489
Family income ($1,000)	77.626
Mother's education	
High school	0.303
Some post-secondary education	0.598
Father's education	
High school	0.243
Some post-secondary education	0.630
PISA reading score	551.614
PISA math score	546.233

Source: Calculations are based on survey data extracted from cohort A of the Youth in Transition Survey (YITS), cycles 1 and 2. For details on sample selections, see text. In 1999-2000 most students were in grade 10, while in 2000-01 most students were in grade 11.

Part III
Persistence

8

Is the Glass (or Classroom) Half-Empty or Nearly Full? New Evidence on Persistence in Post-Secondary Education in Canada

ROSS FINNIE AND HANQING THERESA QIU

Cette étude porte sur la persévérance des jeunes Canadiens dans les études post-secondaires (EPS). Nous apportons de nouvelles données sur ce phénomène, recueillies grâce aux résultats de l'Enquête auprès des jeunes en transition (EJET, cohorte B) ; cette enquête permet de suivre les individus participants pendant un certain nombre d'années, à partir du moment où ils entreprennent des EPS. On observe que, sur une période de cinq ans – quand on inclut les étudiants qui ont changé de programme et ceux qui ont repris leurs études après les avoir abandonnées –, le taux de diplômation a augmenté, passant de 56,5 % à 73,1 % (au niveau collégial) et de 52,1 % à 69,4 % (au niveau universitaire). De plus, si l'on ajoute à ces chiffres les données portant sur les jeunes qui sont toujours aux études, on obtient un taux de persévérance encore plus élevé : il est de 82 % (au niveau collégial) et de 89,8 % (au niveau universitaire). Ces résultats permettent donc de voir la question – ou le « problème » – de la persévérance dans les EPS sous une perspective fondamentalement différente.

This paper provides new evidence on persistence in post-secondary education (PSE) in Canada based on the YITS-B dataset, which allows us to track individuals from their point of entry into PSE. Five-year graduation rates are found to rise from 56.5 and 52.1 percent for college students and university students, respectively, to 73.1 and 69.4 percent when program switchers and leavers who subsequently return to school are included. Total persistence rates, which take into account those still in PSE, push the rates to 82 (college) and 89.8 (university) percent. These results thus provide a fundamentally different view of PSE persistence rates – and the "persistence problem."

Who Goes? Who Stays? What Matters? Accessing and Persisting in Post-Secondary Education in Canada, eds. R. Finnie, R.E. Mueller, A. Sweetman, and A. Usher. Montreal and Kingston: McGill-Queen's University Press, Queen's Policy Studies Series. © 2008 The School of Policy Studies, Queen's University at Kingston. All rights reserved.

Introduction

Entering a (first) post-secondary education (PSE) program is just a beginning, and can be followed by many possible outcomes. Some students continue in their initial program until graduation, some at faster or slower rates than others. Other students change to a new program – at the same institution, at another institution of the same level (college, university), or at a different level of study. Still other students abandon their studies, some to return at a later date.

Understanding these pathways is extremely important for a number of reasons. First, for those interested in the accumulation of human capital at the aggregate or macro level, it is *graduation* rates – actual educational attainment – that represent the more important measure, as opposed to *participation* rates, which are typically defined as referring to whether an individual accesses PSE at some point regardless of whether or not this leads to graduation (Ferrer and Riddell, 2001; Turner, 2004).

Secondly, persistence is important for those interested in the effectiveness of the education system in achieving what is perhaps its main objective: taking individuals from entry through to the successful completion of a diploma that will open up new and better lifetime opportunities in a labour market that is increasingly requiring higher education as a basic credential.

Thirdly, those concerned with equal opportunity in PSE will be interested to know what barriers prevent individuals from completing their PSE schooling, especially if these are related to family background or other such socially determined factors. Other reasons for being interested in persistence in PSE could easily be listed.

But despite this importance, relatively little is known from an empirical perspective about persistence in PSE in Canada. The objective of this paper is, therefore, to provide new empirical evidence on persistence in Canada based on Statistics Canada's Youth in Transition Survey, Cohort B (YITS-B), which is uniquely well suited to such a study as it permits us to follow a representative sample of PSE students from their point of entry through their various PSE pathways, including switches across programs, and stopouts that are followed by a return to PSE.

The evidence we present is intriguing and could change our view of PSE in an important way. We find that five-year graduation rates are just 56.5 percent for college students and 52.1 percent for university students when viewed from the perspective of those who complete their first programs. These figures roughly approximate most of the empirical evidence to date based on records of individual colleges and universities that do not take account of individuals who switch institutions, either immediately or when re-entering PSE after taking a break from their studies.

These rates are quite low, and reflect the basic source of the mounting concerns pertaining to persistence in PSE in Canada. But we then show that, when program switchers and leavers who subsequently return to school are included, graduation rates rise to 73.1 percent at the college level and 69.4 percent at the university level. Furthermore, "total" persistence rates, which also take into account those who are still in PSE, are actually 82 percent (college) and 89.8 percent (university). That is, "persistence" rates rise from just over half to not far from what is perhaps the maximum that could reasonably be expected, given that some rate of leaving PSE must be expected among any population of starting students.

While such numbers may change our view of the persistence issue, they do not necessarily imply that persistence is not still an important issue, and we delve into the underlying dynamics in further detail in order to identify the particular pathways taken, the reasons individuals give for switching or leaving their programs, and the ways in which these dynamics vary with individual characteristics, family background, and schooling experiences at the high school and PSE level.

Taken together, this evidence provides a new perspective of persistence in PSE, with important implications for the related policy issues. While we do not think this is anything like the last word on persistence in PSE in Canada, it should put related discussions on a new empirical footing, and perhaps provides a useful starting point for further research on these issues.

Literature Review: The Existing Evidence

The persistence literature can be classified into two parts: that which focuses on overall rates of graduation, switching, and leaving, and that which analyses these patterns by various characteristics of individual students, their situations, and other relevant factors. We discuss each of these literatures in turn.

Overall Persistence Rates

Persistence in PSE – in Canada as elsewhere – is much less studied than access. Because persistence is essentially a dynamic process, its analysis is considerably more demanding in terms of the data requirements, which essentially include the longitudinal tracking of sufficient numbers of students and their (detailed) PSE outcomes (Long, 2005), along with measures of family background, high school and PSE experiences, and other factors to which it is interesting and important to link persistence. General longitudinal databases, including the Survey of Labour Income Dynamics (SLID) in Canada, tend to lack the required sample sizes of students and detailed PSE information, while more specific student-focused longitudinal databases are rare, precisely because of their narrow relevance, making their high costs (longitudinal data are inherently expensive) more difficult to justify.

Principally due to the lack of good data of a more general nature, a significant proportion of the existing studies have focused on persistence at a single institution. They have thus ignored switching across institutions and other related dynamics, and are in any event not representative of any population more than that of the particular institutions studied. The importance of these limitations is indicated by a number of American studies that suggest that many students have relatively complicated PSE pathways that often involve switching across institutions, and that persistence rates do indeed vary by institution.

Using the Beginning Postsecondary Students Longitudinal Study, Choy (2002) reports on the 1994 status of students who started at four-year institutions in the United States in 1989-90. Five years after their initial enrolment, 47 percent had earned a degree at their first institution, 9 percent were still enrolled at that institution, 28 percent had transferred to other institutions, and 16 percent had left PSE completely. Adelman (2006) uses the National Education Longitudinal Study of 1988 to find that nearly 60 percent of all U.S. undergraduates attended more than one institution within 8.5 years of starting (1992-2000).

In Canada, the even more limited persistence literature includes an early article by Gilbert (1991), who collected answers from 47 Canadian universities to the question: "Of full-time university students enrolled for the first time in the fall of 1985, how many graduated at their institution by the summer of 1990?" From the results he estimated an average five-year non-completion rate of 42 percent.[1] This figure is close to the six-year dropout rate of 46 percent for the 1994 cohort reported by the Consortium of Student Retention Data Exchange (CSRDE) for (principally) U.S. colleges and universities (CSRDE, 2001b) as reported in Grayson and Grayson (2003, 7), which also represents an average dropout rate based on information collected from each individual institution and does not take into account switching across institutions.[2] This 46 percent number in turn corresponds to the sum of the switching rates and leaving rates (28 percent plus 16 percent) reported in Choy (2002), leaving the two different sets of results very close in magnitude, although different in nature due to the varying treatment of switchers.

Wong (1994) finds an average first-year dropout rate of 24 percent for 13 Canadian universities, which is moderately higher than the 20 percent first-year dropout rate reported by CSRDE (2001a) for its 1999 cohort (again as reported in Grayson and Grayson, 2003). Combining this with the five-year non-completing rate of 46 percent from Gilbert (1991), it appears that students in Canada are most likely to leave PSE between the first and the second year, after which the probability of leaving decreases substantially.

In a broader study of all students entering Ontario universities to pursue bachelor or first professional degrees from 1980 to 1984, Chen and Oderkirk (1997) find that 68 percent graduated from their initial programs by 1993. (This represents different numbers of years after starting for the different cohorts included in the sample, but most students could reasonably be expected to have finished their studies by this time.) Another 30 percent had not completed their programs in Ontario by 1991 and were not enrolled in any university in Ontario. A very small proportion of the group, 2 percent, had not completed their programs but were still enrolled in an Ontario university. Note that not only is this study restricted to Ontario students (as opposed to generating nation-wide numbers) but it does not follow students who move outside of Ontario.

None of the Canadian studies discussed above explicitly identifies rates of switching across institutions, and Gilbert himself notes that he was unable to distinguish pure leavers from institutional switchers and temporary stopouts (i.e., those who subsequently return to their studies), and putting all these students into one category made it difficult for him to find significant predictors of the observed profiles. Gilbert concludes that "Canadian universities need to conduct longitudinal research on student learning and eventual destinations, which involves tracking students across institutions in the post-secondary system" (Gilbert, 1991, 18).

Who Leaves and Why: Factors That Influence Persistence Decisions

Two well-known theoretical models are broadly used in the persistence literature. The first is Tinto's (1975; 1993) model of "student integration," according to which students enter PSE with various pre-entry characteristics, such as age, race, gender, family structure, parental education attainment, high school preparation, and their own skills and abilities. These factors contribute to the formation of their initial goals and their level of commitment to their studies. Once enrolled, students then begin to have their specific institution-related PSE experiences, which include their level of academic and social engagement and their academic performance. Students' initial goals and commitments are influenced and modified by these post-entry experiences. These various factors are then taken to determine persistence.

The second well-known model in the literature is Bean and Metzer's (1985) "student attrition model." Its main difference from the Tinto model is that it introduces factors external to institutions, such as finances and peer effects. The student integration model also regards academic performance as an indicator (or determinant) of academic integration, while the student attrition model treats PSE experiences as an outcome (Cabrera, Castaneda, Nora, and Hengstler, 1992) on the grounds that, for example, lower grades can be a symptom of students' detachment from school as they begin the process that leads to their leaving.

In summary, these two models posit that persistence decisions are affected by both pre-entry characteristics and post-entry experiences, but they differ in what they include in the latter and their interpretation of some of the related effects.

In the empirical literature, however, there is no consensus on who drops out and why. In their review, Grayson and Grayson (2003) note that "it is difficult to tell if different results of various studies reflect real differences in explanations for attrition or are simply artefacts of different methodologies … it [therefore] makes more sense to examine findings of individual studies in their own right rather than attempting to fabricate generalizations about attrition." This statement of course points to the need for more empirical work, especially if it employs a dataset that is well suited to the relevant estimation issues, is broadly representative, and uses an appropriate methodology.

Again first turning to the richer U.S. literature, Horn (1998) uses the Beginning Postsecondary Students Longitudinal Study data to find that the education attainment of a student's parents is related to persistence, with students whose parents received no education beyond high school being about twice as likely to drop out at the end of the first year as those with parents with a college degree, and this gap is not narrowed in the following years. The U.S. literature also suggests that students who drop out of their PSE studies appear to have been less academically prepared for their studies than those who persist. For example, using survival analysis techniques on a sample of 8,867 undergraduate students at Oregon State University between 1991 and 1996, Murtaugh, Burns, and Schuster (1999) find that dropout rates decrease with high school GPA.

Post-secondary experiences generally found to be important in the (American) literature include students' GPA and academic and social engagement, and other related measures. For example, using administrative records from Virginia Commonwealth University, Wetzel, O'Toole, and Peterson (1999) find that academic and social integration are the most significant factors determining persistence for all freshmen and sophomore students enrolled at this particular urban public university over the years 1989-1992. This said, and as alluded to above, although the relationship between such PSE indicators and PSE persistence is strong, it is difficult to identify the extent to which these relationships are causal: perhaps being less engaged and obtaining lower grades are simply steps on the path to a student's leaving PSE rather than an exogenous determinant of that outcome.

A national level Canadian study based on the Post-Secondary Education Participation Survey (PEPS) found that among students who left PSE prior to completion, half of them cited "lack of interest in their programs or PSE in general" as the reason for dropping out, whereas 29 percent cited "financial considerations" (Barr-Telford et al., 2003), implying that motivation plays a more important role than financial factors with respect to PSE persistence. This is, however, only a descriptive study, and does not control for other factors or probe into the determinants of these different reasons for leaving, including the various factors (e.g., family background) associated with the two models that have driven the American empirical literature.

Taking one step in this direction, Gilbert and Auger (1988) check the first-year persistence rates for students who entered the University of Guelph in the fall of 1986 to find that financial factors appear to play an important role among students with lower socio-economic status (SES), but not with others. They also find that students from relatively higher SES backgrounds tend to switch to other institutions, while low SES students are more likely to stop out.

Grayson and Grayson (2003) in their review of the literature conclude that the few studies that consider financial constraints as a reason for leaving a PSE program show only a weak relationship between finances and leaving PSE.

The literature thus includes a number of interesting pieces of research, but none of them represents a full analysis of PSE pathways, or "persistence," using any sort of representative national level sample. The principal problem has been the unavailability of relevant data. This sets the stage for the present analysis based on the YITS-B.

The Data and Analytical Approach

The data used in this study come from the Youth in Transition Survey, Cohort B (YITS-B) dataset. The YITS-B is a longitudinal survey designed to facilitate the study of the patterns and determinants of major transitions in young people's lives, particularly with respect to education. The major characteristics of the YITS-B are described elsewhere in this volume (Motte et al., 2008), but it is worth noting that in this analysis we use all four available cycles of the YITS-B, including the last interview in 2006.

The sample frame and longitudinal structure of the YITS-B make it well suited to our purposes of tracking young people as they move through their first PSE experiences, and its focus on PSE-related information (among other early transitions) allows the construction of the detailed PSE profiles required for this analysis with relatively little recall bias.

The analysis essentially uses a survival model setup for each of the two principal dynamics studied. The first (and most important) is students' persistence in their first PSE program, which begins with their entry into that program. The possible transitions are graduation, a switch to another program, or leaving PSE (at least temporarily) before graduation.

The second spell / process analysed is the return to PSE among those who leave their first PSE program before graduation (as just defined). The rest of this section is framed principally in terms of the first dynamic (i.e., what happens in the first program) but the methods discussed extend directly to the re-entry problem (as noted in several places).

The reason for using this setup is that it corresponds to the dynamic nature of the behaviour in question and provides an established method for capturing the relevant transitions. In essence, the transitions in the first model represent departures from an individual's continuation on to the completion of a degree. In the second case, the relevant transition captures the rate of returning to PSE among those who leave. Together these two models capture the most important dynamics related to persistence in PSE in a well-structured framework. However, other results presented essentially cut across other pathways to provide an alternative overview of PSE outcomes with respect to overall graduation rates and continued participation in the system.

A second and related reason for using a survival (or hazard) approach is that the data – due to their longitudinal nature – are in many cases censored. This occurs for three reasons. First, some of the relevant spells are still ongoing at the end of the final survey, which corresponds to the

March-April 2006 cycle 4 interview date. The second source of censoring is the attrition of individuals from the YITS-B that occurs across cycles (interviews) – i.e., they are lost from the data because the individuals cannot be found, or are otherwise not successfully interviewed. Thirdly, in some cases the transition information in the data becomes uncertain at a point in time.

As is standard in survival analysis, spells are censored at the point they can no longer be tracked for any of these reasons, but enter the analysis up to the point of censoring, meaning that all the information available in the data is used in the most efficient manner.[3]

The time frame of the analysis is spell time, not calendar time. Individuals enter PSE (and leave) in different calendar years, but we define the beginning time for anybody starting a spell (for each of the two processes considered) as t_0.[4] We then observe individuals after one year, after two years, etc. (t_1 through a maximum of t_5). The analysis is organized around these event-based one-year intervals.

Figure 1 presents the framework graphically. Individuals start their PSE program at time t_0. After one year, they can be classified according to the four possible outcomes at time t_1: "continuer," "graduate," "switcher," and "leaver." For continuers, a solid arrow depicts their progression to the next time period, t_2, since they did not make any of the relevant transitions during the first year. For those who graduate, switch programs, or leave PSE in the first year, a dashed arrow indicates that these individuals are excluded from further analysis of this process since they have made one of the relevant transitions during the first year, thus terminating the spell. The other "pure" censored observations discussed above (i.e., where the spell is still ongoing as of the last interview at the relevant point in spell time, where the individual

FIGURE 1
Conceptual Framework

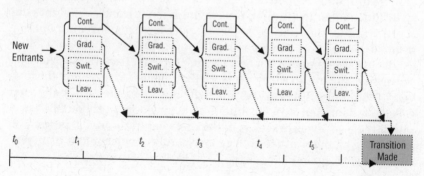

attrites from the sample from one interview to the next, or where there is incomplete information regarding what exactly was happening in terms of the relevant transitions) are also excluded from the point this censoring occurs. This process is repeated in subsequent years.

A similar setup characterizes the re-entry process among leavers, except that the outcomes are simpler: individuals either re-enter or do not (or the spell is censored).

Empirical Findings

Annual Hazard and Cumulative Transition Rates: Persistence in PSE

Table 1 shows the annual hazard (transition) rates for college and university students, respectively, from individuals' point of entry into their first PSE program. The results are broken down by level, college versus university, since the patterns differ substantially, and it is also interesting to observe movements between the two systems.

The calculations shown represent the proportion of students who, during each year of the program (one through five), made each of the relevant transitions, namely that they graduated from the program, switched to a new program, or left PSE. Those who did not make one of these transitions were, by definition, still continuing in the program at the end of the year in question, and these rates are also shown.[5]

Switchers are further differentiated by where they switched to: the same level or (very rarely) a different level in the same institution; or to a different institution, either at the same level or a different one.

For university students (bottom panel), the results show that the first-year "dropout rate" from the point of view of individual institutions – that is, including those who switch to a different institution as well as those who leave PSE entirely – is 14.3 percent. But approximately half of these dropouts, 6.4 percent (if the "don't know" are included) in fact switch to another institution, thus giving a significantly different perspective of the "quit rate" when viewed at the system level rather than from the perspective of a given institution.[6]

Leaving rates among college students (top panel) are higher than for university students in each year (e.g., 12.6 versus 7.9 percent in the first year). Within-institution program switching rates are also higher for college students, but cross-institution switching occurs at about the same rate at the two levels of study: in the first year these are 7.0 percent of all starting students at the college level, and 6.4 percent at the university level (this again includes the "don't know" category).

TABLE 1
Hazard Transition Rates by Year

	Number of Obs.	Continuers (%)	Graduates (%)	Switchers Total (%)	Same Inst. Same level (%)	Same Inst. Diff. level (%)	Diff. Inst. Same level (%)	Diff. Inst. Diff. Level (%)	D.K. (%)	Leavers (%)
College										
Year 1	6,758	62.5	11.7	13.2	5.9	0.4	3.7	1.0	2.3	12.6
Year 2	3,607	48.0	36.8	7.6	3.6	0.3	1.4	0.7	1.7	7.6
Year 3	1,376	32.1	53.2	7.1	1.6	—	3.4	—	1.1	7.5
Year 4	371	37.2	51.0	4.4	1.8	—	—	—	—	7.4
Year 5	99	28.8	53.5	13.9	—	—	—	—	—	3.9
University										
Year 1	4,839	80.9	1.1	10.1	3.0	0.8	3.5	2.0	0.9	7.9
Year 2	3,436	86.2	2.0	7.9	3.4	0.5	1.8	1.3	0.8	3.9
Year 3	2,562	83.4	7.7	5.6	3.5	—	0.5	—	0.9	3.3
Year 4	1,886	47.8	48.5	2.2	1.5	—	0.1	—	0.3	1.5
Year 5	732	31.7	62.6	3.2	1.9	—	—	—	—	2.4

Note: — indicates that results are suppressed to meet the confidentiality requirements of the Statistics Act.

These switchers include 2.8 percent who move from university to college (0.8 percent switching to a different level within a given institution, plus 2.0 percent switching to different level at a different institution), and 1.4 percent who do the reverse. For all the moving between the college and university systems that is sometimes thought to occur, these data suggest that relatively little actually takes place between the beginning of the first year and the beginning of the second, or indeed in any of the subsequent one-year intervals.

One other general finding is that switching and leaving rates are considerably higher in the first year than in the following years, which suggests that dropout rates (from the first PSE program) decline over the course of a program. This decline is greater, and more continuous, among university students, largely because the normal length of their programs tends to be greater.

Graduation rates are, naturally, low in the first year, especially among university students, then rise, sooner for college students (whose programs are generally shorter) than university students.

Table 2 shows the cumulative transition rates by year, which are calculated from the hazard rates shown in Table 1. These take into account those who first continue in their programs but then make a transition in a subsequent year.[7]

The first year rates are by definition the same as those already seen in Table 1, while the second year cumulative rates are of course higher, as the transition rates from the two years are added together, and so on. The five-year dropout rate, defined as including both switchers and leavers (including those who change to a different program in the same institution) is 41.4 percent for college students and 37.5 percent for university students.

But these rates change dramatically when switching is taken into account. For college students they drop from 41.4 to 20.4 percent, or by 50.8 percent in relative terms, and for university students the decline is from 37.5 to 14.9 percent, or a 60 percent reduction. We shall see below how these rates change even further once we take into account those who leave PSE but then graduate from other programs, and those who are still in school in other programs.

Reasons for Switching and Leaving

Table 3 shows the main reasons that individuals who leave their program or switch to another program cite for doing so. These results are reported for the populations of leavers and switchers identified above.

TABLE 2
Cumulative Transition Rates by Year

	Number of Obs.	Continuers (%)	Graduates (%)	Switchers					D.K. (%)	Leavers (%)
				Total (%)	Same Inst.		Diff. Inst.			
					Same level (%)	Diff. level (%)	Same level (%)	Diff. Level (%)		
College										
Year 1	6,758	62.5	11.7	13.2	5.9	0.4	3.7	1.0	2.3	12.6
Year 2	6,758	30.0	34.7	18.0	8.1	0.5	4.5	1.5	3.3	17.3
Year 3	6,758	9.6	50.7	20.1	8.6	0.6	5.6	1.8	3.6	19.5
Year 4	6,758	3.6	55.6	20.5	8.8	0.6	5.7	1.8	3.7	20.3
Year 5	6,758	1.0	57.5	21.0	8.9	0.6	5.7	1.8	4.1	20.4
University										
Year 1	4,839	80.9	1.1	10.1	3.0	0.8	3.5	2.0	0.9	7.9
Year 2	4,839	69.8	2.7	16.5	5.8	1.2	4.9	3.0	1.6	11.1
Year 3	4,839	58.2	8.1	20.4	8.2	1.3	5.3	3.3	2.2	13.4
Year 4	4,839	27.8	36.3	21.7	9.1	1.5	5.3	3.4	2.3	14.2
Year 5	4,839	8.8	53.7	22.6	9.6	1.6	5.5	3.4	2.4	14.9

Note: Calculated from the annual (hazard) transition rates shown in Table 1.

TABLE 3
Main Reason for Leaving

	College			University		
	All (%)	Switcher (%)	Leaver (%)	All (%)	Switcher (%)	Leaver (%)
Number of Obs.		1,971			1,397	
Not enough money	5.9	2.8	9.0	8.5	4.6	15.2
Wanted to work	6.0	2.1	9.9	4.6	2.7	7.8
Marks too low	6.2	3.6	8.8	4.8	4.5	5.3
Didn't like it/not for me	40.5	44.1	37.0	29.1	28.3	30.5
To change schools or programs	17.8	30.4	5.5	29.4	40.5	10.3
"Only missing a few credits, not worth continuing"	2.0	1.1	2.8	—	—	—
Wanted a break	1.8	1.2	2.3	5.5	3.1	9.7
To travel	0.7	—	—	2.2	1.8	2.9
Pregnant/Caring for own child	1.4	—	—	0.9	—	—
Own health	2.3	2.1	2.5	1.7	1.5	2.1
Other	15.4	12.1	18.7	13.0	12.6	13.8

Note: — indicates results are suppressed to meet the confidentiality requirements of the Statistics Act.

In the college sample, "didn't like it/not for me" is by far the most common reason for both switchers (44.1 percent) and leavers (37.0 percent). "To change schools or programs" is the second most common reason for switchers (30.4 percent), for whom it verges on being a meaningless answer but at least does rule out some of the other more specific reasons such as not having enough money. "Not enough money" is, interestingly, cited by just 2.8 percent of switchers and 9.0 percent of leavers. The latter result implies that only 1.8 percent of all those who start a college program leave it because of money problems within their first five years (20.4 percent leave, 9.0 percent of these citing money reasons). Other specific reasons cited by college leavers include "wanted to work" (9.9 percent), and "marks too low" (8.8 percent). Other reasons are less common.

In the university sample, the most common reason for switchers is again "to change schools or programs" (40.5 percent), while 28.3 percent respond "didn't like it/not for me." For leavers, the first and second most important reasons are "didn't like it/not for me" (30.5 percent) and "not enough money" (15.2 percent).[8] The latter number implies that 2.3 percent of all starting university students leave their programs due to funding problems – again a low number, although one that it would nevertheless be desirable to improve upon if effective policy measures could be found to do so, on the grounds that no student should be prevented from continuing in PSE due to financial barriers.

In short, based on what they say, students leave their programs mostly because the schooling is judged not to be the right thing for them or they want to do other things such as work, make a change, or take a break. This group would presumably include those who simply did not see the value of the schooling.

Only 8.8 percent of college leavers and 5.3 percent of university leavers say they left because their marks were too low. Of course this reason – as the others – must be seen in the perspective of the self-report nature of this variable. The true "objective" reasons for leaving and switching may differ from what students say.

How Many Return to PSE after Leaving

Table 4 shows the cumulative rates of returning to PSE among students who left their first program (as identified above) and did not immediately switch to another program. These are derived from the underlying annual hazard rates, which are not shown here.[9]

By one year after first having left school, 22.3 percent of college leavers and 35.6 percent of university leavers have returned to PSE. By three years after leaving (the furthest we can measure with sufficient precision in these data), the returns stand at 40.3 percent and 54.0 percent, respectively, for college and university leavers. These are substantial numbers.

The cumulative rates further indicate that again after three years, just under one-quarter (12.5 percent of the leavers, or 23.1 percent of the 54 percent total who return) of the university returners go back to the same institution (and same level) as their initial (first) program. Another 12.1 percent (22.5 percent of those who return) stay at the same level (i.e., university) but change institutions, 16.7 percent (30.9 percent of the returners) change both level and institution, and 2.4 percent (4.4 percent of the returners) change levels within the same institution.

For college leavers the distributions of where they return are roughly similar, although more change institutions while staying at the same level, and fewer change levels.

194 *Ross Finnie and Hanqing Theresa Qiu*

TABLE 4
Cumulative Rates of Return to PSE among Leavers

	Number of Obs.		Total (%)	Same Inst.		Diff. Inst.		D.K (%)
				Same level (%)	Diff. level (%)	Same level (%)	Diff. level (%)	
College								
Year 1	1,168	Percentage	22.3	5.6	1.1	6.6	3.7	5.2
		Distribution	100.0	25.2	5.0	29.5	16.8	23.6
Year 2	1,168	Percentage	33.2	8.4	1.2	9.7	5.7	8.2
		Distribution	100.0	25.3	3.6	29.3	17.0	24.7
Year 3	1,168	Percentage	40.3	10.1	1.4	11.3	6.9	10.7
		Distribution	100.0	25.0	3.4	28.1	17.1	26.5
University								
Year 1	596	Percentage	35.6	10.4	2.1	8.8	8.7	5.6
		Distribution	100.0	29.1	6.0	24.6	24.5	15.8
Year 2	596	Percentage	48.9	11.8	2.1	12.0	13.5	9.4
		Distribution	100.0	24.2	4.4	24.6	27.6	19.3
Year 3	596	Percentage	54.0	12.5	2.4	12.1	16.7	10.3
		Distribution	100.0	23.1	4.4	22.5	30.9	19.1

Notes: — indicates results are suppressed to meet the confidentiality requirements of the Statistics Act. Results for year 4 and year 5 are omitted due to small sample sizes.

Overall Persistence and Total Graduation Rates

The overall graduation rates shown in Table 5 extend the definition of "persistence" to a more general level to include graduates not just from the first program as seen previously (Table 2), but also those switchers and leavers who go on to graduate from another program that they start either immediately (switchers) or after first being out of PSE (leavers who then return).

Taking these students into account, five-year graduation rates rise from 56.5 percent to 73.1 percent for college students and from 52.1 percent to 69.4 percent for university students.[10] The "persistence" problem as defined with respect to graduation rates is thus seen to be significantly diminished when we track individuals as they move to new programs in different institutions – and new levels of study – rather than being confined to the records of students within a given institution.

Table 6 extends the persistence analysis still further by looking at the status of students at the end of each year after they first enter PSE, categorizing them as (in order) either 1) graduates from the first program, 2) graduates from any other program, 3) still in PSE, or 4) none of the above – i.e., those who are no longer in PSE and left without obtaining a diploma. This table essentially adds those still in PSE to the graduates reported in Table 5, including showing where exactly the ongoing students are enrolled.[11]

After five years, for students who started in a college program, 73.1 percent had graduated, 8.8 percent were still enrolled in PSE, and 18.0 percent were not in PSE (without having earned a degree). For university students, 69.4 percent had earned a degree, 20.4 percent were still in PSE, and just 10.2 percent had left PSE without a degree.

Students still in PSE are further categorized into those in the same (first) program, those in a new program at the same institution (same or different level of study – most are in the former for obvious reasons), and those in a program at a different institution, at the same or different level as the original program. As time passes, fewer students are in the same (first) program and greater numbers become graduates, transfer to another program, or leave PSE.

The summary numbers here are very important. Persistence rates at the university level rise from 52.1 percent to 69.4 percent to 89.8 percent as we add graduates from other programs and those still in PSE (wherever they are enrolled) to those who finish their first programs. Seen the other way around, dropout rates decline to a fraction of their initial level when the broader perspective is adopted. For college students, the comparable persistence rates are 56.5, 73.1, and 81.9 percent.

TABLE 5
Cumulative Total Graduation Rates

		Number of Obs.	Total (%)	Same Prog. (%)	Same Inst. Same level (%)	Same Inst. Diff. level (%)	Diff. Inst. Same level (%)	Diff. Inst. Diff. level (%)	D.K. (%)
College									
Year 1	Percentage	6,758	12.0	11.7	—	—	—	—	—
	Distribution		100.0	97.8	—	—	—	—	—
Year 2	Percentage	6,758	36.9	34.4	1.0	—	0.3	—	1.0
	Distribution		100.0	93.2	2.7	—	0.9	—	2.7
Year 3	Percentage	6,758	57.0	50.1	2.5	0.3	1.8	0.1	2.2
	Distribution		100.0	88.0	4.4	0.5	3.1	0.2	3.9
Year 4	Percentage	6,758	66.2	54.7	3.9	0.3	3.5	0.4	3.4
	Distribution		100.0	82.6	5.9	0.5	5.3	0.6	5.2
Year 5	Percentage	6,758	73.1	56.5	4.9	0.3	5.2	1.8	4.4
	Distribution		100.0	77.3	6.8	0.5	7.0	2.4	6.0
University									
Year 1	Percentage	4,839	1.1	1.1	—	—	—	—	—
	Distribution		100.0	94.1	—	—	—	—	—
Year 2	Percentage	4,839	3.6	2.7	—	—	—	0.4	0.5
	Distribution		100.0	72.8	—	—	—	10.5	12.9
Year 3	Percentage	4,839	11.2	8.1	0.3	—	—	1.2	1.2
	Distribution		100.0	71.9	2.4	—	—	10.9	10.5
Year 4	Percentage	4,839	45.0	35.5	2.3	0.5	1.7	3.0	1.9
	Distribution		100.0	78.9	5.2	1.2	3.8	6.7	4.3
Year 5	Percentage	4,839	69.4	52.1	4.9	1.1	4.4	4.6	2.3
	Distribution		100.0	75.1	7.0	1.6	6.4	6.6	3.3

Note: — indicates that results are suppressed to meet the confidentiality requirements of the Statistics Act.

TABLE 6
Overall Persistence Rates

	Number of Obs.		Graduate (%)	Still in PSE Total (%)	Same Prog. (%)	Still in PSE Same Inst. Same level (%)	Still in PSE Same Inst. Diff. level (%)	Still in PSE Diff. Inst. Same level (%)	Still in PSE Diff. Inst. Diff. level (%)	D.K. (%)	Not in PSE (%)
College											
Year 1	6,758	Percentage	12.0	75.2	62.5	5.6	0.3	3.6	1.1	2.0	12.9
	6,758	Distribution	100.0	100.0	83.1	7.5	0.4	4.8	1.4	2.7	100.0
Year 2	6,758	Percentage	36.9	45.8	29.3	6.3	0.5	5.0	1.6	3.0	17.3
	6,758	Distribution	100.0	100.0	64.1	13.8	1.0	10.9	3.6	6.6	100.0
Year 3	6,758	Percentage	57.0	25.1	9.3	5.1	0.3	5.1	2.8	2.6	17.9
	6,758	Distribution	100.0	100.0	36.9	20.4	1.2	20.3	11.0	10.1	100.0
Year 4	6,758	Percentage	66.2	14.8	3.2	2.4	0.2	3.7	3.3	1.9	19.0
	6,758	Distribution	100.0	100.0	21.8	16.0	1.5	25.1	22.6	12.8	100.0
Year 5	6,758	Percentage	73.1	8.8	1.0	1.6	0.1	2.2	2.7	1.2	18.0
	6,758	Distribution	100.0	100.0	11.4	18.4	0.9	25.3	30.0	14.0	100.0
University											
Year 1	4,839	Percentage	1.1	91.0	80.9	2.8	0.8	3.6	2.0	0.9	7.9
	4,839	Distribution	100.0	100.0	88.9	3.1	0.9	3.9	2.2	1.0	100.0
Year 2	4,839	Percentage	3.6	86.7	69.3	5.9	1.1	5.2	3.7	1.6	9.6
	4,839	Distribution	100.0	100.0	79.9	6.8	1.3	5.9	4.2	1.9	100.0
Year 3	4,839	Percentage	11.2	78.8	57.0	8.4	1.0	6.3	4.4	1.7	9.9
	4,839	Distribution	100.0	100.0	72.4	10.6	1.3	8.0	5.6	2.1	100.0
Year 4	4,839	Percentage	45.0	45.2	26.7	7.2	1.1	5.8	3.3	1.1	9.8
	4,839	Distribution	100.0	100.0	59.2	16.0	2.4	12.9	7.3	2.3	100.0
Year 5	4,839	Percentage	69.4	20.4	8.0	4.9	0.5	3.5	2.4	1.1	10.2
	4,839	Distribution	100.0	100.0	39.1	24.2	2.5	17.1	11.8	5.3	100.0

Note: At the end of each year, students are categorized in a sequential manner into three groups: Graduate from a PSE program, Still in PSE, and Not in PSE. Students who are still in PSE are further categorized into the six groups shown.

Transition Rates by Sample Characteristics

Table 1 presented results for first-program transition rates for all students at each level (college and university) taken together. Table 7 extends this analysis by showing cumulative transition rates for the first five years by a number of variables representing individual student characteristics, family background, and schooling experiences.[12]

It should be kept in mind that these are simple two-way relationships, which are liable to change in some cases when a multivariate perspective is adopted. The latter is not shown here, but may be found in Finnie and Qiu (2008), and some of the more important cases where the two sets of results diverge are mentioned here so that the reader is not left with a potentially misleading impression of the relationships in question.

Men tend to have higher leaving rates than women during the first year at both the university level (17.0 percent versus 13.2 percent) and the college level (23.1 percent versus 17.9 percent), although the results remain significant in the regression framework only at the university level. This means that not only do women enter university at higher rates than men (see, for example, Finnie and Mueller, 2008), but they are also more likely to continue in their studies. Final graduation rates will, therefore, be skewed in terms of gender even further than the access rates that we often rely upon as indicators of PSE achievement would indicate.

Immigrants and visible minorities appear to be slightly more likely to leave PSE from their first programs than others at the college level, while the differences run strongly in the other direction among university students. These results seem to be related to other factors, however, because only the lower leaving rates among university level visible minorities hold up in the multivariate analysis.

The most dramatic result by age is that university students who start their programs at age 21 or above have a leaving rate of 45.2 percent by the five year mark, which is almost three times the rate of the next closest group (those who start at age 20). The pattern is in the same direction but not as strong for college students.

In the college sample, individuals who study in Quebec or British Columbia are more likely to switch: by the five year mark, their rates are 29.0 percent in Quebec and 25.6 percent in B.C., versus (for example) 14.3 percent in Ontario. These patterns are presumably at least partly driven by the CEGEP system in Quebec (as individuals move into the university system) and the university transfer system in B.C., where students who seek a university degree can spend the first two years in a college and then switch to a university to continue their studies.

TABLE 7
Five-Year Cumulative Transition Rates by Individual Characteristics

	College (5 yrs)				University (5 yrs)			
	Cont. (%)	Grad. (%)	Swit. (%)	Leave (%)	Cont. (%)	Grad. (%)	Swit. (%)	Leave (%)
Number of Obs.		6,758				4,839		
All Respondents	1.0	57.5	21.0	20.4	8.8	53.7	22.6	14.9
Gender								
Male	1.3	53.6	22.0	23.1	11.1	49.7	22.2	17.0
Female	0.8	61.1	20.2	17.9	6.8	57.2	22.8	13.2
Immigrant Status								
Immigrant	3.2	48.2	24.7	23.8	15.0	54.3	21.0	9.8
Non-Immigrant	0.9	58.2	20.8	20.2	8.0	53.6	22.9	15.6
Visible Minority Status								
Visible Minority	1.7	50.0	25.5	22.8	14.6	55.4	20.6	9.4
Others	1.0	58.4	20.5	20.1	7.6	53.3	23.1	16.1
Age at Enrolment								
Below 18	1.5	60.1	28.3	10.1	27.2	50.3	14.0	8.5
18	0.9	54.9	25.1	19.1	11.5	46.7	26.6	15.2
19	0.6	57.9	14.8	26.7	6.7	60.6	19.9	12.7
20	1.8	55.1	14.9	28.2	7.6	54.3	22.0	16.1
Above 20	0.0	61.0	11.8	27.2	7.1	26.8	20.9	45.2
PSE Region								
Atlantic	0.9	66.7	8.4	24.0	7.1	49.8	27.9	15.2
Quebec	1.0	55.0	29.0	14.9	7.0	76.2	13.1	3.8
Ontario	1.0	57.8	14.3	26.9	7.3	62.4	19.2	11.2
Prairies	0.6	66.2	11.2	22.0	9.2	42.3	27.8	20.8
B.C.	2.5	52.0	25.6	19.9	14.5	42.6	22.8	20.1
Family Type								
Two Parents	1.0	60.2	19.9	18.9	8.0	54.4	23.4	14.2
Single Parent	1.1	47.3	26.6	25.0	15.7	50.2	15.7	18.5
Other	0.0	41.4	14.9	43.6	2.7	48.1	28.4	20.8
Parental Education								
Below HS	1.8	55.1	17.5	25.7	16.9	45.8	18.4	18.8
HS Completed	0.5	55.7	19.6	24.2	8.2	50.2	25.8	15.8
Coll. Completed	1.1	59.3	20.9	18.6	6.9	52.2	24.3	16.6
Univ. Completed	1.0	58.0	24.4	16.6	9.3	56.2	21.3	13.2

... continued

TABLE 7
(Continued)

	College (5 yrs)				University (5 yrs)			
	Cont. (%)	Grad. (%)	Swit. (%)	Leave (%)	Cont. (%)	Grad. (%)	Swit. (%)	Leave (%)
Average Grade in High School								
Below 60%	1.4	64.1	14.0	20.5	0.0	29.1	35.5	35.4
60%-69%	2.2	47.4	19.0	31.5	15.0	26.3	26.4	32.3
70%-79%	1.0	54.3	21.2	23.5	10.2	40.4	27.6	21.8
80% or Above	0.6	65.8	22.1	11.6	8.1	61.1	20.2	10.6
Average Grade in PSE								
Below 60%	1.9	4.9	43.3	49.9	9.8	27.4	31.6	31.2
60%-69%	1.6	28.8	33.6	36.1	10.9	37.9	28.7	22.5
70%-79%	0.6	56.5	22.4	20.5	8.4	58.5	20.0	13.1
80% or Above	1.3	78.7	11.6	8.4	8.2	67.7	17.1	7.0
Scholarship in First Year								
Yes	0.9	63.8	21.4	14.0	7.3	62.1	19.4	11.2
No	1.1	56.6	20.9	21.4	10.7	44.6	25.9	18.8
Grant in First Year								
Yes	0.0	67.8	16.8	15.4	7.1	54.2	24.1	14.6
No	1.1	56.7	21.5	20.7	9.4	53.6	22.0	15.0
Student Loan in First Year								
Yes	0.4	59.5	18.8	21.4	10.8	50.0	22.6	16.6
No	1.3	57.1	22.1	19.4	8.0	55.3	22.5	14.2
Instructors Have Strong Teaching Ability								
None	0.7	42.7	23.6	33.1	14.2	37.3	31.5	17.0
Some	0.3	52.7	26.4	20.7	10.6	54.3	21.7	13.4
Most	1.3	61.6	19.3	17.8	6.8	58.7	20.4	14.1
Student Has Trouble Keeping up with the Workload (First Year)								
Never	0.9	65.3	18.0	15.8	7.9	61.1	19.6	11.4
Sometime	1.1	52.9	21.8	24.2	8.2	54.3	22.9	14.6
Most of the Time	2.1	34.7	34.2	29.0	13.8	39.6	26.7	19.9
There Are People at School to Talk to (First Year)								
Disagree	0.3	49.5	19.8	30.3	11.5	41.8	28.5	18.3
Agree	1.2	59.7	20.9	18.1	8.3	56.7	20.9	14.1
The First Year Helped Student Obtain Skills (First Year)								
Disagree	0.7	37.4	32.0	29.9	10.1	49.3	24.0	16.6
Agree	1.2	64.7	16.9	17.2	8.2	57.1	21.1	13.6

Among university students, leaving rates rise from Ontario (11.2 percent) through Atlantic Canada (15.2 percent) to the Prairie Provinces (20.8 percent) and British Columbia (20.1 percent), and this general pattern holds in the regression analysis as well. Switching rates, however, go roughly in the opposite direction (e.g., lowest in Ontario, higher elsewhere).[13]

In the college sample, individuals from single parent families tend to have substantially higher switching and leaving rates than students from two parent families, and these results hold in the regression analysis. In the university sample, students from single parent families still have higher leaving rates but also lower switching rates, and only the latter holds when other factors are taken into account.

The data show a negative relationship between leaving rates and parental educational attainment for college students, and once again this relationship holds with the multivariate analysis. The positive relationship between switching rates and parental educational attainment is weaker and not so robust. In the university sample, however, again we find a substantially weaker pattern, and again only the differences in switching rates hold in the regression analysis.

Thus, while it is often alleged that family background – as represented by family type and parental education here – plays an important role in persistence patterns, as it does in access rates (see, for example, Finnie and Mueller, 2008), this appears to be the case much more strongly for college students than those at the university level when looking at persistence. This might be largely related to selection effects: once students are selected into the university system, further background effects are nullified because they are an especially talented, accomplished group who have overcome the barriers that often prevent others of their type from making this start, and are therefore able to overcome any additional challenges they may face as they advance through their studies. College students from less advantaged families may, on the other hand, be more "at the margin" even as they go through their studies because the selection process into college is not as strong as for university.

Five-year cumulative switching and leaving rates are negatively related to high school grades in the university sample, but the patterns – especially the leaving rates – are not so clear in the college sample. The patterns are stronger and more uniform for PSE grades, and the multivariate analysis – not surprisingly – indicates PSE grades dominate high school grades in terms of predicting persistence. This said, PSE grades in particular might be endogenous to quitting or switching. Seen alternatively, these different sets of results might point to the pathways of effects: doing better in high school leads to doing better in

PSE, which is related to increased persistence rates. Disentangling these relationships would be an interesting path for further research.

College and university students who report they received a scholarship in their first year appear to be generally less likely to leave, and the same is true for college students who report receiving a grant; students who report receiving a student loan are, conversely, marginally more likely to leave. But most of these effects – excepting the lower leaving rates among college level grant recipients – disappear in the multivariate analysis framework, indicating that these financial aid variables are related to students' other characteristics, including grades.

A number of variables pertaining to the student's first year PSE experiences are available in the YITS-B, these including the student's opinion of the instructors' ability, the student's ability to keep up with the workload, the student's communication with his or her peers, and how much the student thinks useful skills were obtained from the program. The results point to a strong set of relationships between switching and leaving rates and these variables at the college level, and these continue to hold in the regression analysis. Interestingly – and like the family background effects – the relationships are weaker, and mostly become statistically insignificant in the regression analysis, in the case of university students.

Conclusion

This paper has provided new and unique empirical evidence on PSE pathways in Canada based on the Youth in Transition Survey, Cohort B ("YITS-B") database, which has allowed us to track a representative sample of PSE college and university students on a longitudinal basis from their point of entry into PSE. This is the first time this has been done for Canada.

Our analysis has shown that many individuals follow what might be referred to as "non-traditional" pathways, which include switching programs, taking breaks, and otherwise moving in and out of PSE as they work their way through their studies. This evidence stands in clear contrast to previous Canadian studies, which have mostly been based on institution-level data which, by construction, lose track of students when they leave the particular college or university in question. The present research also goes well beyond the small number of other studies where slightly broader tracking has been attempted but only for very limited populations.

Persistence rates are found to be much higher when viewed from this broader perspective. We find, for example, that 25.8 percent of college students and 18.0 percent of university students leave their first PSE program by the end of the first year, but more than half of these switch immediately to another program, and many of those who do leave PSE return to the system in the next few years.

And thus graduation rates are higher, more general persistence rates which include those individuals still in PSE are higher still, and quit rates are much lower than has been found in previous studies – even as these results are consistent with earlier findings to the degree that relatively direct comparisons can be made (e.g., the number who leave their first program at a given institution).

This is not to say that there is no need to be concerned about persistence in PSE. Many individuals may struggle through programs they do not like, others may make changes that turn out not to be good for them, and the reasons for switching and leaving might point to specific problems that could and should be addressed.

Picking up on these ideas, we also provide an analysis of the reasons that students switch and leave; of where exactly students go when they change programs or where they re-enter the system after leaving PSE entirely during their first program; and of the patterns of switching and leaving by a range of personal characteristics, family background, and schooling experience variables.

We do not consider this research to represent anything like the last word on PSE persistence in Canada. On the contrary, it perhaps provides more of a new starting point for further work than anything else – but this new start is one that is based on a fundamentally improved understanding of overall persistence rates, of the dynamics underlying these rates (switching, leaving, returning), of the reasons underlying these patterns, and how they are related to individual characteristics, family background, and schooling experiences.

It will, therefore, be for further research to drill into these relationships more deeply – to probe some of the dynamics in further detail, to identify further associations of interest, to tease out the relevant causal relationships using advanced statistical methods and a good understanding of the institutional settings underlying the observed outcomes, and to otherwise advance our understanding of PSE persistence in Canada.

Such research could be based on the YITS-B dataset used here; on the (younger) YITS-A database as that cohort moves through the PSE system, perhaps taking particular advantage of the even richer set of background variables it has available; on other survey data; on administrative data, including the Postsecondary Student Information System (PSIS) being built at Statistics Canada; on qualitative analyses, which can probe the reasons for students' behaviour in a way that quantitative data cannot; and other methods.

The present work we hope has established a useful starting point for such future investigations while providing, in the meantime, a new empirical basis for ongoing discussions of PSE persistence in Canada.

Notes

This research was financed by the Canada Millennium Scholarship Foundation through the MESA project. The authors gratefully acknowledge the comments received from Christine Neill and other participants at a special MESA session at the 2008 Canadian Economics Association Meetings in Halifax and from Clément Lemellin and others at the MESA conference held in Montreal in October 2007, as well as a set of written comments based on a close read of a later draft of the paper by Rick Mueller and additional comments from Alex Usher. This paper is derived from Finnie and Qiu (2008).

1. The non-completion rate is defined as 100 percent minus the average completion rates from these Canadian PSE institutions.
2. The Consortium for Student Retention Data Exchange (CSRDE) is a cooperative group of colleges and universities that collect and analyze retention and graduation data for institutional benchmarking purposes. These data are analyzed for first-time full-time degree seeking freshmen by the Center for Institutional Data Exchange and Analysis (C-IDEA) at the University of Oklahoma. Data is then made available to the 421 consortium members (including some Canadian universities along with the great majority of American universities) to use for benchmarking with their peers for their internal academic planning purposes.
3. The results presented here reflect our preferred treatment of the data, regarding which further discussion and other ancillary results may be found in Finnie and Qiu (2008).
4. Thus t_0 is mapped to different calendar years for different cohorts. For example, t_0 is mapped to the year 1997 for cohort-1997, to the year 1998 for cohort-1998, and so on.
5. For each year, these rates are calculated for those students who had not yet made a transition by the relevant year and who were not censored in the current year or in a previous one, thus corresponding to the standard hazard analysis methodology.
6. The "don't know" category includes students who have missing values in key variables, such as institution code and/or level of study.
7. These are calculated by adding the first year rates plus the second year rates applied to the proportion of students who had not made a transition in the first year and thus continued forward, plus the third year rates applied to the proportion of the initial population that had still not made a transition, and so on.

8. The proportion citing money reasons is lower in first year, when other reasons are relatively more important, and higher in later years.
9. In Finnie and Qiu (2008), we also analyse the two sets of dynamics (transition from the first program and returning to school) using logit and multinomial logit (multivariate) approaches.
10. The graduation rates from the first program shown here are very close to but not exactly the same as those shown earlier. This is due to a slight shift in the means of making the relevant calculations required when estimating the two different sets of persistence rates.
11. To make these calculations, we continue to use a hazard approach by following students for the period of time they can be followed, meaning we have data on more students for year one, fewer for year two, fewer again for year three, and so on.
12. These rates are calculated from the single year hazard rates for years one through five.
13. The university sample includes very few students from Quebec because most individuals in that province start their PSE careers at the college level, i.e., in a CEGEP.

References

Adelman, C. 2006. "The Toolbox Revisited: Paths to Degree Completion from High School through College." Washington, D.C.: U.S. Department of Education.

Barr-Telford, L., F. Cartwright, S. Prasil, and K. Shimmons. 2003. "Access, Persistence and Financing: First Results from the Postsecondary Education Participation Survey (PEPS)." Statistics Canada, Education Skills and Learning – Research Papers No. 81-595-MIE – No. 7.

Bean, J., and B. Metzer. 1985. "A Conceptual Model of Nontraditional Undergraduate Students Attrition." *Review of Educational Research* 55 (4): 485–540.

Chen, E., and J. Oderkirk 1997. "Varied Pathways: The Undergraduate Experience in Ontario." *Education Quarterly Review* 4 (3), 47-62.

Choy, S.P. 2002. "Access and Persistence: Findings from 10 Years of Longitudinal Research on Students." American Council on Education, Center for Policy Analysis.

CSRDE. 2001a. "First Year Retention Rate: 1999 First-Time Freshman Cohort." Norman: University of Oklahoma.

CSRDE. 2001b. "Six Year Graduation Rate: 1994 First-Time Freshman Cohort." Norman: University of Oklahoma.

Day, K. 2008. "A Tangled Web: The Relationship between Persistence and Financial Aid." In *Who Goes? Who Stays? What Matters? Accessing and Persisting in Post-Secondary Education in Canada,* edited by R. Finnie, R.E. Mueller, A. Sweetman, and A. Usher. Montreal and Kingston: McGill-Queen's University Press and School of Policy Studies, Queen's University.

Ferrer, A.M. and W.C Riddell 2001. "Sheepskin Effects and the Return to Education." In *Towards Evidence-Based Policy for Canadian Education*, edited by P. de Broucker and A. Sweetman. Kingston, Ont.: Queen's University, John Deutsch Institute for the Study of Economic Policy; and Ottawa: Statistics Canada, in cooperation with McGill-Queen's University Press, 423-45.

Finnie, R., and R.E. Mueller. 2008. "The Backgrounds of Canadian Youth and Access to Post-Secondary Education: New Evidence from the Youth in Transition Survey." In *Who Goes? Who Stays? What Matters? Accessing and Persisting in Post-Secondary Education in Canada*, edited by R. Finnie, R.E. Mueller, A. Sweetman, and A. Usher. Montreal and Kingston: McGill-Queen's University Press and School of Policy Studies, Queen's University.

Finnie, R., and H. Qiu. 2008. "The Patterns of Persistence in Post-Secondary Education in Canada: Evidence from the YITS-B Dataset." MESA Research Paper Series, also a forthcoming Statistics Canada Analytical Studies Research Paper.

Gilbert, S.N. 1991. "Attrition in Canadian Universities." Ottawa: Commission of Inquiry on Canadian University Education.

Gilbert, S.N., F.T Evers, and M. Auger 1989. "University Attrition Differentiated: Rates and Institution Influences." Guelph: University of Guelph.

Grayson, J.P., and K. Grayson. 2003. "Research on Retention and Attrition." Millennium Research Series No. 6 (online): Canada Millennium Scholarship Foundation.

Horn, L. 1998. "Stopouts or Stayouts? Undergraduates Who Leave College in Their First Year." (NCES 1999-087). Washington, D.C.: U.S. Department of Education, National Center for Education Statistics, U.S. Government Printing Office.

Long, B.T. 2005. "Contributions from the Field of Economics to the Study of College Access and Success." Harvard Graduate School of Education Working Paper.

Motte, A., H.T. Qiu, Y. Zhang, and P. Bussière. 2008. "The Youth in Transition Survey: Following Canadian Youth through Time." In *Who Goes? Who Stays? What Matters? Accessing and Persisting in Post-Secondary Education in Canada*, edited by R. Finnie, R.E. Mueller, A. Sweetman, and A. Usher. Montreal and Kingston: McGill-Queen's University Press and School of Policy Studies, Queen's University.

Murtaugh, P.A., L.D. Burns, and J. Schuster. 1999. "Predicting the Retention of University Students." *Research in Higher Education* 40 (3): 355-71.

Turner, S.E. 2004. "Going to College and Finishing College: Explaining Different Educational Outcomes." In *College Choices: The Economics of Where to Go, When to Go, and How to Pay for It*, edited by Caroline M. Hoxby, 13-61. Chicago: University of Chicago Press.

Tinto, V. 1975. "Dropout from Higher Education: A Theoretical Synthesis of Recent Research." *Review of Education Research* 45 (1): 89-125.

– 1993. *Leaving College.* Chicago: University of Chicago Press.

Wong, P. 1994. "Student Retention/Attrition at Trent: A Preliminary Report." Peterborough: Trent University.

Wetzel, J.N., D. O'Toole, and S. Peterson. 1999. "Factors Affecting Student Retention Probabilities: A Case Study." *Journal of Economics and Finance* 23 (1): 45-55.

Youth in Transition Survey, 18-20 Year-Old Cohort, Cycle 1, User Guide, May 30, 2003. Human Resources Development Canada.

9

Transitions and Adjustments in Students' Post-Secondary Education

FELICE MARTINELLO

Des études montrent que seulement 50 % à 60 % des étudiants canadiens terminent le premier programme d'études postsecondaires qu'ils ont choisi. Parmi ceux qui ne le terminent pas, certains abandonnent leurs études, mais la plupart se dirigent vers un deuxième programme, de même niveau ou de niveau inférieur ; plusieurs obtiennent alors un diplôme d'études post-secondaires grâce à cet autre programme. Dans cet article, je présente d'abord des données portant sur ces passages d'un programme à un autre chez les étudiants de niveau universitaire et de niveau collégial. Ensuite, grâce à des analyses de régression, j'évalue les corrélats des décisions d'abandonner un premier programme, de s'inscrire (ou non) à un deuxième programme ou de choisir un programme de niveau inférieur. Cela me permet de conclure que les résultats scolaires au niveau secondaire et les moyens utilisés pour financer les études sont en étroite corrélation avec les différents passages ; par contre, les caractéristiques parentales ne sont reliées qu'aux changements que font les étudiants après leur premier programme.

Only 50 to 60 percent of Canadian students complete their first post-secondary program. Some drop out, but most switch to a second program at the same or lower level, and many obtain a post-secondary credential in their second program. This paper documents these transitions for university and college/CEGEP students, and uses regression analysis to estimate correlates of students' decisions to leave their first program, attempt a second program, and/or switch to a lower level. High school grades and methods of financing education are highly correlated with the transitions, while parents' characteristics are only related to adjustments after the first program.

Who Goes? Who Stays? What Matters? Accessing and Persisting in Post-Secondary Education in Canada, eds. R. Finnie, R.E. Mueller, A. Sweetman, and A. Usher. Montreal and Kingston: McGill-Queen's University Press, Queen's Policy Studies Series. © 2008 The School of Policy Studies, Queen's University at Kingston. All rights reserved.

Introduction

Students learn a lot more than the course material when they attend post-secondary education (PSE). They learn about their abilities and preferences at that level of schooling, the course requirements in their programs and others and the likelihood of completing them, and the employment opportunities enabled by various programs and whether that is what they want to do after school. After starting PSE, students use this information to adjust their plans and decisions. They may change their major, institution, level of study, or even leave PSE entirely. Alternatively, they may decide that their current program is still their best choice and continue on to graduation. Even after graduation students use the information gathered to decide whether to pursue another PSE program and, if so, the type of program.

This study examines the adjustments that students make during their PSE programs. A longitudinal sample from the Youth in Transition Survey Cohort B (YITS-B) is used to document the proportions who do not complete their first PSE program, transfer to other types of institutions, switch to programs at higher or lower levels, or leave PSE. Some limited evidence is also presented in this study for the proportions of students who change their major field of study within their first program – another type of adjustment. Regression analysis is then used to estimate correlates of students' decisions to: (a) stop their first program without graduating, (b) attempt a second program (given they did not complete their first), and (c) attempt their second program at the same level as their first or switch to a lower level.[1] Potential correlates include students' personal, family, and high school characteristics; high school achievement; loans for financing PSE; and choice of major in the first program. Separate analyses are done for students who start bachelor's level programs at universities and students who start two or more year programs in colleges or CEGEPs.[2]

The analysis shows that around 30 percent of college/CEGEP and university students attempted second PSE programs without completing their first, and around three-quarters of those tried again at the same level and type of institution. Most of the others switched to lower level programs. The success rates in second programs were higher for students who changed to a program at a different level, regardless of whether it was higher or lower.

The regression estimates show that the types of funding used for PSE were related to many of the first program outcomes and second program decisions. The major field of study in first programs was unrelated to any of the outcomes or decisions for college/CEGEP students, but among the university students, undecided and science students were much less likely to complete their first programs. The effect of first program major did not persist, however, and it was unrelated to the likelihood of attempting a second program or another at its level. Part-time study at university exhibited the same pattern in that part-time university students were less likely to complete their first program, but there was no relation to their subsequent decisions. As for parents' characteristics, students with more educated parents were more likely to attempt second programs if they did not complete their first, but most of the other outcomes and other parental characteristics showed insignificant estimates. High school and personal characteristics showed mixed results in the regression analysis, but it is notable that gender was very important for college or CEGEP students' decisions but not for university students. Finally, regional or provincial differences were generally estimated to be unimportant, although Alberta and B.C. exhibited some differences, likely due to the closer integration of their college and university systems.

Conceptual Model

Comay, Melnik, and Pollatschek (1973) provide the underlying model for the analysis. They specify education as a dynamic, multi-stage process operating under uncertainty. High school graduates decide to enrol in a specific program at a specific institution if they expect the benefits (monetary, non-monetary, and consumption) to outweigh the costs (again, monetary, non-monetary, and consumption). Expected rather than actual costs and benefits are compared because there is uncertainty about:

- the actual requirements and contents of the courses in that and other alternative programs;
- students' abilities: i.e., their ability to progress through and ultimately complete their program or other possible alternative programs;
- how much students will like their program as compared to alternative programs;
- the nature of the personal and social experiences at that institution as compared to other institutions and how much students will enjoy or dislike attending that institution;
- the labour market outcomes enabled by that program and other alternative programs. These include earnings as well as other characteristics of the career and occupation such as job safety, flexibility, prestige, etc.;

- the alternative labour market outcomes that result from not doing PSE. Again, these include earnings and other characteristics of the career and occupation;
- the costs of education and students' abilities to finance them;
- new alternatives (e.g., previously unknown programs) that may become available during the students' PSE.

Students gain more information about all of these uncertainties after starting their post-secondary education. They also suffer unexpected shocks in all these areas. Thus, at each stage and even after graduating or dropping out, students re-weigh expected costs and benefits, given the information available, to decide whether to acquire more education within the same program or some alternative program or to stop education.

Some students find, in the midst of their first post-secondary program, that their original decision turned out to be a poor one. They may become academically ineligible for their program or continuing may no longer be their first choice. Their new best feasible alternative may be another PSE program, and so they transfer to that other program, institution, or level of study and persist in their post-secondary education. Alternatively, their new best feasible alternative may be to cease post-secondary education and do other things such as paid work in the labour market or unpaid work in the home. Anything increasing the likelihood that another PSE program is their best alternative (e.g., by reducing the costs of transferring to alternative programs) increases the likelihood of students persisting in their post-secondary education.

To keep the analysis simple, some of the temporal aspects of the underlying model are assumed away. How long students persist in their first program and whether they spend time outside of PSE between their first and second PSE programs are not considered. Students still make a sequence of decisions over time, but the timing is collapsed so that students choose a discrete first PSE program and then a discrete second PSE program, if there is one.

Survey of the Literature

There is a large, mainly American literature examining students' progress through their PSE. One area of the literature adopts the approach of Comay et al. (1973) and explicitly models the sequence of decisions that students make over time.[3] Students in these models are allowed to update and change their education decisions as they accumulate more information over the course of their PSE. These studies explicitly model and estimate students' decisions over whether to attend PSE, how long to attend, the quality of the school chosen, major field of study, and whether to interrupt PSE and then re-enrol.

Another area of the literature contains purely empirical studies of student decisions and switches in PSE. American studies such as Adelman (2006), Grubb (1989), and Cabrera, Burkum, and La Nasa (2005) use longitudinal data on individual students to examine their persistence in PSE, degree completion, changes of major, and transfers across institutions. Choy (2002) surveys the findings of three other studies of U.S. high school and PSE students, and Simpson (1987) tracks changes in students' major fields of study at a very detailed level using data from a large American university.

In this work one must distinguish between studies that concentrate on one institution and studies that follow students' decisions across institutions. The former count a transfer to another institution as a dropout, thereby overstating the attrition rate and understating the amount of adjustment (switching) that students do in their PSE. Of the studies cited above, only Simpson (1987) is of the former type. Another complication arises because some U.S. studies include the progression or transfer from two-year to four-year colleges. This sort of progression occurs in Canada (more so in the western provinces) but not nearly as often as in the United States. Thus U.S data often show more transfers across institutions than comparable Canadian data.

Most Canadian contributions to this area of the literature focus on program completion, and there is much less work on changes in major, level of study, or following transfers across institutions. An important reason for this difference is that before the YITS survey there were no Canadian longitudinal surveys of students' activities equivalent to those available for U.S. students. But some Canadian studies do report evidence on these issues, and they are noted below, including Finnie and Qui (2008), who examine students' program changes as one element of a more general analysis of students' trajectories after entering post-secondary education.

Gilbert (1991) uses data provided by several Canadian universities on students who enrolled full time in the fall of 1985. He reports that the percentage of students who did not complete a degree program within five years of starting university (i.e., the five-year non-completion rate) was 42 percent and increasing, mainly due to increases in the time required for degree completion. Gilbert (1991) uses more limited data to estimate that 10 percent of the initial cohort transferred to another institution.

Gilbert and Auger (1988) follow students entering the University of Guelph in 1986 for two years. After two semesters, 76 percent of the initial cohort were continuing their university studies at Guelph. The 24 percent who quit their studies at Guelph (i.e., the leavers) were split evenly between voluntary leavers and those required to withdraw. A telephone survey of the leavers estimated that 67 percent of them transferred to other institutions, 38 percent re-enrolled at Guelph or another PSE institution after spending some time out of PSE, and only 13 percent left PSE completely.

Shaienks, Eisl-Culkin, and Bussière (2006) examine education and transition to work from the mid-1990s to 2003 using three cycles of the YITS-B survey. This is a follow-up to Zeman, Knighton, and Bussière (2004) who do similar analysis using cycles 1 and 2. The studies report students' completion, dropout, and re-enrolment rates for high school and PSE. They also show full- and part-time labour market participation rates. Shaienks et al. (2006) report that nearly half of PSE dropouts returned within the period of the survey, often to a different institution.

Lambert, Zeman, et al. (2004) is a similar study, using the first two cycles of YITS-B, but with more analysis of the characteristics of leavers and why they left. After two cycles approximately 15 percent of PSE students left without completing their program. This is very close to the 15.7 percent that can be calculated from Shaienks et al. (2006). By far the most common reasons for leaving are "did not like it/not for me" and "wanted to change programs." Only 11 percent of leavers cited financial concerns, 7 percent left because they wanted to work, and 6 percent preferred to rest or travel. The authors note that many leavers will return to PSE.

Chen and Oderkirk (1997) use data from the University Student Information System (USIS) on students entering Ontario universities between 1980 and 1984 to estimate completion rates and time to degree. The data follow transfers across Ontario universities, but transfers to colleges or other provinces are classified as leavers. By 1993 (i.e., after eight to 12 years) 68 percent had graduated from a university in Ontario, 2 percent were continuers, and 30 percent had not graduated and were not continuing. Of the leavers, 51 percent left after one year, 19 percent after two years, 10 percent after three years, and 20 percent after four years.

Butlin (2000) uses data on 22- to 24-year-old Canadian youths from the 1995 School Leavers Followup Survey to run logistic regressions on the probability of dropping out of PSE versus the probability of graduating or continuing in PSE. Transfers across institutions are followed, and separate regressions are estimated for university and college/ CEGEP students. Demographic and socio-economic regressors were mostly insignificant for university students while mostly significant for college/CEGEP students. The estimated regional effects were very large, and some variables covering experiences in high school or elementary school (e.g., low grades, problems with science, failed a grade in elementary school) were positively related to the probability of dropping out for both college/CEGEP and university students.

In summary, in contrast to the substantial literature examining students' progress through PSE using the large longitudinal datasets available for U.S. students, much less work has been done in Canada, mainly due to limited data. However, the development of the YITS, along with other datasets such as the Expanded Student Information Survey (ESIS) which extends the USIS, and the Post-Secondary Education Participation Survey (PEPS), has enabled rapid recent growth in the literature. This paper contributes to the Canadian literature by reporting the proportions of students who do not complete their first post-secondary program, transfer to different types of institutions, or switch to programs at higher or lower levels. In addition, it reports estimates of the correlates of students' decisions to not complete their first program, attempt (or not) a second program, and switch to a lower level program. Finally, university and college/CEGEP students are analysed separately, something previously done only by Butlin (2000) and Finnie and Qui (2008).

Data

Data on students' PSE programs, 1995 to 2003, are taken from the first three cycles of the Youth in Transition Survey Cohort B (YITS-B). Respondents must appear in all three cycles to be included, and respondents are excluded if the PSE program reported in one cycle is declared ineligible in a later cycle. The rules for declaring programs ineligible are complex, but generally ineligibility occurs when respondents contradict or refuse to confirm program information that was given in the previous cycle. The data are also restricted to students who either graduated from or left their first PSE program within the time frame of the survey. If the outcome of a student's first program is not known (i.e., he/she is classed as a first program continuer by the end of the third YITS-B cycle), then he/she is excluded from the sample. All observations are weighted by the population weights provided in the survey.

Students' PSE programs are the basic unit of observation and analysis. YITS-B defines students' first post-secondary program as their first formal education above the high school level; towards a diploma, certificate or degree; and requiring three months or more to complete. A new (second) program is recorded if students enrol in another institution, change their level of study (e.g., from a bachelor's level to a diploma or certificate), change to a program with a different name (e.g., from a bachelor of arts to a bachelor of education or science), or interrupt their studies and the interview occurs during the interruption.

It is important to note that, if students change their major field of study, e.g., from economics to philosophy, but the program retains the same name (e.g., both are bachelor of arts programs), then they are not deemed to have changed their program. Similarly, if students change from full- to part-time study (or vice versa) or change the level of study within a YITS-B category, they are not deemed to have changed their program. Examples of this latter type of change include transfers from a three-year to a two-year college diploma program, or from a pass/general type university program to an honours program with more required courses and higher minimum grades.

YITS-B also asked students whether they changed their major field of study in each program. Unfortunately the question was only asked for programs started in that cycle, so the variable undercounts the true number of changes. The results from this question are still reported, however, because although the numbers of changes are understated, the rates of change reported by different groups of students can be compared and significant differences identified.

A major complication arises from the Quebec CEGEP system. Under this system, students generally complete two years of CEGEP (in an academic stream) before entering university, and their time in CEGEP is considered a valid post-secondary program in the YITS survey. Thus, most first PSE programs in Quebec are classified as college/CEGEP according to YITS-B.[4] In contrast, students in other provinces usually enter university directly after high school. Correspondingly, YITS shows that, outside of Quebec, many students (usually well over 50 percent) have first PSE programs at universities. The proportion of Quebec students attending universities in their second program is within the range shown for first programs outside of Quebec; thus the PSE programs of Quebec university students are lagged one program compared to students in other provinces in the YITS.

The following adjustment is done to include Quebec students in the sample of students whose first program is bachelor's level at a university. All students whose first post-secondary program: (a) was in a Quebec college or CEGEP, (b) had an expected length of two years, and (c) was classified as college/CEGEP level (around 80 percent of the cases) or a university transfer program (around 20 percent of cases) have their programs moved forward by one so that their second program is re-classified as their first and their third is re-classified as their second. Then the analysis is restricted to students whose first program (given the adjustment) is bachelor's level at a university. Table 2 shows that the adjustment is only partially successful, and Quebec students are still underrepresented in the sample of first program bachelor's students.

No adjustment for the CEGEP system is required for students en-rolled in three-year (or more) first programs at colleges or CEGEPs, but an adjustment is required for those in two-year programs. This group includes large numbers of Quebec students who are in the academic stream and ultimately headed for university. But the observations from other provinces are a different group: namely, students enrolled in two-year college level programs after completing high school. A rough so-lution is to remove all students enrolled in two-year college/CEGEP first programs in Quebec. Thus the college/CEGEP sample analysed below contains students whose first PSE program was in a college or CEGEP, with an expected length of two or more years of full time study, but Quebec college/CEGEP students in two-year programs are excluded.

It is important to emphasize that although lengths of programs are used to discriminate between different sorts of college programs, the analysis below does not follow cohorts over each year of their studies. Once students have been selected into the sample, the number of years they spend in or between their PSE programs is ignored. See Finnie and Qui (2008) for a study that explicitly examines students' PSE choices and outcomes over each year of their programs.

The sample started with 12,101 students enrolled in PSE programs with expected lengths between two and five and a half years. Of those, only 9,019 were interviewed in all three cycles, and only 5,584 of those had resolved first programs. Of that 5,584, 2,333 chose bachelor's pro-grams at universities for their first program (including 191 Quebec stu-dents who had their second program renamed as their first). Deletion of 152 ineligible programs left a final sample of 2,181 university bach-elor's students. The remaining 2,530 (of the 5,584) were college/CEGEP students in two or more year programs. Deletion of 118 students with ineligible programs and 602 two-year Quebec college/CEGEP students left a final sample of 1,810 college/CEGEP students.

Although some definitions have been given above, it is helpful to reiterate that a leaver is a student who stops his/her program before it is completed and does not enrol in another PSE program within the time frame of the YITS-B survey. A changer or switcher is a student who stops his/her first PSE program before completion and enrols in another (second) PSE program. The second program can be started immediately after the first or after a period of time out of PSE. If the most recent information from the survey reports that a student has neither left nor completed his/her program, then that student is called a continuer (i.e., presumably continuing in the program), and the program is considered unresolved. Conversely, a student's program is said to be resolved if its outcome is known and the student either completed or left the program.

Documenting the Flows

Students in Bachelor's Level Programs in Universities

Figure 1 shows outcomes for students whose first PSE program was bachelor's level at a university. Of those with resolved first programs, 60 percent graduated, while 40 percent left or changed their program within the time frame of the survey. Recall that YITS under-reports the number of changes of major, but as the under-reporting occurs in a systematic way, rates across different groups of students can be compared. Not surprisingly, leavers/changers were more likely to change their major field of study. Figure 1 shows that 18.2 percent of leavers/changers changed their major as compared to 11 percent of students who completed their bachelor's program, and the difference is statistically significant.

Only 8.7 percent of the initial university students left their first program without graduating and stopped post-secondary education entirely (i.e., they did not attempt a second program) during the time frame of the sample. This low percentage occurs because more than three-quarters (78.3 percent) of the leavers/changers enrolled in a second PSE program. Of that group, almost a third subsequently graduated, 42.5 percent were continuing, and 25.2 percent left without completing their second program.

The second program outcomes imply that 70.1 percent (60.0 plus 10.1) of all initial bachelor's students were able to complete a PSE program within the YITS-B survey time frame, and 10.1 of those percentage points resulted from students' second programs. Another 13.3 percent were continuing in their second program, and only 16.6 percent (8.7 plus 7.9) of all initial bachelor's students left without a PSE credential after two program attempts. Some of those students will retry PSE by attempting a third program, but that analysis is left for future work.

FIGURE 1
Outcomes for Bachelor's Level First Programs in Universities (Continuers Excluded)

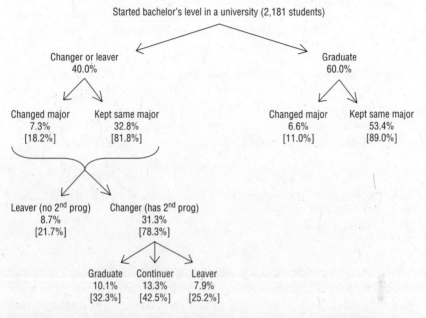

Notes: The upper number is the percentage of all 2,181 students in this category. Square brackets show the percentage of students in the category immediately above. Note that changes of major are under-reported in the YITS.
Source: Author's compilation.

Figure 2 shows the destinations and outcomes for bachelor's students who pursued second programs after not completing their first. Most attempted second programs at the same level and type of institution. namely, another bachelor's program at a university. It would be interesting to examine how many students changed institutions or simply changed programs within their original institution, but large numbers of missing institution codes make this problematic. Figure 2 shows that 72.1 percent of changers started a second program at the bachelor's level or above, with almost all of these at the bachelor's level. The few "above bachelor's" programs include some professional programs (e.g., students starting law school after their second undergraduate year and before completing their first degree). The rest are classified as "graduate level diploma or certificate programs above bachelors and below masters" by YITS.

FIGURE 2
Second Program Destinations and Outcomes: Bachelor's Level Students Who Stopped Their Program Before Completion

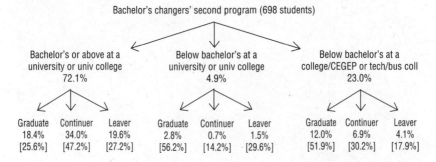

Bachelor's changers' second program (698 students)

| Bachelor's or above at a university or univ college 72.1% | Below bachelor's at a university or univ college 4.9% | Below bachelor's at a college/CEGEP or tech/bus coll 23.0% |

Graduate	Continuer	Leaver	Graduate	Continuer	Leaver	Graduate	Continuer	Leaver
18.4%	34.0%	19.6%	2.8%	0.7%	1.5%	12.0%	6.9%	4.1%
[25.6%]	[47.2%]	[27.2%]	[56.2%]	[14.2%]	[29.6%]	[51.9%]	[30.2%]	[17.9%]

Notes: The upper number is the percentage of all 698 students in this category. Square brackets show the percentage of students in the category immediately above.
Source: Author's compilation.

Less than 5 percent of the changers switched to certificate or diploma programs at universities or university colleges, and most of these were at universities. The remaining 23 percent of changers transferred to a college, CEGEP, or public trade, technical, or vocational institute, with most enrolling in college-level programs at colleges or CEGEPs.

Figure 2 shows that transfers to second programs provide a non-trivial source of PSE graduates. Of first program changers, 18.4 percent completed bachelor's degrees (or higher) in their second program, and another 34 percent were continuing. In addition, 14.8 percent (2.8 plus 12.0) of first program changers completed other PSE programs (below bachelor's level), with another 7.6 percent (0.7 plus 6.9) continuing.

The larger percentage completing bachelor's (or higher) second programs was due to the large number of students who chose another bachelor's program and not to their success rate. In fact, students were much more successful in their second programs if they switched to programs below the bachelor's level. Comparing success rates is difficult because of the different proportions of continuers in each stream. One solution is to ignore the continuers and compare "grad/leaver rates," which equal the percentage of graduates among those with resolved programs (i.e., 100 times the number of graduates divided by the number of graduates plus leavers). The grad/leaver rate for below bachelor's second programs was 72.5 percent, compared to 48.5 percent for second programs at the bachelor's level or above, and the difference was statistically significant using a Wald test.

Students in College/CEGEP Programs of Two or More Years

Figure 3 shows outcomes for students whose first program was two or more years in a college or CEGEP. Of those with resolved programs, 53 percent graduated while 47 percent left or changed their program. This is a lower graduation rate than for university bachelor's students, and the difference is statistically significant.

As with university students, first program leavers or changers at the college level were significantly more likely to change their major than were graduates. Very few (2 percent) college graduates reported changing their major, and their rate was significantly lower than that reported by university graduates.

In addition to being less likely than university students to complete their first program, college students were discouraged from PSE more easily. Of the college students who did not complete their first program,

FIGURE 3
Outcomes for Two or More Year First Programs in a College or CEGEP (Continuers Excluded)

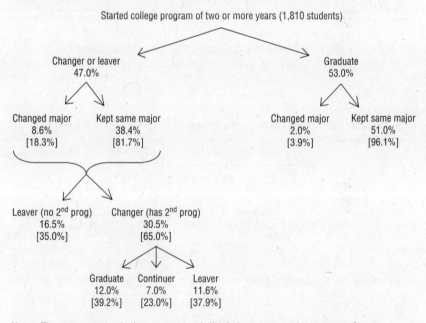

Notes: The upper number is the percentage of all 1,810 students in this category. Square brackets show the percentage of students in the category immediately above. Note that changes of major are underreported in the YITS.

Source: Author's compilation.

35.0 percent did not attempt a second during the time frame of the sample. This compares to 21.7 percent for university students, and the difference is statistically significant. Out of the 65.0 percent of college leavers/changers who did attempt a second program, 39.2 percent subsequently graduated, 23.0 percent were continuing, and 37.9 percent left without completing their second program. Overall, 65.0 percent (53.0 plus 12.0) of all initial college/CEGEP students completed a post-secondary program, with 12.0 of those percentage points coming in second program attempts. Another 7.0 percent were continuing their second program, and some second program leavers will attempt third programs.

Figure 4 reports the destinations and outcomes for students who pursued a second program after not completing their first. College/CEGEP students are similar to university students in that most (72.1 percent) attempted second programs at the same level and type of institution as the first. The percentage is slightly higher than for university changers, but it rounds to the same number. In the college changers group, 9.3 percent transferred to bachelor's level programs at universities or university colleges, but almost all were at universities. Another 4.3 percent started second programs below bachelor's level at universities or university colleges, and again most of these were at universities. The remaining 14.2 percent transferred to technical, trade, or vocational institutes or private business colleges, and their programs were split fairly evenly between college level programs and certificates/diplomas/

FIGURE 4
Second Program Destinations and Outcomes: College/CEGEP Students Who Stopped Their Program before Completion

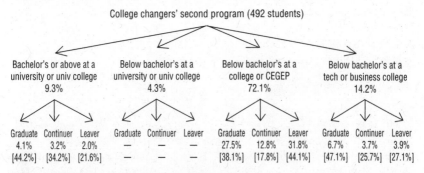

Notes: The upper number is the percentage of all 492 students in this category. Square brackets show the percentage of students in the category immediately above. — indicates suppressed to maintain confidentiality.

Source: Author's compilation.

licences from private business schools, training institutes, or professional associations in business or finance.

As for outcomes, 4.1 percent of college changers completed a bachelor's degree, and another 3.2 percent were continuing in bachelor's programs. The outcomes for second programs below bachelor's at a university or university college are suppressed because there are too few observations in one of the cells to meet Statistics Canada's confidentiality requirements. However, one can still conclude that more than 34.2 percent (27.5 plus 6.7) of college changers completed a PSE credential below bachelor's level, with more than 16.5 percent (12.8 plus 3.7) continuing. Thus, second programs also provided a non-trivial source of PSE graduates for initial college/CEGEP students.

College changers attempting second college programs had a grad/leaver rate of 46.4 percent, and they were less successful in their second programs than those who transferred to a bachelor's program. Their grad/leaver rate was 67.2 percent, but the difference is only significant at the 5.2 percent level due to the small numbers who switched to bachelor's programs. This differs from university changers who had better success if they transferred to a college or CEGEP rather than a second program at the bachelor's level. College changers who started a second program at a technical, trade, or vocational institute or private business college also had a much higher grad/leaver rate (63.5 percent) than those re-trying in college or CEGEP, but the difference was not statistically significant.

To recap this section, Figures 1 to 4 show that around 30 percent of initial PSE students switched to second programs (as defined by YITS) before they completed their first, and those second programs provided a significant source of PSE credentials. Almost three-quarters of the students who switched programs tried again at the same level and type of institution. Most of the others switched to lower level programs, but all who switched to different level programs (higher or lower) enjoyed higher average success rates in their second programs.

Correlates of Student Decisions

Students in Bachelor's Level Programs in Universities

Three probit regressions are estimated. The first includes all students whose first program was bachelor's level at a university, and its dependent variable equals one if the student graduated from that first program and zero if he/she did not. The second regression is restricted to students who discovered, ex post, that their first program decision was not a good one, and so did not complete their first program. Its dependent variable equals one if the student attempted a second program and zero if he/she did not pursue any more PSE over the YITS survey period. The third is restricted to students who, after stopping their first PSE program, attempted a second. Its dependent variable equals one if the second program was also at the bachelor's level and zero if it was below bachelor's level, regardless of the type of institution where the second program was taken.

The regressions are estimated independently even though the three decisions are clearly interdependent, with many aspects decided simultaneously rather than sequentially. The three binary choices specified, however, capture the essence of the students' decisions and simplify the econometrics and interpretations of the estimates enormously.

Table 1 provides definitions of the variables used in the regression analysis, while Table 2 reports means and standard deviations for the full samples. The right hand side variables are typical of those specified in PSE persistence or completion studies. They include students' personal characteristics (gender, urban/rural, mother tongue, province/region), their parents' characteristics (highest level of education, PSE important to them, number and type of parents in the home during high school), and high school variables (average grades, attended a private high school, did co-op, took a break between high school and PSE). The effect of student aid and PSE financing is an important topic in the literature, so a dummy variable is included to show whether the student received a government-sponsored student loan. Another dummy variable indicates whether the student received a bank loan, a line of credit, or a loan from parents or other family members. The last financing dummy variable indicates whether the student received funds that did not have to be repaid from a partner, a family member, or other people. As most of the funds in this category come from partners and family, it is referred to as family funding with no repayment. Note that this last category does not include other non-repayable funds such as grants, bursaries, scholarships, or other awards. Finally, students' decisions about their major, changing their major, part-time study, and moving out of their parents' home are also included as possible correlates.

Table 3 reports estimates of the marginal effects of the right hand side variables for the three probits. Rather than considering each equation separately, it is more instructive to look at the estimates for each right hand side variable across the three regressions. Starting at the bottom of Table 3, students' province or region was uncorrelated with completion of their first program or attempts at a second. But among

TABLE 1
Right Hand Side Variables Used in the Regression Analysis

Personal Characteristics
male   male
rural   gave rural address
other mother tongue   French or English is not the first language learned

Characteristics of High School
private HS   attended private high school for at least one year
did co-op in HS   took a work experience course in high school
HS grade average   average grade in last year of high school in tens
took break before PSE   interrupted schooling for at least 12 months after end of high school

Characteristics of Parents
parents' highest educ   index of the highest level of education achieved by either parent
PSE important to parents   index of how important PSE is to parents. Four increasing categories.
had one or no parents   lived with only one or fewer parents in high school
two parents, but step   lived with two parents in high school, but not both biological

Decisions during First PSE Program
moved out   permanently moved out of parents' home before end of first PSE program
part time   was a part time student for some portion of their first PSE program
changed major   changed their major field of study in their first PSE program

PSE Financing
family funding,   received funds for PSE from partners, parents, or other people during
   no repayment   first PSE program that did not have to be repaid
student loan   received a government sponsored student loan during first PSE program
other loan   received a loan from a bank, a line of credit, or from parents or other
                                 family members during first PSE program

Major Field of Study (agriculture, recreation, health, transportation are omitted categories)
humanities major   majored in humanities, education, fine arts, comm. in first PSE program
social science major   majored in social, behavioural sciences or law in first PSE program
business major   majored in business management or public admin in first PSE program
science major   majored in math, science, engineering, architecture in first PSE program
undecided major   was undecided, did not have a major field of study in first PSE program

Province or Region of Institution of First Program (Ontario is the omitted province/region)
Atlantic   Newfoundland, PEI, Nova Scotia, New Brunswick
Quebec   Quebec
Manitoba, Saskatchewan   Manitoba or Saskatchewan
Alberta   Alberta
British Columbia   British Columbia

Source: Author's compilation.

TABLE 2
Means and Standard Deviations, Full Samples

	First program is bachelor's level at a university		First program is two or more years in college or CEGEP	
	mean	standard deviation	mean	standard deviation
male	0.4438	0.0193	0.4825	0.0214
rural	0.1580	0.0127	0.2339	0.0148
other mother tongue	0.1311	0.0132	0.0800	0.0142
private HS	0.0922	0.0103	0.0925	0.0126
did co-op in HS	0.2241	0.0170	0.2967	0.0209
HS grade average	8.4341	0.0241	7.8105	0.0323
took break before PSE	0.1083	0.0121	0.2164	0.0184
parents' highest educ	7.6144	0.0951	6.2165	0.1250
PSE important to parents	3.8041	0.0213	3.6900	0.0301
had one or no parents	0.1113	0.0126	0.1758	0.0163
two parents, but step	0.0676	0.0094	0.0886	0.0149
moved out	0.3895	0.0191	0.2585	0.0179
part time	0.0523	0.0076	0.0741	0.0131
changed major	0.1185	0.0112	0.0970	0.0117
family funding, no repayment	0.8101	0.0148	0.6814	0.0207
student loan	0.3868	0.0186	0.3917	0.0209
other loan	0.2604	0.0168	0.1511	0.0140
humanities major	0.1517	0.0134	0.1362	0.0147
social science major	0.2012	0.0152	0.0852	0.0122
business major	0.1145	0.0127	0.1694	0.0164
science major	0.3167	0.0181	0.2286	0.0174
undecided major	0.1258	0.0114	0.2467	0.0190
rec, agric, health major	0.0901	0.0121	0.1339	0.0138
Atlantic	0.1493	0.0094	0.0404	0.0047
Quebec	0.1128	0.0114	0.4114	0.0211
Ontario	0.4424	0.0199	0.4013	0.0215
Manitoba, Saskatchewan	0.0920	0.0074	0.0253	0.0040
Alberta	0.0938	0.0118	0.0679	0.0089
British Columbia	0.0973	0.0105	0.0506	0.0089

Source: Author's compilation.

TABLE 3
Probit Estimates of Marginal Effects: Bachelor's Students in University

Sample:	First program is bachelor's level at a university	Left/changed first program	Took a second PSE program
Dependent variable:	1 = Grad from 1st prog 0 = Left/changed 1st prog	1 = Did 2nd prog 0 = No 2nd prog	1 = 2nd prog at bach level 0 = 2nd prog below bach
male	-0.0462 (-1.23)	-0.0431 (-0.99)	-0.0225 (-0.39)
rural	-0.0663 (-1.10)	-0.0993 (-1.34)	-0.1428** (-1.97)
other mother tongue	0.0476 (0.81)	0.0907* (1.76)	0.1842** (2.98)
private HS	0.0362 (0.63)	0.0852* (1.81)	0.1546** (2.11)
did co-op in HS	-0.0578 (-1.24)	0.0700* (1.66)	-0.0550 (-0.83)
HS grade average	0.1274** (5.00)	0.1066** (3.78)	0.1659** (4.32)
took break before PSE	-0.0004 (-0.01)	-0.1089 (-1.56)	-0.0452 (-0.51)
parents' highest educ	0.0036 (0.52)	0.0173** (2.17)	0.0068 (0.67)
PSE important to parents	-0.0035 (-0.12)	0.0629* (1.77)	-0.0800 (-1.50)
had one or no parents	0.0527 (0.96)	0.0237 (0.45)	-0.0688 (-0.74)
two parents, but step	-0.2367** (-3.25)	-0.0332 (-0.45)	0.0667 (0.75)
moved out	0.1189** (3.11)	-0.1069** (-2.04)	0.0857 (1.45)
part time	-0.2228** (-2.87)	-0.0455 (-0.51)	0.0082 (0.09)
changed major	-0.0831 (-1.45)	0.0595 (1.35)	0.0980 (1.39)
family funding, no repayment	0.1674** (3.42)	-0.0826** (-2.23)	0.1556** (2.13)
student loan	0.0981** (2.37)	0.0343 (0.88)	0.0438 (0.72)
other loan	0.0073 (0.17)	0.0055 (0.12)	-0.0118 (-0.18)

... continued

TABLE 3
(Continued)

Sample:	First program is bachelor's level at a university	Left/changed first program	Took a second PSE program
Dependent variable:	1 = Grad from 1st prog 0 = Left/changed 1st prog	1 = Did 2nd prog 0 = No 2nd prog	1 = 2nd prog at bach level 0 = 2nd prog below bach
humanities major	-0.1337* (-1.73)	-0.0996 (-0.90)	0.1187 (1.06)
social science major	-0.1347* (-1.74)	-0.0666 (-0.68)	0.0451 (0.38)
business major	-0.0785 (-0.79)	-0.1289 (-0.80)	-0.0233 (-0.15)
science major	-0.1823** (-2.67)	-0.0221 (-0.24)	0.0572 (0.47)
undecided major	-0.2396** (-3.14)	0.0427 (0.55)	0.0429 (0.38)
Atlantic	-0.0548 (-1.14)	0.0282 (0.55)	-0.0135 (-0.19)
Quebec	0.0376 (0.58)	0.0674 (1.01)	-0.1303 (-0.79)
Manitoba, Saskatchewan	-0.0563 (-1.09)	0.0697 (1.58)	-0.1295 (-1.59)
Alberta	-0.1144 (-1.35)	0.0391 (0.63)	-0.1381 (-1.09)
British Columbia	0.0796 (1.43)	-0.1016 (-1.01)	-0.3967** (-2.97)
N	1750	632	511
Mean of dependent variable	0.6736	0.8048	0.7053

Notes: ** (*) indicates statistically significant at the 5 percent (10 percent) level. Robust z statistics are in parentheses.
Source: Author's compilation.

those who attempted a second program, B.C. students were less likely to re-try at the bachelor's level and more likely to enter a program below bachelor's level, compared to the omitted province of Ontario. Although the third regression ignores the type of institution where the second program was taken, the large university college system in B.C. (compared to other provinces) may account for this effect, providing more opportunities for certificate and diploma level programs than are available in other provinces. The other western provinces also provide more university college type opportunities than the rest of Canada, and their coefficients and standard errors also suggest a negative effect, but they are not significantly different from zero at conventional levels.

First program completion rates varied significantly across the major fields of study. Undecided and science students were much more likely to leave or change their first program than those in the omitted group of "agriculture, recreation, health." Humanities and social science students were also more likely to leave or change than the omitted group, but the differences were only significant at the 8.5 percent level. Other differences across majors were statistically insignificant. While students' majors were strongly associated with the decision to leave or change their first program, they had no effect on subsequent decisions about whether to attempt a second program or on the level of that program. Science and undecided students were just as likely as other students to attempt a second program at a bachelor's or lower level if they did not complete their first.

The PSE financing variables show big differences across the various sources of funding compared to the implicit alternative that students are paying for PSE with grants, scholarships, or bursaries or out of their current income or savings. Table 3 shows that students with student loans or family funding that will not be repaid were much more likely to graduate from their first program. But students with the non-repayable family funding in their first program were less likely to attempt a second program if they did not complete their first (a parental/family recrimination effect, perhaps). Second programs were also more likely to be at the bachelor's level if students received non-repayable family funds in their first programs. Receipt of a student loan in the first program was uncorrelated with decisions made after that program, and other types of loans were not correlated with any of the decisions or outcomes considered.

Given the results in Figure 1, one would expect a lower probability of graduation from students who changed their major in their first program. The point estimate in Table 3 is consistent with that expectation, but controlling for the other factors, it is not statistically significant at conventional levels. Further, changing major is not significantly related to the decision to attempt second programs or the level of any subsequent programs, but these results may be due to under-counting of changes in major.

Part-time study in students' first PSE program was strongly associated with leaving or changing that program before completion, but it was unrelated to re-enrolment or the levels of subsequent PSE programs. As for living arrangements, students who permanently moved out of their parents' home before the end of their first program were more likely to graduate from that program. But those who did not graduate were less likely to attempt a second program, and there was no relation to the level of their second program.

The presence of parents during high school was generally uncorrelated with all three of the dependent variables, but students who lived with two adults who were not both biological parents were much less likely to graduate from their first PSE program. Surprisingly, parents' education and the importance of PSE to parents were unrelated to students' success in their first program. Apparently parents with higher education did not bring better information or decision-making to students' first program choices. For students who stopped their first program, however, parents' education was positively and significantly correlated with the decision to re-enrol in another PSE program. Thus parents' education appears to be related to students' ability to adjust to adversity in their first program by finding and undertaking alternative programs. PSE being important to parents was also positively related to students' decision to try a second program, but only at the 7.6 percent significance level. Neither parents' education nor the importance of PSE to parents was significantly related to the level of second programs.

High school characteristics generated surprisingly few statistically significant coefficients for the outcome of students' first programs. High school grades were strongly correlated with completion, but the other high school variables were insignificant. High school grades were also strongly correlated with attempting a second program – at the bachelor's level – if the first was not completed. Students who attended a private high school were more likely to start a second program if they did not complete their first, although the estimate is only significant at the 7.1 percent level, and they were also more likely to choose bachelor's level second programs. Surprisingly, spending more than 12 months out of school before PSE was not significantly related to any of the decisions.

An unexpected result was the insignificance of gender for all three of the student decisions. Other personal characteristics – rural address and first language not French or English – were not related to first program outcomes. Students whose mother tongue was other than French or English were more likely to start a second program at the bachelor's level, while rural students were more likely to choose second programs below bachelor's level if they attempted a second program after quitting their first.

Students in College/CEGEP Programs of Two Year or More Years

The first two regressions are repeated for students who started two or more year programs in a college or CEGEP, regardless of the reported level of their program. The changed major variable is omitted from the first regression because very few graduates changed major (see Figure 3), and so it is almost perfectly correlated with the dependent variable. The third regression (examining the level of second programs) is omitted because the variation in the dependent variable is small and too closely correlated with province/region and major. Estimated marginal effects are reported in Table 4.

The results differ from those for university students. Starting from the bottom of Table 4, college students in Alberta and B.C. were much less likely to graduate from their first program compared to the omitted province of Ontario, although the B.C. coefficient is only significant at the 10.2 percent level. B.C. students were also much more likely to start a second program if they did not complete their first. These results may be due to the greater integration of programs across colleges and universities in those provinces. More students may have transferred from colleges to universities, and a change in institution constitutes a program change in the YITS. This would also explain why the levels of second programs were so closely correlated with province/region in the unreported third regression.

College or CEGEP students' first program major was not related to any of the outcomes considered, which again contrasts with university students who experienced big differences in first program completion rates across majors.

The financing of PSE also provided different and surprising estimates. As with university students, college or CEGEP students with student loans or family funding that will not be repaid were more likely to complete their first program, although the former was only significant at the 10 percent level. Unlike university students, college students with other types of loans were also much more likely to graduate from their first program, but (as with university students) this had no effect on second programs. Non-repayable family funding was not related to second program attempts for those who did not complete their first, while student loans made second program attempts less likely.

For college students, unlike university students, moving out of the parents' home or part-time study were not significantly related to either first program completion or pursuit of a second program. Also unlike university students, college students who lived with one (or no)

TABLE 4
Probit Estimates of Marginal Effects: Students in Two Year or More Year College/CEGEP Programs

Sample:	First program two or more years in college/CEGEP	Left or changed first program
Dependent variable:	1 = Grad from 1st prog 0 = Left/changed 1st prog	1 = Took 2nd prog 0 = No 2nd prog
male	-0.1298** (-2.83)	-0.2141** (-3.66)
rural	-0.0537 (-1.23)	-0.0242 (-0.38)
other mother tongue	0.0301 (0.33)	0.0997 (0.91)
private HS	0.0558 (0.84)	0.1018 (1.18)
did co-op in HS	-0.0265 (-0.49)	-0.1010 (-1.34)
HS grade average	0.1169** (4.36)	-0.0006 (-0.02)
took break before PSE	-0.0119 (-0.22)	-0.0512 (-0.73)
parents' highest educ	-0.0111 (-1.27)	0.0282** (2.36)
PSE important to parents	0.0381 (1.10)	0.0260 (0.70)
had one or no parents	-0.2505** (-4.62)	-0.0362 (-0.47)
two parents, but step	0.0238 (0.28)	-0.0361 (-0.30)
moved out	0.0751 (1.55)	0.1040 (1.59)
part time	-0.1401 (-1.54)	-0.1215 (-0.99)
changed major		0.1695** (2.82)
family funding, no repayment	0.0981** (2.06)	-0.0044 (-0.07)
student loan	0.0737* (1.65)	-0.1532** (-2.12)
other loan	0.1758** (3.64)	-0.0446 (-0.54)

... continued

TABLE 4
(Continued)

Sample:	First program two or more years in college/CEGEP	Left or changed first program
Dependent variable:	1 = Grad from 1st prog 0 = Left/changed 1st prog	1 = Took 2nd prog 0 = No 2nd prog
humanities major	0.0099 (0.13)	-0.0725 (-0.53)
social science major	-0.0733 (-0.70)	-0.2608 (-1.60)
business major	-0.0890 (-1.13)	-0.1121 (-0.85)
science major	-0.0800 (-1.11)	0.0066 (0.06)
undecided major	-0.1070 (-1.50)	-0.1942 (-1.58)
Atlantic	0.0199 (0.27)	0.0763 (0.90)
Quebec	-0.0617 (-1.10)	0.0862 (1.08)
Manitoba, Saskatchewan	-0.1323 (-1.44)	-0.0192 (-0.17)
Alberta	-0.2697** (-3.58)	0.0462 (0.53)
British Columbia	-0.1673 (-1.64)	0.2495** (4.88)
N	1213	472
Mean of dependent variable	0.5908	0.6915

Notes: ** (*) indicates statistically significant at the 5 percent (10 percent) level. Robust z statistics are in parentheses.

Source: Author's compilation.

parent during high school were less likely to complete their first programs, while other living arrangements yielded insignificant estimates. However, college students mimicked university students in that family status in high school was unrelated to attempts at second PSE programs.

College and university students are similar in that parents' education and the importance of PSE to parents were unrelated to students' achievements in their first programs, but higher parental education made students more likely to attempt a second program if they did not finish their first. The two groups are also similar in that more than 12 months out of school before PSE had no significant correlation with any of the outcomes that followed.

College students with higher high school grades were much more likely to graduate from their first program but, unlike university students, high school grades were unrelated to second program attempts if the first was not completed. Attending a private high school or doing co-op yielded insignificant effects on later PSE decisions.

Gender was strongly related to outcomes for college/CEGEP students but insignificant for university students. Male college students were much less likely to graduate from their first program and much less likely to try a second program if they did not complete their first. Other personal characteristics – rural address and other mother tongue – were not significantly related to first program outcomes or the decision to pursue a second program.

Conclusions

Out of the PSE students with resolved first program outcomes, only 50 to 60 percent graduated from their first program. This suggests that there is room for helping students to improve the decisions they make about their first programs. University students were more likely than college students to complete their first program and, out of those who did not, university students were also more likely to attempt second programs. Ten to 12 percent of initial PSE starters obtained a PSE credential by completing a second program within the time frame of the YITS survey, and 7 to 13 percent were still continuing their second programs. Thus second programs provide an important route for students to complete PSE credentials.

College/CEGEP and university students who stopped their first programs before completion followed similar strategies for their second. Almost three-quarters of both groups tried another program at the same level and type of institution. Most of the rest tried lower level programs, but almost 10 percent of college/CEGEP changers transferred to bachelor's level second programs. In general, students who transferred to programs at different levels (up or down) had higher success rates than those who tried again at the same level and type of institution. This provides further evidence of poor first decisions and room for improving the matching of students to first PSE programs.

As for the regression estimates, the province/region variables were insignificant with the exception of some coefficients for Alberta and

B.C. The estimated differences for those provinces likely reflect the greater integration of their college and university systems, but some of the results were mixed and not statistically significant. First-program major field of study was unrelated to any of the outcomes for college or CEGEP students, but university science and undecided students were much less likely to complete their first programs. The effect was short-lived, however, and subsequent decisions were unrelated to their first program major.

PSE outcomes and student decisions varied with how students financed their PSE. Students receiving government-sponsored student loans or non-repayable funds from family were generally more likely to complete their first program. However, those who encountered difficulties and did not complete their first program sometimes appeared to be discouraged by those sorts of funding. University students were less likely to attempt second programs if they received non-repayable family funding while college students were less likely to pursue a second program if they received a student loan.

Surprisingly, parents with more education did not appear to help students make better initial decisions about their PSE. Parents' education was not correlated with successful completion of first programs. However, more parental education was correlated with the probability that students attempted second programs if they did not complete their first. Thus students whose parents have more education appear more able to adjust to adversity or surprises within their PSE, and any overall relation between parents' education and PSE completion occurs via this mechanism.

Not surprisingly, high school grades are highly correlated with most of the PSE outcomes and student decisions, and in the expected directions. Family status and living arrangements have some statistically significant coefficients, but the estimates vary across university and college students. A striking result was that for university students the outcomes and decisions were unrelated to gender, while male college/CEGEP students were much less likely to complete their first program and start a second.

The analysis above suggests that PSE persistence and completion could be increased by policies that improve students' decisions about their first PSE programs. Providing more and better information about PSE programs and all of the other uncertainties outlined above is an obvious way to help improve those decisions. Other policies such as delaying decisions about PSE or defining more general programs of study would likely have similar effects. However, all of these policies have costs, and the costs should be weighed against the benefits.

The analysis above is also meant to highlight the fact that facilitating transfers and switches can improve PSE persistence and completion. Students' ability to obtain PSE credentials in their second programs shows that stopping a first program and transferring to another institution or program level should not be considered a failure of the individual or the system. It is a response to the uncertainties inherent in the process and the accumulation of more information during the process. Unfortunately a negative view of student transfers has been reinforced by the current practice of collecting and publishing institution-specific retention and graduation rates as performance indicators for institutions. Less emphasis on institution-specific statistics and greater emphasis on the institutions' contributions to the overall accumulation of human capital by students would encourage more transfers and greater PSE persistence and completion. In theory there should be optimal rates of stoppage and transfers that correctly weigh costs and benefits within the context of the uncertainties and randomness of the system. While this paper stops far short calculating such optimal rates, the flows and correlations presented above may contribute to their development.

Notes

I would like to thank Clément Lemelin, Ross Finnie, and the MESA Research Review Committee for helpful comments, Theresa Qui for excellent research assistance and advice, and the MESA research program for financial, institutional, and research support.

1.   Figures 3 and 4 show that some students switch to second programs that are at higher levels than their first before completing their first program. For example, some college/CEGEP students quit their programs before completion and switch to bachelor's level programs in universities. Likewise some students in bachelor's programs transfer to professional programs before completing their bachelor's degree. However, there are too few of these cases to include in the regression analysis.

2.   The definitions of the groups are slightly different for post-secondary students in Quebec due to the CEGEP system. See the data section.

3.   For example: Altonji (1993); Arcidiacono (2004); DesJardins, Ahlburg, and McCall (2002); Cameron and Heckman (1998); and Light (1996). A Canadian contribution is Montmarquette, Mahseredjian, and Houle (2001).

4.   The few first post-secondary programs occurring in a university in Quebec are likely students who graduated from high school in another province and transferred to a Quebec university for their first PSE program.

References

Adelman, C. 2006. "The Toolbox Revisited: Paths to Degree Completions from High School through College." Washington, D.C.: U.S. Department of Education.

Altonji, J.G. 1993. "The Demand for and Return to Education When Education Outcomes Are Uncertain." *Journal of Labor Economics* 11 (1), part 1: 48-83.

Arcidiacono, P. 2004. "Ability Sorting and the Returns to College Major." *Journal of Econometrics* 121 (1-2): 343-75.

Butlin, G. 2000. "Determinants of University and Community College Leaving." *Education Quarterly Review* 6 (4): 8-23.

Cabrera, A.F., K. Burkum, and S.M. La Nasa. 2005. "Pathways to a Four-Year Degree." In *College Student Retention: Formula for Student Success*, edited by A. Seidman, 155-214. Washington, D.C.: American Council on Education.

Cameron, S.V., and J.J. Heckman. 1998. "Life Cycle Schooling and Dynamic Selection Bias: Models and Evidence for Five Cohorts of American Males." *Journal of Political Economy* 106 (2): 262-333.

Chen, E., and J. Oderkirk. 1997. "Varied Pathways: The Undergraduate Experience in Ontario." *Education Quarterly Review*, Statistics Canada Catalogue 81-003-XPB, 4, no. 3, 47-62.

Choy, S.P. 2002. *Access and Persistence: Findings from Ten Years of Longitudinal Research on Students*. Washington, D.C.: American Council on Education.

Comay, Y., A. Melnik, and M.A. Pollatschek. 1973. "The Option Value of Education and the Optimal Path for Investment in Human Capital." *International Economic Review* 14 (2): 421-35.

DesJardins, S.L., D.A. Ahlburg, and B.P. McCall. 2002. "Simulating the Longitudinal Effects of Changes in Financial Aid on Student Departure from College." *Journal of Human Resources* 37 (3): 653-79.

Finnie, R., and H.T. Qiu. 2008. "Is the Glass (or Classroom) Half-Empty or Nearly Full? New Evidence on Persistence in Post-Secondary Education in Canada." In *Who Goes? Who Stays? What Matters? Accessing and Persisting in Post-Secondary Education in Canada*, edited by R. Finnie, R.E. Mueller, A. Sweetman, and A. Usher. Montreal and Kingston: McGill-Queen's University Press and School of Policy Studies, Queen's University.

Gilbert, S. 1991. *Attrition in Canadian Universities*. Research Report no. 1, Commission of Inquiry on Canadian University Education, June 1991.

Gilbert, S.N., and M. Auger. 1988. *Student Finances and University Attrition*. Ottawa: Department of the Secretary of State of Canada, PCS-6-00173.

Grubb, N.W. 1989. "Dropouts, Spells of Time, and Credits in Postsecondary Education: Evidence from Longitudinal Surveys." *Economics of Education Review* 8 (1): 49-67.

Lambert, M., K. Zeman, M. Allen, and P. Bussière. 2004. "Who Pursues Post-Secondary Education and Why: Results from the Youth in Transition Survey." Ottawa: Statistics Canada 81-595-MIE no. 26.

Light, A. 1996. "Hazard Model Estimates of the Decision to Reenroll in School." *Labour Economics* 2 (4): 381-406.

Montmarquette, C., S. Mahseredjian, and R. Houle. 2001. "The Determinants of University Dropouts: A Bivariate Probability Model with Sample Selection." *Economics of Education Review* 20 (5): 475-84

Shaienks, D., J. Eisl-Culkin, and P. Bussière. 2006. "Follow-up on Education and Labour Market Pathways of Young Canadians Aged 18 to 20: Results from YITS Cycle 3." Ottawa: Statistics Canada 81-595-MIE no. 45.

Simpson, W.A. 1987. "Tracking Students through Majors." *Journal of Higher Education* 58 (3): 323-43.

Zeman, K., T. Knighton, and P. Bussière. 2004. "Education and Labour Market Pathways of Young Canadians between Age 20 and 22: An Overview." Ottawa: Statistics Canada 81-595-MIE no. 18.

10

University Attainment, Student Loans, and Adult Life Course Activities: A Fifteen-Year Portrait of Young Adults in British Columbia

LESLEY ANDRES AND MARIA ADAMUTI-TRACHE

Cette étude est basée sur les données du projet Paths on Life's Way, échelonné sur 15 ans. Nous y analysons l'incidence des prêts étudiants sur l'éducation et d'autres activités qui ont marqué la vie des participants au projet. Nous nous concentrons sur les macroforces qui ont influencé cette cohorte ; nous adoptons une perspective fondée sur le concept de « parcours d'une vie » et nous avons recours à l'analyse factorielle de correspondance. Nous établissons ainsi la nature, le choix du moment et la durée de diverses voies qui permettent de mener à terme des études universitaires, en lien avec le montant de prêts étudiants reçus et avec diverses étapes de la vie (le mariage, par exemple), réalisées ou non. Les résultats montrent la nécessité, en matière de politiques publiques, de mettre en place de meilleurs services d'orientation professionnelle, et, sur le plan des prêts étudiants, de créer des mécanismes qui permettent aux étudiants de prévoir l'aide dont ils auront besoin pour ainsi planifier des études universitaires sans s'endetter de façon excessive.

We employ the 15-year longitudinal Paths on Life's Way database to examine the relationship between student loans and educational and other life course outcomes. By framing the study within the macro structural and policy forces affecting this cohort, then adopting a life course perspective and employing correspondence analysis, we identify the nature, timing, and duration of various paths to university completion in relation to the amount of student loans incurred and participation in other adult life activities (e.g., marriage). Implications for policy include the need for stronger counselling services and for loan schemes that provide predictable assistance measures to allow for university planning and relief against unreasonable debt loads.

Who Goes? Who Stays? What Matters? Accessing and Persisting in Post-Secondary Education in Canada, eds. R. Finnie, R.E. Mueller, A. Sweetman, and A. Usher. Montreal and Kingston: McGill-Queen's University Press, Queen's Policy Studies Series. © 2008 The School of Policy Studies, Queen's University at Kingston. All rights reserved.

Introduction

Among the multiple elements that conspire to facilitate or prevent post-secondary participation and completion, this paper focuses on three macro forces in relation to a cohort of youth in British Columbia as they left high school and negotiated the next 15 years of their lives. First, we locate the analysis in the policy debate beginning with the Access for All initiative in B.C. in the mid-1980s. Second, we highlight the B.C. student financial assistance program available to students as they left high school in 1988 in relation to tuition fees, and document how this program evolved over time. Third, we describe the changing nature of the B.C. post-secondary system from the 1980s onwards. As we examine how these elements likely impacted the post-secondary educational opportunities, experiences, and outcomes of this group, our conceptual focus changes to a life-course perspective. Taking into account characteristics such as social class, gender, and geographic location, we reveal the different paths taken by individual lives.

Capturing the ongoing dance between structure and agency across time is a major challenge. Over the span of 15 years, nothing remains static, and many changes have occurred in post-secondary structures, policy agendas and directions, and the individuals themselves as they matured and took on adult roles.

The Paths on Life's Way database used as the basis for this study was initially part of an endeavour in the 1980s in the province to further understand post-secondary participation and completion patterns. In 1989, the British Columbia Research Corporation and the British Columbia Institute of Technology, under contract with the Ministry of Education and the Ministry of Advanced Education and Job Training, undertook a survey of new Grade 12 graduates. Two of the primary purposes of this survey were to "collect fundamental, student-based information" (British Columbia Research Corporation, 1990, 2) and "to investigate reasons why students choose to go, or not to go, to post-secondary education" (4). This baseline study was transformed into the Paths on Life's Way longitudinal project (Andres, 2002a; 2002b; 2002c; 2002d).

British Columbia Access Policy

In the mid-1980s, educational policy-makers in B.C. were troubled by the low numbers of young people making the transition from high school to post-secondary education and, in particular, the low transition rate to university. The Report of the Standing Committee on

National Finance (1987) indicated that of all of the provinces in 1985-86, British Columbia had the lowest proportion of students directly entering university. Of this total cohort, 29 percent continued on to community college, and 17 percent entered university; in other words, 55 percent of those graduating from high school did not continue directly to post-secondary studies. In contrast, other provinces had much higher transition rates (i.e., Ontario at 32 percent for community college and 25 percent for university).

The structure of post-secondary education in British Columbia could account for some of these differences. Even in the 1980s, students were able to complete one or two years of university-equivalent courses at community colleges, thus lowering the numbers entering university directly. However, in Alberta, with similar post-secondary transfer arrangements and the second lowest transition rate to university, 27 percent of high school graduates continued directly to university. This figure was much closer than that of British Columbia to the national average of 29 percent.

In the 1980s, transfer rates between community colleges and universities in B.C. were also considered problematic. Of the Grade 12 graduates in the province who entered the post-secondary system in the 1985-86 year, 64 percent entered community colleges and 36 percent directly entered universities (Standing Senate Committee on National Finance, 1987). In 1985, the estimated total transfer rates from British Columbia community colleges to universities ranged from 14 to 51 percent with a median rate of 29 percent (B.C. Ministry of Advanced Education and Job Training, 1987). Degree completion rates of students transferring from college to university were estimated to range from 8 to 32 percent, compared with 29 to 56 percent for those students directly entering university (10). The Ministry of Advanced Education and Job Training (1987) concluded that "on average less than one in four full-time students who begin college academic programs can expect to end up with a first degree. Looking at it another way, those who begin studies at university have twice the chance of completion as those who begin college" (11).

These concerns led to a governmental review from which the Provincial Access Committee was established. This committee produced the report *Access to Advanced Education and Job Training in British Columbia: Report of the Provincial Access Committee* (1988) which, in turn, led to the establishment in 1989 of Access for All – a six-year, $690 million fund targeted at expanding access to all types of education throughout the province. The impact of this report is arguably second only to that of the MacDonald Report (1962) in changing the face of post-secondary education in British Columbia. Its focus on access in the broadest sense resulted in dramatic structural changes such as the establishment of five university colleges. In addition, the B.C. Council on Admissions and Transfer (BCCAT) was created and given a mandate to ensure that the various post-secondary institutions worked together as an integrated and coordinated system (Andres and Dawson, 1998).

The B.C. Provincial Access Committee (1988) questioned the extent to which the province's post-secondary system provided equitable opportunities for successful degree completion. They pointed out that quotas were placed on both the number of students admitted to universities and the number of transfer students accepted from colleges. Thus, those who were currently overrepresented in the community college system were the most likely to be affected by these policies. This finding supported claims in the research literature that community colleges only exacerbated the problem of less equitable outcomes for disadvantaged youth. As Karabel (1986) lamented, "the implications of this pattern of overrepresentation – one in which individuals from working-class and minority backgrounds tend to be concentrated in the very institutions that offer them the least chance of obtaining a bachelor's degree – are sobering" (17). Others commented on the paradox of the increasing availability of post-secondary places together with a concomitant escalation of competition for, in particular, university places (Coleman and Husén, 1985).

In subsequent reports over the years, attention was directed toward the relationship among the economy, the post-secondary system, and the labour market. These reports focused on topics ranging from structural unemployment as a result of the shifting economy (*An Analysis of Career, Technical, Vocational and Basic Training Needs in British Columbia,* 1989-93), the qualification/skills gap (*Access for Equity and Opportunity,* 1992), skills (*Skills Now: Real Skills for the Real World,* 1994), and skills and employability (*Training for What?,* 1995). However, it was the focus on equality of opportunity of access – based on theories of human capital and social justice that drove the dramatic expansion of post-secondary education in Canada and B.C. – that probably had the greatest impact on the B.C. high school graduating class of 1988.

British Columbia Student Financial Aid and Related Tuition Policies

In contrast to extensive attention to issues of access and transfer, in the 1980s the B.C. student financial aid system was in disarray. In 1984, the provincial grant portion of available financial aid was eliminated and replaced by the B.C. Student Loan (*Review of BC Student Assistance and Barriers to Post-Secondary Participation: Final Report*, 1992). As a result of this change and related meagre loan remission policies, until 1987 British Columbia ranked tenth among the provinces in financial aid expenditures per full-time enrolment (Table 1). In 1987, a new student financial aid scheme was adopted, which included equalization grants to students during their first two years of study, supplementary grants for students in college preparatory programs, and an improved loan remission program. As a result of these changes, B.C. moved from tenth to sixth place in terms of financial aid expenditures per full-time enrolment (Table 1). It was this student financial-aid milieu that confronted the Class of '88.[1]

TABLE 1
Provincial Student Financial Aid Expenditure per Full-time Enrolment ($)

	1985-86	1986-87	1987-88	1988-89	1989-91	1991-92
British Columbia	81	52	345	522	622	735
British Columbia[a]	NA	45	394	574	637	NA
Alberta	1,141	1,465	1,550	1,595	1,389	1,227
Saskatchewan	548	981	567	853	988	1,660
Manitoba	294	374	386	676	733	726
Ontario	489	547	609	606	607	626
Quebec	776	672	656	642	656	834
New Brunswick	555	558	617	738	811	850
Nova Scotia	395	372	382	419	444	482
PEI	725	816	816	731	776	818
Newfoundland	521	643	803	751	903	1,028
Yukon[b]	10,898	15,365	9,440	6,914	6,830	8,418
NWT[b]	10,639	16,718	15,392	16,750	14,893	17,500
Canada	553	648	673	753	793	899

Notes:
[a]Provincial figures use the B.C. government definition of post-secondary education, which differed from that of Statistics Canada; hence the two entries for B.C.
[b]Yukon and NWT data were not used to calculate the Canadian averages.
Source: *Review of BC Student Assistance and Barriers to Post-Secondary Participation*, 1992, 59.

However, student aid policies did not remain static. In 1992, a 15-member committee was appointed by the Minister of Advanced Education to review the B.C. Student Assistance Program, identify financial and other barriers to post-secondary participation, and recommend improvements to the existing scheme (*B.C. Provincial Access Committee*, 1988, i). Despite putative improvements, the committee identified numerous problems. In particular, it highlighted how equalization payments, loan remission, and timely completion policies created hardships for "mature students, ... single parents, students with disabilities, and educationally disadvantaged students" (1988, 11). In addition, the committee described the B.C. student financial aid scheme as "a complex, very difficult-to-understand web of programs" (5) that students, parents, and "even professionals in the student aid field" (11) struggled to comprehend. The final report in 1992 advanced 173 recommendations to improve the existing system; of these, 80 were flagged as priorities.

In 1997, the committee chair wrote a "report card" to assess the extent to which the recommendations had been implemented. Orum (1997) reported that although a few improvements to the system (e.g., more flexible repayment arrangements with lending institutions; reduced turnaround times in processing loan remission applications) had been implemented, the vast majority of recommendations were not endorsed. Moreover, some changes implemented by the B.C. government, such as limiting loan remission to apply only to B.C. student loans, further reduced the extent to which students could be relieved of onerous debt loads.

Between 1988 and 2003, both the Canada Student Loans Program and what is now called StudentAid BC evolved. Despite an announcement in the 2004 provincial budget that student grants would be eliminated and replaced with an enhanced student loan scheme (Malcolmson and Lee, 2004, 16), a limited and for the most part specifically targeted grant program is still in place. In addition, since 2000, bursaries have been available through the Canada Millennium Scholarship Foundation for full-time undergraduate students who have successfully completed at least 60 percent of a year of post-secondary studies and are eligible for student financial assistance in their province or territory of residence (http://www.millenniumscholarships.ca/en/index.asp).

B.C.'s Tuition Fee Policy

As the Class of '88 was about to embark on post-secondary studies, tuition fees in B.C. posed a constraint to access. In 1990 the median domestic undergraduate tuition fees in Canada were $1,545, ranging from a low of $904 in Quebec and a high of $1,941 in Nova Scotia. In B.C. this figure was $1,808. Within five years, tuition rates in B.C. had increased by 25 percent to $2,563. In 1996-97, in an attempt to enhance access to the post-secondary system, the provincial government imposed a freeze on tuition fees. This freeze remained in place until 2002-03; since then, tuition rates have risen steadily (Figure 1).

FIGURE 1
Undergraduate Domestic Tuition Fees for Full-time Students by Selected Provinces, 1990-2007

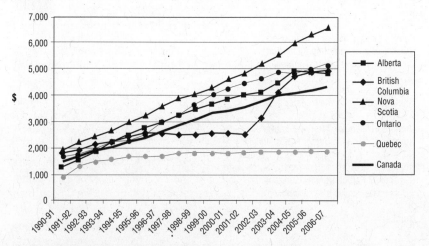

Source: Statistics Canada, 2005; 2006; 2007.

Structure of the B.C. Post-Secondary System

Finally, the evolving structure of the B.C. post-secondary system must be considered when examining issues of student financial aid policies in relation to post-secondary participation and completion rates. In the late 1980s, B.C. students leaving high school had a wide array of available post-secondary choices. As Table 2 demonstrates, the post-secondary system was extensive, highly diversified, and advanced in terms of inter-institutional articulation. In 1988 the system included four public universities, one private university, 15 community colleges, four public institutes, an Open University, an Open College, and hundreds of private colleges and trade schools.

However, like student financial aid and tuition fees, the structure of the system did not remain static. Over a 15-year period, both the structure and the nature of post-secondary institutions and the number of available seats changed dramatically. The figures in Table 2 indicate overall expansion of the system, increased numbers of institutions awarding university degrees, and increased inter-institutional transfer. According to Malcolmson and Lee (2004), between 1991-92 and 2003-04 the number of full-time equivalent spaces in B.C. colleges and universities increased by 42,700, an increase of 38 percent (7). Enrolments

TABLE 2
The B.C. Transfer System

	1989-90	2000-01	2004-05	2005-06*
Public post-secondary institutions	23	28	26	26
Public degree granting institutions	4	14	15	17
Out of province public institutions	1	1	1	1
Private degree granting institutions	1	1	3	4
Private non-degree granting institutions	3	3	3	3
Total institutions in the transfer system	27	33	33	34
Number of "sending" transfer courses	5,000	7,254	7,921	8,757[a]
Number of current transfer equivalencies	16,000	47,000	57,520	55,656
Number of transfer agreements per course	3.2	6.5	7.3	6.4
Number of grandparented transfer agreements			27,506	36,208[b]
Documented block transfer agreements	N/A	600	774	759
Associate degree block transfer		N/A	N/A	
Number of changes made to the database		20,234	9,721[c]	

Notes:
[a]As of 31 March 2006.
[b]With an end-date prior to 31 March 2006.
[c]Compares to 6,427 in 2002-03; 7,227 in 2003-04.
Source: Gelin, 2006.

at universities grew from 49,482 in 1990-91 to 71,134 in 2003-04, representing an unweighted increase of 44 percent or a weighted increase of 51.4 percent.[2] At first glance, such expansion could be interpreted as a positive development for enhancing post-secondary participation. However, during this period, funding support for B.C. students decreased by a total of 17.3 percent (unweighted) or 21.4 percent (weighted). Translated into constant 2003 dollars, funding declined from $11,374 per student in 1990-91 to $9,407 in 2003-04, a drop of almost $2,000 per student (10). As Malcolmson and Lee point out, although the B.C. post-secondary system experienced enormous expansion throughout the 1990s, the extra seats created were not adequately funded. They conclude that "provincial policy may reduce one barrier to accessing post-secondary education while simultaneously increasing another barrier (the financial cost of attending)" (8). As Finnie (2005) demonstrates, understanding the capacity / demand / funding nexus is critical.

It is within these evolving sets of policies, practices, and institutional changes that we examine the post-secondary trajectories of the Class of

'88. Rarely are we able to take a 15-year retrospective look at the life trajectories of individuals with the intent to inform our current educational policies and practices. Few studies exist that assess the impact of policies such as student financial aid on educational and occupational outcomes in relation to both the factors affecting those outcomes (e.g., gender, academic capital, socio-economic status, and geographic location), and the adult life events (e.g., marriage, family, home ownership) affected by these factors.

However, conducting analyses of longitudinal data presents considerable conceptual and methodological challenges. Most often, structures are treated as unchanging, which clearly is not the case. In addition, study participants age, get married, have children, become mature students; structures and related policies will have different impacts on those passing through the system at different times. To take up this challenge, we employ a life course framework. First, we specify our research questions, followed by a brief overview of a life course perspective used to address these questions.

Purpose

In this empirical structural study, we employ Paths on Life's Way longitudinal data to examine the interrelationships among background characteristics, post-secondary educational participation and attainment, student financial assistance (i.e., student loans), labour force participation, and adult life course activities. We address the following research questions:

- Who was eligible for university studies (i.e., gender, social class), and how did this relate to the post-school status of respondents one year after high school graduation?
- What were the educational attainment levels of young women and men over a 15-year period following high school graduation? What are the costs incurred by those who obtained a university education?
- How are the timing and sequences of paths taken to obtain a university degree related to various individual factors? How are they related to the level of student debt incurred?
- How are various paths to university completion associated with family background, eligibility for university, student debt incurred, educational attainment, timing of marriage and parenthood, home ownership, and job characteristics 15 years following high school graduation?

In other words, how can 15 years of data on education, work, debt load, and other life events of British Columbian youth contribute to a better understanding of the current post-secondary trends?

Conceptual Framework

We adopt a sociological life course perspective to address the questions listed above. Rather than examining changes in one or more dependent variables in relation to a fixed set of independent variables, we endeavour, as Hunt (2005) specifies, to "attempt to comprehend the human experience in terms of the institutional context . . . or the 'processes' which forge the lives of individuals, and the life chances and opportunities of particular social constituencies" (7). The following concepts are central to this approach: individuals as agents and their related "choices"; social structure; "linked social lives" such as "family, education, and work" (23); and the "timing of lives," which Hunt defines as "a strategic adaptation to external events and the resources available to an individual" (23).

The transition from adolescence to adulthood depends on the interplay of given characteristics of individuals and the demographic, economic, social, and cultural contexts through which they pass. As we described above, from a structural perspective, the ways in which society and its related institutions are constructed, organized, and defined in successive periods provides the macrosociological context for studying the life courses of individuals. Cohort characteristics (e.g., the generation to which they belong), government policies related to education and the labour market, public sentiment toward education and work, changing conceptions of the family, economic conditions such as recession and unemployment, and the changing structure of the educational system and labour market all shape transitions from one life stage to another.

To understand the impact of social institutions and structures on individuals' lives, we need, as Hodgkinson (1985) asserts, to begin to examine social institutions from the perspective of the people who move through them. Social theory and the life course literature highlight the dynamic relationship between macrosocial and cultural forces and contexts and individuals as purposive actors (Bourdieu, 1990; Giddens, 1984; Hunt, 2005). These theoretical perspectives provide us with the conceptual tools to expand and deepen our understandings of how individuals seize, ignore, or resist opportunities and how they are constrained by structures, policies, and practices of the larger society. To detect the impact of a given set of social forces on a given cohort at both the micro and macro levels, it is essential to conduct analyses across time. This requires the availability of databases that lend themselves to analyses of cohorts.

Research Design

The longitudinal datasets of Paths on Life's Way include information on education, careers, and family formation patterns of female and male high school graduates of the British Columbia Class of '88 who answered four follow-up surveys (Andres, 2002a; 2002b; 2002c; 2002d). A total of 733 respondents (60 percent of them women) answered all four waves of surveys (administered in 1989, 1993, 1998, and 2003), which represents about 3 percent of the entire Class of '88 graduates. Over time, the sample has been affected by attrition, with a slight bias toward women and respondents coming from more educated backgrounds and with better high school performance. However, overall, the longitudinal sample remained remarkably representative of the original respondent group (Andres, 2002a). Hence, the results of this study represent the best-case scenario in terms of education and work, which suggests that the findings are even more relevant in explaining existing social inequities in schools, post-secondary institutions, and the labour market.

Variables

Although post-secondary participation, credentials obtained, and occupations are recorded year by year, for the purpose of this study only the 1989 post-secondary destinations and highest credentials earned by 1993, 1998, and 2003 are employed. The variables are introduced briefly in this section.

High school achievement is directly related to respondents' chances of continuing post-secondary education. Grade point average (GPA) scores and eligibility for university admission are measures of achievement during the senior high school years. These indicators from student high school records were matched with survey data and used in the current analysis.

Post-secondary participation one year after high school graduation is an indicator of purposeful planning, fulfilment of requirements, aspirations to continue to post-secondary education, and availability of resources. Respondents are classified into three groups: non-participants, non-university participants (i.e., those attending community colleges, institutes, or university colleges), and university participants. Educational attainment by 1993, 1998, and 2003 refers to the highest credential earned by respondents at five, 10, and 15 years since high school graduation. We distinguish five categories: non-participants, non-completers (i.e., those who attended but did not obtain any credential), those who possess non-university credentials, those who completed bachelor's degrees, and those who obtained first professional or graduate degrees. Most of the analyses are conducted with university graduates (N=433) only – the last two groups described above. We further divide the sub-sample of university graduates into three groups: those who obtained bachelor's degrees by 1993 (early bachelor's), those who obtained bachelor's degrees after 1993 (delayed bachelor's), and those who obtained degrees beyond the bachelor's level (graduate degrees). We anticipate that the timing and/or duration of university completion is strongly related to financing and student loans.

The focal variable of the study is the government student loan. First, we determine whether students have government student loans, and second, the amount of student loans received over time. We anticipate that various social and cultural factors affect the way individuals manage the funding of their university studies. Other financial burdens that occur over life course (e.g., buying a house) are included in the study. In addition, the analysis includes whether respondents are married and have children (yes/no) by 2003.

Occupational status is the current or most recent job held by respondents in 2003. Three categories of occupational prestige have been derived by aggregating the Pineo-Porter-McRoberts (Pineo and Goyder, 1988) socio-economic classification of occupations scale of 16 prestige categories. We distinguish occupations as unskilled and semi-skilled, technical and skilled, and management and professional.

Methods of Analysis

In the first analysis, we provide an overview of post-secondary participation and completion rates of the Class of '88 longitudinal sample, and of student loans incurred by respondents within five, 10, and 15 years after high school graduation. University completion and student financial assistance information is analyzed in relation to gender and family background.

In the second analysis, we employ correspondence analysis to unveil the associations among university completion paths (i.e., differentiated by level of education and timing), student loans, individual characteristics (e.g., gender, high school academic capital), family background (e.g., parental education, geographical location), and other life circumstances (e.g., marital status, parenthood, home ownership, job characteristics) of university graduates from the high school graduating class of 1988. We conclude this analysis with a descriptive profile of those who graduate from university with and without student debt.

Correspondence Analysis Method

Correspondence analysis (CA) is the most effective analytical technique to describe data patterns and explore relations among the categorical data of the Paths on Life's Way Project. This multivariate technique analyzes two-way contingency tables in which columns correspond to the variable to be explained (e.g., university completion paths) and rows correspond to various explanatory variables (e.g., gender, parental education, high school academic capital). It offers a visual representation of the data distribution in a two-dimensional CA map where points correspond to each category (row or column profile) of variables included in the analysis (Greenacre, 1993). The location of these profiles in a multidimensional space is computed from data in contingency tables, and the dispersion of profiles is described by a variance-type measure called *inertia*. Correspondence analysis is viewed as a method for decomposing the overall inertia along principal axes. The CA map used for analysis is usually based on the pair of principal axes that explain the largest amount of inertia. Because there are no dependent variables in CA, no causal claims on relationships are made. We used XLSTAT to compute the chi-square coordinates of profile points and the statistical tests of the analysis. Elsewhere we offer more details on the use of this method in analyzing educational data (Adamuti-Trache and Andres, 2008; Andres, Adamuti-Trache, et al., 2007).

For the purpose of this paper, we refer primarily to the so-called *dimensional* or *factor-analytic* interpretation of the map that examines the most likely row or column profiles aligned along principal axes in order to identify a latent "hidden" variable along each axis, and then establish how other sets of profiles are associated with this structure. Additional CA tests obtained with XLSTAT provide exact information on the contributions of row and column profiles to inertia that support the *factor-analytic* interpretation. Occasionally we use a *descriptive* approach to identify similar categories corresponding to sets of points that are close on the map, and contrast them with dissimilar categories corresponding to points situated far apart from each other.

Findings

We begin with a descriptive analysis of the variables described above. We then employ correspondence analysis to examine relationships among the variables.

Analysis 1[3]

The post-school status of high school graduates is only partially determined by their educational histories as reflected in overall school assessments of eligibility for university education. Table 3 demonstrates that within about one year following high school graduation only 50 percent of those who were eligible to commence study at a university actually did, while 40 percent enrolled in non-university institutions, and 11 percent did not participate in any post-secondary studies. Percentages differ by gender, with eligible men more likely to enrol in university (i.e., 59 percent of men vs. 43 percent of women). Among those not eligible for university, there are also clear gender differences. Whereas 63 percent of women attended community colleges and institutes, only 51 percent of their male counterparts chose this route. Also, larger proportions of men (41 percent) than women (28 percent) in this group were post-secondary non-participants in 1989. A small proportion of women (9 percent) and men (8 percent) attended university studies even though they were assessed as non-eligible based on their high school performance.[4]

TABLE 3
University Eligibility versus 1989 Post-School Status by Gender

| 1989 status | Eligible for university | | | | | | Non-eligible for university | | | | | |
| | All | | Female | | Male | | All | | Female | | Male | |
	N	%	N	%	N	%	N	%	N	%	N	%
Non-participant	47	11	31	12	16	9	95	33	47	28	48	41
Non-university	178	40	120	45	58	32	167	58	108	63	59	51
University	221	50	116	43	105	59	25	9	16	9	9	8

Note: Rounding up produces a total greater than 100 percent.
Source: Authors' compilation.

When contrasting post-secondary participation within one year after high school graduation with parental educational attainment, it is evident that respondents with university-educated parents were more effective than those with non-university educated parents in turning eligibility for university into university enrolment. According to Table 4, 61 percent of the former group enrolled in universities compared to 44 percent of the latter group. Even if they were eligible for university, 45 percent of individuals from families where one or more parent had not completed university enrolled in non-university institutions. Among those not eligible for university, respondents with educated parents were again more likely to participate in either non-university (65 percent) or university (14 percent) institutions. In contrast, lower proportions of those with non-university educated parents enrolled in non-university institutions (58 percent) and universities (8 percent). Respondents with non-university educated parents who were not eligible for university were the most likely to be non-participants (35 percent) one year after high school graduation.

TABLE 4
University Eligibility versus 1989 Post-school Status by Parental Education

1989 status	Eligible for university				Non-eligible for university			
	Parents – no univ		Parents – univ		Parents – no univ		Parents – univ	
	N	%	N	%	N	%	N	%
Non-participant	29	11	14	9	70	35	13	21
Non-university	116	45	50	31	116	58	41	65
University	113	44	99	61	15	8	9	14

Notes: The Ns in Tables 3 and 4 differ due to missing data on parental education.
Source: Authors' compilation.

These analyses indicate that social class (i.e., parental education), gender, and academic ability as measured by eligibility for university played a significant role in the paths chosen by high school graduates. Although women and men were equally eligible for university (i.e., about 60 percent), more women tended to enrol in community colleges and institutes directly after high school graduation. Similarly, even if they were eligible for university, students with non-university educated parents were more likely to commence their studies at non-university institutions such as community colleges. Although high school academic histories as reflected by eligibility for university had a strong influence on respondents' post-school choices, other factors also influenced whether and where respondents continued to study at post-secondary institutions. These findings confirm that there is a relationship between university participation and family background (Drolet, 2002) and support the concerns raised by the B.C. Provincial Access Committee (1988) regarding equitable opportunities to attend university for disadvantaged young adults. This suggests that "reserves of talent" (Härnqvist, 1978) remained untapped.

The "one year out of high school" picture changed over time, and the question is whether government student assistance programs had any impact on this change. Indeed, the proportion of B.C. young women and men who completed post-secondary studies increased considerably over the 15 year period following high school graduation. By 2003, 59 percent of all respondents (N=733) obtained university degrees (i.e., 37 percent obtained bachelor's degrees and 22 percent professional and graduate degrees). Only 4 percent of respondents had never participated in post-secondary education, 9 percent did not complete their studies by 2003, and 27 percent obtained only non-university credentials. This distribution suggests a high educational profile for this sample, with 96 percent having participated in post-secondary studies and 59 percent obtaining university degrees. As Figures 2a and 2b reveal, the change in educational attainment occurred primarily within the first 10 years or less after high school graduation.

The 1993 and 1998 pictures are very different, showing that women were likely to complete university degrees in a more timely fashion than men. In 1993, 35 percent of women versus 28 percent of men obtained bachelor's degrees or higher, with only 5 percent of women versus 9 percent of men not yet participating in post-secondary education. By 1998, more men than women were non-participants (i.e., 6 percent vs. 4 percent) or non-completers (i.e., 15 percent vs. 11 percent). However, university completion was quite similar for men and women (i.e., 55 percent and 56 percent), and results did not change dramatically between 1998 and 2003.

Elsewhere (Andres and Adamuti-Trache, 2006) we have specified the variety of educational trajectories followed by this longitudinal sample – in part, as a consequence of a highly articulated post-secondary system in B.C. that allows individuals to tailor their educational journeys according to their life circumstances. In principle students are not constrained by their original choices and can negotiate their way through the system. Overall we notice that the proportion of respondents who completed non-university credentials at community colleges and institutes varied slightly, with most of the change occurring with increasing proportions of female and male respondents completing university degrees. Since university education is associated with more significant costs, we focus our attention on determining to what extent financial issues affected university completion. What were the costs incurred by those who obtained a university education and how were they intertwined with the dynamics of completing a university degree? The research sample consists of those who obtained a bachelor's degree or higher by 2003 (N=433, 60 percent women), from which sub-samples are selected to analyze the 1993 results (N=242, 65 percent women) and 1998 results (N=409, 60 percent women).

FIGURE 2a
Highest Educational Attainment – Females

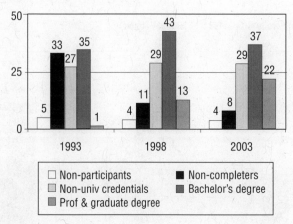

FIGURE 2b
Highest Educational Attainment – Males

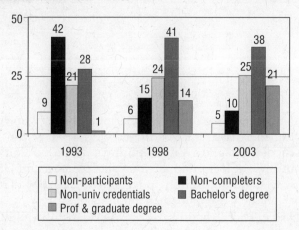

Source: Authors' compilation.

By 1993, about 34 percent of all university graduates received government assistance and other financial aids to fund their post-secondary education. As Figure 3 shows, this proportion increased to 52 percent by 1998 and to 54 percent by 2003. There are slight differences by gender. More female respondents (36 percent), who were more likely to start and complete education earlier but were also more likely to commence their studies at non-university institutions, borrowed money by 1993. The comparable figure for men was 30 percent. By 2003, 56 percent of men and 53 percent of women who obtained university degrees reported that they had taken out student loans.

FIGURE 3
Proportion of University Graduates with Student Loans

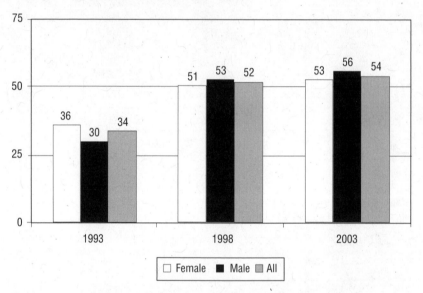

Source: Authors' compilation.

The substantial increase in the number of students who relied on government financial assistance occurred before 1998, within 10 years after high school graduation. Table 5 portrays the proportion of those who took out student loans and the total debt load accumulated over time by those who graduated from university by 2003. For all respondents, a 71 percent increase in median amounts of borrowing occurred between 1993 (i.e., $8,200) and 1998 (i.e., $14,000), with an additional 30 percent increase between 1998 and 2003 (i.e., $18,000).

TABLE 5
Median Debt Load from Student Loans and Amount Owed in 2003

	Median debt load by each year									Still owing		
	By 1993			By 1998			By 2003			2003		
	N	%	$	%	N	$	N	%	$	%	N	$
Female	55	69	9,500	125	61	15,000	138	59	18,000	34	53	15,000
Male	25	31	6,900	81	39	13,500	95	41	18,000	30	47	10,000
All	80	100	8,200	206	100	14,000	233	100	18,000	64	100	11,500

Source: Authors' compilation.

Although debt incurred in the first stage until 1993 is related to the costs of completing a bachelor's degree, higher costs that occur in later stages are likely to be related to either pursuing graduate studies or to delayed or prolonged study. By 2003, regardless of gender, the median debt load for those with student loans was $18,000. Of the total of 233 university graduates who borrowed money, about 73 percent (i.e., 75 percent of women and 68 percent of men) had repaid their debt. In 2003, less than one-third of university graduates had not yet repaid their student loans.

Our analyses indicate that respondents used multiple sources to finance their education. In Tables 6a and 6b, we report various sources of financial support received by those who were university graduates by 2003, and we contrast by social class and gender the two groups of respondents who did or did not rely on student loans. Overall, we notice that in both 1993 and 1998, those who pursued and completed university education relied mainly on parental support, scholarships or bursaries, personal savings, and, to large extent, earnings from full-time summer work or part-time work during the academic year. There is some variation in the proportion of respondents who indicate various sources of support by gender and parental education. Although steady trends are not clear, a drop in parental support over time is evident; also, larger proportions of male respondents report earnings from full-time work as a source to finance education. Perhaps more significant for our study is that those who took out student loans were for the most part more likely to rely on earnings from work (all gender and social class groups) and less likely to rely on parental support (those with less educated parents). Very few respondents were employed full-time during the academic year. However, in the five years following high school graduation, the vast majority – and in particular those with student loans – were employed full time during the summer months.

TABLE 6a
University Graduates by 2003 with Student Loans Declared by 1993 by Sex and Parental Education

	No loans percent				Loans percent			
	Parents no univ		Parents univ		Parents no univ		Parents univ	
	Female (n=71)	Male (n=37)	Female (n=61)	Male (n=47)	Female (n=48)	Male (n=38)	Female (n=36)	Male (n=17)
Direct support from parents or other relatives	80	62	72	49	65	55	61	53
Direct support from spouse	7	0	0	2	6	0	3	0
Repayable loans from family	13	16	5	11	21	21	33	24
Scholarships or bursaries	62	49	53	36	58	50	69	53
Earnings from full-time work (including summer employment)	63	76	69	70	79	92	86	100
Repayable loans from employer (including repayment in time)	0	0	0	0	0	0	0	6
Non-repayable loans/assistance from employer	1	5	0	0	0	0	0	6
Part-time work during the academic year	58	54	53	40	63	61	78	35
Full-time work during the academic year	9	5	7	6	8	5	6	6
Personal savings	49	51	48	55	52	47	39	59
Other	9	8	16	9	4	5	11	12

N=355

Source: Authors' compilation.

TABLE 6b
University Graduates by 2003 with Student Loans Declared by 1998 by Sex and Parental Education

	No loans percent				Loans percent			
	Parents no univ		Parents univ		Parents no univ		Parents univ	
	Female (n=66)	Male (n=38)	Female (n=52)	Male (n=40)	Female (n=68)	Male (n=57)	Female (n=52)	Male (n=30)
Direct support from parents or other relatives	61	63	54	53	43	42	52	57
Direct support from spouse	12	5	8	5	4	11	4	7
Repayable loans from family	14	3	8	10	15	21	8	13
Scholarships or bursaries	39	24	38	55	56	46	62	50
Earnings from full-time work (including summer employment)	50	58	56	66	60	75	79	70
Repayable loans/assistance from employer	0	0	0	0	0	0	0	0
Non-repayable loans from government	0	0	0	0	3	2	1	3
Non-repayable loans/assistance from employer	0	3	0	0	3	0	0	3
Part-time work during the academic year	42	37	46	28	57	56	62	40
Full-time work during the academic year	9	11	16	5	4	4	0	0
Personal savings	41	34	38	43	35	30	31	33
Other	9	3	6	18	4	9	8	17

N=403

Source: Authors' compilation.

In Table 7, we examine student loan patterns by entry into and exit from the post-secondary system, by social class as determined by whether at least one parent had earned a university degree, and by gender. We developed a typology by first specifying the original high school destination of respondents by 1989 as non-participants, non-university participants, or university participants. We then categorized bachelor's degree completion as *early* if respondents completed their studies within five years of high school graduation (i.e., by 1993) or *delayed* if they completed bachelor's degrees after 1993 but by 2003. Finally, we distinguished between those who completed bachelor's

TABLE 7
Student Loan Status by Parental Education, Initial Post-High School Status, and Gender

	Females				Males			
	No loan %	Loan %	Median amount of loan $	N	No loan %	Loan %	Median amount of loan $	N
University educated parents								
University completion (%)								
Univ – early bachelor's	77	23	15,000	26	69	31	8,000	16
Univ – delayed bachelor's	33	67	20,000	6	67	33	5,000	12
Univ – graduate	33	67	23,000	18	47	53	24,500	15
Non-univ – early bachelor's	53	47	12,000	17	50	50	3,175	4
Non-univ – delayed bachelor's	59	41	16,500	17	56	44	23,000	9
Non-univ – graduate	23	77	13,500	13	57	43	27,500	7
Non-part – early bachelor's	NA	NA	NA	0	0	100	45,000	1
Non-part – delayed bachelor's	0	100	40,000	4	50	50	20,000	2
Non-part – graduate	50	50	25,000	6	0	100	52,500	4
Non-university educated parents								
University completion (%)								
Univ – early bachelor's	74	26	16,000	23	47	53	9,800	17
Univ – delayed bachelor's	50	50	31,500	8	30	70	22,000	10
Univ – graduate	41	59	23,500	27	43	57	34,500	21
Non-univ – early bachelor's	32	68	12,000	25	25	75	7,000	8
Non-univ – delayed bachelor's	55	45	23,000	22	44	56	17,000	18
Non-univ – graduate	40	60	13,100	20	40	60	20,000	10
Non-part – early bachelor's	50	50	18,000	2	100	0	NA	1
Non-part – delayed bachelor's	50	50	32,500	4	25	75	16,500	8
Non-part – graduate	0	50	11,500	4	0	100	21,500	2

Source: Authors' compilation.

degrees and those who earned graduate degrees. This classification is a modified version of a typology used by the authors in a paper that explored the educational trajectories of Paths respondents (Andres and Adamuti-Trache, 2008).

One clear finding emerges: those who complete university studies in a timely fashion – either as direct entry students from high school, as transfers from non-university institutions, or in the rare instance as non-participants, incur lower levels of student debt than do those who delay degree completion regardless of entry point. The exceptions were male university participants in 1989 who delayed completion; they had one of the lowest median debt levels at $5,000. The mean income of males who had university-educated parents and were university non-completers in 1998 was considerably higher than others who had not earned university credentials (Andres, 2002a), which supports the speculation that this group had been lured away from university study into lucrative careers. Eventually, however, most completed their university studies. This group of males was far more likely than females in the same category to have not taken out student loans.

Across most groups the median amount of student loans is higher for women. The exception is in relation to the completion of graduate studies where the debt load carried by males is considerably higher.

It is not necessarily the case that respondents whose parents had less than university education were more likely to have taken out student loans. This may mean that parental education level is not a good proxy for parental income level, or it may mean that more students from the middle class are applying and qualifying for student loans. However, as Table 7 indicates, gender is a key factor as there are much greater differences between males from educated and non-educated families than there are between women from these two groups. Overall, most of those with student loans and whose parents have not completed university had higher debt loads.

If our analysis had stopped in 1993, five years after respondents graduated from high school, the story told by the Paths data would show a discrepancy in university completion rates by gender (i.e., 37 percent of women compared to 29 percent of men, Figures 2a, 2b), a moderate proportion of university graduates with student loans (i.e., 36 percent of women and 30 percent of men), and relatively modest debt loads (i.e., $9,500 for women and $6,900 for men).[5] However, the results portrayed above indicate that following respondents over 15 years changes the story considerably.

In summary, in this section we have demonstrated that data collected over a period of five years following high school provide an incomplete picture of the post-secondary education trajectories, completion rates, and borrowing patterns of students. To better understand these dynamics over a longer time frame, we continue the analyses to include other aspects of individuals' lives, such as work, marriage, and parenthood. Only Paths respondents who completed university degrees by 2003 are included in the following analysis.

Analysis 2

The first analysis has revealed that the majority of Paths respondents have reached high levels of university education (i.e., 37-38 percent had earned bachelor's degrees and 21-22 percent graduate degrees) with median student loans of $18,000 over 15 years. However, we hypothesize that by examining the variety of educational paths that lead to degree completion in relation to other adult life activities, we will be able to cast a different light on the student loan story. For the purpose of this analysis, the university graduate sample is divided into three groups: those who obtained bachelor's degrees by 1993 (early bachelor's degree), those who took a longer time period to obtain bachelor's degrees (delayed bachelor's degree), and those who obtained graduate degrees any time before 2003 (graduate degree).

Results in Table 8 indicate that those completing a bachelor's degree "early" – that is, within five years following high school graduation – were in a better position to graduate with no loans or a very small debt load. The slight increase in median student debt by 1998 and 2003 for this "early bachelor's" group is due to participation in other levels of education, either as extra credentials at non-university level or in graduate programs that had not yet been completed by 2003. Meanwhile, those who had not completed bachelor's degrees by 1993 incurred larger amounts of debt across all time periods. The largest increase in student debt for this group occurred between 1993 and 1998. Regardless of the timing of bachelor's degree completion, women incurred higher median student debt at all times.

Those who completed first professional or graduate degrees by 2003 are located in the last two columns of Table 8. Men who obtained such credentials reported the highest median student debt by 2003 ($26,000) as opposed to men who obtained bachelor's degrees within five years ("early bachelor's") and reported a median debt load of only $8,000 by 2003. In 1998 and in 2003, the median student debt incurred by men who obtained graduate degrees surpassed that reported by women.

TABLE 8
University Completion and Student Loans by Gender

		Early bachelor's		Delayed bachelor's		Graduate degrees	
		Female (n=97)	Male (n=51)	Female (n=65)	Male (n=61)	Female (n=97)	Male (n=62)
Student loans (1989-2003) percent	Yes	43	49	54	52	63	61
Median student debt ($)	1993	8,600	6,330	12,250	7,400	12,000	11,000
	1998	9,750	6,830	21,000	15,000	15,000	19,500
	2003	12,500	8,000	24,000	18,000	19,000	26,000

Source: Authors' compilation.

As indicated at the outset of this paper, we employ a life course perspective when examining university completion and student financial burden. In the ensuing correspondence analysis, many factors related to life course events such as academic capital accumulated in high school, various demographic characteristics, and occupational status are included.

The correspondence analysis map in Figure 4 positions the points corresponding to the three-column profiles assigned to the university completion categories (i.e., early bachelor's, delayed bachelor's, graduate degrees) in relation to the 30-row profiles corresponding to gender (2), parental education (2), family geographic location (3), high school GPA (3), university eligibility (2), 1989 post-school status (3), debt load (2), amount of student loan (4), marital status by 2003 (2), parenthood by 2003 (2), home ownership by 2003 (2), and occupational status in 2003 (3). The two-dimensional CA map is an exact representation of all profile points, and the two principal axes explain 100 percent of the dispersion of points.

The horizontal axis accounts for 55 percent of the average total inertia. It opposes the group that completed a university degree by 1993 (early bachelor's) to the left and the groups who took longer to completion (delayed bachelor's and graduate degrees) to the right side of the map. The "hidden" variable can be identified as time to university completion – with shorter time to completion to the left side of the map and longer time to completion to the right. The row profiles that align best to the horizontal axis (based on map and CA statistical tests of row contributions to inertia) are those describing the

FIGURE 4
University Completion, Student Debt, and Life Course Characteristics

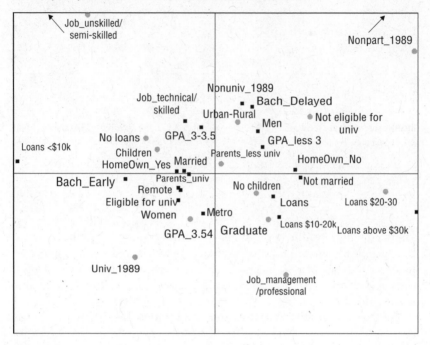

Source: Authors' compilation.

amount of student loan: the "loans < $10k" category to the left is far apart from the "loans above $30k" category to the right side of the map. The correspondence analysis shows clearly that the timing of university completion is associated with the amount of student loan incurred by respondents (these row profiles contribute by 35 percent to the horizontal axis inertia).

Overall, the "no loans" and "loans" categories are situated symmetrically and closer to the centre of the map that corresponds to an average profile since respondents are quite evenly distributed in these two groups (i.e., 54 percent had student loans by 2003; see Figure 3). What differentiates groups most is the amount of student loan incurred. One can also notice that "no loans" or lower amounts of loans profiles (left side) are associated with being married, having children, or owning a home by 2003, while larger amounts of loans profiles (right side) are likely to correspond to not having engaged in these adult life activities by 2003.

The vertical axis accounts for 45 percent of the total inertia and mainly contrasts the column profile that corresponds to "delayed bachelor's" (up) and "graduate degrees" (down), thus differentiating the two groups that take longer to complete university studies. Two sets of row profiles contribute the most to the vertical axis. First, 1989 post-school status, that describes post-secondary participation directly out of high school, contributes about 29 percent to the axis. It shows clearly that those who delay completion are likely to have started in non-university post-secondary institutions or (very few) to have never participated in post-secondary studies. Some respondents may not have been eligible for university admission due perhaps to lower GPA, lack of prerequisites, or both. Geographical location may also be a contributing factor in delaying completion. The second set of row profiles, which contributes about 40 percent to the vertical axis, is related to occupational status by 2003, a consequential variable. The CA map shows that those who delayed bachelor's degree completion are more likely to occupy technical/skilled occupations and (very few) unskilled/semi-skilled jobs rather than occupations at the management/professional level. Perhaps those who delay university entry or take prolonged routes through the system were established in lower level jobs and so degree completion did not guarantee a transition to the professional ranks. Those who completed bachelor's degrees early and did not continue on to graduate studies incurred lower levels of student debt, were more likely to be married with children, and were more likely to have purchased a home.

Appendix I contains additional details on the data distributions of various individual characteristics of female and male respondents who completed university degrees in each of the three categories. The table demonstrates clearly that those who delayed bachelor's degree completion represented a more vulnerable group in terms of high school preparation and post-secondary participation. A slightly higher proportion came from families with less education and were substantially more likely to have come from urban-rural areas. Overall, they incurred higher levels of student debt, a burden that is difficult to carry considering that return to education is less evident for these individuals. Only 20 percent of women in the delayed bachelor's completion category were in management or professional jobs. When compared to the other two groups, both women and men in this category were less likely to be married, have children, and own homes.

We conclude this section by contrasting the profiles of respondents who completed their university education with or without student loans. In Table 9, we report the composition of the two loan status groups by

TABLE 9
Student Loan Status by Gender

	Females			Males		
	No loan (n=122)	Loan (n=137)	Tests*	No loan (n=77)	Loan (n=97)	Tests[a]
University completion (%)						
Early bachelor's	46	25	p<0.05	33	27	ns
Delayed bachelor's	25	30		36	34	
Graduate degrees	29	45		31	39	
Academic achievement (%)						
GPA 1.0 – 3.0	26	24	ns	20	33	ns
GPA 3.0 – 3.5	23	27		29	26	
GPA 3.5 – 4.0	51	48		52	41	
University eligibility (%)						
No	22	27	ns	20	21	ns
Yes	78	73		80	79	
1989 PSE participation (%)						
Non-participant	7	10	ns	7	14	ns
Non-university	43	53		33	34	
University	50	37		61	52	
At least one parent has university education (%)						
No	55	57	ns	49	64	p<0.1
Yes	45	43		51	36	
Family geog. location (%)						
Metropolitan area	48	25	p<0.001	53	35	p<0.1
Urban-rural area	34	46		27	39	
Remote area	18	29		20	26	
2003 Home ownership (%)						
No	28	26	ns	27	30	ns
Yes	72	74		73	70	
1993 mean salary ($)	12.4	11.2	ns	13.5	11.8	ns
1998 mean salary ($)	19.0	18.2	ns	23.1	18.2	p<0.05
2003 mean salary ($)	29.4	29.4	ns	32.5	35.1	ns

Note:
[a]We used chi-square tests to compare proportions and one-way ANOVA tests to compare means.
Source: Authors' compilation.

gender in relation to various factors in order to determine whether graduates with student loans are essentially different from those who completed their studies without loans. Of the 137 female respondents who had student loans, 25 percent obtained early bachelor's degrees, 30 percent were in the delayed bachelor's degree completion category, and 45 percent had earned graduate degrees. The composition of the group of women who did not have student loans is quite different: most (46 percent) obtained early bachelor's degrees. The chi-square test of independence shows that there is a significant association between loan status and university completion paths for female respondents. Quite similar but less pronounced patterns are evident for male respondents.

Family geographical location is another factor for which a significant difference between the student loan group distributions can be demonstrated. Those coming from urban-rural areas were the most likely to receive student loans, and this pattern is stronger for women. Most respondents without loans had parents living in metropolitan areas, and this pattern is stronger for men. There is a modest association between family background (parental education) and student loan status, with about 57 percent of women and 64 percent of men who had loans coming from less educated families. However, this relationship is significant only for males. There is no significant difference between the student loan groups by GPA or university eligibility status; since all of the respondents in this analysis are university graduates, their high school academic characteristics are quite similar. This suggests that all being relatively equal in terms of academic ability, other factors do contribute to delayed or prolonged study for some talented individuals. For example, most women who received student loans over time began their studies in 1989 in non-university institutions (53 percent), while the majority (52 percent) of men who received loans entered university directly in 1989. Similar patterns are evident within the group of respondents without student loans, which supports a previous observation that women are more likely than men to go through a university transfer route. Few differences are detected between groups on variables related to home ownership and mean salary.

Discussion and Conclusion

The complexity of the analyses above attests to the challenges in portraying the various routes through the post-secondary system in relation to an examination of debt load incurred over time and in relation to evolving individual, institutional, and system characteristics. In an articulated system such as that of B.C. which encourages participation in post-secondary education by all age groups, multiple entry and transfer points must be taken into account. Individuals' actions reflect the structure of the system, which means that if we focus on only one entry point (e.g., direct entry after high school graduation) or one exit point (e.g., completion of a bachelor's degree), some key components of the post-secondary attainment/student debt story remain concealed. Also, it is critical to account for where someone commences post-secondary studies and whether the journey through to degree completion is swift, delayed, or extended.

One key finding of this paper is that an extended time to degree completion – due to delayed entry into the post-secondary system, a prolonged period of study, or transfer from a non-university institution to university – is costly in terms of overall student debt incurred. Our findings show clearly that those students requiring student financial assistance who complete university degrees within five years of high school graduation incur far less overall debt than those who fall into the "delayed bachelor's" category. This finding is even more remarkable given that B.C. had a tuition freeze in place for most of the years that students in this category would have studied in post-secondary institutions. However, the less than generous B.C. student assistance policies and, in particular, a loan remission policy restricted to only B.C. student loans as well as limited access to grants and bursaries may have offset any intended financial relief through frozen tuition fees. In addition, expansion of the number of post-secondary places outside the large metropolitan areas may have encouraged students to begin post-secondary studies in their local communities, which may, in turn, have resulted in prolonged completion times. Problems with transfer from non-university institutions to universities, such as difficulty in gaining access to useful information about the transfer process and in choosing courses that are transferable to receiving institutions, are well documented (Andres, 2001). However, our findings also reveal that those students who begin their studies at non-university institutions *and* complete their studies within five years incur the lowest amounts of student debt. In B.C., this is considered an indication that the transfer system is working very well and as intended.

However, gender differences in median debt loads are evident for this group. Elsewhere, Andres (1999) has demonstrated that women are more likely than men to work part-time during the academic year, which suggests that men are able to earn more during the summer and as a result are perhaps less likely to need high levels of student financial assistance. However, our study shows that those who hold student loans are also more likely to work, either full-time or part-time, which appears to be associated with high costs of obtaining a university education and limited parental financial support.

The correspondence analysis confirms that there is an association between the timing and duration of paths to university completion and the amount of student loans incurred. In addition, commencing post-secondary studies within one year of high school graduation matters. The types and duration of paths taken to university completion have consequences for other spheres of respondents' lives (e.g., marriage, children, home ownership, occupational status). This analysis demonstrates that high school achievement is a relevant explanatory variable of educational paths that not only determines what respondents do one year after high school graduation but also has long-term consequences.

In terms of policy implications, it appears that to ensure timely degree completion, adequate student financial assistance is necessary – through scholarships, bursaries, student loans that can be repaid without causing undue hardships for students who are becoming increasingly involved in other facets of adult life, or a combination of all of the above. Implementation requires adequate student services within post-secondary institutions to assist students who have difficulties in planning their way through the system in terms of academic and financial need, but also in relation to their career and life course plans. Especially in articulated post-secondary systems that offer a range of institutional opportunities, it is important to strengthen counselling services. It is a mistake to take for granted that by simply creating an articulated system, students will find optimal ways to navigate it.

The most able students are those who are most likely to finish their studies within five years. Secondary school personnel, policy-makers, students, and parents should be made aware of the relationship between poor preparation in high school – as reflected in low achievement levels and ineligibility for direct entry into universities – and its subsequent impact on time to completion of university degrees, related debt load, and the ability to engage in adult life tasks. In other words, students who plan to earn university degrees would be well advised to take advantage of the educational opportunities offered by the tuition-free segment of the educational system – that is, senior secondary.

We have demonstrated that even though women complete their studies more quickly than men, they are more likely to incur higher levels of student debt. Elsewhere it has been demonstrated repeatedly that women with equivalent levels of education as men are much more likely than men to be in lower status jobs and earn less money. Income-contingent repayment schemes, such as those in Australia, could mitigate somewhat the burden of debt repayment in relation to low levels of income, particularly for women. Substantial loan remission for timely completion of university studies could be another strategy of benefit to women.

As we described at the beginning of this paper, policies around access and financial aid and the actual structure of the system are in constant flux. It is thus very difficult for students and their parents to monitor, plan for, and adapt to these changes. Perhaps students who enter the system should be able to "lock in" to certain conditions of funding for a given (e.g., five year) period of time to ensure continuity and provide some guarantee that their saving strategies over the years leading up to post-secondary participation are adequate to fund entry into the post-secondary system and timely program completion. An "education mortgage" scheme would both introduce predictability into borrowing patterns and reinforce the idea that education is truly an investment in one's future. A scheme that intertwines educational and financial goals could also serve as an incentive for students to complete each educational level more quickly and earn a credential over a shorter period of time.

Two factors may have potentially confounded our findings about the relationship between "delayed" bachelor's degree and total student debt. First, delayed bachelor's are likely to spend more time than early bachelor's in post-secondary institutions as independent students. Independent student status increases the amount of student financial assistance available to these individuals because parental income is not a determining factor (Usher, 2004). Second, in 1994 Canada loan limits increased from $105/week to approximately $180/week for first and second year students and $270/week for students beyond second year. The impact of this one-time change to the student financial system requires additional investigation in relation to our findings. However, it does not change the fact that those in the delayed bachelor's category accumulate more student debt.

Similarly, rural students accumulate more debt because urban students in general have the option of living with their parents. While this may indeed be in keeping with the intentions of government policy, it costs rural students more to complete university studies. From an equity of access perspective, rural students are disadvantaged due to ascription.

Why do women complete their studies more quickly, yet incur more student debt? Why do males who take prolonged routes through the university system graduate with relatively lower levels of debt? Why are a relatively high proportion of respondents from middle-class backgrounds taking out student loans to complete their studies? How does the nature of the B.C. transfer system enhance or hinder timely completion of university studies? Although the results of our analyses have allowed us to speculate about possible explanations, further research is required to explore answers to these questions in depth. Our findings not only suggest directions for further research but indicate the nature and duration of data collection required.

Finally, the story told in this paper is clearly a British Columbia story. As highlighted at the beginning of the paper, the structure of the system, the nature of the student financial aid system, and the structure of provincial tuition fees clearly influence the way in which a given cohort manoeuvres through a given post-secondary system. Although analyses of data drawn from a Canadian sample such as is available in the Youth in Transition Survey Cohort B (YITS-B) (see Andres and Adamuti Trache, 2007, and other chapters in this volume) can provide an indication of overall trends, it is much more difficult to pinpoint reasons for high debt loads incurred by students and to devise policies to enhance the financial well-being of post-secondary graduates without locating the analysis within the relevant provincial context. However, even when considering the B.C. system alone, it is clear that student financial assistance policies were not in step with the intentions of the Access for All initiative and its enduring legacy.

Notes

1. In addition, the Ministry of Education provided a limited number of scholarships to students who wrote and achieved high scores on scholarship examinations. Scholarships were awarded to students on the basis of Standard Ministry Scores. In 1987-88, 1,174 of the 6,372 students who wrote scholarship examinations received these awards. Also, school districts offered awards ($500 value) to 1 percent of their students. In 1987-88, the Passport to Education program was introduced, which, according to the Ministry of Education (1988), "was designed both to recognize current achievement and to promote greater effort and achievement in the future" (22). It allowed students to accumulate award credits over the four years of high school to a maximum of $800. However, it had limited impact on 1988 graduates as eligible students would have earned $275 at most (British Columbia Ministry of Education, 1988).
2. A weighted full-time equivalent (WFTE) is adjusted to account for variations in tuition fees, for example between an undergraduate arts student and a medical student (Malcolmson and Lee, 2004, 20).
3. In several tables, cells contain a small "n" indicating small numbers. These results must be interpreted with caution. However, when compared with other cells in a table (e.g., Table 6), a small "n" demonstrates that some trajectories are very infrequently embarked upon.

4. It is likely that these students were admitted as exceptional admissions (e.g., without the necessary prerequisites). We do not have precise information about admission decisions.
5. We compared these results with data from the Youth in Transition Survey Cohort B (YITS-B). The YITS-B longitudinal study of youth has much in common with the 1989 and 1993 surveys of the Paths on Life's Way project. Comparable findings between Paths and YITS data within first five years after the high school graduation of each cohort support the credibility and generalizability of the B.C. longitudinal results.

References

Adamuti-Trache, M., and L. Andres. 2008. "Embarking on and Persisting in Scientific Fields of Study: Cultural Capital, Gender, and Curriculum along the Science Pipeline." *International Journal of Science Education* 30 (12): 1557-84.

Andres, L. 1999. "Multiple Life Sphere Participation by Young Adults." In *From Education to Work: Cross-National Perspectives*, edited by W. Heinz, 149-70. Cambridge: Cambridge University Press.

– 2001. "Transfer from Community College to University: Perspectives of British Columbia Students." *Canadian Journal of Higher Education* 31 (3): 35-74.

– 2002a. *Educational and Occupational Participation and Completion Patterns of the Class of '88*. Vancouver: British Columbia Council on Admissions and Transfer.

– 2002b. *Paths on Life's Way: Base Line Study (1988) and First Follow-up (1989)*. Vancouver: Department of Educational Studies, University of British Columbia.

– 2002c. *Paths on Life's Way. Phase II Follow-up Survey, 1993, Five Years Later*. Rev. ed. Vancouver: Department of Educational Studies, University of British Columbia.

– 2002d. *Paths on Life's Way: Phase III Follow-up Survey of 1998, Ten Years Later*. Vancouver: Department of Educational Studies, University of British Columbia.

Andres, L., and M. Adamuti-Trache. 2006. *Youth Transitions through Education, Work and Life: British Columbia High School Graduates of the Class of '88*. Paper presented at the 16th World Congress of Sociology, Durban, South Africa, 23-29 July.

– 2007. *For Whom Does Student Financial Assistance Make a Difference? A Fifteen Year Portrait of British Columbia Young Adults*. Paper presented at the Measuring the Effectiveness of Student Aid (MESA) Conference, Canada Millennium Scholarship Foundation, Montreal, 19 October.

– 2008. "Life Course Transitions, Social Class, and Gender: A Fifteen Year Perspective of the Lived Lives of Canadian Young Adults." *Journal of Youth Studies* 11 (12): 115-45.

Andres, L., M. Adamuti-Trache, E.-S. Soon, M. Pidgeon, and J.-P Thomsen. 2007. "Educational Expectations, Parental Social Class, Gender, and Post-Secondary Attainment: A Ten Year Perspective." *Youth and Society* 39 (2): 135-63.

Andres, L., and J. Dawson. 1998. *Investigating Transfer Project. Phase III: A History of Transfer Policy and Practice in British Columbia*. Research report prepared for the B.C. Council on Admissions and Transfer. Vancouver: B.C. Council on Admissions and Transfer.

B.C. Ministry of Advanced Education and Job Training. 1987. *Completion, Transfer, and Retention*. Paper No. 8 in the Access, Completion and Transition to Work Series. Victoria: B.C. Ministry of Advanced Education and Job Training.

B.C. Provincial Access Committee. 1988. *Access to Advanced Education and Job Training in British Columbia*. Report to the Ministry of Advanced Education and Job Training.

Bourdieu, P. 1990. *In Other Words. Essays toward a Reflexive Sociology*. Translated by M. Adamson. Stanford: Stanford University Press. (Original work published in 1982, 1987).

British Columbia Ministry of Education. 1988. *Ministry of Education Annual Report*. British Columbia: Ministry of Education.

British Columbia Research Corporation. 1990. *A Follow-up Survey of 1987/88 Grade 12 Graduates*. Technical Report. Vancouver: B.C. Research.

Coleman, J.S., and T. Husén. 1985. *Becoming Adult in a Changing Society*. Paris: OECD.

Drolet, M. 2002. "Can the Workplace Explain Canadian Gender Pay Differentials?" *Canadian Public Policy* 28 (Supplement 1): 41-63.

Finnie, R. 2005. "Access to Post-Secondary Education: An Analytical Framework and New Evidence on Background Effects." In *Preparing for Post-Secondary Education: New Roles for Governments and Families*, edited by R. Sweet and P. Anisef, 17-54. Montreal and Kingston: McGill-Queen's University Press.

Gelin, F. 2006. "The British Columbia Council on Admissions and Transfer and Its Role in the BC Post-Secondary System." Paper presented at the BCCAT Orientation for New Council Members Meeting. Thompson Rivers University, Kamloops, B.C.

Giddens, A. 1984. *The Constitution of Society*. Berkeley: University of California Press.

Greenacre, M. 1993. *Correspondence Analysis in Practice*. London: Academic Press and Hartcourt Brace and Co.

Härnqvist, K. 1978. *Individual Demand for Education*. Paris: OECD.

Hodgkinson, H.L. 1985. *All One System: Demographics of Education, Kindergarten through Graduate School*. Washington, D.C.: Institute for Educational Leadership.

Hunt, S. 2005. *The Life Course: A Sociological Introduction*. Hampshire: Palgrave Macmillan.

Karabel, J. 1986. "Community Colleges and Social Stratification in the 1980s." *New Directions for Community Colleges* 54 (2): 13-30.

Macdonald, J. 1962. *Higher Education in British Columbia and a Plan for the Future*. Vancouver: University of British Columbia.

Malcolmson, J., and M. Lee. 2004. *Financing Higher Learning: Post-Secondary Education Funding in BC*. Vancouver: Canadian Centre for Policy Alternatives.

Orum, J. 1997. *Review of BC Student Assistance and Barriers to Post-Secondary Participation*.

Pineo, P.C., and J. Goyder. 1988. "The Growth of the Canadian Educational System: An Analysis of Transition Probabilities." *Canadian Journal of Higher Education* 17 (2): 37-54.

Review of BC Student Assistance and Barriers to Post-Secondary Participation, Final Report. 1992. Victoria: B.C. Ministry of Advanced Education, Training, and Technology.

Standing Senate Committee on National Finance. 1987. *Federal Policy on Post-Secondary Education*. Ottawa: Minister of Supply and Services Canada.

Statistics Canada. 2005. University Tuition Fees, *The Daily* (1 September 2005). Accessed 21 September 2007. http://www.statcan.ca/Daily/English/050901/d050901a.htm.

– 2006. University Tuition Fees, *The Daily* (1 September 2006). Accessed 21 September 2007. http://www.statcan.ca/Daily/English/060901/d060901a.htm.

– 2007. Average Undergraduate Tuition Fees for Full-Time Students, by Discipline, by Province: Statistics Canada. Accessed 21 September 2007. http://www40.statcan.ca/l01/cst01/educ50a.htm?sdi=tuition percent20fees percent20provinces.

Usher, A. 2004. *Are the Poor Needy? Are the Needy Poor?* Toronto: Educational Policy Institute.

APPENDIX
Determinants and Consequences of University Completion Paths
(Column Percentages)

University completion		Early bachelor's		Delayed bachelor's		Graduate degrees	
Gender		Female	Male	Female	Male	Female	Male
Academic achievement (GPA)							
1.0 – 3.0		23	22	31	31	24	27
3.0 – 3.5		23	33	31	30	25	19
3.5 – 4.0		55	45	39	39	52	53
University eligibility	Yes	81	88	65	75	76	77
1989 PSE participation							
Non-participant		2	4	14	18	10	6
Non-university		44	26	65	44	42	18
University		54	71	22	38	47	38
Student loans (1989-2003)							
None		57	51	46	48	37	39
<$10,000		18	31	14	10	13	3
$10-20,000		11	12	8	18	20	13
$20-30,000		8	4	14	15	17	18
Above $30,000		6	2	19	10	13	27
Parents have university degree							
No parent		54	55	56	61	58	56
At least one parent		46	45	44	39	42	44
Parents' geographical location							
Metropolitan area		37	45	28	38	39	47
Urban- Rural area		36	31	54	38	36	32
Remote area		27	24	19	25	25	21
2003 Occupational status							
Unskilled/Semi-skilled		10	12	13	15	3	0
Technical/Skilled		55	46	67	42	44	31
Management/Professional		35	41	20	42	53	69
2003 Marital status	Yes	78	82	71	75	70	73
2003 Children	Yes	77	55	51	44	39	40
2003 Home ownership	Yes	77	78	74	65	67	68
Sample size (N)		**97**	**51**	**65**	**61**	**97**	**62**

Source: Authors' compilation.

Part IV
Financial Issues

11

Why Are Lower-Income Students Less Likely to Attend University? Evidence from Academic Abilities, Parental Influences, and Financial Constraints

MARC FRENETTE

Cette étude avait pour but de permettre une meilleure compréhension des différences importantes qui existent, selon les différents degrés de la répartition du revenu, entre les jeunes qui entreprennent ou non des études universitaires. Grâce aux données de l'Enquête auprès des jeunes en transition (EJET, cohorte A), je montre que l'on peut expliquer 96 % de l'écart total qui sépare les jeunes du quartile supérieur de revenu et ceux du quartile inférieur grâce à des caractéristiques observables. Par exemple, les différences dans les facteurs à long terme – comme les résultats aux tests normalisés de lecture et les résultats scolaires obtenus à 15 ans, l'influence des parents et la qualité de l'établissement fréquenté au secondaire – expliquent 84 % de l'écart. En revanche, seulement 12 % de l'écart est relié aux contraintes financières.

This study attempts to shed light on the large gap in university attendance that exists across the income distribution. Using YITS-A, I find that 96 percent of the total gap in university attendance between youth from the top and bottom income quartiles can be accounted for by differences in observable characteristics. Differences in long-term factors such as standardized test scores in reading obtained at age 15, school marks reported at age 15, parental influences, and high school quality account for 84 percent of the gap. In contrast, only 12 percent of the gap is related to self-reported financial constraints.

Who Goes? Who Stays? What Matters? Accessing and Persisting in Post-Secondary Education in Canada, eds. R. Finnie, R.E. Mueller, A. Sweetman, and A. Usher. Montreal and Kingston: McGill-Queen's University Press, Queen's Policy Studies Series. © 2008 The School of Policy Studies, Queen's University at Kingston. All rights reserved.

Introduction

It is well known that while participation in non-university post-secondary programs varies little by parental income, university participation tends to rise substantially with parental income (Figure 1). Only 31.0 percent of youth in the bottom 25 percent of the income distribution attend university, compared to 50.2 percent in the top 25 percent and 43.4 percent in the third quartile. Even youth in the second quartile are at a considerable disadvantage compared to youth in the top half of the income distribution. In fact, they are only slightly more likely to attend university than youth in the bottom quartile. The steepness of the income gradient in university participation has raised concerns among student groups, parents, policy analysts, and education planners, since it potentially has negative implications for the intergenerational transmission of earnings.

Why does university participation vary so much by parental income levels? Is it because a university education is more costly than other forms of post-secondary education? Alternatively, is it because the minimum grade requirements to enter university are much higher than for most college and trade school programs? The answers to such questions

FIGURE 1
Post-Secondary Participation Rate by Parental Income Quartile

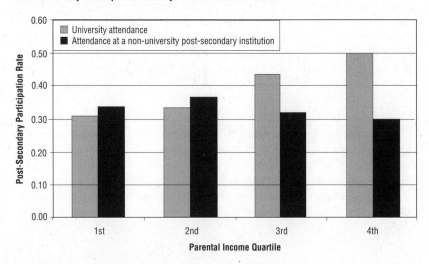

Note: Parental income is adjusted for family size of youth at age 15.
Source: Statistics Canada, Youth in Transition Survey, Cohort A.

are important, because there are many potential levers available to address the gap in university participation, such as tuition fees, student loans, scholarships, early learning intervention, and programs geared towards increasing awareness of the benefits of a university education. Given that some of these levers address financial constraints while others address knowledge gaps (i.e., academic performance or awareness of benefits), a more complete understanding of the reasons why lower-income youth are less likely to attend university is important for Canadian policy design.

An often-cited explanation for the gap revolves around credit constraints (e.g., Kane, 1994; Ellwood and Kane, 2000; Card, 2001). Essentially, it is argued that economically disadvantaged youth cannot afford to pay for the cost of a university education through their own means and must rely on student loans. However, they may not be able to secure enough loan money to comfortably cover the full cost of attending.[1]

An alternative explanation advanced by others (e.g., Carneiro and Heckman, 2002) suggests that youth from economically disadvantaged families are lacking in parental resources or influences, which can have a negative impact on cognitive abilities, motivation, study habits, perception of the benefits of a university education, and social environment. According to this view, disadvantaged youth often do not choose to attend university because they do not perform well in school; they do not have any interest in furthering their education; their friends are less likely to go on to university; and so on. Even if they are able to borrow enough money, some may be averse to debt because they underestimate the economic benefits of a university education over a lifetime.

In the United States, the empirical evidence on credit constraints on university attendance has been mixed. There appears to be a consensus in the literature that credit constraints on attendance were small or nonexistent in the past, as demonstrated by Carneiro and Heckman (2002) who follow teenagers from the 1979 cohort of the National Longitudinal Survey of Youth for several years. However, data from the 1997 cohort of the same study suggest an increasing importance of credit constraints (Belley and Lochner, 2007).

In Canada, it was impossible to examine the issue until recently because of lack of available data. With the release of the third cycle of the Youth in Transition Survey (YITS), Cohort A, it is now possible to link university attendance of 19-year-old youth to a plethora of information on this group when they were aged 15, including results from standardized tests, high school marks, sense of control (or mastery) over their lives, self-esteem, parental income, parental education, parental expectations, peer influences, high school attended, and financial con-straints, among others. In other words, it is now possible to assess the extent to which disadvantaged students are less likely to attend uni-versity because of factors such as their performance on standardized tests, overall marks, parental influences, peer influences, or financial resources. The purpose of this study is to attempt to further understand the income gap in university participation with this new data source.

In the next section, I describe the basic methodology employed in the study. I then turn to the data, beginning with a breakdown of how stu-dents from various parts of the income distribution have different standardized test scores, school marks, parental influences, etc. Next, I describe how such characteristics tend to mediate the income–enrolment relationship. In the core of the paper I formally decompose the gaps in university participation across different parts of the income distribu-tion into explained and unexplained components (i.e., the portions of the gap that are accounted for and those that are not accounted for by differences in observable characteristics, respectively). The result of this exercise is unequivocal: I find that 96 percent of the total gap in univer-sity attendance between youth from the top and bottom income quar-tiles can be accounted for by differences in observable characteristics.

Differences in long-term factors such as standardized test scores in reading obtained at age 15, school marks reported at age 15, parental influences, and high school quality account for 84 percent of the gap. In contrast, only 12 percent of the gap is related to financial constraints. In my conclusion, I put these results into perspective. I argue that the find-ings suggest that the evidence on the existence of widespread credit constraints is quite weak and, as a result, our focus should now shift towards trying to further understand why students from lower-income families tend to perform more poorly on standardized and scholastic tests than students from higher-income families. An additional path that research may take is to examine how the gap in parental influences can be closed, since it too contributes towards the gap in university participation.

Methodology

Data for the study are drawn from the Youth in Transition Survey (YITS), Cohort A, which is described in detail by Bussière, Motte, Qiu, and Zhang (2008).[2] In the current study, I focus on students who were in Grade 10 on 31 December 1999 (the usual grade for students turning 15 years old in a given year), and who held a high school diploma on 31 December 2003 (when students were 19 years old), since credit constraints are operative following high school when students must decide whether or not to go on. The main outcome is university participation by 31 December 2003.

Two measures of academic abilities are used in the study. The first is the Programme for International Student Assessment (PISA) overall reading score. Note that I also used mathematics and science test scores (Frenette, 2007) and found similar results. The second is the student's overall mark in Grade 10. Conditional on one's performance on a standardized test, school marks may reflect one's ability to capitalize on these skills in a more structured setting (Jacob, 2002). Jacob goes further and treats school marks as "non-cognitive" abilities, once cognitive abilities are taken into account.

The YITS contains two additional measures of "non-cognitive abilities." The first is feeling control (or mastery) over one's life. Respondents were asked seven questions related to the extent that they felt they could change their destiny or success in life. A scalar measure was constructed from the seven responses. The second measure is self-esteem. Respondents were asked 10 questions related to how they felt about themselves. Again, a scalar measure was constructed from the responses. Both measures were standardized to have a mean of zero. I use the average of the two measures in the analysis. Heckman, Stixrud, and Urzua (2006) use a similarly constructed variable in their study.

Five other pieces of information were taken from the student questionnaire. First, students were asked how many of their friends were planning to pursue their education after high school. This information can capture peer influences on student educational outcomes. For the purposes of this study, the answers were grouped into three categories: "some or none," "most," or "all." Second, students were asked to what extent they agreed with the notion that getting a good job later in life depends on their success in school now. This is the closest measure in the survey of the student's perception of the returns to schooling. For the purposes of this study, students who disagreed (or strongly disagreed) are deemed to have a low (or a very low) perception of the returns to schooling, while those who agreed (or strongly agreed) are deemed to have a high (or a very high) perception of the returns to schooling. The region of residence (Atlantic provinces, Quebec, Ontario, Manitoba–Saskatchewan, Alberta, and British Columbia) and the student's gender are also used in the study. Finally, students are categorized as financially constrained or not. All respondents are asked, "What is the highest level of education you would like to get?" and then, "Is there anything standing in your way of going as far in school as you would like to go?" I define financially constrained youth as those who did not attend university despite wanting to do so, and who cited finances as one reason why they did not go as far in school as they would like to.[3]

The parents of the students were also administered a questionnaire in 2000. Four pieces of information are used in this study: the quartile of total income in 1999 (including earnings, investment income, and government transfer income), the presence of parents in the home (for the purposes of this study: one parent present, two parents present with one or none being a birth parent, or two birth parents present), the highest level of education of either parent (for the purposes of this study: no post-secondary certificate, a non-university post-secondary certificate, an undergraduate degree, or a graduate or professional degree), and parental expectations of the highest level of educational outcome of the child (for the purposes of this study: a university degree or not).

To account for differences in family size and their associated economies of scale, I calculated "equivalent" income by dividing parental income by the square root of the family size.[4] Based on equivalent income, students were separated by quartile. The threshold levels of equivalent income for each quartile are $20,409 (25th percentile), $30,531 (50th percentile), and $41,000 (75th percentile).[5]

Another important factor to consider is the quality of the high school attended. Although most schools in Canada are publicly funded, not all jurisdictions fund education equally. There may also be teacher selection according to neighbourhood and/or student quality. Furthermore, many schools rely in part on fundraising campaigns organized by parents (e.g., book sales, bake sales). To the extent that schools located in well-to-do neighbourhoods can generate more funds from these campaigns, it is possible that students from more favourable backgrounds may benefit from more school resources. Finally, universities may be more likely to recruit from certain schools. In an attempt to account for differences in high school quality, I created an index of the propensity of a high school to generate university-bound students, accounting for the composition of students in the high school. To do so, I regressed a binary university participation variable on a set of dummy variables indicating the high school attended and a set of control variables for the student's characteristics. The coefficients on the high school dummies can be interpreted as the school's intrinsic ability to produce a university-bound student, after accounting for the student's characteristics. The coefficients were then used as a measure of high school quality (i.e., the propensity to generate university-bound students).

As in Frenette and Zeman (2008), the goal of this study is to decompose the gap in university attendance into an explained component and an unexplained component. The explained portion of the gap provides an estimate of the reduction in the total gap that we would expect to see if the two groups had the same observable characteristics. Specifically, the explained portion is simply the difference in the characteristics of youth from different parts of the income distribution, multiplied by the "impact" that the characteristic has on the probability of university attendance.[6]

Results

The large enrolment gaps shown in Figure 1 suggest that some students have a clear advantage in terms of attending university, and that this advantage is somehow related to parent income. But what distinguishes students from different parts of the income distribution, and how do these factors influence their probability of attending university? In Table 1, I show sample means of variables used in the analysis by quartile of parental income.

What is evident from Table 1 is that university participation rises with parental income, but so too does the likelihood of possessing characteristics that may foster higher educational attainment. Moreover, the increases are monotonic, in the sense that they tend to increase at every level of income.

In terms of reading abilities, students in the top income quartile (Q4) are far more likely to be at the top of the reading distribution compared to students in the bottom income quartile (Q1). For example, 7.2 percent of students in Q4 perform in the top 5 percent of all youth on the reading test, compared to only 2.9 percent of students in Q1. Conversely, only 2.9 percent of students in Q4 perform in the bottom 5 percent on the reading test, compared to 7.4 percent of students in Q1.

If we use the top and bottom 25 percent of the reading distribution as a yardstick, the difference in performance across the income distribution is equally compelling. Among students in Q4, 32.8 percent perform in the top 25 percent on the reading test, while only 18.8 percent perform in the bottom 25 percent. In contrast, only 18.0 percent of students in Q1 perform in the top 25 percent, while 32.3 percent of these youth perform in the bottom 25 percent. Similar patterns emerge from the distribution of overall marks.

Differences in the mastery/self-esteem score across the income distribution are much smaller. Among students in Q4, 27.1 percent are in the top 25 percent of the mastery/self-esteem distribution, while only 23.1 percent are in the bottom 25 percent. In contrast, only 22.0 percent

TABLE 1
Means of Variables by Parental Income Quartile

	Parental income quartile			
	1st	*2nd*	*3rd*	*4th*
University participation	0.310	0.335	0.434	0.502
Reading score<P5	0.074	0.045	0.051	0.029
P5 Reading score<P10	0.064	0.055	0.044	0.037
P10 Reading score<P25	0.184	0.159	0.122	0.122
P25 Reading score<P50	0.266	0.260	0.244	0.225
P50 Reading score<P75	0.232	0.250	0.262	0.258
P75 Reading score<P90	0.114	0.143	0.162	0.187
P90 Reading score<P95	0.036	0.045	0.051	0.069
Reading score P95	0.029	0.042	0.064	0.072
Overall mark<60%	0.056	0.049	0.046	0.041
60% Overall mark 69%	0.167	0.161	0.135	0.143
70% Overall mark 79%	0.352	0.332	0.337	0.301
80% Overall mark 89%	0.301	0.339	0.357	0.383
Overall mark 90%	0.064	0.074	0.092	0.106
Mastery/self-esteem<P5	0.058	0.058	0.043	0.041
P5 Master y/self-esteem<P10	0.061	0.053	0.043	0.043
P10 Master y/self-esteem<P25	0.166	0.142	0.146	0.147
P25 Master y/self-esteem<P50	0.220	0.229	0.232	0.224
P50 Master y/self-esteem<P75	0.276	0.270	0.276	0.273
P75 Master y/self-esteem<P90	0.132	0.154	0.159	0.155
P90 Master y/self-esteem<P95	0.045	0.046	0.050	0.058
Mastery/self-esteem P95	0.043	0.049	0.051	0.057
One parent	0.303	0.148	0.082	0.050
Two parents, one or more not from birth	0.097	0.107	0.119	0.119
Two birth parents	0.600	0.745	0.799	0.831
Parents have no PS certificate	0.469	0.350	0.246	0.175
Parents have a non-university PS certificate	0.355	0.434	0.379	0.313
Parents have an undergraduate degree	0.118	0.149	0.242	0.296
Parents have a graduate or professional degree	0.045	0.058	0.127	0.210
Parents expect university degree	0.620	0.652	0.729	0.794
Very low perception of returns to schooling	0.017	0.016	0.017	0.016
Low perception of returns to schooling	0.067	0.067	0.061	0.064
High perception of returns to schooling	0.499	0.496	0.504	0.485
Very high perception of returns to schooling	0.417	0.421	0.419	0.436
Few or no friends plan to further education after high school	0.205	0.194	0.150	0.140

... *continued*

TABLE 1
(Continued)

	Parental income quartile			
	1st	*2nd*	*3rd*	*4th*
Most friends plan to further education after high school	0.505	0.485	0.515	0.485
All friends plan to further education after high school	0.290	0.321	0.335	0.375
Atlantic provinces	0.123	0.096	0.060	0.052
Quebec	0.177	0.185	0.156	0.150
Ontario	0.361	0.384	0.443	0.483
Manitoba or Saskatchewan	0.097	0.089	0.078	0.058
Alberta	0.087	0.097	0.113	0.125
British Columbia	0.156	0.150	0.150	0.132
Female	0.549	0.529	0.523	0.501
High school quality P5	0.054	0.057	0.045	0.040
P5 High school quality<P10	0.045	0.046	0.055	0.055
P10 High school quality<P25	0.146	0.174	0.140	0.135
P25 High school quality<P50	0.247	0.270	0.258	0.234
P50 High school quality<P75	0.262	0.230	0.256	0.251
P75 High school quality<P90	0.142	0.129	0.150	0.174
P90 High school quality<P95	0.058	0.046	0.047	0.052
High school quality P95	0.046	0.048	0.049	0.058
Financially constrained	0.134	0.109	0.079	0.059
Sample size	4,327	3,930	3,298	3,147

Note: Percentiles are denoted by "P."
Source: Statistics Canada, Youth in Transition Survey, Cohort A.

of students in Q1 are in the top 25 percent of the mastery/self-esteem distribution, while 28.4 percent are in the bottom 25 percent.

In terms of parental presence, only 5.0 percent of students in Q4 have only one parent in the home, compared to 30.3 percent of youth in Q1. Among families with two parents present, students in Q4 are also far more likely to have two birth parents present.

Not surprisingly, parental education is very unequally distributed across income quartiles. Students in Q4 are almost five times more likely to have at least one parent who possesses a graduate or professional degree than students in Q1 (21.0 percent compared to 4.5 percent).

Slightly more than half of all students in Q4 (50.6 percent) have at least one parent who possesses a university degree. Among students in Q1, only 16.3 percent have at least one parent who possesses a university degree. At the other end of the spectrum, 46.9 percent of students in Q1 do not have a parent who possesses a post-secondary certificate, compared to only 17.5 percent of students in Q4.

Given the large differences in parental education, it is not surprising that parental expectations vis-à-vis a university education tend to rise with family income. In fact, 79.4 percent of students in Q4 have parents who expect them to obtain a university degree. Among students in Q1, only 62.0 percent of parents expect them to obtain a university degree.

Despite the fact that students at the bottom of the income distribution are not raised by highly educated, highly paid parents, they tend to attribute as much importance to schooling in determining their future success in the labour market as students at the top of the income distribution do. Of course, this could be the result of seeing their low-educated parents work in low-paying jobs (i.e., they see the negative impact of *not* pursuing higher education).

Students with higher levels of parental income also tend to report a larger proportion of friends planning to pursue further education after high school. Among students in Q4, 37.5 percent state that all of their friends plan to further their education after high school, compared to only 29.0 percent among students in Q1. Students who are higher up in the income distribution are also less likely to live in the Atlantic provinces, Quebec, Manitoba–Saskatchewan, or British Columbia, and are more likely to live in Ontario and Alberta. These students are also slightly less likely to be female, largely because girls tend to live with their mothers following divorce, and families headed by lone mothers generally have lower levels of income than other family types. Students at the top of the income distribution are somewhat more likely to have attended a high school with a relatively high propensity to produce university-bound students.

Finally, and not surprisingly, youth from lower-income families are more likely to report being financially constrained with respect to university attendance than others (13.4 percent compared to 5.9 percent). Overall, only 9.5 percent of youth report being financially constrained. An earlier Statistics Canada study (Bowlby and McMullen, 2002) reported that 70.7 percent of high school graduates with no post-secondary education cited financial barriers to going as far in school as they would like. Although the data and methods are slightly different, a similar estimate can be generated from the data used in the current study, although as I demonstrate in Figure 2, it only applies to a very select

FIGURE 2
Incidence of Reporting a Financial Barrier to Attending University among High School Graduates

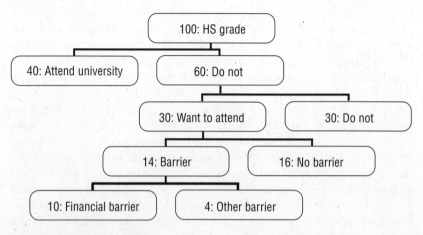

Note: All numbers are percentages.
Source: Statistics Canada, Youth in Transition Survey, Cohort A.

group of youth. Out of 100 high school graduates, 40 attend university by age 19 and 60 do not. Only half (or 30) of the 60 youth who did not attend university report wanting to attend university. Of these, only 14 report some sort of barrier to attending, 10 of which cite their financial situation. So, 10 of the original 100 high school graduates claimed facing a financial barrier to attend university. Of the very small number of students (i.e., 14) who claimed facing a barrier of some sort to attend university, 10 of them cited a financial barrier (roughly 70 percent).

Whether the large differences in socio-economic characteristics described above can go some distance in explaining the large gaps in university participation across the income distribution also depends on the extent to which these characteristics influence the decision to attend university. The detailed regression results are available in Frenette (2007). To summarize these results, university participation tends to increase substantially with the reading score. High school marks are also positively associated with university participation, especially beyond 80 percent. University participation is generally not associated with the mastery/self-esteem score.[7] The number and type (birth or other) of parents present in the home play minimal roles in the decision to attend university. Parental education, on the other hand, is very strongly associated with university participation. Youth with at least one university-educated parent enjoy a large advantage in university participation over youth with no post-secondary-educated parent. The same is true for parental expectations: students whose parents expect them to complete a university degree are far more likely to do so. Perceptions of the returns to schooling are generally not associated with university participation. Students who report that all of their friends plan to pursue further education after high school are generally more likely to pursue university than students who report that few or none of their friends plan to do so. Some regional differences appear to be evident, although the differences are not large by any means since we control for student composition and high school quality. Females are more likely to go on to university than males even after conditioning on reading abilities, high school marks, parental influences, and detailed socio-economic characteristics. There are also very large differences in university participation based on the type of high school attended. Finally, and obviously, being financially constrained is associated with a large decline in university participation, all else being equal.

So far I have shown that students whose parents have different levels of income tend to have very different academic abilities, parental influences, and peer influences. Furthermore, they tend to grow up in different parts of the country, attend different types of high schools, and are more or less likely to be financially constrained. Many of these observable characteristics tend to influence the decision to attend university, although some more than others. I now turn to the main focus of the paper, which is to attempt to explain the gap in university attendance across various income quartiles with the observable characteristics.

In Figure 3 I show the decomposition results between youth from the top and the bottom income quartiles. Recall from Figure 1 that the gap in university participation between these two groups of youth is 19.2 percentage points. Almost all of this gap can be explained by differences in observable characteristics (96 percent). Only 12 percent is related to financial constraints. In contrast, 84 percent is related to long-term factors. The most important of these characteristics is parental education, which accounts for 30 percent of the gap. Reading scores account for 20 percent of the gap, while marks account for 14 percent. Note that, collectively, reading abilities and marks account for 34 percent of the total gap, which is slightly greater that the portion explained by parental education. Parental expectations account for 12 percent. The remaining factors do not account for a large proportion of the total gap (less than 9 percent in the category "other").

FIGURE 3
Proportion of University Participation Gap Explained by Differences in
Characteristics (Q4-Q1)

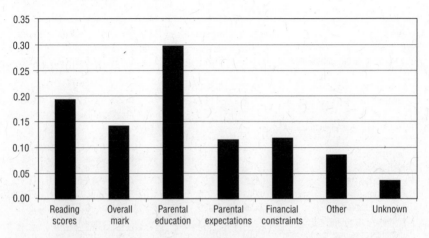

Source: Statistics Canada, Youth in Transition Survey, Cohort A.

Results of the decompositions between all combinations of youth from
different income quartiles appear below in Table 2. The gap in university attendance between students in Q3 and students in Q1 is also substantial (about 12 percentage points). Again, differences in observable
characteristics account for almost all of the gap (94 percent), and the
same factors come into play. Similar results hold when I decompose the
gap between other income quartiles. In general, most of the gap can be
explained by differences in observable characteristics. Moreover, financial constraints never play a larger role than student and parental
characteristics.

To substantiate the results, I performed three robustness checks. First,
results for models using mathematics and science standardized test
scores as measures of academic abilities are similar, except that a somewhat smaller proportion of the total gap in university participation can
be explained by differences in test scores (Frenette, 2007).[8]

Second, I also ran the decompositions by dropping Quebec residents,
given substantial differences in the schooling system in that province.
This exercise yielded no qualitative change in the results.

Third, it may be argued that asking youth to identify barriers (e.g.,
their financial situation) to attending university is a subjective exercise.
In fact, about one-half of all youth who did not attend university despite

TABLE 2
Decomposition of the University Participation Gap across Parental Income Quartiles

Decomposition across parental income quartiles						
	4th-1st	3rd-1st	2nd-1st	4th-2nd	3rd-2nd	4th-3rd
Total gap in university participation	0.192	0.123	0.025	0.167	0.099	0.068
Explained proportion of gap	0.962	0.943	1.587	0.902	0.770	0.970
Unexplained proportion of gap	0.038	0.057	-0.587	0.098	0.230	0.030
Proportion of gap explained by differences in:						
Reading scores	0.197	0.211	0.598	0.131	0.103	0.151
Overall mark	0.143	0.171	0.475	0.118	0.103	0.121
Mastery/self-esteem	-0.001	-0.002	0.058	0.001	0.001	0.003
Parental presence	0.001	0.016	0.188	0.009	0.005	0.009
Parental education	0.299	0.268	0.312	0.284	0.197	0.295
Parental expectations	0.116	0.124	0.198	0.115	0.116	0.136
Perceptions of returns to schooling	0.004	0.002	0.007	0.004	-0.001	0.010
Peer influences	0.017	0.008	0.032	0.009	0.018	0.017
Region	0.024	0.026	-0.010	0.001	0.022	0.004
Female	-0.017	-0.011	-0.048	-0.013	-0.003	-0.024
High school quality	0.058	-0.002	-0.522	0.142	0.126	0.160
Financial constraints	0.120	0.133	0.298	0.099	0.083	0.086

Source: Statistics Canada, Youth in Transition Survey, Cohort A.

wanting to do so claimed that nothing was standing in their way of attending (Figure 2). However, it is clear that these students did not perform as well in high school as university participants did. At age 15, 68.4 percent of future university attendees reported an overall mark of 80 percent or higher, and 91.6 percent reported a mark of 70 percent or higher. In contrast, only 34.7 percent of youth who claimed no barriers to attending reported an overall mark of at least 80 percent (a key threshold for university attendance), which is about half of the proportion of future university attendees. Moreover, only 74.2 percent of them reported an overall mark of 70 percent or higher. Interestingly, youth who claimed financial barriers to attending university reported even poorer grades in high school. Only 29.3 percent of them reported an overall mark of 80 percent or higher, and only 68.7 percent of them reported scoring 70 percent or higher. Given the potential problems in interpreting responses to such questions, I ran the models by dropping the financial constraints variable as a further test of robustness. In that case, 88 percent of the gap between the top and the bottom income quartiles was accounted for by differences in academic performance, parental influences, and other socio-economic characteristics. Thus, the main conclusion holds: differences in academic performance and parental influences account for the bulk of the gap in university attendance.

Conclusion

It is well known that economically disadvantaged students in Canada are less likely to pursue university education than students from well-to-do families. This has raised concerns among student groups, parents, policy analysts, and education planners, since it potentially has negative implications for the intergenerational transmission of earnings. Until recently, data limitations made it very challenging to understand the reasons behind this gap. With the release of the third cycle of the Youth in Transition Survey, Cohort A, it is now possible to link university attendance of 19-year-old youth to a plethora of information on these youth when they were aged 15, including results from standardized tests, high school marks, sense of control (or mastery) over their lives, self-esteem, parental income, parental education, parental expectations, peer influences, and high school attended, among others. The purpose of this study is to attempt to further understand the income gap in university participation with these new data.

I find that 96 percent of the total gap in university attendance between youth from the top and bottom income quartiles can be accounted for by differences in observable characteristics. Differences in long-term factors such as standardized test scores in reading obtained at age 15, school marks reported at age 15, parental influences, and high school quality account for 84 percent of the gap. In contrast, only 12 percent of the gap is related to financial constraints.

What do the results mean? To answer this question, it is important to realize that family income may pose different barriers to attending university. First, differences in academic performance across the income distribution may themselves be the result of differences in family income. Families with more financial resources may spend more money on books for children, take their children to museums, spend more on daycare in the early years, or locate in neighbourhoods with better schools, for example. These actions may result in higher performance on standardized and scholastic tests and thus in a higher probability of attending university in the future. Second, upon deciding to attend university, students may be faced with another barrier that is related to their family's financial position: credit constraints. However, the evidence presented in this study casts some doubt on the *widespread* existence of credit constraints in Canada.

Despite the weak evidence on credit constraints, there are two important caveats to keep in mind. First, even if credit constraints do not matter a lot for the population of youth as a whole, they may matter for certain groups of students in some instances. For example, Ontario students from middle-class backgrounds saw a large decline in their probability of pursuing a professional degree following the large and sudden tuition fee deregulation in these programs in Ontario universities (Frenette, 2008). Another example is students who grew up living out of commuting distance from a university. The additional cost of attending a university away from the parental home is greater than $5,000 (Barr-Telford et al., 2003), which appears to reduce enrolment among students from lower-income families who must move away to attend (Frenette, 2004). Second, even if credit constraints could be ruled out, it is important to note that this would be conditional on the existing financial aid system. The current system of financial aid in Canada is quite extensive and includes such elements as student loans, grants, tax credits, and scholarships. Removing any component of the system may (or may not) introduce credit constraints.

What the findings of the study suggest is that, given the weak evidence on the existence of widespread credit constraints, our focus should now shift towards trying to further understand why students from lower-income families tend to perform more poorly on standardized and scholastic tests than students from higher-income families. An additional path that research may take is to examine how the gap in parental influences can be closed, since it too contributes towards the gap in university participation.

Notes

This article is adapted from Frenette (2007). The author gratefully acknowledges helpful comments by Miles Corak, Darren Lauzon, René Morissette, Christine Neill, Garnett Picot, and Klarka Zeman. The author is responsible for all remaining errors.

1. There are other types of financial constraints (e.g., not having enough money to help children learn; returns to schooling that are too low to justify the cost). However, this study focuses primarily on the financial constraints associated with the ability to pay for a university education.

2. Note also that to account for the complex survey design of YITS, all variance measures were bootstrapped with 1,000 replicate weights.

3. In a separate specification, only students who cited finances as the only reason for not attending were deemed financially constrained. This yielded no substantial changes in the results. Also, note that the measure may *overstate* the number of students who are financially constrained from attending university, since some students may plan to attend university later, and hope to continue beyond an undergraduate degree, but then cannot for financial reasons. These students are not financially constrained from attending university per se but rather only from attending a graduate or professional program. Unfortunately, the nature of the question asked does not allow us to identify these cases.

4. See Skuterud, Frenette, and Poon (2004) for a more detailed discussion of equivalent income. Note that the general conclusions in this article do not change when I use raw (unadjusted) parental income.

5. For a family of four, these are equivalent to twice these levels in unadjusted terms: $40,819 (25th percentile), $61,062 (50th percentile), and $82,000 (75th percentile).

6. For more technical readers, please see Frenette (2007) for a more detailed description of the approach used. Note that I only show results from method 3 in the current study since the findings are largely invariant to the choice of method.

7. In a recent study, Heckman, Stixrud, and Urzua (2006) demonstrate that non-cognitive abilities are a very strong determinant of the probability of males being university graduates by age 30. Since I can only look at university participation by age 19, it is possible that non-cognitive abilities may have longer-term effects on the probability of attending university that I cannot capture with the data at hand. Alternatively, non-cognitive abilities may be reported with considerable error, which would bias estimates towards zero if the error is random. Another possibility is the correlation between academic and non-cognitive abilities. To address this, I ran models after dropping academic abilities from the specifications. As a result, the association between non-cognitive abilities and university participation became stronger and more statistically significant, yet their explanatory power was still not large by any means.

8. One possible reason for the lower explanatory power of the mathematics and science test scores is that the PISA evaluation focused mainly on reading. Alternatively, it may actually be the case that reading abilities are a more discriminating factor in university attendance than mathematics or science abilities.

References

Barr-Telford, L., F. Cartwright, S. Prasil, and K. Shimmons. 2003. *Access, Persistence and Financing: First Results from the Postsecondary Education Participation Survey (PEPS)*. Culture, Tourism and the Centre for Education Statistics Research Papers No. 81-595-MIE2003007. Ottawa: Statistics Canada.

Belley, P., and L. Lochner. 2007. "The Changing Role of Family Income and Ability in Determining Educational Achievement." *Journal of Human Capital* 1 (1): 37-89.

Bowlby, J.W., and K. McMullen. 2002. *At a Crossroads: First Results for the 18 to 20-Year-Old Cohort of the Youth in Transition Survey*. Culture, Tourism and the Centre for Education Statistics Research Paper No. 81-591-XIE. Ottawa: Statistics Canada.

Card, D. 2001. "Estimating the Return to Schooling: Progress on Some Persistent Econometric Problems." *Econometrica* 69 (5): 1127–60.

Carneiro, P., and J.J. Heckman. 2002. "The Evidence on Credit Constraints in Post-Secondary Schooling." *Economic Journal* 112 (482): 705–34.

Ellwood, D.T., and T.J. Kane. 2000. "Who Is Getting a College Education? Family Background and the Growing Gaps in Enrollment." In *Securing the Future: Investing in Children from Birth to College*, edited by S. Danziger and J. Waldfogell. New York: Russell Sage Foundation.

Frenette, M. 2004. "Access to College and University: Does Distance to School Matter?" *Canadian Public Policy* 30 (4): 427–43.

– 2007. *Why Are Lower-Income Students Less Likely to Attend University? Evidence from Academic Abilities, Parental Influences, and Financial Constraints*. Analytical Studies Research Paper Series No. 11F0019MIE2007295. Ottawa: Statistics Canada.

– 2008. "University Access amid Tuition Fee Deregulation: Evidence from Ontario Professional Programs." *Canadian Public Policy* 34 (1): 89-109.

Frenette, M., and K. Zeman. 2008. *Why Are Lower-Income Students Less Likely to Attend University? Evidence from Academic Abilities, Parental Influences, and Financial Constraints*. Analytical Studies Research Paper Series No. 11F0019MIE2007295. Ottawa: Statistics Canada.

– 2008. "Understanding the Gender Gap in University Attendance: Evidence Based on Academic Performance, Study Habits, and Parental Influences." In *Who Goes? Who Stays? What Matters? Accessing and Persisting in Post-Secondary Education in Canada*, edited by R. Finnie, R.E. Mueller, A. Sweetman, and A. Usher. Montreal and Kingston: McGill-Queen's University Press and School of Policy Studies, Queen's University.

Heckman, J.J., J. Stixrud, and S. Urzua. 2006. "The Effects of Cognitive and Noncognitive Abilities on Labor Market Outcomes and Social Behavior." *Journal of Labor Economics* 24 (3): 411–82.

Jacob, B.A. 2002. "Where the Boys Aren't: Non-Cognitive Skills, Returns to School and the Gender Gap in Higher Education." *Economics of Education Review* 21 (6): 589–98.

Kane, T.J. 1994. "College Entry by Blacks since 1970: The Role of College Costs, Family Background, and the Returns to Education." *Journal of Political Economy* 102 (5): 878-911.

Motte, A., H.T. Qiu, Y. Zhang, and P. Bussière. 2008. "The Youth in Transition Survey: Following Canadian Youth through Time." In *Who Goes? Who Stays? What Matters? Accessing and Persisting in Post-Secondary Education in Canada,* edited by R. Finnie, R.E. Mueller, A. Sweetman, and A. Usher. Montreal and Kingston: McGill-Queen's University Press and School of Policy Studies, Queen's University.

Skuterud, M., M. Frenette, and P. Poon. 2004. *Describing the Distribution of Income: Guidelines for Effective Analysis.* Income Research Paper Series No. 75F0002MIE2004010. Ottawa: Statistics Canada.

12

How Is Variation in Tuition across Canadian Provinces Related to University Participation in the Youth in Transition Survey?

DAVID JOHNSON

L'Enquête auprès des jeunes en transition permet de définir une série de points de prise de décision que traversent les jeunes en lien avec leurs études : pendant la dernière année des études secondaires ou collégiales, pour décider s'ils entreprendront ou non des études universitaires l'année suivante ; et pendant des études universitaires, pour décider de poursuivre ces études l'année suivante ou de les abandonner sans obtenir de diplôme. Cette étude montre qu'un changement dans les frais de scolarité semble avoir peu d'effet sur la probabilité qu'un jeune Canadien décide d'entreprendre ou non des études universitaires immédiatement après avoir terminé ses études secondaires ou collégiales, et aucun effet sur le fait que, une fois à l'université, il abandonne ses études sans obtenir son diplôme.

The Youth in Transition Survey identifies decision points at which a youth in Canada completing high school or CEGEP decides whether to attend university in the next academic year and decision points at which a youth in university continues into the next academic year or leaves without graduating. This paper finds little evidence that tuition levels play an important role in the decision by Canadian youth to immediately attend university after graduation from either high school or CEGEP, and no evidence that tuition levels or a change in tuition alters the probability that a Canadian youth, once in university, leaves university without obtaining a degree.

Who Goes? Who Stays? What Matters? Accessing and Persisting in Post-Secondary Education in Canada, eds. R. Finnie, R.E. Mueller, A. Sweetman, and A. Usher. Montreal and Kingston: McGill-Queen's University Press, Queen's Policy Studies Series. © 2008 The School of Policy Studies, Queen's University at Kingston. All rights reserved.

Introduction

In most countries, including Canada, tuition fees at public universities are significantly less that the cost of attending university. Taxpayers heavily subsidize university attendance. Yet increases in tuition fees are controversial, giving rise to claims that students will be forced to leave university or that many students will choose not to attend when fees are increased.

In making a university access decision, students who have just completed high school or CEGEP either proceed to university in the next academic year or do not. Once in a university bachelor's program, students make a persistence decision at the end of each academic year. Students who are not graduating either leave without completing their degree or persist into their next year of study. Each access or persistence decision takes place at a specific time in a specific province in which each student pays an amount of tuition and fees varying across provinces and over time within the same province. It is this variation that allows measurement of the association of higher tuition with access and with persistence.

Do fewer young people attend university directly from high school when tuition fees are higher? Do more students drop out of university after fees are increased or when the level of fees is higher? This paper makes a very specific contribution to this policy debate by measuring the effect of variation in tuition fees, both levels and changes, on access and persistence decisions made by respondents to the Youth in Transition Survey.

The effect of higher tuition on student access and persistence behaviour is small in the period from 1996 to 2003, when tuition fees rose rapidly in many provinces. The evidence strongly suggests that tuition variation was not a central issue in access or persistence decisions by youth in attending university in Canada at that time.

When opponents of tuition fee increases claim that fewer young people will participate at university, they likely have one of two thoughts in mind. First, they may think of students attending university because university participation raises future wages. If university participation is more costly, then fewer students, all else being equal, should decide to attend, as higher tuition reduces the gap between future benefits and current costs. However, in this way of thinking, it is less likely that the level of tuition affects the persistence decision. The student who entered university understood the need to pay tuition over the three or four years, and even though the level of tuition is higher in one province than in another, once the initial decision has been made to attend because benefits exceed costs, choices about staying at university should not be much affected by the level of tuition. However, it is then surprising that even quite large increases or decreases in tuition are unrelated to decisions to continue. If changes in tuition were unexpected, at least some students should decide to leave university because the perceived expected net benefit of participation has swung from positive to negative when tuition was unexpectedly higher than when the initial decision to attend was made. Thus a higher level of tuition is predicted to reduce access, and increases in tuition are predicted to reduce persistence when youth are balancing monetary benefits and costs of university participation.

A second way of thinking about the potential impact of higher tuition or increases in tuition on access and persistence is to recognize that students can and do borrow to pay for university. Such loans will be repaid out of higher future wages. It is possible that the large numbers of students borrowing to attend university face an overall limit, called a "binding credit constraint," on the loans they can access. Such a maximum may exist in each academic year or over the years of obtaining a degree. In this situation, an increase in tuition fees might prevent some students from continuing, and a reduction in tuition would allow some extra students to continue. If everything else is equal across Canadian provinces, a similar credit constraint on borrowing to attend university in all provinces should be more likely to affect the access decision in a high-tuition province. If students already at their credit constraints face an unexpected increase in tuition, they may be forced to drop out. If two similar students in different provinces are at the same credit constraint and one fails to get a summer job and faces higher tuition, then that credit constraint combined with higher tuition may prevent the student in the higher-tuition province from continuing.

The result that neither the university access nor university persistence decision is associated with changes in tuition or the level of tuition fees has several policy interpretations. First, it may be that tuition fees are set so low and the net benefit of participation is so large that the observed increases or variations in the level across provinces are not large enough to move any student from attendance to non-attendance. Second, it may be that there are relatively few credit constraints to prevent already enrolled or potential students from attending university when tuitions rise. This would be the case if the various publicly funded grant and loan programs for university students function well or if students are able to obtain the additional funds needed from other sources such as work, parents, or non-government loans.[1]

It is important to stress that simply finding that levels or changes in levels of tuition costs do not change access or persistence behaviour cannot be interpreted as proving that lower tuition (or higher tuition) is good or bad policy. The present results say nothing about whether tuition in any Canadian province is at the optimum level. The choice of the appropriate level of tuition is complex and depends on the sharing of private and public benefits of a university education. If access and persistence were affected by tuition, then tuition policy would relate strongly to issues of social mobility. The one small but potentially important piece of evidence in this research finds a weak but statistically significant relationship between reduced access and overall higher tuition for youth who come from families where neither parent has university-level educational experience.

Thus even if for society as a whole access and persistence are unrelated to tuition, there are important equity issues related to tuition policy. Use of university is positively related to both current family income and the future income of graduated students. If university attendance is positively correlated with current family income for reasons other than a financial barrier to university attendance, then a low tuition policy for all students is an overall transfer to better-off families in society. But a low tuition policy for all students may have a weak effect that slightly increases access by students from families where parents have no university education. This is the policy discussion that needs to take place when more evidence is brought to bear. We may also want to know how higher tuition fees are paid: Are students taking out more loans? Are students working more? Are parents making larger contributions to their children's university education? These issues are not addressed in this paper, and YITS data do not allow them to be addressed at this time.

This paper makes three contributions to the literature on the relationship between university participation and tuition in the United States and Canada. First, the existing literature does not usually directly connect the access decision or the persistence decision at a point in time to variation in tuition, which is a time-and-place dependent variable. Second, although there is a literature on persistence and a much larger literature on participation at university, the research presented in this chapter clearly separates persistence and access as components of overall participation at university. Third, combining the YITS-A and YITS-B surveys provides a large and long sample of access and persistence decisions where the maximum amount of variation in tuition over time and across provinces can be observed. This allows the most opportunity for tuition levels and changes to interact with those decisions.

The American literature on post-secondary participation and tuition fees is reviewed in Leslie and Brinkman (1988) and Heller (1997) and updated in Heller (1999). Measures of participation like the proportion of persons within a certain age bracket at university (or with university degrees) would increase if more students were to access or persist; then a larger proportion would be enrolled and a larger proportion would obtain degrees. The large body of Canadian evidence on tuition and overall participation is reviewed in Looker and Lowe (2001) as well as in Junor and Usher (2002, 2004). In many ways the Canadian studies are more useful to the present study, since the role of private universities in Canada is very small, and in most provinces tuition fees have been set by provincial policy at the same level across all universities within a province, but fees are at very different levels in different provinces.

The studies that relate overall participation to tuition have not produced the clear result that participation falls in jurisdictions with higher tuition fees. More recent studies of the Canadian data make use of individual data on university participation and find that higher tuition fees do reduce overall participation by a very small amount in well-specified models. Neill (2006) and Johnson and Rahman (2005) use the individual data from the Labour Force Survey (LFS) from 1976 onwards and find a statistically significant negative response for university participation to an increase in tuition. Neither effect is large in an economic sense, the participation rate falling between 1 and 3 percentage points per $1,000 (measured in 1992 dollars) increase in tuition. Johnson and Rahman find this negative effect on participation only relative to strong positive province-specific time trends in university participation between 1976 and 2003. Their study has a very poor proxy for student aid at the provincial level (the proportion of university expenditures spent on student aid), since there is no data on the amount of student aid received by individuals. Neill includes Canada-wide, year-fixed effects as well as province-fixed effects in obtaining her estimates of the negative effect of higher tuition levels on enrolment probabilities.

Another limitation of the LFS is that very little information is available on family background. Coelli (2004) makes some progress around this important limitation by using individual responses concerning post-secondary choices in the Survey of Labour Income Dynamics (SLID). He finds that access by lower-income families is reduced when tuition is increased. The number of low-income youth in SLID is very small, particularly in the provincial sub-samples used. One advantage of the present study is that YITS provides a large sample of youth over many years.

The literature studying the university persistence decision is much smaller, particularly in Canada. Reviews of both U.S. and Canadian literature are found in Grayson and Grayson (2003), McElroy (2005), and Mueller (2007). Administrative records of specific post-secondary institutions indicate that the most common dropout point is the end of year one. There is a strong correlation between family background and university completion. Marks (2007) concludes that, in Australia, once students enter the university system, their socio-economic backgrounds play little direct role in completion. This is indirect evidence that financial factors are not central in persistence. The present study finds similar evidence in Canada. Stinebricker and Stinebricker (2007), using direct survey evidence for a sample from Berea College, conclude that financial issues are not central in the persistence decision. There is, as far as I know, no separate literature linking the access decision to the level of tuition facing potential students at the time of the access decision. YITS allows analysis of the role of tuition at decision points.

This study is not the first to use the YITS or similar data to consider participation and persistence issues in Canada. Barr-Telford et al. (2003), using data from a survey similar to YITS, the Postsecondary Education Participation Survey (PEPS), report that of the PEPS respondents who started post-secondary education in September 2000, 75 percent were still in post-secondary education 18 months later. Of the 16 percent that left without graduation, only 29 percent reported leaving for financial reasons. Five papers to date, Bowlby and McMullen (2002), Lambert et al. (2004), Shaienks et al. (2006), Day (2007), and Finnie and Qiu (2007), use YITS to consider various aspects of persistence. The first three papers do not estimate a model of persistence; they describe the data. There is a general sense that the same social factors that are associated with post-secondary access decisions are those associated with post-secondary dropout decisions. YITS does ask if respondents perceive a financial barrier to post-secondary participation. For the persons who leave post-secondary education, 34 percent report financial barriers to continuing. For those who stay in post-secondary education, 29 percent report a financial barrier. Day (2007) limits her study of persistence in YITS to students who enrol in a post-secondary program in September 1999 and then measures the effect of financial aid variables on the status of these students as of 31 December 2001; she finds that leavers are less likely to have received financial aid. Finnie and Qiu (2007) take a long view of persistence using YITS-B responses from 1996 to 31 December 2003. They focus on the role of family variables and on the variation in dropout rates by age of enrolment in a post-secondary program. Students who are older when starting a program are more likely to drop out. All studies find substantial variation across provinces in the rate at which respondents leave post-secondary education after commencing. The very specific contribution of the present study is to link the level and changes in tuition (as well as changes in the tax treatment of tuition) in the sample years across Canadian provinces to the respondent decision points and then to ask whether the level or change in tuition and tax treatment has, given the other observable characteristics of the respondent, any impact on the decision to access or persist at university.

The paper proceeds as follows. The extraction and description of measures of access, persistence, and stage of education at university from the Youth in Transition Survey is described in the next section. The third section describes a statistical model linking access and persistence decisions to tuition and other variables. The details of the methodology and a variety of robustness checks on these results are presented in Johnson (2008a, 2008b).

Access and Persistence in YITS

YITS is a Canadian longitudinal survey with two groups of youth: YITS-A, aged 15 on 31 December 1999 (26,055 participants as of 31 December 1999) and YITS-B, aged 18, 19, or 20 on 31 December 1999 (22,378 participants as of 31 December 1999). The data can be used to create an educational history of this group of Canadian youth to the end of 2003. A YITS respondent completes high school (CEGEP in Quebec) in the first of the pair of academic years in Table 1 and then may or may not proceed to a bachelor's program at university in the second of the pair of years making an access decision. The number of access decisions in the first column of Table 1 shows a particularly large number of decisions following the 2001-02 academic years. A member of the larger and younger Cohort A sample would normally complete Grade 12 in June 2002 and enter post-secondary education in September 2002, the "normal" path for students in eight of 10 Canadian provinces. In Ontario and Quebec YITS-A (or YITS-B) have a different "normal" path. In both provinces, university entry in this period took place two years after Grade 11 completion, in Ontario through a formal Grade 13 and in Quebec through two years of CEGEP. Thus YITS-A respondents in these two provinces on the normal path to university completed Grade 13 or the second year of CEGEP in June 2003 and would enter university in September 2003. Those access decisions are observed in the final row of Table 1.[2]

Table 1 shows the percentages of students who access in each pair of academic years. "Access" here means that the respondent who finished high school or CEGEP either did or did not attend university in that province in the next year.[3] One noteworthy observation is that the access rate is so much lower in 2000-01 to 2001-02. This reflects the complicated sequencing of the YITS cohorts. Given the age structure of YITS, none of the YITS respondents would normally obtain a high school (or two-year CEGEP) graduation in 2001-02. Thus Table 1 shows that persons whose high school graduations are outside the normal path have lower access rates.

TABLE 1
Access to and Persistence in University in the Combined YITS-A and YITS-B Sample

Transition years	Access: Percent entering university directly from high school or CEGEP completion		Persistence: Percent continuing in university to next academic year		
	Number of observations rounded to nearest 100	Canadian percentages using survey weights	Number of observations rounded to nearest 100	Canadian percentages using survey weights	Percent in Year One
1996-97 to 1997-98	3,500	20.9	suppressed	99.0	69.4
1997-98 to 1998-99	5,500	25.7	1,900	93.8	32.9
1998-99 to 1999-2000	6,000	30.4	5,000	88.2	33.3
1999-2000 to 2000-01	1,700	28.7	7,300	90.2	29.9
2000-01 to 2001-02	1,600	14.5	8,200	91.2	25.3
2001-02 to 2002-03	12,500	24.3	6,000	95.2	21.8
2002-03 to 2003-04	3,900	36.5	8,000	94.8	22.3

Notes: Samples are constructed from combined samples of YITS-A and YITS-B as described in the text. Counts are rounded to nearest 100 in accordance with Statistics Canada protection of confidentiality. Percentages are for the Canadian population of youth aged 15, 18, 19, and 20 on 31 December 1999. Access means that a youth completed high school or CEGEP in the first of the pair of academic years in question and then continued into university in the next academic year. Persistence means that a youth in university in the first of the pair of academic years continued into university in the next academic year and had not graduated in the first academic year.

Table 2 presents provincial access rates in the two left-hand columns. These are provincial access rates for YITS-B and YITS-A respondents. The aggregate access rate for YITS-B varies from 42.6 percent in Nova Scotia to 21.6 percent in Ontario. Quebec has the lowest access rate for YITS-A, and Nova Scotia has the highest rate. Access to university in Quebec is a different process, but it is clear even at this point in the analysis that since Nova Scotia is the province with some of the highest tuition levels and Quebec is the province with the lowest tuition levels, it will be difficult to find a simple negative relationship between access rates and the level of tuition. Table 2 also shows that the access rate is higher in seven of 10 provinces for those born in 1984 (YITS-A) than for those born earlier (YITS-B); that is, access rates in Canada appear to increase even over this relatively short period of time.

YITS is also used to create a sample to study the persistence decision. Persistence and transition issues at university usually take place between academic years. The summer between two academic years is treated as a decision point where one new piece of information is the level of tuition in the second academic year of each pair. Respondents persist if, when enrolled in a bachelor's program, they stay for an additional academic year towards obtaining the bachelor's degree.[4] If they

TABLE 2
Variation in Access and Persistence Rates across Canadian Provinces

Province	Access: Percent entering university directly from high school or CEGEP completion		Persistence: Percent continuing in university to next academic year	
	YITS-B	YITS-A	Overall persistence	Year One persistence
British Columbia	30.9	30.5	87.6	82.0
Alberta	24.9	25.9	83.5	81.5
Saskatchewan	31.3	29.6	87.2	83.3
Manitoba	29.4	33.6	87.1	82.7
Ontario	21.6	28.7	91.2	86.4
Quebec	25.4	14.9	95.2	94.7
New Brunswick	35.4	41.8	86.7	84.5
Prince Edward Island	34.9	44.6	90.6	84.2
Nova Scotia	42.6	52.3	85.5	81.5
Newfoundland	33.7	35.8	82.8	76.4

Notes: See Table 1.

leave without obtaining a bachelor's degree in the first of the pair of academic years studied, they do not persist. The number of observations of persistence decisions between academic years is listed in the third column of Table 1.[5]

Because YITS-B and YITS-A have such a specific age structure, the number and type of observations of persistence decisions between a specific pair of academic years vary as the components of YITS age. All samples except the first pair of years have a large number of persistence decisions to observe. This is not surprising, as the persons in YITS-A are 12 years old and the oldest person in YITS-B is 17 years old on 31 December 1996. The probability in this small group of unusual students that continued into university in 1997-98 was 99 percent. In the remainder of the table, the persistence rates range from 88.2 to 95.2 percent. The last column of Table 1 also presents one measure of the characteristics of the particular group of decision-makers in each pair of academic years. The variable constructed from YITS counts the number of academic years since the respondent was a full-time high school student (this value is adjusted by two years in Quebec).[6] Each academic year for each respondent was identified as 1, 2, 3, 4, 5, 6, and 7 years after last high school attendance. These variables were used in the analysis of persistence.[7] To begin, Table 1 shows that the two years with the highest percentage of Year One students are the two years with the highest leaving rates. This is consistent with the administrative data on university dropout rates. This feature of Table 1 illustrates the composition effect in YITS data. We are following, over time, groups that age over time.

Table 2 illustrates composition effects in a different way. Although average persistence rates vary widely from province to province, in every province the persistence rate for university students who are respondents in Year One is lower than the overall persistence rate. The remainder of the paper presents estimates of the role of tuition and other variables in explaining the variation in access and persistence rates across years and across provinces. However, Tables 1 and 2 remind us that effects associated with the year of analysis (composition effects) and the province must be considered seriously.

Association of Tuition and Access and Persistence Decisions

Two different measures of the level of university tuition in the province are created to link to the observations of access and persistence decision. Figure 1 is the result of adjusting Usher's (2006) nominal measure of the direct cost of university attendance, which includes compulsory

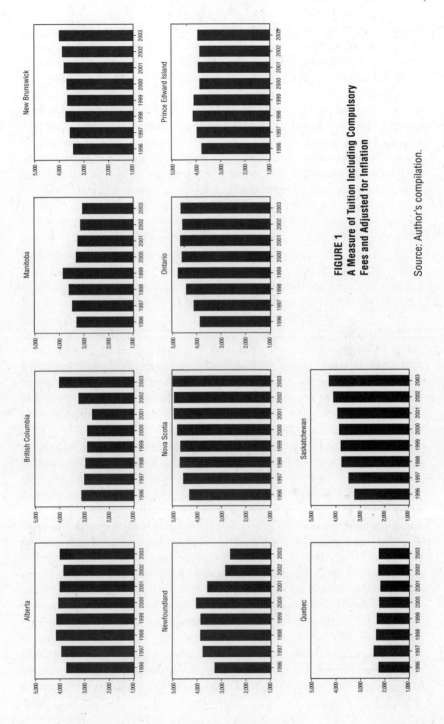

FIGURE 1
A Measure of Tuition Including Compulsory Fees and Adjusted for Inflation

Source: Author's compilation.

fees for inflation. Usher (2006) also calculates a measure of the reduction in taxes due associated with a year of university attendance in a province. This measure is adjusted for inflation and presented in Figure 2. When the values in Figure 1 are subtracted from those in Figure 2, the result is a net of tax measure of tuition. Figure 3 shows the change in the gross real level of tuition and fees, the values illustrated in Figure 1. A similar measure of the change in net of tax real tuition and fees could be constructed. These four variables that measure the level and change in real gross and net tuition are added to a general model of the access and persistence decisions (including an important discussion about province and year fixed effects).

The estimated equations take the very general form

$$
\begin{aligned}
\text{Decision}_{i,j,t} = {} & f \text{ (Observable Personal Characteristics)} \\
& + i \text{ (indicator variables representing year and province} \\
& \quad \text{fixed effects)} \\
& + t \text{ (tuition measures) +} \\
& + u \text{ (unemployment measure) + an error term} \qquad (1)
\end{aligned}
$$

For persons who do not think in mathematical terms, think of equation (1) as a list of factors associated with the access and persistence decisions. The variable $\text{Decision}_{i,j,t}$ equals 1 if the individual "i" in province "j" between pairs of academic years "t" either accesses university in the year after high school completion or, in the analysis of persistence, continues his or her studies into the next academic year. Otherwise the value of the variable "Decision" equals zero.

Table 3 presents coefficient estimates for the models implicit in equation 1. The focus in Table 3 is to understand what social and economic variables other than tuition have a clear association with access and persistence decisions. Table 3 also highlights the importance of year fixed effects and province fixed effects. Table 4 then moves to the discussion of tuition effects. The left-hand sides of Tables 3 and 4 refer to access decisions and the right-hand sides to persistence decisions. All the coefficients listed in these tables measure the change in the probability of access with a one-unit change in the relevant variable on the right-hand side of equation (1).[8] A very large proportion of the variables are indicator variables, so in both models the relevant change is from zero to the state indicated when the value of the indicator variable is one.

For example, the first row of Table 3 reports coefficients on a variable called "Female" that takes on a value of 1 if the respondent is female and is zero otherwise. A negative sign in the table indicates that when

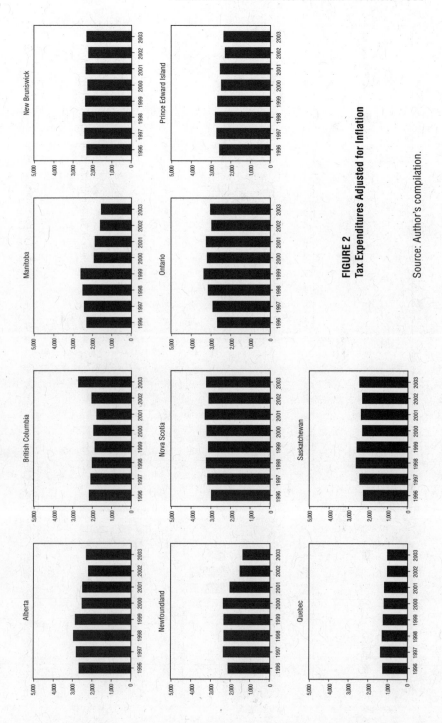

FIGURE 2
Tax Expenditures Adjusted for Inflation

Source: Author's compilation.

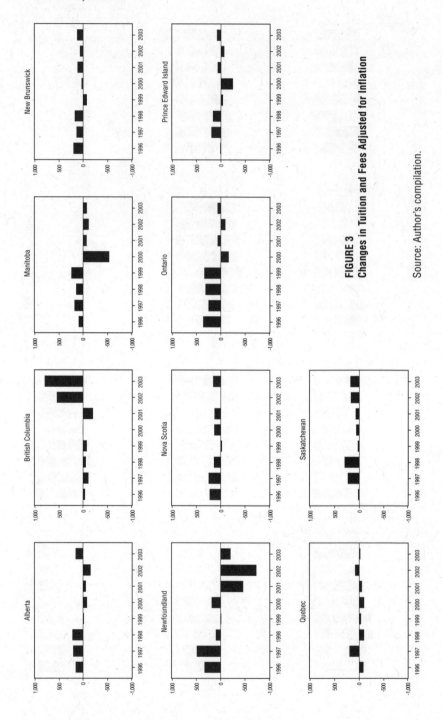

FIGURE 3
Changes in Tuition and Fees Adjusted for Inflation

Source: Author's compilation.

TABLE 3
Access and Persistence Coefficients on Social and Economic Variables in Linear Probability Models Estimated without Tuition Variables (Prob. Values in parentheses)

Variable	Access Model	Persistence Model
Female	-0.0138 (0.36)	0.017 (0.36)
Born in Canada	-0.0076 (0.74)	-0.011 (0.62)
Visible minority	0.072 (0.00)	0.026 (0.19)
Single parent	-0.026 (0.03)	0.029 (0.04)
Number of high schools	-0.041 (0.00)	0.003 (0.73)
Parent with university	0.145 (0.00)	0.007 (0.66)
Positive parental attitude	0.089 (0.00)	-0.004 (0.75)
High school grade	0.114 (0.00)	0.064 (0.00)
High school math grade	0.032 (0.00)	0.005 (0.48)
Year One	NA	-0.023 (0.11)
Year Two	NA	-0.001 (0.92)
Year Three	NA	0.015 (0.11)
Unemployment rate for youth	-0.022 (0.00)	-0.003 (0.82)
British Columbia	0.128 (0.00)	-0.027 (0.21)
Alberta	0.029 (0.15)	-0.060 (0.02)
Saskatchewan	0.074 (0.00)	-0.035 (0.17)
Manitoba	0.036 (0.12)	-0.033 (0.24)
Quebec	0.085 (0.00)	0.020 (0.14)
Ontario	Omitted	Omitted
New Brunswick	0.250 (0.00)	-0.015 (0.51)
Nova Scotia	0.320 (0.00)	-0.038 (0.17)
Prince Edward Island	0.240 (0.00)	0.032 (0.38)
Newfoundland	0.420 (0.00)	-0.028 (0.56)
1996-97 to 1997-98	-0.186 (0.00)	0.067 (0.01)
1997-98 to 1998-99	-0.134 (0.00)	-0.110 (0.00)
1998-99 to 1999-00	-0.106 (0.00)	-0.090 (0.00)
1999-00 to 2000-01	-0.125 (0.00)	-0.070 (0.00)
2000-01 to 2001-02	-0.182 (0.00)	-0.066 (0.00)
2001-02 to 2002-03	-0.159 (0.00)	-0.010 (0.15)
2002-03 to 2003-04	Omitted	Omitted
R^2	0.190	0.064
Sample size	26,137	13,548

Notes: Access and persistence are 0-1 variables defined in the text where a 1 denotes a student attending university immediately after high school graduation and persistence indicates a student in university who remains in university in the next academic year. Female equals 1 if respondent is female. Born in Canada equals 1 if respondent is born in Canada. Visible minority equals 1 if respondent is a member of a visible minority. Single parent equals 1 if respondent spent most of high school with one adult. If at least one parent had some university, then Parent with University equals 1. If the youth perceived that the value of education beyond high school was either "fairly important" or "very important" to either parent, the value of Positive Parental Attitude equals 1. The variables High School Grade and High School Math Grade take on values of 1 through 7 where 7 is the highest grade (over 90 percent) and 1 is the lowest grade of less than 50 percent. Year Effects are Canada-wide dummy variables for the pairs of academic years. Province effects are dummy variables for all observations from that province. Standard errors are estimated robustly using survey weights and, for the persistence model, with clusters at the individual level.

TABLE 4
Coefficients on Tuition Variables in Different Specifications of Fixed Effects in Models of Access and Persistence Using the Linear Probability Model (Prob. Values in parentheses)

Fixed effect specification	Access Model		Persistence Model			
	Real tuition and fees	Net real tuition	Real tuition and fees	Change in real tuition and fees	Net real tuition	Change in real tuition
No year fixed effects and no province fixed effects	-0.0088 (0.13)	-0.018 (0.01)	-0.0037 (0.53)	0.028 (0.013)	-0.0078 (0.24)	0.026 (0.12)
No year fixed effects and province fixed effects	0.058 (0.00)	0.023 (0.23)	0.024 (0.21)	0.045 (0.07)	-0.032 (0.12)	0.031 (0.16)
Year fixed effects and no province fixed effects	-0.019 (0.00)	-0.023 (0.00)	-0.0050 (0.038)	0.0062 (0.74)	-0.0040 (0.053)	0.025 (0.27)
Year fixed effects and province fixed effects	-0.032 (0.15)	-0.0005 (0.98)	-0.0014 (0.94)	0.016 (0.54)	0.0086 (0.70)	0.028 (0.37)

Notes: The variables added to the list of social and economic variables in Table 3 are the tuition measures in the left-hand column. The level or change in tuition is measured in 1992 dollars where the units are thousands of dollars. These are added separately to the models estimated and presented in Table 3. Standard errors are estimated robustly with survey weights and individual clusters in the models of persistence.

the variable is positive rather than zero (or when the variable in question increases by one unit), then access or persistence is less likely. The value in parentheses beside each coefficient is a guideline on the probability that the coefficient is statistically different from zero. Low Prob. Values indicate it is very likely; high Prob. Values near to unity indicate it is very unlikely. The Prob. Value of 0.36 on the coefficient Female in the access equation indicates that only at a 36 percent level of significance would the null hypothesis that being female alters the access rate be rejected. This may be surprising, since females outnumber males at Canadian universities. The association of female with access is to be interpreted as a change in only that variable from male to female, holding all other variables at the same value. To be concrete, if females have higher grades in secondary schools than males, and that is why they access more successfully, then this factor is included in the model. The statement that it makes no difference in access to be female is only true at the same level of high school grades. This is true for all other coefficients and variables in Tables 3 and 4.

Nine variables from YITS measure various aspects of respondents' personal and family characteristics. The coefficients on these variables are read as described above. Being female and being born in Canada does not affect access or persistence. Members of a visible minority are 7.2 percentage points more likely to access university but are not significantly more likely to persist. Single parenthood is an indicator variable set equal to 1 if the YITS respondent spent most of high school with one parent. Youth from such families are less likely to access but, oddly enough, more likely to persist. A youth who has attended more than one high school is 4.1 percentage points less likely to access; there is no association of an additional high school with persistence. YITS asked a question about youths' perception concerning the attitude of their parent(s) to the value of education beyond high school. If that perception is either "fairly important or very important," then the parental attitude variable takes on a value of 1. This increases the probability of access by 8.9 percentage points but does not affect persistence. The effect of having at least one parent with some university is similar. This increases the probability of access by a huge amount, 14.5 percentage points, but does not change the probability of persistence.

Finally, the dominant variables in both the access and persistence equation are the respondents' high school grades. Grades are measured so that an increment of one unit is an increase from an overall average (last grade in high school mathematics) from 50-59 percent to 60-69 percent and the like for similar increments in grades. A 10 percentage point increase in a student's overall high school grade raises the access probability by 11.4 percentage points and persistence probability by 6.4 percentage points. A 10 percentage point increase in a high school mathematics grade increases the probability of access by 3.2 percentage points but does not affect persistence.

The variables capturing the number of years after high school (or CEGEP) completion enter only the persistence equation. As expected, persistence is lower in Year One, but the effect is statistically significant only at the 11 percent level. Persistence is similarly higher in Year Three. However, the general point is clear: the further along a student is in a program, the less likely he or she is to drop out.

Finally, in Table 3 there is a measure of the unemployment rate in each province in the 12 months preceding the access or persistence decision. There is no strong prior effect of high unemployment on the two decisions. Higher unemployment seems to make obtaining higher education a more desirable choice at the access decision. Higher unemployment could make summer employment more difficult and reduce persistence, but the association of unemployment and persistence is not statistically significant. The provincial unemployment rates also control for business cycle effects. This may help clarify the interpretation of the coefficients on the province and year fixed effect variables in Table 3.

Table 3 presents coefficients on province fixed effect variables. These variables have values of 1 for all observations from that province in all years and 0 otherwise. The coefficient on the province fixed effect has a similar interpretation to the coefficients discussed above. If a respondent is from a specific province, all else being equal, then the coefficient is the increase in the probability of access because the indicator variable for that province increases from 0 to 1. One important point is that this change in the probability of access or persistence is a change relative to the province omitted from the list of province fixed effect variables. In both columns Ontario is the omitted province. Thus the coefficient of 0.128 on the British Columbia fixed effect in the access model (the left side) means that, holding other factors constant, a respondent from British Columbia is 12.8 percentage points more likely to access than the same respondent in Ontario. The Prob. Value of 0.00 indicates this is a very precisely estimated effect.

The string of positive coefficients on the province fixed effects coefficients says that access is higher in all non-Ontario provinces when all other factors in the model are taken into account. These coefficients are not estimates of average access rates in each province; these are found in Table 2, which shows that access rates in British Columbia are 9.3 percent higher for YITS-B and only 1.8 percent higher for YITS-A. Neither value is the 12.8 percentage points discussed above. The coefficient 0.128 on the British Columbia fixed effects means only that, for a respondent with the same characteristics in the same pair of years in Ontario and in British Columbia, access rates are then different and usually lower in Ontario. The reasons for lower access in Ontario for the same types of YITS respondents relative to all other provinces are not made precise in the model. The fixed effect simply means that, whatever those reasons are, they are not related to the factors already included in the model – that is, to the respondent's gender, place of birth, visible minority status, and the other variables already discussed – and that they are in effect over all periods.

In the access model, it is very plausible that the larger college system in Ontario relative to other provinces reduces the probability of university access.[9] Alberta has a relatively low access rate relative to other provinces (similar to Ontario's access rates, in fact) because the coefficient on the Alberta fixed effect is only 0.029. Relative to British Columbia, a respondent is much less likely to access in Alberta because the coefficient on the Alberta fixed effect is only 0.029, clearly smaller than the 0.128 coefficient representing the British Columbia fixed effect.

The lower access rate in Alberta cannot be associated with lower unemployment rates there, since unemployment rates are included in the model. One possibility is that relative wages for high school graduates are much higher in Alberta than in British Columbia, and so the opportunity cost of university attendance is higher in Alberta throughout this whole period. If we added wages of a high school graduate to the model, this hypothesis could be tested. Fixed effects represent a variable or variables affecting decisions in that province in all time periods not already in the list of variables in the model. There are many possible reasons why the provinces would have different access rates. These are reflected in the precise estimates of provincial fixed effects. It is equally possible that provinces would have very different persistence rates, although the coefficients representing province fixed effects in the persistence model are by and large not statistically different from zero. The only exception is Alberta, where persistence is 6 percentage points lower than in Ontario, all else being equal.

The coefficients on the year fixed effects in both the access equation and the persistence equations are clearly different from zero. Most coefficients are negative relative to the omitted pair of years, the last pair of years in the data. A negative coefficient means that access or persistence is lower between that pair of years relative to the omitted pair of years. These fixed effects are part of the description of observations in all the years in all the observations across Canada; that is, the fixed effect for the access pair of years 1996-97 to 1997-98 means that access is 18.6 percentage points lower in that pair of years relative to the omitted pair of years for reasons not already associated with other variables in the model. The coefficient on the fixed effect for the specific pair of years discussed in Table 1, 2000-01 to 2001-02, in the access model has a very large negative coefficient of -0.182. This coefficient means that a respondent who graduated from high school in 2000-01 relative to a respondent who graduated in 2002-03 has an 18.2 percentage point lower probability of attending university in the year after high school graduation. In Table 1, it was argued that the persons in this pair of years are the students in the sample who are not finishing high school along the "normal" path in Canada – that is, the sample that requires an extra year of high school. This is an example of a composition effect where, because the observations in YITS all start at specific ages, they all remain in a specific age pattern over time.

Beyond the pair of years starting in 2000-01, the negative values of the other year-effect coefficients are much more difficult to interpret. The year fixed effects are simply factors that affect access all across Canada which are not in the variables already in the rest of the model.

The year effects on persistence likely relate to the very imperfect measure of stage of study in the data and changes in the composition of the sample. Aside from the first peculiar year of data on persistence, they generally indicate an increase over time in persistence rates that occurs across the country. The interpretation of the fixed effects relating to both year and province is sufficiently difficult that in presenting the association of higher tuition and changes in access rates, models are estimated with different combinations of fixed effects. This is because tuition levels are the same in a province in a year for all respondents and because, on average, real tuition levels rise over time. Thus a provincial fixed effect could be capturing the effect of a high-tuition province relative to a lower-tuition province in a model where tuition variables are not included, as is the case in Table 3.[10] A year fixed effect could be capturing increases in tuition that took place all across Canada. The only way to test this hypothesis is to add the measures of tuition to the model estimated in Table 3. The coefficients measuring the association of tuition, access, and persistence are presented in Table 4.

Because it is very difficult to provide an absolutely clear interpretation of either the Canada-wide year effects or the province fixed effects, Table 4 presents coefficients on the tuition variables in four specifications and asks if there is any robust evidence that the level of tuition, however measured, tends to reduce the probability of access or persistence. Tuition is measured in thousands of constant (1992) dollars, so a change in one unit of tuition corresponds to $1,000. This is an enormous change in tuition. Consider Figures 1 to 3: the average level of tuition over the sample in the non-Quebec provinces is about $2,500, so a $1,000 change is a 40 percentage point increase in real tuition.

If higher levels of tuition or increases in tuition (gross or net) in the different specifications with combinations of year and province fixed effects were associated with lower access rates or lower persistence rates, then Table 4 would be filled with large negative coefficients statistically different from zero, that is, with low Prob. Values. While there are some negative coefficients, they are small, and most are not statistically significant; some coefficients are positive. It is thus very difficult to argue from Table 4 that higher levels of real tuition are a substantial impediment to access, and impossible to conclude that higher levels of real tuition or increases in tuition reduce persistence.

The strongest evidence that higher tuition reduces access is found in the third row. Read literally, the first two entries in that row indicate that a $1,000 increase in real (net) tuition reduces the probability of access by 1.9 (2.3) percentage points. Recalling that $1,000 is a 40 percentage point increase in tuition, there is a sense that this is a very small effect. It is more important that this result is obtained only when there are no province fixed effects so that all of the variation in provincial access rates is laid at the feet of variation in tuition. The coefficients in Table 3 suggest this is an incorrect assumption. If province fixed effects are included in the models of access (the second and fourth rows), there are no statistically significant effects of real tuition on access. If there are no year fixed effects but there are province fixed effects (the second row), then the coefficients relating access and tuition levels are actually positive and significant. This is not surprising, since access seems to have risen over time and, as is clear in Figure 1, so has real tuition. The most important result on access is found in the fourth row of Table 4 where there are (as is almost certainly appropriate) both year and province fixed effects. In this specification, a $1,000 increase in the level of gross real tuition reduces the probability of access by 3.2 percentage points. The Prob. Value is only 0.15, indicating that this is not a precisely estimated coefficient and that it is not statistically different from zero. But it is negative, and it is similar in magnitude to the results cited earlier from Neill (2006) and Johnson and Rahman (2005). It is interesting and requires further investigation that the coefficient relating net real tuition to access is clearly zero. This suggests that reducing tuition through tax credits is not an effective policy to increase access.

Finally, if a sample of persons is created in which neither parent has a university educational experience, then Johnson (2008a) shows that a $1,000 increase in real tuition and fees is associated with a reduction in the access probability of 4.8 percentage points for this group and the effect is statistically significant in the specification with province and year fixed effects. The association of net real tuition and access is not statistically significant in the sample of youth drawn from parents without a university education. There is some further work to be done on the interaction of tuition, access, the tax system, and a more precise measure of socio-economic status. However, the general message from the coefficients presented in Table 4 is that the level of tuition, gross or net, is not strongly associated with access.

There is even less evidence in Table 4 that the level of gross or net tuition or changes in gross or net real tuition have any impact on persistence. Only three of the estimated coefficients have Prob. Values less than 0.10. One is positive, suggesting that in these specifications a higher level of tuition is associated with increased persistence rates. If there are no province fixed effects and there are year fixed effects, then the coefficient estimates found in the third row would associate a $1,000 increase in the level of real tuition with a decrease in the persistence rate of approximately one-half of one percentage point. This, as pointed out in the introduction, is quite difficult to interpret. Since students entering university should be aware of the need to pay multiple years of tuition, a higher level of tuition on entry should not affect the persistence rate. The interpretation of any such effect rests on the possibility of credit constraints so that a negative shock to income, such as lack of a summer job, would be more likely to induce a decision not to persist. However, if this is the path, we would have expected a higher provincial unemployment rate to be associated with lower persistence in Table 3, and this is not the case. Further, if credit constraints were the issue, it would be reasonable to expect increases in tuition to reduce persistence, and this is clearly not the case. These are the string of insignificant coefficients in the fourth and sixth column of Table 4. There is simply no convincing evidence of an association between tuition and persistence behaviour.

Conclusion

The YITS survey covering the activities of a large sample of Canadian youth aged 15, 18, 19, and 20 on 31 December 1999 through to December 2003 allows identification of specific points in time when youths exit high school (CEGEP in Quebec) and make an access decision to attend or not attend university. Once in attendance at university, at the end of each academic year when they have not obtained their degree, they make a persistence decision: Should they continue into the next academic year? This paper provides measures of the association of the level or the change in tuition fees at the time of decision-making and the access or persistence decisions. This is a useful way to engage the issue of the effects of higher tuition on the Canadian student population.

Opponents of increases in tuition often claim that students will drop out and not complete their degrees after tuition increases. The evidence provides no support for this assertion. Once students enter university, there is no relationship between tuition levels or changes in tuition levels and persistence decisions. This suggests that, once in university, existing student aid programs have functioned well in Canada as a whole. It suggests, in particular, that when tuition is increased, students are able to remain in university. Students simply do not drop out more when tuition is increased.

There are important unanswered questions. If students are borrowing more to stay in university, from whom and how much are they borrowing? On what terms are they borrowing? Are parents paying a larger share of the costs of university? Are students working more during school? Is work during school good or bad for students?

Many opponents of tuition increases also claim that higher levels of tuition mean students will decide not to go to university; that is, higher tuition is said to reduce access. The evidence simply does not support this claim for young persons in Canada who graduated from high school or CEGEP over the period studied. This result suggests existing student aid programs are working fairly well and that financial barriers to access are small, at least for the student population as a whole. The policy discussion around the correct level of tuition should move past overall accessibility issues to other criteria for the correct level of tuition. I suggest three large issues for future research.

Some interesting preliminary evidence mentioned in this study needs further investigation. Consider the population of young people in two groups: in the first group, at least one parent has exposure to university-level education, while in the second group neither parent does. If we look at young persons from families where neither parent has university experience, then the evidence indicates that a higher level of tuition does slightly reduce access for young people from this group. This is an important piece of evidence and needs much more research to understand its implications. In particular, the research in the present study, in common with other studies of the interrelationship of tuition and access issues in Canada, does not have good measures of student aid. We do not know the effect of student aid on the access behaviour by these different groups in different provinces because the student aid data in YITS is limited. This is an important area for future research.

The second large issue, also beyond the scope of this paper, is to consider the following policy tradeoff. If tuition is lowered for all students, and this is done without an increase in government grants per student, the available level of resources per student is lowered for all students. While there is a gain in access for a subgroup of students, there is no gain in overall access. The access gain for the subgroup takes place at the cost of fewer resources per student for all students. What is the correct policy choice? Are there better ways to address the access needs for the subgroup?

Third, there is a strong intergenerational and interpersonal equity aspect in a decision to fund an overall reduction in tuition. Consider the case where the government grant is increased to compensate for the tuition reduction. Thus taxes must be increased to fund this policy, or government spending must be lowered in another area. More importantly, it is clear that the probability of university attendance rises considerably with the education level of the parents sending youth to university. Thus the immediate benefits of lower tuition are received

by families with higher than average incomes. Since university graduates make higher than average salaries after graduation, if they pay
less tuition, their net gain is larger. These are transfers to graduates and
their families from the average taxpayer. These equity issues relating to
tuition policy also need further investigation.

What is clear from the research presented in this chapter is that the
level of tuition is not the central issue in the determination of overall
access rates to university and overall persistence rates at university in
Canada. The debate about the appropriate level of tuition, access, and
persistence should move on to more fertile ground.

Notes

I owe an enormous debt to Alex Usher and Ross Finnie, coordinators of the
Measuring the Effectiveness of Student Aid (MESA) project. In particular the
work of Ross, Theresa Qui, and Yan Zhang in the documentation of the YITS-A
and YITS-B surveys was and is an invaluable contribution for all YITS users.
Theresa's programming to create the persistence measures is particularly ap-
preciated. Pat Newcombe-Welch and Cindy Tremblay, at the South-Western
Ontario Research Data Centre and its branch at Laurentian University, are also
to be thanked for their help.

Useful comments were made by participants and discussants at both the
preliminary MESA meeting held at the Canadian Economics Association conference in June 2007 and the subsequent MESA meeting in October 2007, as well as at
the Higher Education Meeting at the National Bureau of Economic Research. This
work was partly done as the Fulbright Visiting Chair at the University of California, Santa Barbara. Any errors are, of course, my responsibility.

1. The results do not then apply to adult students at university who are not
    included in the Youth in Transition Survey.
2. Table A-1 in the appendix follows the typical YITS-A respondent after
    Grade 10 attendance in December 1999 and the typical YITS-B respond-
    ent, assuming they were 15 years of age in Grade 10. The very end of the
    time period studied is complicated by the ending of the formal Grade 13
    year in Ontario in 2002-03 because the group of Ontario students who
    were in Grade 10 in December 1999 graduated from Grade 13 in June 2003.
    A group of Grade 12 students in Ontario also graduated in June 2003 and
    was eligible for university. These groups of Grade 12 and Grade 13 stu-
    dents constitute the "double cohort." The year fixed effects and the prov-
    ince fixed effects may be partly associated with the complications around
    the ending of Grade 13 in Ontario.
3. Thus this paper does not consider access to other forms of post-secondary
    education beyond university programs leading to a bachelor's degree. This

is the YITS definition of university. Since the focus of the research in this paper relates to the effect of the level and change in university level tuitions on university access and participation, the evidence is only about access to and persistence in university. There is further work to do on the interaction of college and university choices. This interaction, we know, varies by province. This leads to the introduction of province fixed effects later in the analysis.

4. It is also possible in the data to work with a series of start and end dates at specific post-secondary institutions, colleges, and universities. In earlier versions of this study, all results also used definitions of persistence defined by institutions rather than program. No results were affected by this choice.

5. Respondents also exit YITS at the end of Cycle 1 on 31 December 1999 and at the end of Cycle 2 on 31 December 2001. Persistence choices from 1998-99 to 1999-2000 could be recorded for those who exit on 31 December 1999 using the Fall Term information from September 1999 to December 1999. Persistence choices from 2000-01 to 2001-02 can be recorded for those who exit on 31 December 2001 using the Fall Term information from September 2001 to December 2001. This adds about 10 percent more observations of persistence but means that analysis with weights so that the sample represents the Canadian population is no longer possible. There is no difference in the analysis of the effect of tuition between the weighted and unweighted samples. Results are presented in the paper only for weighted samples.

6. Since all Quebec persistence respondents are in university, they have graduated from CEGEP. The assumption is made here that most of these university students took two years of CEGEP, the normal path in Quebec. That is, a Quebec student in university where Year One=1 is a student in university in the third year after Grade 11.

7. Two other variables were used in the analysis. A dummy variable was created if the academic year in the first of the pair of academic years was the first year of the bachelor's program. A dummy variable was created if the persistence decision observed in one pair had been immediately preceded in time by a previous persistence decision. Results on tuition were not sensitive to the choice of stage of PSE variable used.

8. These are estimated using a linear probability model. The working papers referred to earlier contain a more complete set of results and include estimates from probit models.

9. It is important not to ascribe any analytical or policy or optimality statements from these fixed effects. Suppose it was the larger college system in Ontario that lowers access to university in that province: it may be better or worse for students to have more college places relative to university

places. We do not know the answer to this question. This may be an optimal system for society, but there could be some other factor in play in Ontario. The fixed effect simply says whatever that factor is, it is in play for all periods in the sample.

10. This does not occur, but if we imagine each province had the same constant level of tuition over all years and that tuition levels were the *only* difference across provinces, then the province fixed effect would be the effect of tuition. To re-emphasize, this is not what occurs. Precisely because there is variation in provincial tuition levels over time and thus changes in those levels, the project is able to ask how the level of tuition is associated with access and persistence decisions. If provinces did not vary tuition over time, we could not measure the effect of variation in tuition. There would be no variation to observe.

References

Barr-Telford, L., F. Cartwright, S. Prasil, and K. Shimmons. 2003. "Access, Persistence and Financing: First Results from the Postsecondary Education Participation Survey (PEPS)." Statistics Canada, Human Resources Development Canada: Education, Skills and Learning Research Paper No. 81-595-MIE2003007.

Bowlby, J.W., and K. McMullen. 2002. "At a Crossroads: First Results for the 18 to 20-Year-Old Cohort of the Youth in Transition Survey." Human Resources Development Canada and Statistics Canada, No. 81-591-XPE.

Coelli, M. 2004. *Tuition Increases and Inequality in Post-Secondary Education Attendance*. Vancouver: University of British Columbia.

Day, K. 2007. "The Effect of Financial Aid on the Graduation Rate of College and University Students in Canada." Paper prepared for the MESA Conference, Montreal, October 2007.

Finnie, R., and T. Qiu. 2007. "The Patterns of Persistence in Post-Secondary Education in Canada: Evidence from the YITS. Paper prepared for the MESA Conference, Montreal, October 2007.

Grayson, J.P., and K. Grayson. 2003. "Research on Retention and Attrition." Millennium Research Series No. 6 (online): Canada Millennium Scholarship Foundation.

Heller, D.E. 1997. "Student Price Response in Higher Education: An Update to Leslie and Brinkman." *Journal of Higher Education* 68 (6): 624-59.

– 1999. "The Effects of Tuition and State Financial Aid on Public College Enrollment." *Review of Higher Education* 23 (1): 65-89.

Johnson, D.R. 2008a. "Interprovincial Variation in University Tuition and the Decision to Attend University Immediately after High-School Graduation: Evidence from Youth in Transition Survey in Canada." Paper in preparation for Measuring the Effectiveness of Student Aid.

– 2008b. "Inter-Provincial Variation in University Tuition and the Decision to Continue to Attend University: Evidence from Youth in Transition Survey in Canada." Paper in preparation for Measuring the Effectiveness of Student Aid.

Johnson, D.R., and F. Rahman. 2005. "The Role of Economic Factors, Including the Level of Tuition, in Individual University Participation Decisions in Canada." *Canadian Journal of Higher Education* 35 (3): 101-27.

Junor, S., and A. Usher. 2002. *The Price of Knowledge: Access and Student Finance in Canada*. Montreal: Canada Millennium Scholarship Foundation Research Series.

– 2004. *The Price of Knowledge: Access and Student Finance in Canada*. Montreal: Canada Millennium Scholarship Foundation Research Series.

Lambert, M., K. Zeman, M. Allen, and P. Bussière. 2004. "Who Pursues Postsecondary Education, Who Leaves and Why: Results from the Youth in Transition Survey." Research paper, Culture, Tourism and Centre for Education Statistics. Statistics Canada. Human Resources Development Canada. No. 81-595-MIE-No. 026.

Leslie, L.L., and P.T. Brinkman. 1988. *The Economic Value of Higher Education*. New York: American Council of Education, Macmillan.

Looker, E.D., and G.S. Lowe. 2001. "Post-Secondary Access and Student Financial Aid in Canada: Current Knowledge and Research Gaps." Canadian Policy Research Network. http://www.cprn.ca/cprn.html.

Marks, G.N. 2007. "Completing University: Characteristics and Outcomes of Completing and Non-Completing Students." Australian Council for Educational Research.

McElroy, L. 2005. "Student Aid and University Persistence: Does Debt Matter?" Canada Millennium Scholarship Foundation.

Mueller, R.E. 2007. "Access and Persistence of Students from Low-Income Backgrounds in Canadian Post-Secondary Education: A Review of the Literature." Paper prepared for the Educational Policy Institute's MESA Program.

Neill, C. 2006. Tuition Fees and the Demand for University Places. Waterloo, Ont.: Wilfrid Laurier University. http://www.wlu.ca/documents/17295/Enrol_Fee.pdf.

Shaienks, D., J. Eisl-Culkin, and P. Bussière. 2006. "Follow-Up on Education and Labour Market Pathways of Young Canadians Aged 18-20: Results from YITS Cycle 3." Culture, Tourism and Centre for Education Statistics Research Papers: Statistics Canada No. 81-595-MIE2006045.

Stinebricker, T.R., and R. Stinebricker. 2007. "The Effects of Credit Constraints on the College Drop-Out Decision: A Direct Approach Using a New Panel Study." National Bureau of Economic Research, Working Paper 13340.

Usher, A. 2006. "Beyond the Sticker Price: A Closer Look at Canadian University Tuition Fees." Toronto: Educational Policy Institute.

APPENDIX

TABLE A-1
Structure of the "Normal" Path through Four Years of University in the YITS Surveys

Initial year	Next year	Age in initial year YITS A	Grade (non ON, QC)	Grade ON(QC)	Age in initial year YITS B	Grade (non ON, QC)	Grade ON(QC)	Age in initial year YITS B	Grade (non ON, QC)	Grade ON(QC)	Age in initial year YITS B	Grade (non ON, QC)	Grade ON(QC)
1996-97	1997-98	12			15	10	10	16	11	11	17	12	12(CEGEP 1)
1997-98	1998-99	13			16	11	11	17	12	12(CEGEP 1)	18	Year 1	13(CEGEP 2)
1998-99	1999-2000	14			17	12	12(CEGEP 1)	18	Year 1	13(CEGEP 2)	19	Year 2	Year 1
1999-2000	2000-01	15	10	10	18	Year 1	13(CEGEP 2)	19	Year 2	Year 1	20	Year 3	Year 2
2000-01	2001-02	16	11	11	19	Year 2	Year 1	20	Year 3	Year 2	21	Year 4	Year 3
2001-02	2002-03	17	12	12(CEGEP 1)	20	Year 3	Year 2	21	Year 4	Year 3	22		Year 4
2002-03	2003-04	18	Year 1	13(CEGEP 2)	21	Year 4	Year 3	22		Year 4	23		
2003-04	Na	19	Year 2	Year 1	22		Year 4	23			24		

Notes: Age refers to the normal age of the respondent in the first academic year of the pair of academic years. Eight provinces, excluding Ontario and Quebec (ON and QC), normally graduate students from high school at the end of Grade 12. Students are normally 15 years of age in Grade 10. In Ontario, during the period studied, students normally graduated high school at the end of Grade 13. In Quebec, students who are university bound normally graduate high school at the end of Grade 11 (Year 5 in Quebec terminology, since high school starts in Grade 7) and then complete two years at CEGEP. University programs are normally either three of four years to degree completion.

13

A Tangled Web: The Relationship between Persistence and Financial Aid

KATHLEEN DAY

Cet article examine les moyens qu'utilisent les chercheurs pour analyser les effets de l'aide financière sur la persévérance des jeunes pendant leurs études postsecondaires. Mes observations replacent ainsi dans une perspective différente – et en général critique – les études existantes dans ce domaine. Même dans le cas de la présente étude, dont les résultats reposent sur l'utilisation des précieuses données de l'Enquête auprès des jeunes en transition (EJET, cohorte B), les difficultés, sur le plan méthodologique, restent énormes ; les résultats sont donc, au mieux, sujets à interprétation. L'étude conclut que, étant donné les interactions complexes – et donc très difficiles à définir – qui existent entre la persévérance et l'aide financière, évaluer de façon précise l'impact de l'aide financière sur la persévérance des jeunes pendant les études postsecondaires exigera des données mieux appropriées, plus probablement de nature expérimentale.

This paper addresses questions related to how to estimate the effects of student financial aid on persistence in post-secondary education. In doing so, it also casts most existing research into a different – and generally critical – perspective. New estimates are generated using the extremely rich YITS-B dataset, but even here the methodological challenges remain daunting and the findings are ambiguous at best. The paper concludes that due to the nature of the complex interactions between persistence and financial aid and the related "identification" issues, obtaining an accurate estimate of the impact of financial aid on post-secondary persistence in Canada will require better data, quite likely of an experimental type.

Who Goes? Who Stays? What Matters? Accessing and Persisting in Post-Secondary Education in Canada, eds. R. Finnie, R.E. Mueller, A. Sweetman, and A. Usher. Montreal and Kingston: McGill-Queen's University Press, Queen's Policy Studies Series. © 2008 The School of Policy Studies, Queen's University at Kingston. All rights reserved.

Introduction

Financial aid directed in various forms towards post-secondary students is nothing new. Universities have long used scholarships as a means of attracting the best students, while government-financed student loans were first introduced in Canada in 1964.[1] A variety of private organizations also have a history of offering scholarships, grants, and bursaries to students who meet certain criteria.[2]

Over the past two decades, as tuition fees have risen while at the same time both governments and individuals have become increasingly convinced of the importance of post-secondary education to the economic well-being of individuals and the Canadian economy as a whole, the adequacy of existing financial aid programs has been regularly called into question.[3] Unless increases in financial aid keep pace with increases in tuition fees, young people from lower-income families will find it increasingly difficult to invest in post-secondary education, which may potentially lead to a higher degree of income inequality in the future. As part of its response to these concerns, in 1998 the federal government created the Canada Millennium Scholarship Foundation to distribute bursaries and scholarships to post-secondary students in Canada.[4]

Yet despite the widespread belief that financial aid is important to removing barriers to post-secondary education, there have been surprisingly few empirical analyses of the impact of that aid on the acquisition of post-secondary education in Canada. Most of the studies that do exist are descriptive in nature and fail to control for many of the factors that may affect post-secondary outcomes. This paper will help to fill this gap by reviewing the results of previous studies using U.S. and Canadian data, as well as examining new results for Canada presented in Day (2007). Although the effect of financial aid on access to post-secondary education is also of interest, this study focuses on persistence – in other words, how financial aid influences outcomes for students who begin a post-secondary program.

As the paper will show, measurement of the impact of financial aid on post-secondary persistence is fraught with difficulties. It is difficult, if not impossible, to disentangle the effects of financial aid from those of other determinants of persistence using existing data, in large part because many of those other determinants also influence the amount of financial aid received. These interrelationships no doubt explain why there are so many conflicting results about the effects of financial aid in the literature.

As a consequence, this paper is unable to answer questions like "How much would persistence rates increase in Canada if student loans were increased by $1,000?" Although simple descriptive analyses suggest that there is indeed a positive correlation between post-secondary persistence and aid in the form of scholarships and awards, grants and bursaries, and government-sponsored student loans, more sophisticated statistical techniques, some of which attempt to control for the interrelationships between the determinants of persistence and financial aid, lead to contradictory results. Both the direction and magnitude of the effect of financial aid on post-secondary persistence in Canada remain unclear.

The next section of the paper looks at what simple descriptive analyses based on recent surveys of Canadian high school graduates reveal about the nature of the correlation between financial aid and post-secondary persistence. I then review attempts to quantify the relationship between financial aid and persistence, and discuss the difficulties that researchers encounter in trying to do so. Finally, I summarize the state of our knowledge about the effect of financial aid on post-secondary persistence in Canada, and suggest some directions for future research.

Persistence and Financial Aid in Canada: A First Look at the Data

Common sense as well as economic models of investment in human capital suggests that the effect of financial aid on post-secondary persistence should be positive. Non-repayable forms of aid such as scholarships, bursaries, and grants have the effect of reducing the cost to the individual of acquiring a post-secondary education. Consequently, all other things being equal, one would expect an individual who received this type of aid to invest in more post-secondary education. In other words, such individuals would be more likely to begin post-secondary education (PSE), would likely stay in school longer, and would be more likely to complete their post-secondary programs.

Like scholarships, bursaries, and grants, student loans should also encourage enrolment in post-secondary education and increase persistence. Individuals contemplating a post-secondary program face an investment decision similar to that of a firm considering investing in new plant and equipment; firms will take on a loan and make the investment as long as the expected future profits more than offset the cost of repaying the loan. Similarly, successfully completing a post-secondary program should raise future income by more than the amount of loan payments, making it rational for individuals to take on loans to finance their post-secondary education. Of course, because student loan repayments reduce the net increase in earnings due to post-secondary education, one would expect a given dollar increase in non-repayable aid to have a larger positive impact on persistence than the same dollar increase in loans. However, while there has often been debate about the optimal design of government-sponsored student loan programs, most observers would agree that, like scholarships, student loans should increase both rates of participation and rates of completion of post-secondary programs.[5]

What do the data for Canada tell us about the effects of financial aid on persistence? Bowlby and McMullen (2002, 56-57), using early data from Cohort B of Statistics Canada's Youth in Transition Survey (YITS-B), note that 33 percent of PSE continuers reported the receipt of scholarships, as opposed to only 18.6 percent of PSE leavers. Similarly, 14.6 percent of continuers as compared to 9.3 percent of leavers reported receiving grants or bursaries, while 29.2 percent of continuers as opposed to 26.7 percent of leavers reported receiving government-sponsored student loans. PSE graduates were also more likely to report receipt of financial aid than PSE leavers, although the only category of aid they were more likely to report than continuers was government-sponsored student loans. These numbers certainly suggest a positive correlation between financial aid and persistence, although the numbers for scholarships (and to a lesser extent, grants) may overstate the importance of financial aid, since scholarship recipients are also likely to have greater academic ability and/or be better prepared for post-secondary education.

Consistent with the evidence from YITS-B, Barr-Telford et al. (2003, 10), reporting on Statistics Canada's Postsecondary Education Participation Survey, find that 29 percent of individuals who left their post-secondary program by March 2002 (survey respondents began their studies in September 2000) cited "financial reasons" for doing so. This figure, which amounts to almost one-third of leavers, may overestimate the proportion of students who face financial constraints, however, because "financial reasons" included not only the respondent's financial situation and the inability to obtain a student loan, but also wanting or needing to work. Finnie, Laporte, and Zhang (forthcoming, 2008) find that when "wanting to work" is excluded from financial reasons for leaving, the percentage drops to 21.9 percent. Although smaller, this figure implies that about one-fifth of those who begin a post-secondary program face financial constraints severe enough to prevent them from completing their program.

More recently, in Day (2007) I examine the relationship between receipt of financial aid and persistence using a sample drawn from YITS-B. The sample consists of students who began a post-secondary program in August or September 1999, and who responded to both Cycles 1 and 2 of the survey.[6] Table 1 shows the population estimates of the proportion of individuals who did *not* receive financial aid during the 1999-2001 period. Financial aid is divided into three categories: scholarships and awards, grants and bursaries, and government-sponsored student loans ("aid" refers to total aid received from all three sources). Students are divided into two categories: those who either had graduated by the end of December 2001 or who were continuing their studies, and those who had left PSE by December 2001 without graduating. Students are also sorted by the type of institution attended: university, college (i.e.,

TABLE 1
Percentage of Students with No Financial Aid, by Type of Institution and Persistence, Canada, 1999-2001

	Leaver	Graduate/Continuer	Total
University			
Scholarships	57.7	38.8	40.9
Grants	73.7	65.4	66.3
Student loans	61.4	68.2	67.4
Aid	33.6	21.4	22.8
College			
Scholarships	85.7	79.6	80.9
Grants	91.4	75.0	78.5
Student loans	80.1	67.0	69.9
Aid	66.4	49.8	53.4
Other			
Scholarships	68.6	54.1	56.5
Grants	84.0	72.8	74.6
Student loans	83.3	73.7	75.3
Aid	51.8	40.9	42.7
Total			
Scholarships	74.6	56.7	59.6
Grants	84.9	70.2	72.6
Student loans	75.2	68.6	69.7
Aid	54.3	35.3	38.4

Source: Day, 2007, Table 3. Author's compilations based on data from YITS-B. Numbers are weighted estimates for the population constructed using Cycle 2 sampling weights.

community college or CEGEP), or another type of institution.[7] The table shows that, with only one exception, leavers are less likely to have received financial aid than those who persist. The exception is at the university level, where persistent students are less likely to receive student loans than leavers. Interestingly, the table also shows that more than half – 61.6 percent, to be exact – of Canadian post-secondary students received at least one of the three types of financial aid. At the university level, this percentage was even higher: 77.2 percent.

In addition to calculating the percentage of students who did not receive aid, I also computed the average amount of aid received by aid recipients, classified by type of aid, type of institution, and persistence status. These amounts are presented in Table 2. In general, the results are consistent with those of Table 1, in that in almost all cases persistent

TABLE 2
Average Amount of Aid Received by Aid Recipients, by Type of Institution and Persistence, Canada, 1999-2001

	Leaver	*Graduate/Continuer*	*Total*
Scholarships			
University	2,228	3,454	3,356
College	1,506	1,241	1,285
Other	2,200	2,314	2,300
All students	2,004	2,862	2,773
Grants			
University	1,633	2,060	2,023
College	1,292	1,880	1,829
Other	2,090	2,373	2,343
All students	1,610	2,050	2,011
Student loans			
University	7,818	11,957	11,413
College	5,913	7,571	7,332
Other	7,546	9,264	9,070
All students	6,966	9,846	9,460
Total Aid			
University	6,618	8,445	8,270
College	4,475	6,412	6,108
Other	4,736	7,013	6,692
All students	5,434	7,634	7,367

Source: Day, 2007, Table 5. Author's compilations based on data from YITS-B. Numbers are weighted estimates for the population constructed using Cycle 2 sampling weights.

students (i.e., graduates and continuers) receive on average larger amounts of aid than do leavers (the one exception is scholarship aid for college students). This is true even for student loans at the university level – on average, university students who persisted received $11,957 in government-sponsored student loans while university students who left their PSE program received only $7,818. Of course one should bear in mind when examining Table 2 that part of the explanation for the higher amounts received by persistent students may simply be that these students remained in PSE longer than their counterparts and therefore were eligible to receive more money.

Nonetheless, all of these findings for Canada, derived from two different surveys, suggest that there is indeed a positive correlation between financial aid and persistence. However, financial aid is not the only factor likely to influence persistence, which raises the question of whether or not the observed positive correlation would remain after other potential influences on persistence have been taken into account. Indeed, the one anomaly in Table 1 – the finding that continuing university students are less likely to receive student loans than those who leave university – highlights the dangers of jumping to conclusions too quickly based on simple tabulations or computed correlations. University students may be less likely to receive student loans because they are more likely to receive other forms of financial support. Table 1 also shows that university students are far more likely to receive aid in the form of scholarships than are college students, for example – only 41 percent of university students report that they did not receive any scholarship income, as compared to 81 percent of college students. Furthermore, for policy-making purposes it would be desirable to have a numerical estimate of the effect of financial aid on persistence. The next section of this paper addresses the problems inherent in trying to produce such a numerical estimate.

Measuring the Impact of Financial Aid on Post-Secondary Persistence

The calculation of a numerical estimate of the effect of financial aid on post-secondary persistence requires the use of more complex statistical techniques. While a number of studies have attempted the task, most are based on U.S. data.[8] Many of these studies use administrative data from universities and colleges and employ a variety of models and estimation techniques. Persistence itself is often represented as a variable that takes on the value 1 if the individual chooses to continue his or her post-secondary education, and 0 otherwise. The time frame over which persistence is examined varies from one year to as many as six or seven years. Thus some studies look at persistence in the short term, while others focus on the completion of post-secondary studies.

While models and estimation techniques may vary, the list of variables deemed to influence persistence is more consistent across American studies. Indicators of racial background, gender, and age at commencement of studies are typically included. If the data are available, studies often include parental income, high school grade point average, results of the Scholastic Assessment Test (SAT), and other variables including whether the student is from out of state or lives on campus. However, the results of these studies with respect to the impact of financial aid have been less consistent and sometimes surprising. For example, DesJardins, Ahlburg, and McCall (1999), examining the persistence of a sample of University of Minnesota students (Minneapolis campus) who commenced their studies in the fall of 1986, use a complex event history model that allows one to estimate the separate effects of the explanatory variables on each year of study. They find that for these students, grants did not have a statistically significant effect on dropout behaviour; the amount of scholarship aid received significantly reduced dropouts only in year 2, and student loans significantly reduced dropouts only in year 3 or after five or more years. However, in a separate model examining the time to the first temporary "stopout" from the post-secondary program, they find that scholarships and student loans are more important in reducing stopouts.

In a later study, in which they again use data on University of Minnesota students (Twin Cities campus), this time for students who entered university in the fall of 1991, Desjardins, Ahlburg, and McCall (2002) estimate a more complex model in which both stopouts and graduation are jointly examined. Financial aid is again divided into several categories in their estimating equations: loans, state grants, merit aid (i.e., scholarships), federal gift aid, other aid, and work/study. This time they find that only aid in the form of work/study programs has any impact on graduation rates; they conclude that work/study programs appear to promote graduation over time.[9] However, they do find that both merit aid and loans have statistically significant effects on stopout behaviour. In this study, an increase in loans actually *increases* the probability of a stopout, while an increase in merit aid reduces the probability of a stopout. They conclude that although neither loans nor merit aid have a direct effect on graduation rates, they do have an indirect effect on graduation rates through their impact on stopout rates. Students who do not stop out will be more likely to graduate, or will tend to graduate sooner. However, the fact remains that not only does the study find that some other types of aid have no significant effect but it also finds that one type of aid, loans to students, appears to have counterintuitive effects on persistence.

McElroy (2005) is one of the few Canadian studies that attempts to control for other factors in measuring the effect of financial aid on persistence. Like Desjardins, Ahlburg, and McCall (1999, 2002), she uses administrative data; her dataset is from six Canadian universities and covers students who entered university in 1997 or 1998. The students are followed for five years. She divides financial aid into two categories, repayable aid (loans) and non-repayable aid (scholarships, awards, grants, and bursaries), and estimates models based on two different measures of persistence: the percentage of required credits completed, and a 0-1 variable equal to 1 if the individual graduated by the end of the five-year period and 0 otherwise. To control for the fact that students who remained in school longer could potentially receive more aid, she uses as her aid measure the amount of aid received divided by the number of years completed.

Due to the limited nature of her dataset, McElroy (2005) could not include in her model as many control variables as did the American studies discussed above. In addition to the financial aid variables, the only variables she could include were indicators of gender, students' age at entry into the post-secondary program, and an indication of whether the program was four or five years in length rather than just three years. However, she included a number of aid-related variables including the types of aid received and the annualized amounts received.

McElroy (2005) does not actually indicate in her study which variables had a statistically significant effect on persistence. However, she computes the predicted effect on persistence of different amounts of aid of different types. Her calculations show that the predicted rate of degree completion decreased with the amount of aid received for students who received loans; for students who received only non-repayable aid, completion rates did not vary much with the amount of aid received. Similarly, the proportion of credits completed decreased as the amount of aid increased for students who received loans, while there was no clear pattern for students who received only non-repayable aid. McElroy hypothesizes that the observed negative relationship between repayable aid and persistence may be due to efforts on the part of students to avoid assuming high levels of debt, or may reflect a higher level of unmet financial needs among loan recipients.

One limitation of McElroy's (2005) study is that the institutional dataset that she used did not include many individual or family characteristics. By way of contrast, YITS-B includes a considerable amount of information about individual characteristics, and thus allows one to test whether financial aid still has an impact on persistence after controlling for these characteristics. In Day (2007), using data from YITS-B, I estimate a model of post-secondary persistence in which students who began PSE in August or September 1999 are defined to be persistent if they were graduates or continuers as of December 2001. The dependent variable in the model is set equal to 1 if the individual is persistent and 0 otherwise, and probit estimation is used. In addition to financial aid, the explanatory variables include the student's age at the time of enrolment, the number of children the student has, and years since the student immigrated to Canada (defined to be 0 for the Canadian-born). In addition, a number of 0-1 variables indicate whether or not the student is female; has French as a mother tongue; has a mother tongue other than English or French; is married; is a member of a visible minority; changed province or city to begin PSE; whether PSE is important to the student's parents; whether the student's overall high school average was between 90 percent and 100 percent, 80 percent and 89 percent, or 70 percent and 79 percent; an additional variable indicates in which province the student lived. Probit models were estimated for all post-secondary students, for university students, and for college students, with either total financial aid received over the 1999-2001 period or the amounts received of three types of aid: scholarships, grants, and student loans.[10]

The results of these models of persistence, some of which are presented in Table 3, indicate, somewhat surprisingly, that few of the personal characteristics included, other than marital status, have a statistically significant impact on persistence over the period examined.[11] Being married has a strong negative impact, reducing the probability of persistence by almost 40 percentage points for post-secondary students, university students, and college students alike. Having parents who think PSE is important has a more moderate, positive impact on persistence, at least for college students. However, the overall high school average, the best indicator of ability available in the dataset, has a more important impact: having an average grade in the 90-100 percent range increases the probability of persistence by at least 20 percentage points for university students, 30 percentage points for college students, and 15 percentage points for all students.

The most interesting results, however, involve financial aid. Holding all else constant, total financial aid has a positive and significant effect on persistence. However, the effect is rather small in magnitude: the parameter estimates imply that a $1,000 increase in total aid will increase the persistence of university students by less than one percentage point,

TABLE 3
Predicted Effect on the Probability of Persistence: Selected Results for Canada, 1999-2001

Variable	All students	University students	College students	All students	University students	College students
French	-0.093	-0.272*	-0.048	-0.090	-0.269*	-0.047
Other language	0.014	0.076	0.109	0.012	0.068	0.096
Married	-0.396***	-0.390**	-0.403***	-0.402	-0.405**	-0.417***
PSE important to parents	0.075***	0.051	0.163***	0.073**	0.050	0.169***
High school average						
90%-100%	0.163***	0.226**	0.301***	0.154***	0.206*	0.312***
80%-89%	0.075*	0.175**	0.123*	0.072*	0.166	0.129*
70%-79%	-0.027	0.073	0.027	-0.025	0.071	0.031
Financial aid						
Total aid	0.010***	0.006**	0.021***			
Scholarships				0.012	0.017	-0.007
Grants				0.028**	0.022	0.096**
Student loans				0.006**	0.003	0.016**
Probability of persistence of reference individual	0.779	0.734	0.595	0.785	0.744	0.597

Note: These results are drawn from Table 7 of Day (2007), which is derived from the author's estimates based on data from YITS-B. For variables other than financial aid, the "predicted effect" is the difference between the probability of persistence of an individual for whom the variable equals 1 and the probability of persistence for the reference individual. For the financial aid variables, the "predicted effect" is the effect on the probability of persistence of increasing the financial aid of the reference individual by $1,000. The reference individual is a male who lives in Ontario, with English as his mother tongue, who is not a member of a visible minority, whose average grade in high school was below 70 percent, whose parents do not consider post-secondary education to be very important, who is unmarried and has no dependent children, and did not change city or province to attend PSE. In addition, the reference individual is assumed to be of average age, with average income but no financial aid. All equations were estimated using sampling weights. Finally, * indicates significance at the 10 percent level, ** significance at the 5 percent level, and *** significance at the 1 percent level.

of all post-secondary students by one percentage point, and of college students by about two percentage points. When aid is disaggregated into three categories, none of the three types of aid has a statistically significant impact on the persistence of university students, but both grants and loans have a significant impact on the persistence of all students and college students. As one would expect, the predicted effect of a $1,000 increase in non-repayable grants is larger than that of an equivalent increase in government-sponsored student loans, with the difference amounting to as much as eight percentage points for college students.

While these results seem more consistent with prior expectations than those of McElroy (2005), they are still somewhat surprising. First, the magnitude of the effects is small. Second, when aid is disaggregated into three categories, it appears to have no effect on the persistence of university students, and scholarships have no significant effect for any group of students. While one can explain the lack of effect of scholarship aid as a statistical artifact – it is likely to be highly correlated with the academic performance variables – it is harder to explain why the other types of aid have no effect on the persistence of university students. Do these results accurately measure the causal effect of student aid on post-secondary persistence?

There are at least two reasons why one should be careful about attaching a causal interpretation to these results. First of all, human capital theory suggests that not all students will be affected by changes in financial aid. Only students just on the margin between continuing and not continuing – in other words, students for whom the expected benefits of continuing are almost equal to the expected costs – are likely to be affected by changes in financial aid. For the majority of students, the expected benefits of PSE may so far exceed the expected costs that it would take a very large change in financial aid to have any impact on their decision to continue. Thus the relatively small magnitude of the predicted effect of a change in financial aid may simply reflect the fact that for most individuals in the sample, changes in financial aid were not large enough to have much impact on persistence.[12]

Second, as Bettinger (2004) and Alon (2005) have pointed out, unobservable factors that have not been included in the model may influence both persistence and the amount of financial aid received. If so, financial aid must be treated as an endogenous determinant of persistence. If this endogeneity is not taken into account in the estimation process, estimates of the effect of financial aid (and the other explanatory variables) on persistence will be biased. Dealing with this problem would require the construction of a more detailed structural model of post-secondary persistence in which both the determinants of financial aid and the determinants of persistence are modelled. From an econometric point of view, what is needed is a variable (or better yet, several variables) that influences the amount of financial aid received but *not* the persistence decision. In their papers, both Bettinger and Alon try to identify and make use of such variables. Bettinger's solution to the problem is to regress financial aid on a quartic function of variables that determine financial aid, such as family income and assets, family size, and the number of children attending college; he then uses the residuals from this equation as an instrumental variable.[13]

Needless to say, identifying such variables in YITS-B (or any other dataset) is not easy. First consider financial aid in the form of scholarships. Scholarships are supposed to be awarded primarily on the basis of merit. The primary measure of academic merit available to granting agencies is probably the overall high school average. However, this variable has already been included in the models of persistence, since it is the best available indicator of ability, an important determinant of success at the post-secondary level. Although YITS-B contains many other variables, none of them seems likely to be a more important determinant of the amount of scholarship aid than overall high school average. Thus good instruments for scholarships may not exist in YITS-B.

In the case of grants and student loans, both of which are allocated at least in part on the basis of financial need, it is a little easier to identify some potential instruments. These include variables related to family structure, such as whether or not the student lives with a single parent or two biological parents, how many siblings the student has, and whether or not the student lives at home. Although parental income is not available, the dataset does include information on the level of education of parents or guardians, which is likely to be highly correlated with income. In addition, data on the student's income in 1999 are available. These variables are clearly related to the amount of student loans received – in fact, applicants to the Canada Student Loans Program are required to supply information about family size, earned income, parental income, and whether or not the student still lives at home.[14]

Thus it is possible to find in the YITS-B dataset some variables that are likely to be correlated with student financial aid, which can potentially be used as instruments for student aid in re-estimating the models of persistence. Similar variables – in particular, family income and family size – were used to generate instruments for financial aid by Bettinger (2004), although he used them somewhat differently. In Table 4, I show how the results reported earlier change when instrumental variable methods are used to re-estimate the persistence models presented in Table 3.[15] As before, both marital status and high school average continue to have important impacts on persistence. For marital status the effect is also similar in magnitude, although the positive effect of overall high school average is now even greater. However, the most surprising feature of the results in Table 4 is that with respect to financial aid they are completely different. For all post-secondary students, total financial aid now has a statistically significant negative, not positive, effect on persistence. For university and college students, total financial aid no longer has a statistically significant effect at all.

340   *Kathleen Day*

TABLE 4
Predicted Effects on the Probability of Persistence When Aid Is Treated as Endogenous: Selected Results for Canada, 1999-2001

Variable	All students	University students	College students
French	-0.071	-0.259	-0.027
Other language	0.045	0.086	0.120
Married	-0.268**	-0.327	-0.314**
PSE important to parents	0.064*	0.047	0.120*
High school average			
90%-100%	0.310***	0.264	0.358***
80%-89%	0.147***	0.200	0.136**
70%-79%	-0.009	0.085	0.011
Financial aid			
Total aid	-0.028**	-0.001	-0.027
Probability of persistence of reference individual	0.601	0.695	0.543

Note: These results are drawn from Table 9 of Day (2007), which is derived from the author's estimates based on data from YITS-B. For variables other than financial aid, the "predicted effect" is the difference between the probability of persistence of an individual for whom the variable equals 1 and the probability of persistence for the reference individual. For the financial aid variables, the "predicted effect" is the effect on the probability of persistence of increasing the financial aid of the reference individual by $1,000. The reference individual is a male who lives in Ontario, with English as his mother tongue, who is not a member of a visible minority, whose average grade in high school was below 70 percent, whose parents do not consider post-secondary education to be very important, who is unmarried and has no dependent children, and did not change city or province to attend PSE. In addition, the reference individual is assumed to be of average age, with average income but no financial aid. All equations were estimated using sampling weights. Finally, * indicates significance at the 10 percent level, ** significance at the 5 percent level, and *** significance at the 1 percent level.

How can one explain this complete reversal in the results for all post-secondary students? Most likely the problems lie in the choice of instruments for financial aid. First of all, the chosen instruments may not be relevant to all students in the sample. For example, instrumental variables related to financial need may be irrelevant to those students with high levels of ability who rely largely on scholarship income. If the instruments are only relevant to a sub-sample of individuals, then the estimated effects cannot be viewed as representative of the population as a whole.

Second, the instruments may be "weak." Even if it is plausible that the chosen instrumental variables influence the amount of aid received but not the probability of persistence, they must have a high degree of explanatory power – in other words, they must do a good job of explaining the amount of aid received – in order to be good instruments. Day (2007) tests the strength of the instruments using two alternative tests recently proposed by Stock and Yogo (2005), and finds that although the chosen instruments do have some explanatory power in equations for the amount of financial aid, they cannot really be considered strong instruments. There remains too much unexplained variation in the financial aid equations based on these variables.[16] Consequently, there may remain considerable bias in the estimates in Table 4.

Finally, although the instruments selected appear to be comparable to those used in other studies, one could still argue that they really belong in the persistence equation as well, in which case they would not be good instruments.[17] Parental financial support, which has not been explicitly included in the persistence equations, may also depend on family structure. Holding parental income constant, parents may choose to support only the child who has the best chance of success at the post-secondary level, or they may divide the available resources more evenly among their children, resulting in less financial support for children with many siblings. In either case, family size influences the amount of parental support. Parental education may also influence persistence independently of its effect on parental income, if highly educated parents put more pressure on their children to succeed at the post-secondary level, or if they are better informed about sources of aid. If highly educated parents are better informed about aid sources, their children may be more likely to apply for aid than children of less educated parents, and hence more likely to receive it.

On the other hand, parental pressure may already be captured in the indicator of the importance of post-secondary education to parents, and parental decisions regarding the financial support they provide their children may be made prior to admission to university. If so, the chosen instruments for financial aid may still be useful when studying persistence. However, some doubt remains as to the adequacy of the instruments used. It is also worth noting that while some of Bettinger's (2004) results suggest that financial aid in the form of Pell grants in the United States tends to increase persistence, this result is not always robust to changes in the sample or estimation method used. Thus the problem of sensitivity of the sign as well as the magnitude of the effect of financial aid is not restricted to the YITS-B data.

Conclusions

While simple cross-tabulations reveal a positive correlation between financial aid and post-secondary persistence in Canada, separating the effect of financial aid from the effects of other factors influencing persistence is not an easy task. When models of persistence that include a variety of control variables are estimated, total financial aid as well as grants and student loans are still positively correlated with persistence, although the magnitude of the effect is small. Furthermore, aid in the form of scholarships does not seem to have a statistically significant effect, most likely because of the strong correlation between scholarship aid and high school grades. When the models were re-estimated allowing for the potential endogeneity of financial aid arising from the simultaneous dependence of both financial aid and persistence on the same unobservable factors, the positive correlation between financial aid and persistence disappeared, and in some cases was replaced by a negative correlation.

Given the strong likelihood that financial aid is indeed endogenous, and the limitations of the instrumental variables used, these contradictory results are not surprising. Not only the original probit estimates but also the instrumental variable estimates based on weak instruments are likely to be biased. Unfortunately the direction of the bias is hard to predict, and it is not possible to say which set of estimates is the most biased. Thus although common sense suggests that financial aid should have a positive impact on persistence for at least some students, the magnitude of the effect and the characteristics of the students most likely to benefit from it remain unknown. Furthermore, although it is in many ways a very rich dataset, it is unlikely that YITS-B contains any further information that could help to disentangle these effects.

How, then, can future research lead to better estimates of the effect of financial aid on persistence? The problem that researchers in this area must face is that there are many possible ways to finance a post-secondary education, which interact with each other and academic performance in different ways. For example, students' decisions about how much time to spend working part time will have repercussions for both their eligibility for government-sponsored student loans and their academic performance, and may also influence their eligibility for merit-based forms of aid later on. In addition, as discussed above, some of the unobservable factors that influence persistence may also influence the amount of aid received, not to mention the student's allocation of time. There are thus many endogenous variables that need to be taken into account when analyzing the effect of financial aid on post-secondary persistence. Finally, persistence and financial aid share many of the same determinants, or appear to, because the channels through which some variables operate are not fully understood. For example, parental education is highly correlated with persistence but may also influence financial aid if highly educated parents provide more financial support or help their children apply for financial aid.

Part of the problem empirical researchers face, then, is finding exogenous variables that they can use as instruments for the many variables that are endogenous to the student decision-making process. What are needed are variables that influence one endogenous variable but not the others. Better theoretical models of persistence could perhaps help to identify such variables, but few theoretical models of the relationship between persistence and the financing of post-secondary education exist, no doubt because of the complexity of the problem.[18] More empirical studies that focus on how students finance their post-secondary education might also be helpful in identifying the factors that influence the amount of financial aid received, but data limitations may pose a problem here too. Although it provides more information on the financing of post-secondary education than many other surveys, YITS does not in fact provide details on the amounts obtained from all sources of finance.

Another approach to identifying the magnitude of the effect of financial aid that has not hitherto been discussed would be the use of a natural experiment. Dynarski (2003), in her study of the effect of the 1982 elimination of the Social Security Student Benefit Program in the United States, uses such an approach to estimate the effect of financial aid on college attendance and rates of completion. She finds evidence of a statistically significant impact of financial aid on college attendance, although the effect on persistence is less clear. In order to apply this approach in Canada, one would need to find some change in financial aid to students that affected a clearly identifiable group of students but not a comparison group.

Unfortunately, I am unaware of such a natural experiment for Canada that could be exploited in this fashion. Inter-provincial variation is unlikely to constitute such a natural experiment. Even if important differences in financial aid existed across provinces, it would be difficult to disentangle the effect of those differences from the effect of other provincial differences related to post-secondary education, such as differences in tuition fees. Thus obtaining an accurate estimate of the impact of financial aid on post-secondary persistence in Canada may have to wait until better data, in the form of a more complete survey or a suitable natural experiment, become available.

In the meantime, it would be a mistake to conclude that the results discussed in this paper imply that financial aid has little or no effect on post-secondary persistence. While some forms of aid may have other impacts – for example, scholarships may have a greater impact on the choice of post-secondary institution than on persistence per se – the sudden elimination of all forms of student financial aid would likely have a dramatic negative effect on post-secondary enrolment and persistence in Canada. As better data become available, future studies will likely be able to shed more light on the relationship between financial aid and post-secondary persistence in Canada without having to resort to such a dramatic experiment.

Notes

I would like to thank Theresa Qiu for her invaluable assistance in compiling the data, as well as her help with computer programming. I would also like to thank Statistics Canada's RDC program for providing access to the Youth in Transition Survey data, the MESA Project for its research support, as well as the MESA Research Review Committee, Hans Vossentyn, other participants in the MESA conference of 19 October 2007, colleagues at the University of Ottawa, and the editors of this volume for their helpful comments and suggestions. All remaining errors in the paper are my own responsibility.

1. See Human Resources and Social Development Canada (2006) for a very brief overview of the history of the Canada Student Loans Program.
2. For example, some companies offer scholarships to the children of their employees. On the website of the Association of Colleges and Universities of Canada (http://www.aucc.ca/scholarships/index_e.html), children of employees of MDS Nordion and NAV Canada can apply online for scholarships.
3. For a recent example, see Canadian Federation of Students (2007).
4. See Canada Millennium Scholarship Foundation (2007) for a brief overview of the objectives of the Canada Millennium Scholarship Foundation.
5. See Finnie and Schwartz (1996) for a comprehensive study of the Canada Student Loans Program and a discussion of various policy options related to student loans.
6. Only individuals for whom all the required data for a more complex statistical analysis were available were included in the sample. For further details regarding the characteristics of the sample, see Day (2007).
7. Other institutions include university colleges, publicly funded technical institutes, trade/vocational colleges, private business schools or training institutes, Quebec secondary schools or school boards, or any other school

above high school. Note that the YITS-B variable used to categorize institutions (TYPEID2 from the Cycle 2 Institutions roster) includes Quebec CEGEPs with community colleges.

8. For a more comprehensive review of the literature on post-secondary persistence, see Mueller (2008).
9. This conclusion is based on a model in which graduation and stopout are modelled jointly. See p. 570 of their paper for further discussion.
10. For further details regarding the variables, see Day (2007).
11. There also were no significant provincial differences.
12. This point was raised by several participants at the MESA conference entitled All in the Family? Evidence from the YITS on PSE Access and Persistence, 19 October 2007.
13. Alon (2005) does not seem to specify which variables were used as instruments.
14. See the Canada Student Loans Program website, maintained by Human Resources and Social Development Canada, for information about current eligibility requirements for student loans and grants offered by the program (http://www.hrsdc.gc.ca/en/learning/canada_student_loan/index.shtml#loans).
15. The estimation of probit models with endogenous explanatory variables is discussed in Newey (1987) and Rivers and Vuong (1988).
16. Note that in addition to the highlighted instruments, all the explanatory variables in the Table 3 equations were included in the financial aid equations. See Day (2007) for the complete specification of these equations.
17. Alon (2005) also uses instrumental variable methods to estimate models of persistence similar to those discussed in this paper. However, Alon's paper does not seem to identify the exact variables used as instruments.
18. Bettinger (2004) does make an attempt to construct one.

References

Alon, S. 2005. "Model Mis-Specification in Assessing the Impact of Financial Aid on Academic Outcomes." *Research in Higher Education* 46 (1): 109-25.

Barr-Telford, L., F. Cartwright, S. Prasil, and K. Shimmons. 2003. "Access, Persistence, and Financing: First Results from the Postsecondary Education Participation Survey (PEPS)." Statistics Canada Education, Skills and Learning Research Papers, Statistics Canada No. 81-595-MIE–No. 007, Ottawa, Canada.

Bettinger, E. 2004. "How Financial Aid Affects Persistence." In *College Choices: The Economics of Where to Go, When to Go, and How to Pay for It*, edited by Caroline M. Hoxby, 207-37. Chicago: University of Chicago Press.

Bowlby, J.W., and K. McMullen. 2002. *At a Crossroads: First Results from the 18- to 20-Year-Old Cohort of the Youth in Transition Survey.* Ottawa: Human Resources Development Canada and Statistics Canada.

Canadian Federation of Students. 2007. *Strategy for Change: Money Does Matter.* Ottawa: Canadian Federation of Students (October). http://www.cfsadmin. org/quickftp/Strategy_for_Change_2007.pdf .

Canada Millennium Scholarship Foundation. 2007. "About the Millennium Scholarships." www.millenniumscholarships.ca/en/aboutus/index.asp, accessed 14 January 2008.

Day, K. 2007. "The Effect of Financial Aid on the Persistence of University and College Students in Canada." Paper prepared for the MESA Project.

DesJardins, S.L., D.A. Ahlburg, and B.P. McCall. 1999. "An Event History Model of Student Departure." *Economics of Education Review* 18: 375-90.

– 2002. "A Temporal Investigation of Factors Related to Timely Degree Completion." *Journal of Higher Education* 73 (5): 555-81.

Dynarski, S.M. 2003. "Does Aid Matter? Measuring the Effect of Student Aid on College Attendance and Completion." *American Economic Review* 93 (1): 279-88.

Finnie, R., C. Laporte, and Y. Zhang. Forthcoming. 2008. "Access to Post-Secondary Education: Evidence from the Post-Secondary Education Participation Survey." Analytical Studies Branch Research Paper, Statistics Canada.

Finnie, R., and S. Schwartz. 1996. *Student Loans in Canada.* Toronto: C.D. Howe Institute.

Human Resources and Social Development Canada. 2006. "About the Canada Student Loans Program." http://www.hrsdc.gc.ca/en/hip/cslp/about/ 01_ab_missionprogram.shtml, accessed 14 January 2008 .

McElroy, Lori. 2005. *Student Aid and University Persistence: Does Debt Matter?* Montreal: Canada Millennium Scholarship Foundation.

Mueller, R.E. 2008. *Access and Persistence of Students from Low-Income Backgrounds in Canadian Post-Secondary Education: A Review of the Literature.* Department of Economics, University of Lethbridge. A MESA Project Research Paper. Toronto: Educational Policy Institute.

Newey, W.K. 1987. "Efficient Estimation of Limited Dependent Variable Models with Endogenous Explanatory Variables." *Journal of Econometrics* 36: 231-50.

Rivers, D., and Q.H. Vuong. 1988. "Limited Information Estimators and Exogeneity Tests for Simultaneous Probit Models." *Journal of Econometrics* 39: 347-66.

Stock, J.H., and M. Yogo. 2005. "Testing for Weak Instruments in Linear IV Regression." In *Identification and Inference for Econometric Models: Essays in Honor of Thomas Rothenberg,* edited by D.K. Andrews and J.H. Stock, 80-108. Cambridge: Cambridge University Press.

14

Family Income, Access to Post-Secondary Education and Student Grants: Why Equal Access Requires More Than Loans

LORNE CARMICHAEL AND ROSS FINNIE

Certains jeunes de milieux défavorisés qui ont les capacités nécessaires pour faire des études universitaires décident pourtant de ne pas entreprendre de telles études. Pour expliquer ce phénomène, on invoque souvent des facteurs comme le manque d'information, la « crainte de l'endettement », le faible degré d'instruction des parents ou le fait que les études universitaires coûtent trop cher. Dans cet article, nous avançons qu'il existe une autre explication : les difficultés associées aux faibles revenus avec lesquels ces jeunes devront vivre pendant leurs études. Avant de décider de poursuivre leurs études, ils doivent donc pouvoir espérer un taux de rendement supérieur (en comparaison avec les jeunes plus favorisés), et ce, même dans les cas où les prêts étudiants sont faciles à obtenir et peu coûteux. Nous vérifions nos résultats de façon empirique, et concluons que des bourses ciblées sont nécessaires pour égaliser les chances de poursuivre des études post-secondaires pour les jeunes de milieux défavorisés.

Factors such as lack of information, "debt aversion," low parental education, or unaffordability are commonly invoked to explain why some qualified students from lower income families do not go to university. We argue that another cause is the hardship associated with the limited resources that these students must live on while in school. To attend, they will need a higher measured rate of return than their peers, even when student loans are cheap and widely available. We test our idea empirically and conclude that targeted grants are needed to even the PSE playing field for youth from lower income families.

Who Goes? Who Stays? What Matters? Accessing and Persisting in Post-Secondary Education in Canada, eds. R. Finnie, R.E. Mueller, A. Sweetman, and A. Usher. Montreal and Kingston: McGill-Queen's University Press, Queen's Policy Studies Series. © 2008 The School of Policy Studies, Queen's University at Kingston. All rights reserved.

Introduction

For a young person who qualifies, a post-secondary education (PSE) typically carries many benefits. Estimates of the private returns to a university degree in Canada and elsewhere regularly top 10 percent (see, e.g., Blondal et al., 2002), while university graduates also benefit from their schooling in non-financial ways.[1] Apart from the pure consumption value of the education – the pleasure of the learning itself, enjoying the social life on campus – which is difficult to quantify, they enjoy better health (Kenkel, 1991), spend less time in jail (Lochner and Moretti, 2001), and benefit in a range of other ways (Haveman and Wolfe, 1984).

Economists therefore tend to view schooling as an "investment" in "human capital" that can yield substantial future "returns," and argue that qualified young people who are likely to succeed in PSE and go on to enjoy these sorts of benefits should be willing to pay the associated costs of the schooling, just as individuals would be willing to invest in other assets. Nonetheless, post-secondary education throughout the world is supported through a complex array of private bursaries, government grants, and subsidized student loans. Why should we be paying students to undertake an investment that is already so profitable for them?

One justification for public support of qualified students – including direct support of institutions – is based on the belief that educating a talented subset of the population will have external benefits for all members of society. For example, the effect of higher education on economic growth seems sure to be positive, although estimates are imprecise (Bassanini and Scarpenta, 2001). As well, low-skilled workers might earn higher wages due to the presence of university graduates (Moretti, 2004), which could be due to complementarities in production among workers (Johnson, 1984). Higher education is also linked to participation in community affairs, the democratic process, and volunteer work (Bynner and Egerton, 2000). Other such effects could be listed.

These "externality" arguments, however, justify subsidies to all qualified students – not just those who are deemed to have financial need, who come from lower income families, or who otherwise tend to merit targeted funding. They further suggest that those students who are expected to generate the greatest external benefits should get the largest subsidies, which may provide a rationale for merit-based scholarships or differential levels of support for those students undertaking the kinds of education (level and field of study) likely to have the greatest external benefits.

Other arguments for general grants, low tuition fees, and other forms of public support for students are based on the idea that the financial hardships they endure during university make them deserving of such assistance. Economists generally discount this argument, however, noting that those who qualify tend to come from richer than average families, are fortunate enough to possess a greater ability to achieve at school, and will eventually take their place among the financially fortunate in society – and will therefore have "lifetime incomes" well above the norm. Thus there seems to be no convincing equity-based reason to justify those who do not have these advantages and who will not benefit from attending university subsidizing those who do (Finnie and Schwartz, 1996; Finnie, 2005).

A more technical argument for general grants for students (Boskin, 1975; Carmichael, 1999) is based on the argument that such transfers can help to produce a more neutral system of taxation with respect to investments in human capital (i.e., schooling). Under a progressive income tax system, the returns from a university education are taxed at a higher rate than the opportunity cost – i.e., the wages that potential students would earn if they did not attend university. Grants could correct this distortion, and the potential under-investment in schooling that could result, by providing an offsetting subsidy. Once again, such grants should not be income based, and again it is those who stand to benefit the most from the schooling (and thus eventually have the highest marginal tax rates) who should receive the most.

Another case for more targeted grants is based on the idea that some students, especially those from lower income families or those where education is less valued (perhaps because the parents did not go on to PSE), will have poor information about the benefits (and perhaps the costs) of education or will otherwise have different "preferences" for PSE (Usher, 2006) than their fellow students. The ideal solution to problems such as these, however, would be to deliver better information or to otherwise attack the related "cultural" biases, although grants may be a reasonable "second best" instrument that could encourage attendance, especially in the short run (Finnie, 2005).

Alternatively, grants targeted toward students from poorer families are often supported as a means to help these individuals afford their schooling – or in more technical terms, to overcome the liquidity constraints that may prevent them from attending university.[2] However, since these students are blessed with academic ability and are likely to do well after graduation, most economists argue that the student loan system (and an unsubsidized one at that) is a more equitable tool for ensuring access.

One way to organize these arguments is to recognize that the economic role of general tuition subsidies and certain targeted grants should be to ensure that the expected private rate of return faced by any student deciding to attend university reflects the true social return. That is, the first role of a student financial aid system should be to provide all qualified students with the funds they require to attend, preferably at a cost that reflects the social cost of those funds, and academic screening (i.e., admission standards) should be used to prevent under-qualified students from wasting their time – and society's resources.

These are all "efficiency" arguments: their goal is to ensure that those people (and only those people) for whom the net personal and social benefit is positive will in fact choose to attend PSE. Meanwhile, we have suggested that equity based arguments for student support are less compelling, given the privileged status that university graduates generally enjoy in society – in the future (over their lifetimes) if not necessarily while they are students (depending on their parents' income level).

In this paper we suggest another argument for grants – one based principally on the normative goal of ensuring equal access to education, but also consistent with efficiency goals, by equalizing schooling opportunities for those from lower income families. The argument depends on the fact that the decision to invest in a university education is not purely a financial one but also requires that individuals attend an institution for four years and adopt a lifestyle during that period that will tend to be more frugal than what could be enjoyed were they not students. Most importantly, we will argue that the "hardship" of attending university will be greater for those from lower income families, thus restricting their participation, and that grants are the means of equalizing schooling chances.

In order to make this argument, we first need to discuss the meaning of "equal access to education." To do so we develop a simple model of PSE decision-making that takes into consideration the student's standard of living while at school, which will generally be related to family income. We then show that equal access requires more than a student loan system and leads to the case for targeted grants. We proceed to discuss some predictions of this approach, and test some of these predictions using data from the Youth in Transition Survey, Cohort A (YITS-A) database. A final concluding section completes the paper.

Equal Access

The concept of "equal access to post-secondary education" is not usually intended to mean that everyone should go to university (or college), but rather that those who would truly benefit from the schooling and for whom the benefits of it outweigh the costs should have the opportunity to go. One way to develop the relevant concepts is to use the supply and demand analysis of human capital choice that forms the basis of Becker's well known theory of the distribution of income (1975).

In this set-up, demand for education is given by the marginal rate of return expected from a particular level of schooling: individuals will invest up to the point where the marginal benefit of the schooling equals the marginal cost. Presented graphically (see Figure 1), years of schooling is on the horizontal axis, and the rate of return on the vertical axis. Students who are better at school or who otherwise have more to gain from the education (including its non-pecuniary benefits) will have higher demand curves, but any given individual will have a downward sloping demand curve because successively higher levels of schooling will eventually lead to lower marginal rates of return (if only because education takes time and working careers are finite).

The height of the individual's supply curve is, meanwhile, given by the marginal cost of the funds required to pay for the investment. Higher levels of education require more money and require the individual to access successively more expensive pools of capital, first perhaps from parents, then from other sources such as student loans or, eventually, private banks, and so on. Individuals' supply curves are, therefore, generally upward sloping, but students from higher income families will tend to have supply curves that are further to the right and flatter because they have access to relatively less expensive sources of financing for their schooling.

Educational choices at the individual level are – as usual – determined by the intersection of supply and demand. To illustrate this, and to frame the equity issue, let us suppose that we have two individuals with the same demand for education because they have similar ability – and are therefore "equally deserving" – but that they come from different backgrounds. What will happen? Figure 1 shows this situation and the unequal access that results.

The schooling of student 1 is assumed to be able to be completely financed with parental savings at a low opportunity cost (the horizontal supply curve S_1), while student 2 needs to resort to student loans and eventually private loans, which are increasingly expensive (the different steps in the supply curve), in order to achieve the same levels of education (S_2). As a result, the poorer student chooses less education ($E_2 < E_1$).

A natural definition of "equal access" in this framework would be represented by a different situation, where the marginal cost of the funds

FIGURE 1
Unequal Access to Schooling by Family Background

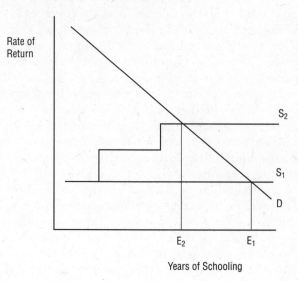

Source: Authors' compilation.

needed to attend university would be the same for both students – i.e., the supply curve faced by the two students would be identical (Becker, 1975, 123). More generally, students with more to gain from their schooling (the "more able") would choose more education than others (as should be the case), but the cost of the funds to finance their schooling would be the same, and as a result different students with the same ability would get the same amount of education. In particular, family income would no longer be a factor in determining schooling choices.

One could go further and ask that policies be designed to ensure that the marginal cost of funds be set equal to the social cost of those funds, and that students be able to borrow as much as they wished at this rate – that is, the supply curve should be perfectly elastic at the relevant level. This could in principle be achieved with a generous student loan system – without the use of grants – as long as even students from wealthier families had to repay any money they received from their parents at a cost at least equal to the social cost of the funds that holds for others. This situation is illustrated in Figure 2, where S represents the social cost of funds – and the supply curve – for all students.

In fact, many students will receive money absolutely free from their parents, meaning that ensuring equal access, by equalizing the cost of

FIGURE 2
Equal Access

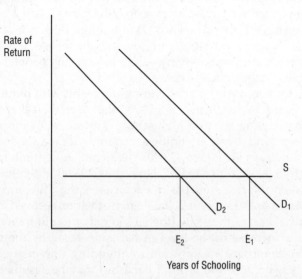

Source: Authors' compilation.

funds, will require grants rather than loans, and this is surely the case in reality.

Here, though, we wish to focus on a different point, one that is rooted in demand curves rather than supply curves and the manner in which demand curves for higher education might vary with family income even for students with the same underlying ability (and other attributes). More specifically, consider a situation in which two students do in fact face the same cost of funds (i.e., the same supply curve), but one comes from a higher income family than the other. Suppose, furthermore, that these potential students are identical in every other respect: they have had the same kind of upbringing, possess the same academic abilities, face the same employment opportunities both during school and after (as a graduate or non-graduate), and so on. Importantly, even though their family income differs, each also receives the same level of financial support from their family *conditional* on their attendance at university or college. (We make this assumption because it allows us to focus on the particular point we wish to make – relaxing it only strengthens the case for grants, almost in a trivially obvious way.)

Young people of PSE age may receive financial support from their parents whether or not they attend university. Richer ones may be given a car, be covered by a family dental plan, or receive a monthly allowance. This *unconditional* family support does not affect the financial calculations associated with deciding to go to university, since it is received whether the student attends or not and therefore does not affect the (net) financial rate of return to the schooling. Nonetheless, it will affect the lifestyle – the standard of living – that these young people are able to afford at this stage in their lives.

Suppose (for simplicity) that attending university will require a reduction in yearly expenditures of $5,000 relative to the alternative of taking a job immediately after high school. The student from a lower income background, while attending school, might face a reduction in spending from (say) $10,000 to $5,000. The richer student might face a reduction from $20,000 to $15,000. Note the $10,000 difference in incomes between the two students in each case – the difference in the unconditional financial support given them by their respective families.

The financial cost is the same (the $5,000 reduction in living standards), but the increase in the level of hardship faced by the student from the lower income background in attending university will be greater. This is because the level of hardship may be assumed to increase in a non-linear fashion at lower levels of income, and so this student faces a higher personal cost of attending university.[3] Even though the financial costs and benefits are assumed to be the same in absolute dollar terms, the lower income student faces greater hardship and will therefore be less likely to choose the schooling – or will need an extra incentive to do so.

To emphasize, this effect works through the demand side of Becker's (1975) model. Two students who face the same financial rate of return from going to university and who are identical in all other respects apart from the unconditional financial support they get from their parents will not face the same personal or "psychological" rate of return for the schooling. Students from lower income families will demand less education and, precisely, because the effect works through the demand side, access to a fully efficient and equitable loan system (as described above) that equalizes the financial cost of attendance for rich and poor will not change the result.[4]

It may not be immediately clear why access to a fully efficient loan system does not change the result. Why can't lower income students just borrow money to reduce the hardship of attendance? The answer is that they can, and will do so. Indeed, higher income students may borrow as well. But lower income students will need to borrow more money and therefore have to pay back more money in the future. There is as well always the chance that students will not succeed and not gain access to the higher income stream of a university graduate. In this event students from poorer families will again experience a higher level of hardship than will richer students, since the required loan repayments are higher.

At this point the normative issue becomes quite simply "Is this fair?" Some might argue that there is in fact no normative issue. Rich people have more access to most things, including various other kinds of investments, than poor people, and this applies for their children too, in the form of better pre-PSE schooling and other kinds of activities with a career investment component.

However, inherent in most concerns regarding "equal access to PSE" is the belief that university education should be treated as a "merit good," much like medical care. Higher income families would, in a free market, demand more medical care because they could afford it, but Canadians have decided that they would prefer to see this good allocated through assessed need rather than by willingness (and ability) to pay. It can be argued on similar grounds that university education should be allocated in a like manner – according to potential benefit and the desire to go rather than money.

PSE, especially for those who have the ability to benefit but are at the margin of attendance due to low family income levels, can be a life-transforming event. Our normative perspective is that the relative hardship a student experiences due entirely to coming from a lower income family should not be a factor in determining who goes to university and who does not. For those who share this normative position, evidence that hardship is a factor in educational decisions will provide an important rationale for the use of grants to low income students in order to achieve equal access to education.

Implications

It has been well established that students from more affluent backgrounds are more likely to attend university than those from less affluent families. However, when other background influences such as parental education are considered, the effects of parental income fall off sharply (Mueller, 2008). The standard interpretation of this finding is that for reasons of nature or nurture, parents who have higher levels of education tend to raise children who themselves also prefer to go on to PSE and have the ability and preparation to do so, but when these measures are omitted from the analysis, they are picked up by parental income (i.e., a classic "omitted variables" problem).

Even after including the proper background controls such as parental education, parental income may still affect university attendance because it will tend to relax the liquidity constraints that could prevent a qualified student from going. But in the absence of financial barriers to attendance (e.g., in the presence of a good student loan system), the relationship between income and attendance should disappear.

Our approach has developed the idea that – even after these "taste" / ability and liquidity effects – family income will still affect university attendance through another route: the unconditional transfers that families bestow on their children, whether or not they go on to PSE. Families with higher incomes transfer more money and therefore imply less student hardship. The reason is that the value of a dollar of current expenditure is higher when a person has less money, and therefore the hardship of going to school is greater for students from lower income families.

All else being equal, giving up $5,000 of expenditure per year to go to school (our example from above) is more of a barrier when the person has less money to start with. So, if our approach is correct, the effect of family income on attendance will never completely disappear, no matter what else is included in the analysis. The YITS data, with their particularly rich set of background variables, will allow us to test this hypothesis.

A second implication of our model concerns the effects of student loans on the effort students put into their studies. Students with larger loans will expect to have lower net expenditure levels in the future due to their loan payments, and it will also be more important for them to graduate and get a well-paying job to pay off their loans. To the extent that study effort leads to higher future incomes and a greater likelihood of graduating, it follows that more indebted students should put greater effort into their studies. This implication can also be tested with the YITS data.

A final implication of our model is that the costs of going to university, including both direct costs (tuition fees and so on) and opportunity costs, will have greater disincentive effects for students from less affluent backgrounds due to the same income non-linearities that drive the parental income effects, and any increase in costs will have more of an impact on these students than others.[5] This is not an implication that we can test with the YITS data directly, since there is little exogenous variation in costs that can be readily identified in a statistical sense, but in the next section we will briefly discuss evidence from the literature that supports it.

The Evidence

In this section we report the results of some empirical tests of these propositions. We test the first two propositions using the Youth in Transition Survey, Cohort A (or YITS-A). These data are described in detail in Motte, Qiu, Zhang, and Bussière (2008). We note here simply that – of particular importance to our tests – the quality of the background variables is especially high. We have detailed information on student grades and attitudes, and information about family background is also plentiful and accurate, gathered as it is by interviews with the respondents' parents.[6]

Family Income Effects on Access

Our approach suggests that family income will affect access by shifting the demand for education, in addition to any effect it might have by making the schooling more affordable. We test this hypothesis using the YITS-A dataset, Cycle 3, which captures this cohort at age 19, when they have begun to enter PSE in large numbers. These data are well suited to our purposes because of their rich background information, as well as that pertaining to their participation in PSE. The latter data include information on the constraints that have affected access, including financial ones, for those who do not participate in PSE. This allows us to examine the effects of family income on access to PSE while taking financial barriers into account.

The dependent variables used in our access models represent a bit of a turning of the usual set-up on its head. This is done in order to facilitate the investigation of the precise hypotheses being examined. Whereas access models usually consist of using a logit or probit (or sometimes simply a linear probability) model where participating in PSE (or a specific level of PSE such as university) takes the value of 1 and not participating is given a 0, we turn those relationships around and, at least in the first case, accessing PSE is given a value of 0 and non-access is given a value of 1 – thus simply reversing the nature of the usual relationships (e.g., higher parental income will be expected to have a negative rather than positive effect).

The reason for this approach is to allow us to study the effects of income (and the other variables included in the models) on the different reasons for non-participation – corresponding to the different implications of our model. We thus use a multinomial logit model set-up where 0 is participation in PSE, 1 is non-access and the individual cites a financial barrier as the reason for non-participation (i.e., affordability is the issue), and 2 is non-access but the person does not cite a financial constraint as the reason for non-participation. (In the raw data, of those who did not attend PSE, 18.0 percent of the males and 27.3 percent of the females cited financial barriers as the reason.)

We would thus expect family income to affect the financial constraint non-access outcome if the student financial aid system is not doing an effective job or there is otherwise some set of factors that generate such an income-financial barrier relationship. We would, however, also expect family income to affect the no-financial-constraint non-access outcome if it also plays a role in the participation decision for the reasons we have argued above. Income might also operate through other channels (such as high school outcomes), but we believe the YITS-A dataset is sufficiently rich that effects such as these are likely controlled for, thus leaving us to at least tentatively conclude that we are in fact estimating "pure" or "direct" income effects.

The results of this estimation are shown in Tables 1 and 2. Table 1 shows the results of the simpler access ("0") versus non-access ("1") model, while Table 2 breaks the latter into those citing a financial barrier ("1") and those giving a reason other than the lack of financing for their non-participation in PSE ("2").

In each case, two sets of results are presented, one in which the PSE outcome includes both college and university students, and another in which only university students are included among the participants, and college students are excluded from the models. We focus on the latter specification because the literature has clearly established that university access is the more highly differentiated PSE outcome where family background and other effects matter more, and hence we expect to find sharper results with this model (see, e.g., Finnie and Mueller, 2007).

Each set of models is estimated with parental education first excluded and then included in order to show how much of the "raw" or "total" family income effects appears in fact to be parental education effects – and also to show the general magnitude of these other background effects. In all cases the models include as well controls for sex, province, family type, and visible minority and immigration status, although the results for these variables are not reported here.

The most interesting and general finding from Table 1 is that family income is indeed significantly related to non-participation in PSE when parental education is omitted from the model, but that these effects are significantly attenuated when the latter is added (the second column in each set of results). Still, significant income effects remain. So, for

TABLE 1
Access Models: Simple Case of Non-Participation in PSE

	University only			College and university		
	1	2	3	1	2	3
Parent/guardian education (HS completed)						
Less than HS		0.1302*** [0.0239]	0.0504** [0.0251]		0.1425*** [0.0254]	0.0682** [0.0267]
Some PSE		-0.0857*** [0.0277]	-0.0450** [0.0223]		-0.0751*** [0.0242]	-0.0497** [0.0230]
Trade/college		-0.0906*** [0.0189]	-0.0332** [0.0154]		-0.0696*** [0.0169]	-0.0325** [0.0158]
University-below BA degree		-0.2603*** [0.0330]	-0.0912*** [0.0306]		-0.1781*** [0.0288]	-0.0833*** [0.0304]
University-BA		-0.3340*** [0.0195]	-0.1304*** [0.0165]		-0.2286*** [0.0166]	-0.1066*** [0.0165]
University-grad		-0.4127*** [0.0222]	-0.1476*** [0.0227]		-0.2841*** [0.0198]	-0.1291*** [0.0236]
Other/unknown		0.2299** [0.1066]	-0.0582 [0.1036]		0.3124** [0.1383]	0.012 [0.1248]
Parent/guardian income level ($50,000 to $75,000)						
Extremely low ($0-$5,000)	0.0985 [0.0744]	0.1021 [0.0721]	0.0238 [0.0682]	0.0973 [0.0653]	0.0874 [0.0653]	0.0761 [0.0574]
$5,000 to $25,000	0.1880*** [0.0274]	0.0895*** [0.0286]	0.0177 [0.0256]	0.1504*** [0.0264]	0.0709*** [0.0262]	0.0188 [0.0246]
$25,000 to $50,000	0.1137*** [0.0183]	0.0570*** [0.0180]	0.0271* [0.0150]	0.0779*** [0.0167]	0.0376** [0.0165]	0.0105 [0.0156]
$75,000 to $100,000	-0.1096*** [0.0179]	-0.0476*** [0.0171]	-0.0381*** [0.0136]	-0.0789*** [0.0155]	-0.0393** [0.0154]	-0.0347** [0.0143]
$100,000 and up	-0.2178*** [0.0185]	-0.0930*** [0.0201]	-0.0682*** [0.0164]	-0.1574*** [0.0159]	-0.0843*** [0.0175]	-0.0766*** [0.0165]

Notes: Average marginal effects shown. Standard errors in brackets.
*** $p<0.01$, ** $p<0.05$, * $p<0.1$.
Model 1 includes basic background variables such as gender, high school location in urban/rural area, province of high school, French minority outside Quebec, family structure, visible minority, immigrant status, and being both visible minority and immigrant.
Model 2 adds parental education.
Model 3 adds the full set of YITS scale variables and high school grade variables.
In the university only results, college students are excluded from the estimation. In the college and university results, both types of PSE students are included.
The effects shown should be interpreted as the effect of the indicated variables on the probability of not participating in PSE.
Source: Carmichael and Finnie, 2008.

TABLE 2A
Access Models: Reasons for Non-Participation (University Only)

	1		2		3	
	Financial barrier	Financial situation not a barrier	Financial barrier	Financial situation not a barrier	Financial barrier	Financial situation not a barrier
Parent/guardian education (HS completed)						
Less than HS			0.0265 [0.0247]	0.1037*** [0.0295]	0.0061 [0.0240]	0.0447 [0.0275]
Some PSE			-0.019 [0.0188]	-0.0672* [0.0361]	-0.0304* [0.0182]	-0.015 [0.0271]
Trade/college			-0.0119 [0.0123]	-0.0789*** [0.0236]	-0.0107 [0.0130]	-0.0228 [0.0174]
University- below BA degree			-0.0572*** [0.0182]	-0.2033*** [0.0504]	-0.0407* [0.0227]	-0.0509 [0.0396]
University-BA			-0.0620*** [0.0099]	-0.2722*** [0.0259]	-0.0334*** [0.0119]	-0.0976*** [0.0195]
University-grad			-0.0918*** [0.0085]	-0.3218*** [0.0365]	-0.0678*** [0.0118]	-0.0796** [0.0325]
Other/unknown			-0.0831* [0.0473]	0.3187*** [0.1107]	-0.0786 [0.0585]	0.0241 [0.1323]
Parent/guardian income level ($50,000 to $75,000)						
Extremely low ($0-$5,000)	0.0723 [0.0536]	0.024 [0.0772]	0.0746 [0.0542]	0.026 [0.0729]	0.0418 [0.0560]	-0.0167 [0.0510]
$5,000 to $25,000	0.1045*** [0.0256]	0.0813** [0.0334]	0.0824*** [0.0243]	0.0049 [0.0326]	0.0776*** [0.0247]	-0.0607** [0.0256]
$25,000 to $50,000	0.0616*** [0.0132]	0.0497** [0.0247]	0.0506*** [0.0127]	0.0041 [0.0234]	0.0503*** [0.0132]	-0.0251 [0.0175]
$75,000 to $100,000	-0.0092 [0.0095]	-0.1009*** [0.0262]	0.0021 [0.0099]	-0.0502** [0.0246]	0.0024 [0.0100]	-0.0407** [0.0172]
$100,000 and up	-0.0392*** [0.0079]	-0.1785*** [0.0294]	-0.0182* [0.0095]	-0.0747** [0.0298]	-0.012 [0.0102]	-0.0564*** [0.0206]

Notes: Average marginal effects shown. Standard errors in brackets.
*** $p<0.01$, ** $p<0.05$, * $p<0.1$.
Model 1 includes basic background variables such as gender, high school location in urban/rural area, province of high school, French minority outside Quebec, family structure, visible minority, immigrant status, and being both visible minority and immigrant.
Model 2 adds parental education.
Model 3 adds the full set of YITS scale variables and high school grade variables.
In the university only results, college students are excluded from the estimation.
The effects shown should be interpreted as the effect of the indicated variables on the probability of not participating in PSE.
Source: Carmichael and Finnie, 2008.

TABLE 2B
Access Models: Reasons for Non-Participation (College and University)

	1		2		3	
	Financial barrier	*Financial situation not a barrier*	*Financial barrier*	*Financial situation not a barrier*	*Financial barrier*	*Financial situation not a barrier*
Parent/guardian education (HS completed)						
Less than HS			0.0289 [0.0188]	0.1136*** [0.0332]	0.0107 [0.0178]	0.0580* [0.0306]
Some PSE			-0.0174 [0.0136]	-0.058 [0.0354]	-0.0255* [0.0133]	-0.0244 [0.0315]
Trade/college			-0.0095 [0.0092]	-0.0605** [0.0236]	-0.0098 [0.0097]	-0.0229 [0.0204]
University- below BA degree			-0.0401*** [0.0143]	-0.1384*** [0.0469]	-0.0367** [0.0161]	-0.047 [0.0462]
University-BA			-0.0426*** [0.0079]	-0.1863*** [0.0244]	-0.0291*** [0.0090]	-0.0777*** [0.0225]
University-grad			-0.0663*** [0.0071]	-0.2185*** [0.0346]	-0.0557*** [0.0088]	-0.0721* [0.0385]
Other/unknown			-0.0568 [0.0360]	0.3774*** [0.1396]	-0.0623* [0.0369]	0.0807 [0.1790]
Parent/guardian income level ($50,000 to $75,000)						
Extremely low ($0-$5,000)	0.0637 [0.0428]	0.0312 [0.0771]	0.0628 [0.0424]	0.0227 [0.0739]	0.0479 [0.0434]	0.0286 [0.0632]
$5,000 to $25,000	0.0831*** [0.0202]	0.0648* [0.0344]	0.0647*** [0.0190]	0.0037 [0.0332]	0.0633*** [0.0196]	-0.0459 [0.0281]
$25,000 to $50,000	0.0459*** [0.0102]	0.0296 [0.0247]	0.0384*** [0.0098]	-0.0032 [0.0237]	0.0379*** [0.0103]	-0.0295 [0.0206]
$75,000 to $100,000	-0.0055 [0.0075]	-0.0739*** [0.0247]	0.0019 [0.0078]	-0.0417* [0.0243]	0.0027 [0.0080]	-0.0377* [0.0208]
$100,000 and up	-0.0285*** [0.0064]	-0.1289*** [0.0273]	-0.0158** [0.0073]	-0.0685** [0.0285]	-0.0119 [0.0078]	-0.0654*** [0.0241]

Notes: Average marginal effects shown. Standard errors in brackets.
*** p<0.01, ** p<0.05, * p<0.1.
Model 1 includes basic background variables such as gender, high school location in urban/rural area, province of high school, French minority outside Quebec, family structure, visible minority, immigrant status, and being both visible minority and immigrant.
Model 2 adds parental education.
Model 3 adds the full set of YITS scale variables and high school grade variables.
In the college and university results, both types of PSE students are included.
The effects shown should be interpreted as the effect of the indicated variables on the probability of not participating in PSE.
Source: Carmichael and Finnie, 2008.

example, when only the sharper university versus no PSE comparison is made (the left-hand columns) the top two family income categories ($75,000-$100,000 and greater than $100,000) are associated with 11.0 and 21.8 percent lower probabilities of not participating in university as compared to the comparison middle income group ($50,000-$75,000) when parental education is excluded, while these effects fall to considerably lower but still significant (and important) 4.8 and 9.3 percentage points when parental education is added. These results hold, if perhaps not quite as strongly, when college students are included and grouped with university students in the PSE participation group – as expected.

We now turn to what are perhaps the more important propositions pertaining to our model: the effect of family income on participation for those who face financial barriers to their participation in PSE (which the student financial aid system is of course meant to rectify) versus those who are not financially constrained from going to PSE but do not participate anyway (for other reasons). The results reported in Table 2 show the findings of this model.

The results suggest, first, that the student financial aid system does indeed seem to be doing a good job in the sense that being constrained from going to PSE due to financial barriers is only relatively weakly related to family income, with many of the income-related coefficients in the first equation ("Financial barrier") not statistically significant, and those that are significant relatively small in magnitude, especially once the parental education variables are added.

Family income is, however, in general significantly related to not going to PSE even though the person is not financially constrained from going (the "Financial situation not a barrier" equations). This is especially true, again, when the university option is isolated. The implication of this finding is that the student financial aid system might need to go beyond pure "affordability" criteria if it wants to level the PSE access playing field for young people from lower income families.

Student Loans and Effort

We now turn to the effects on effort of having a student loan. We define effort as the number of hours spent on school work out of class, and this is estimated using a tobit framework since the endogenous variable is left-censored at zero (although a simple ordinary least squares (OLS) approach generated very similar findings). The same sets of controls are included as in the access models, but we report only the student financial aid variables. These are shown in Table 3.

TABLE 3
Student Financial Aid and Hours Spent on School Work outside of Class

	1	2	3	4
	College			
Scholarships	1.099***	0.590**	0.571**	0.642***
	[0.24]	[0.23]	[0.23]	[0.23]
Grants	0.503*	0.326	0.262	0.255
	[0.30]	[0.29]	[0.29]	[0.29]
Student loans	0.271	0.147	0.137	0.145
	[0.19]	[0.18]	[0.18]	[0.19]
Constant	8.677	8.598	8.780	9.408
No. of observations	6,412	6,395	6,395	6,395
	University			
Scholarships	2.070***	1.040***	0.820***	0.800***
	[0.24]	[0.24]	[0.25]	[0.24]
Grants	0.332	0.207	0.162	0.177
	[0.29]	[0.27]	[0.27]	[0.27]
Student loans	0.272	0.419	0.526**	0.531**
	[0.28]	[0.27]	[0.27]	[0.26]
Constant	12.683	11.430	11.319	10.788
No. of observations	4,451	4,436	4,436	4,436

Notes: Only the results for the student financial aid variables included in the models are reported. The other variables are listed below.
Model 1 includes basic background variables such as gender, visible minority status, region of schooling, family structure, and parental education.
Model 2 adds high school grade and high school engagement variables.
Model 3 adds PSE grade variables.
Model 4 adds PSE engagement variables.
The model is for full-time students only.
Source: Carmichael and Finnie, 2008.

The coefficients on the student loan variables conform to the predictions of the model. University students with loans spend on average in the range of .5 or .6 more hours per week (outside of class) on their school work than do those without loans – this on a mean value of around 10 hours per week. For college students, the effects are slightly smaller, in the range of .3 or .4 hours, but this is in a context where mean hours are also lower, and the effects are still statistically significant. Note that the final regression includes measures of high school grades and engagement as well as university grades and engagement, and the effect of loans on effort is strongest in this regression. We may thus conclude that this evidence is in fact consistent with the predictions of our model regarding student loans and student effort.

Access and Costs

The one prediction we do not test directly using the YITS-A is that pertaining to the effects of the costs of PSE on participation, for the reasons mentioned above (i.e., the lack of exogenous variation in costs that can be identified in the YITS-A). However, we note that this is an old issue in the economics of education literature.[7] Researchers such as Hoenack (1971), Bishop (1977), McPherson and Shapiro (1991), and others have noted that changes in cost variables such as transportation costs, tuition fees, and student aid all have a larger effect on access for students from lower income families. These papers do not provide much in the way of a theoretical framework, but to the extent that they are concerned with the distribution of income, they tend to speak in terms of income rather than "hardship" or utility effects. Even though their (implicit) models are linear, the empirical result is not surprising and could be driven by the financial constraints that prevent poorer students from attending university.

More interesting, perhaps, is the fact that changes in the alternative wage (Corazzini et al., 1972) also have a greater effect on access for lower income students. Changes in the alternative wage do not alter the amount of money one needs to subsist at university, and a change in the alternative wage will change the financial return to education by the same amount for students from both higher and lower income families. In our approach a change in the alternative wage has a greater effect on the return for the lower income student. It might be expected, therefore, to have a greater effect on behaviour, even in a system that provides unlimited and cheap access to educational loans. While we believe this does have normative implications for the use of targeted grants, it is not a prediction that we are able to test directly with the YITS data.

Conclusion

Various arguments can be made in favour of general public grants for the support of PSE. Probably the strongest one is based on the belief that higher education provides external benefits to all of society and should therefore be encouraged. Another argument is based on the idea that grants can help to provide a more neutral tax system and thus bring investments in human capital more in line with investments in financial or physical capital in this respect. Grants may also serve as a second-best response to informational problems related to the benefits (and costs) of education, which may be of particular importance for lower income students.

These arguments do not, however, imply that PSE should be free, since the personal benefits of higher education are substantial, and the incentives for good students to pursue their studies are already considerable. Further arguments for grants, or for education to be free, are normally dismissed by economists as ideological statements about the appropriate role of the state in society (if they come from colleagues in academe) or as self-serving calls for undeserved and regressive public transfers (if they come from students).

As for more targeted grants aimed at lower income students with the goal of helping them afford the schooling investments they may wish to make, economists generally recognize again that university students – even those from lower income families – are likely to benefit greatly from these investments on a personal level, and are likely to be wealthy in a lifetime sense, since they will tend to go on to higher than average incomes after their schooling. Thus such support should come in the form of loans rather than grants paid for by the average taxpayer.

This paper has, however, developed an alternative argument in favour of targeted grants based on family income, founded on the idea that income will affect access to education through its effect on the personal rate of return to schooling. Students from lower income families are likely to experience greater hardship during their schooling, as compared to those from higher income families, due to the greater income transfers that higher income families make to their children whether or not they go to school. This hardship will act as a deterrent and will tilt the access playing field away from lower income students. Grants, not loans, would be required to equalize opportunities.

The idea has empirical implications for the effects of family income on access. In particular, we would expect to see a positive relationship between family income and access to higher education after taking other background effects into account (including parental education) even among those students who are not actually constrained by financial barriers. A second implication is that students with loans would be expected to work harder to graduate and otherwise do better at school. We have tested these propositions using the YITS-A data and found support. The model also predicts that students from lower income families will be more responsive to changes in costs, and our appeal to other studies on this matter (which is not readily testable with the YITS-A) suggests this is indeed the case.

Our proposition has implications for programs aimed at providing equal access to post-secondary education. In particular, student loans will not correct this problem – grants are required. Policy-makers may, furthermore, need to go beyond "affordability" in fashioning student aid packages, and provide grants even when affordability per se does not appear to be an issue, since students from lower income families may need extra incentives to attend.

In short, equal access may require that we provide grants to students from lower income backgrounds. Our paper does not, however, tell us how large these grants should be. That can only be answered by further research.

Notes

The authors are grateful to MESA for financing this research, to Theresa Qiu and Yan Zhang for their excellent research assistance, and to Richard Mueller, Alex Usher, Arthur Sweetman, and other participants at the MESA conference in Montreal in October 2007 for their many useful comments.

1. The same is true, although to a lesser degree, for college students, where college is defined in the Canadian sense of meaning post-secondary education programs "below" university – programs that tend to be shorter and more vocationally focused.

2. Advocates sometimes make this argument to justify grants for all students, including those rich enough to face no liquidity constraint. This is a bad argument because it wastes money, precisely because the assistance is not needed and involves transfers from a less well off segment of society (the average taxpayer) to one that is better off, especially in a lifetime sense (PSE students from higher income families).

3. "I've learned to appreciate every single thing I have, and it's hard for me to see people here throwing away hundreds of dollars on clothes and parties and stuff. I just don't get it" (student at Queen's University, quoted in *The Journal*, Queen's University, 30 November 2006).

4. Our companion paper (Carmichael and Finnie, 2008) uses a mathematical set-up to establish this result and the implications discussed in the next section. The assumptions we use are simply that the utility of consumption is concave (students are risk averse) and that there is a chance that the student will not graduate. Independent evidence for the non-linearity that

underlies the result is contained in the effects of student loans on study effort, which we examine in the next section of this paper.

5. These three implications are worked out explicitly in Carmichael and Finnie (2008).

6. See also Finnie and Mueller (2008), who estimate similar access models using the YITS-A, but with a different focus than ours.

7. We thank the MESA referees for these references.

References

Bassanini, S., and S. Scarpenta. 2001. "Does Human Capital Matter for Growth in OECD Countries? Evidence from Pooled Mean-Group Estimates." Technical Report 282, OECD working paper.

Becker, G.S. 1975. *Human Capital: A Theoretical and Empirical Analysis, with Special Reference to Education.* New York: Columbia University Press.

Bishop, J. 1977. "The Effect of Public Policies on the Demand for Higher Education." *Journal of Human Resources* 30 (4): 285-307.

Blondal, S., S. Field, and N. Giroard. 2002. "Investment in Human Capital through Upper Secondary and Tertiary Education." OECD Economic Studies 34: 41-89.

Boskin, M.J. 1975. "Notes on the Tax Treatment of Human Capital." In *Conference on Tax Research 1975.* Washington D.C.: Department of the Treasury.

Bynner, J., and M. Egerton. 2000. "The Social Benefits of Higher Education: Insights Using Longitudinal Data." Technical report, Centre for Longitudinal Studies, Institute of Education, London.

Carmichael, H.L. 1999. "Restructuring the University System: What Level of Public Support?" *Canadian Public Policy* 25 (1): 133-40.

Carmichael, L., and R. Finnie. 2008. "Grants for Students: Equal Access to Post-Secondary Education Requires More Than a Student Loan Program." Accessed 19 November 2008 at http://www.mesa-project.org/pub/pdf/MESA_Carmichael_Finnie.pdf.

Corazzini, A., D.J. Dugan, and H.B. Grabowski. 1972. "Determinants and Distributional Aspects of Enrollment in U.S. Higher Education." *Journal of Human Resources* 7 (1): 39-59.

Finnie, R. 2005. "Student Financial Aid: The Roles of Loans and Grants." In *Taking Public Universities Seriously,* edited by F. Iacobucci and C. Tuohy, 476-97. Toronto: University of Toronto Press.

Finnie, R., and R.E. Mueller. 2007. "The Effects of Family Income, Parental Education and Other Background Factors on Access to Post-Secondary Education in Canada: Evidence from the YITS." Accessed 19 November 2008 at http://www.mesa-project.org/pub/pdf/MESA_Finnie_Mueller.pdf.

– 2008. "The Backgrounds of Canadian Youth and Access to Post-Secondary Education: New Evidence from the Youth in Transition Survey." In *Who Goes?*

Who Stays? What Matters? Accessing and Persisting in Post-Secondary Education in Canada, edited by R. Finnie, R.E. Mueller, A. Sweetman, and A. Usher. Montreal and Kingston: McGill-Queen's University Press and School of Policy Studies, Queen's University.

Finnie, R., and S. Schwartz. 1996. *Student Loans in Canada: Past, Present and Future.* Toronto: C.D. Howe Institute.

Haveman, R.H, and B.L. Wolfe. 1984. "Schooling and Economic Well-Being: The Role of Nonmarket Effects." *Journal of Human Resources* 19 (3): 377-407.

Hoenack, S.A. 1971. "The Efficient Allocation of Subsidies to College Students." *American Economic Review* 61 (3): 302-11.

Johnson, G.E. 1984. "Subsidies for Higher Education." *Journal of Labor Economics* 2 (3): 303-18.

Kenkel, D.S. 1991. "Health Behavior, Health Knowledge, and Schooling." *Journal of Political Economy* 99 (2): 287-305.

Lochner, L., and E. Moretti. 2001. "The Effect of Education on Crime: Evidence from Prison Inmates, Arrests, and Self Reports." Technical Report 8605, National Bureau of Economic Research.

McPherson, M.S., and M.O. Schapiro. 1991. "Does Student Aid Affect College Enrollment: New Evidence on a Persistent Controversy." *American Economic Review* 81 (1): 309-18.

Moretti, E. 2004. "Estimating the Social Return to Higher Education from Longitudinal and Repeated Cross Sectional Data." *Journal of Econometrics* 121 (1-2): 175-212.

Motte, A., H.T. Qiu, Y. Zhang, and P. Bussière. 2008. "The Youth in Transition Survey: Following Canadian Youth through Time." In *Who Goes? Who Stays? What Matters? Accessing and Persisting in Post-Secondary Education in Canada,* edited by R. Finnie, R.E. Mueller, A. Sweetman, and A. Usher. Montreal and Kingston: McGill-Queen's University Press and School of Policy Studies, Queen's University.

Mueller, R.E. 2008. "Access and Persistence of Students in Canadian Post-Secondary Education: What We Know, What We Don't Know, and Why It Matters." In *Who Goes? Who Stays? What Matters? Accessing and Persisting in Post-Secondary Education in Canada,* edited by R. Finnie, R.E. Mueller, A. Sweetman, and A. Usher. Montreal and Kingston: McGill-Queen's University Press and School of Policy Studies, Queen's University.

Usher, A. 2006. "Grants for Students: What They Do, Why They Work." Technical report, Educational Policy Institute, Toronto.

About the Authors

MARIA ADAMUTI-TRACHE obtained a doctoral degree in theoretical physics from the University of Bucharest (Romania), where she taught physics for 15 years. She also received an M.A. in higher education from the University of British Columbia and is currently a Ph.D. candidate in educational studies. She has expertise in life course research, which explores the impact of gender, age, social class, and immigrant status on education and work transitions. Her current research focuses on the socio-economic integration of recent immigrants and further education and labour market outcomes of university graduates. She continues to do research jn math and science education, gender, and science-related careers. Currently, she is research manager with Edudata Canada, and statistical consultant in the Faculty of Education, University of British Columbia.

LESLEY ANDRES is a professor in the Department of Educational Studies at the University of British Columbia. She is also the principal investigator of the *Paths on Life's Way* project, a 15-year longitudinal study of B.C. young adults. Her research and teaching interests include the sociology of education, foundations of higher education, issues of inequality and access, the transition from high school to post-secondary education and work, life course research, and quantitative and qualitative research methods. Her research focuses on the intersecting domains of participation in post-secondary education, equality of educational opportunity, and the relationship between institutional structures and individuals as agents.

PATRICK BUSSIÈRE is chief of post-secondary education research in the National Learning Policy Research Group (NLPRG) of the Learning Policy Directorate in Human Resources and Social Development Canada (HRSDC). His current responsibilities include the development of research evidence for policies related to post-secondary education in

Canada as well as the management of many surveys – including YITS and PISA – in collaboration with Statistics Canada and other organizations such as the Council of Ministers of Education, Canada, and the Organization for Economic Co-operation and Development (OECD). He is a graduate of Sherbrooke University, where he specialized in education and labour economics.

LORNE CARMICHAEL received a B.A. (hons.) from the University of Western Ontario in 1976, where he also won the gold medal in mathematics. He received his Ph.D. in economics from Stanford University in 1981. Since then he has been a professor of economics at Queen's University, serving as department head from 1994 to 2000. He has studied academic tenure, promotion contests, and piece rates, and has written on the Japanese labour market. More recently, he has developed models of fairness based on territoriality and has been an advocate of a graduate tax for the funding of post-secondary education.

LOUIS CHRISTOFIDES joined the Department of Economics at the University of Guelph in 1972 and served as chair of the department from 1987 to 1997; since 2004, he has been professor emeritus. He is currently professor of economics and dean of the Faculty of Economics and Management at the University of Cyprus. He received a B.A. in economics from the University of Essex (1968), an M.A. from the University of Essex (1969), and a Ph.D. from the University of British Columbia (1973). His teaching and research interests are in labour economics, econometrics, and macroeconomics. He is a research associate of CLLRNet and CESifo and a research fellow at IZA.

KATHLEEN DAY is currently an associate professor in the Department of Economics at the University of Ottawa. She has a Ph.D. in economics from the University of British Columbia. Her research has involved applied econometric work on a variety of Canadian issues, including inter-provincial labour mobility, volunteerism, regional disparities, the relationship between pollution and economic growth, and most recently, post-secondary education in Canada.

ROSS FINNIE was educated at Queen's University, the London School of Economics, and the University of Wisconsin-Madison. He is currently an associate professor in the Graduate School of Public and International Affairs at the University of Ottawa and a visiting fellow at Statistics Canada. His current interests in post-secondary education include access and barriers to PSE, persistence and pathways to completion, student financial aid, immigrant participation in PSE, the measurement of quality in PSE, students' adjustment to the PSE experience, and other topics. One of the principals of the MESA project, he is also the project's research director.

MARC FRENETTE is a research economist with the Business and Labour Market Analysis Division at Statistics Canada. His primary areas of interest include the economics of education and income inequality. He has published research papers on both topics in government publications as well as in several Canadian and international scientific journals. His work in education has mainly focused on post-secondary access, with particular emphasis on the role of distance to school, family background, academic achievement, and tuition fee deregulation. His current research agenda focuses on understanding the factors linked to learning.

JORGEN HANSEN is an associate professor of economics at Concordia University. He also holds appointments as research fellow at IZA and research associate at CIRANO and CIREQ and is a member of the management committee of the McGill-Concordia QICSS satellite. His research on education, welfare use, and labour supply has been funded by SSHRC and FQRSC, and his work has been published in leading economics journals.

MICHAEL HOY received his Ph.D. in economics from the London School of Economics (1982) and is a professor in economics at the University of Guelph where he has been since 1985. His research spans a number of areas in public economics, including equity implications of post-secondary education policy, the design and regulation of insurance markets, and tax policy. He has also made contributions in the area of inequality and poverty measurement.

DAVID JOHNSON is professor of economics at Wilfrid Laurier University and Education Policy Scholar at the C.D. Howe Institute. He was Fulbright Visitor at the University of California, Santa Barbara, in 2008. His other educational research includes comprehensive analyses of elementary school test scores in Ontario, Alberta, and British Columbia. He is co-author of *Macroeconomics* (3rd Canadian edition) and is particularly interested in the use of spreadsheets in the teaching of intermediate macroeconomics. He received his B.A. from the University of Toronto in 1978, his M.A. from the University of Western Ontario in 1979, and his Ph.D. from Harvard University in 1983. Before coming to Wilfrid Laurier in 1985, he worked for two years at the Bank of Canada.

ZHI (JANE) LI is a Ph.D. candidate in the economics department at the University of Guelph. She obtained her B.A. in economics from Nankai University, China. Her Ph.D. thesis is about subjective measurements of well-being. The first chapter compares the performance of subjective measurements (a group of self-reported life satisfactions) and objective measurements such as income and age on marriage survival analysis. The second chapter studies comparison of relative income effects on subjective well-being. These two chapters make use of the German Social-Economic Panel. The final chapter, based on the study in this volume, is an extended exploration of the evolution of aspirations to post-secondary education attendance.

FELICE MARTINELLO was educated in economics at the University of Western Ontario and the University of British Columbia and is currently professor of economics at Brock University. He has written on labour unions, wage determination, and union organizing, and has recently turned his attention to post-secondary education.

ANNE MOTTE joined the Canada Millennium Scholarship Foundation in 2006 as a policy and research officer. Among other research projects, she is responsible for the Millennium access bursary evaluation (the MESA project), Canada's largest evaluation of an ongoing student financial aid program. She also co-authored the latest edition of the Foundation's flagship publication, *The Price of Knowledge*. She is a graduate of economics from McGill and Université du Québec à Montréal with a keen interest in education and labour market issues.

RICHARD E. MUELLER is an associate professor of economics at the University of Lethbridge. His current research interests include the various determinants of entry into post-secondary education and other related education issues. His other major research focus is on the determinants of international migration. He also dabbles in issues related to the labour market outcomes of individuals in same-sex couples and the labour market effects of Aboriginal residential school attendance. He holds degrees from the University of Calgary and the University of Texas at Austin, and has held visiting academic positions throughout the world. His work has appeared in a number of economics and Canadian studies journals and edited volumes.

HANQING THERESA QIU is currently a research assistant for the Measuring the Effectiveness of Student Aid (MESA) Project. She holds an M.A. in economics from the University of Ottawa. Her research interests include labour economics and health economics. Her current research is focused on students' access to and persistence in post-secondary education. She is the co-author with Ross Finnie of *The Pattern of Persistence in Post-Secondary Education in Canada: Evidence from the YITS-B Dataset.*

THANASIS STENGOS is a university research professor in the Department of Economics at the University of Guelph. His research interests include theoretical and applied econometrics and in particular nonparametric methods applied to the empirics of economic growth, labour economics, economics of education, applied demand analysis, and financial economics. He is the author of many scholarly articles and a forthcoming book, *Human Capital and Economic Growth*, from Stanford University Press.

ARTHUR SWEETMAN is the director of the School of Policy Studies at Queen's University, where he holds the Stauffer-Dunning Chair in policy studies. Additionally, he has appointments in Queen's Department of Economics and the Department of Community Health and Epidemiology. He has a Ph.D. in economics, and much of his research addresses empirical issues related to education and the labour market. Recent volumes distributed by McGill-Queen's University Press that he has co-edited include: *Towards Evidence-Based Policy for Canadian Education/ Vers des politiques canadiennes d'éducation fondées sur la recherche*; and *Fulfilling Potential, Creating Success: Perspectives on Human Capital Development.* He also works on a range of other topics including immigration, social and health policy. One of the principals of the MESA project, he is also the chair of the research advisory committee.

ALEX USHER is the vice-president (Research) and director (Canada) of the Educational Policy Institute (EPI), a non-partisan research organization with offices in Toronto, Virginia Beach, and Melbourne. A graduate of McGill University and Carleton University, with an academic background in history, economics, and political science, he is the author of many articles and monographs on higher education, including *The Price of Knowledge* and *The Price of Knowledge 2004*, which are well-known as broad summaries of access and student finance in Canada. One of the principals of the MESA project, he is also responsible for the overall management of the project.

KLARKA ZEMAN has been an analyst at the Centre for Education Statistics of Statistics Canada for the past four years. She holds a bachelor's degree in economics and political science and a master's degree in political science. Her past work has mainly focused on youth transitions from education to the labour market and on youth post-secondary participation. Her current research interests include returns to post-secondary education and youth delinquency.

YAN ZHANG was a research assistant for the Measuring the Effectiveness of Student Aid (MESA) project and currently is a research assistant at Statistics Canada. Her research interests include labour economics and health economics. Her current research is focused on access to post-secondary education, income replacement after retirement, and maternal employment.

Queen's Policy Studies
Recent Publications

The Queen's Policy Studies Series is dedicated to the exploration of major public policy issues that confront governments and society in Canada and other nations.

Our books are available from good bookstores everywhere, including the Queen's University bookstore (http://www.campusbookstore.com/). McGill-Queen's University Press is the exclusive world representative and distributor of books in the series. A full catalogue and ordering information may be found on their web site (http://mqup.mcgill.ca/).

School of Policy Studies

Economic Transitions with Chinese Characteristics: Thirty Years of Reform and Opening Up, Arthur Sweetman and Jun Zhang (eds.), 2009   Paper 978-1-55339-225-5 ($39.95)
Cloth ISBN 978-1-55339-226-2 ($85)

Economic Transitions with Chinese Characteristics: Social Change During Thirty Years of Reform, Arthur Sweetman and Jun Zhang (eds.), 2009   Paper 978-1-55339-234-7 ($39.95)
Cloth ISBN 978-1-55339-235-4 ($85)

Politics of Purpose, 40th Anniversary Edition, Elizabeth McIninch and Arthur Milnes (eds.), 2009   Paper ISBN 978-1-55339-227-9 Cloth ISBN 978-1-55339-224-8

Dear Gladys: Letters from Over There, Gladys Osmond (Gilbert Penney ed.), 2009
ISBN 978-1-55339-223-1

Bridging the Divide: Religious Dialogue and Universal Ethics, Papers for The InterAction Council, Thomas S. Axworthy (ed.), 2008
Paper ISBN 978-1-55339-219-4 Cloth ISBN 978-1-55339-220-0

Immigration and Integration in Canada in the Twenty-first Century, John Biles, Meyer Burstein, and James Frideres (eds.), 2008
Paper ISBN 978-1-55339-216-3 Cloth ISBN 978-1-55339-217-0

Robert Stanfield's Canada, Richard Clippingdale, 2008   ISBN 978-1-55339-218-7

Exploring Social Insurance: Can a Dose of Europe Cure Canadian Health Care Finance?
Colleen Flood, Mark Stabile, and Carolyn Tuohy (eds.), 2008
Paper ISBN 978-1-55339-136-4 Cloth ISBN 978-1-55339-213-2

Canada in NORAD, 1957–2007: A History, Joseph T. Jockel, 2007
Paper ISBN 978-1-55339-134-0 Cloth ISBN 978-1-55339-135-7

Canadian Public-Sector Financial Management, Andrew Graham, 2007
Paper ISBN 978-1-55339-120-3 Cloth ISBN 978-1-55339-121-0

Emerging Approaches to Chronic Disease Management in Primary Health Care,
John Dorland and Mary Ann McColl (eds.), 2007
Paper ISBN 978-1-55339-130-2 Cloth ISBN 978-1-55339-131-9

Fulfilling Potential, Creating Success: Perspectives on Human Capital Development,
Garnett Picot, Ron Saunders and Arthur Sweetman (eds.), 2007
Paper ISBN 978-1-55339-127-2 Cloth ISBN 978-1-55339-128-9

Reinventing Canadian Defence Procurement: A View from the Inside, Alan S. Williams, 2006
Paper ISBN 0-9781693-0-1 (Published in association with Breakout Educational Network)

SARS in Context: Memory, History, Policy, Jacalyn Duffin and Arthur Sweetman (eds.), 2006
Paper ISBN 978-0-7735-3194-9 Cloth ISBN 978-0-7735-3193-2
(Published in association with McGill-Queen's University Press)

Dreamland: How Canada's Pretend Foreign Policy has Undermined Sovereignty, Roy Rempel, 2006
Paper ISBN 1-55339-118-7 Cloth ISBN 1-55339-119-5
(Published in association with Breakout Educational Network)

Canadian and Mexican Security in the New North America: Challenges and Prospects,
Jordi Díez (ed.), 2006   Paper ISBN 978-1-55339-123-4 Cloth ISBN 978-1-55339-122-7

*Global Networks and Local Linkages: The Paradox of Cluster Development in an Open
Economy*, David A. Wolfe and Matthew Lucas (eds.), 2005
Paper ISBN 1-55339-047-4 Cloth ISBN 1-55339-048-2

Choice of Force: Special Operations for Canada, David Last and Bernd Horn (eds.), 2005
Paper ISBN 1-55339-044-X Cloth ISBN 1-55339-045-8

Force of Choice: Perspectives on Special Operations, Bernd Horn, J. Paul de B. Taillon, and
David Last (eds.), 2004   Paper ISBN 1-55339-042-3 Cloth 1-55339-043-1

New Missions, Old Problems, Douglas L. Bland, David Last, Franklin Pinch, and Alan Okros
(eds.), 2004   Paper ISBN 1-55339-034-2 Cloth 1-55339-035-0

*The North American Democratic Peace: Absence of War and Security Institution-Building in
Canada-US Relations, 1867-1958*, Stéphane Roussel, 2004
Paper ISBN 0-88911-937-6 Cloth 0-88911-932-2

Implementing Primary Care Reform: Barriers and Facilitators, Ruth Wilson, S.E.D. Shortt
and John Dorland (eds.), 2004   Paper ISBN 1-55339-040-7 Cloth 1-55339-041-5

Social and Cultural Change, David Last, Franklin Pinch, Douglas L. Bland, and
Alan Okros (eds.), 2004   Paper ISBN 1-55339-032-6 Cloth 1-55339-033-4

Clusters in a Cold Climate: Innovation Dynamics in a Diverse Economy, David A. Wolfe and
Matthew Lucas (eds.), 2004   Paper ISBN 1-55339-038-5 Cloth 1-55339-039-3

Canada Without Armed Forces? Douglas L. Bland (ed.), 2004
Paper ISBN 1-55339-036-9 Cloth 1-55339-037-7

Campaigns for International Security: Canada's Defence Policy at the Turn of the Century,
Douglas L. Bland and Sean M. Maloney, 2004
Paper ISBN 0-88911-962-7 Cloth 0-88911-964-3

Understanding Innovation in Canadian Industry, Fred Gault (ed.), 2003
Paper ISBN 1-55339-030-X Cloth 1-55339-031-8

Delicate Dances: Public Policy and the Nonprofit Sector, Kathy L. Brock (ed.), 2003
Paper ISBN 0-88911-953-8 Cloth 0-88911-955-4

Beyond the National Divide: Regional Dimensions of Industrial Relations, Mark Thompson,
Joseph B. Rose and Anthony E. Smith (eds.), 2003
Paper ISBN 0-88911-963-5 Cloth 0-88911-965-1

The Nonprofit Sector in Interesting Times: Case Studies in a Changing Sector,
Kathy L. Brock and Keith G. Banting (eds.), 2003
Paper ISBN 0-88911-941-4 Cloth 0-88911-943-0

Clusters Old and New: The Transition to a Knowledge Economy in Canada's Regions,
David A. Wolfe (ed.), 2003   Paper ISBN 0-88911-959-7 Cloth 0-88911-961-9

The e-Connected World: Risks and Opportunities, Stephen Coleman (ed.), 2003
Paper ISBN 0-88911-945-7 Cloth 0-88911-947-3

Knowledge Clusters and Regional Innovation: Economic Development in Canada,
J. Adam Holbrook and David A. Wolfe (eds.), 2002
Paper ISBN 0-88911-919-8 Cloth 0-88911-917-1

Lessons of Everyday Law/Le droit du quotidien, Roderick Alexander Macdonald, 2002
Paper ISBN 0-88911-915-5 Cloth 0-88911-913-9

*Improving Connections Between Governments and Nonprofit and Voluntary Organizations:
Public Policy and the Third Sector,* Kathy L. Brock (ed.), 2002
Paper ISBN 0-88911-899-X Cloth 0-88911-907-4

Institute of Intergovernmental Relations

*Canada: The State of the Federation 2006/07: Transitions – Fiscal and Political Federalism
in an Era of Change,* vol. 20, John R. Allan, Thomas J. Courchene, and Christian Leuprecht
(eds.), 2009   Paper ISBN 978-1-55339-189-0 Cloth ISBN 978-1-55339-191-3

Comparing Federal Systems, Third Edition, Ronald L. Watts, 2008 ISBN 978-1-55339-188-3

*Canada: The State of the Federation 2005: Quebec and Canada in the New Century – New
Dynamics, New Opportunities,* vol. 19, Michael Murphy (ed.), 2007
Paper ISBN 978-1-55339-018-3 Cloth ISBN 978-1-55339-017-6

Spheres of Governance: Comparative Studies of Cities in Multilevel Governance Systems,
Harvey Lazar and Christian Leuprecht (eds.), 2007
Paper ISBN 978-1-55339-019-0 Cloth ISBN 978-1-55339-129-6

Canada: The State of the Federation 2004, vol. 18, *Municipal-Federal-Provincial Relations
in Canada,* Robert Young and Christian Leuprecht (eds.), 2006
Paper ISBN 1-55339-015-6 Cloth ISBN 1-55339-016-4

Canadian Fiscal Arrangements: What Works, What Might Work Better, Harvey Lazar (ed.), 2005
Paper ISBN 1-55339-012-1 Cloth ISBN 1-55339-013-X

Canada: The State of the Federation 2003, vol. 17, *Reconfiguring Aboriginal-State Relations,*
Michael Murphy (ed.), 2005   Paper ISBN 1-55339-010-5 Cloth ISBN 1-55339-011-3

Canada: The State of the Federation 2002, vol. 16, *Reconsidering the Institutions of
Canadian Federalism,* J. Peter Meekison, Hamish Telford and Harvey Lazar (eds.), 2004
Paper ISBN 1-55339-009-1 Cloth ISBN 1-55339-008-3

*Federalism and Labour Market Policy: Comparing Different Governance and Employment
Strategies,* Alain Noël (ed.), 2004   Paper ISBN 1-55339-006-7 Cloth ISBN 1-55339-007-5

The Impact of Global and Regional Integration on Federal Systems: A Comparative Analysis,
Harvey Lazar, Hamish Telford and Ronald L. Watts (eds.), 2003
Paper ISBN 1-55339-002-4 Cloth ISBN 1-55339-003-2

Canada: The State of the Federation 2001, vol. 15, *Canadian Political Culture(s) in Transition,*
Hamish Telford and Harvey Lazar (eds.), 2002
Paper ISBN 0-88911-863-9 Cloth ISBN 0-88911-851-5

Federalism, Democracy and Disability Policy in Canada, Alan Puttee (ed.), 2002
Paper ISBN 0-88911-855-8 Cloth ISBN 1-55339-001-6, ISBN 0-88911-845-0 (set)

Comparaison des régimes fédéraux, 2ᵉ éd., Ronald L. Watts, 2002   ISBN 1-55339-005-9

John Deutsch Institute for the Study of Economic Policy

The 2006 Federal Budget: Rethinking Fiscal Priorities, Charles M. Beach, Michael Smart
and Thomas A. Wilson (eds.), 2007
Paper ISBN 978-1-55339-125-8 Cloth ISBN 978-1-55339-126-6

Health Services Restructuring in Canada: New Evidence and New Directions,
Charles M. Beach, Richard P. Chaykowksi, Sam Shortt, France St-Hilaire and Arthur
Sweetman (eds.), 2006   Paper ISBN 978-1-55339-076-3 Cloth ISBN 978-1-55339-075-6

A Challenge for Higher Education in Ontario, Charles M. Beach (ed.), 2005
Paper ISBN 1-55339-074-1 Cloth ISBN 1-55339-073-3

Current Directions in Financial Regulation, Frank Milne and Edwin H. Neave (eds.),
Policy Forum Series no. 40, 2005   Paper ISBN 1-55339-072-5 Cloth ISBN 1-55339-071-7

Higher Education in Canada, Charles M. Beach, Robin W. Boadway and R. Marvin McInnis
(eds.), 2005   Paper ISBN 1-55339-070-9 Cloth ISBN 1-55339-069-5

Financial Services and Public Policy, Christopher Waddell (ed.), 2004
Paper ISBN 1-55339-068-7 Cloth ISBN 1-55339-067-9

The 2003 Federal Budget: Conflicting Tensions, Charles M. Beach and Thomas A. Wilson
(eds.), Policy Forum Series no. 39, 2004
Paper ISBN 0-88911-958-9 Cloth ISBN 0-88911-956-2

Canadian Immigration Policy for the 21st Century, Charles M. Beach, Alan G. Green and
Jeffrey G. Reitz (eds.), 2003   Paper ISBN 0-88911-954-6 Cloth ISBN 0-88911-952-X

Framing Financial Structure in an Information Environment, Thomas J. Courchene and
Edwin H. Neave (eds.), Policy Forum Series no. 38, 2003
Paper ISBN 0-88911-950-3 Cloth ISBN 0-88911-948-1

*Towards Evidence-Based Policy for Canadian Education/Vers des politiques canadiennes
d'éducation fondées sur la recherche,* Patrice de Broucker and/et Arthur Sweetman (eds./
dirs.), 2002   Paper ISBN 0-88911-946-5 Cloth ISBN 0-88911-944-9

*Money, Markets and Mobility: Celebrating the Ideas of Robert A. Mundell, Nobel Laureate
in Economic Sciences,* Thomas J. Courchene (ed.), 2002
Paper ISBN 0-88911-820-5 Cloth ISBN 0-88911-818-3

Our publications may be purchased at leading bookstores, including the Queen's
University Bookstore
(http://www.campusbookstore.com/), or can be ordered online from: McGill-
Queen's University Press, at
http://mqup.mcgill.ca/ordering.php

For more information about new and backlist titles from Queen's Policy Studies,
visit the McGill-Queen's
University Press web site at:
http://mqup.mcgill.ca/